OTTOMAN IMPERIALISM DURING THE REFORMATION: EUROPE AND THE CAUCASUS

NEW YORK UNIVERSITY

STUDIES IN NEAR EASTERN CIVILIZATION

NUMBER 5.

ALSO IN THIS SERIES

Number I: F. E. Peters, Aristotle and the Arabs

Number II: Jacob M. Landau, Jews in Nineteenth-Century Egypt

Number III: Lois Anita Giffen, Theory of Profane Love Among the Arabs: The Development of the Genre

Number IV: Lewis V. Thomas, A Study of Naima
Norman Itzkowitz, *editor*

Ottoman Imperialism During the Reformation:

Europe and The Caucasus

Carl Max Kortepeter

NEW YORK/NEW YORK UNIVERSITY PRESS
LONDON/UNIVERSITY OF LONDON PRESS LTD.
1972

Library of Congress Catalog Card Number: 72–075005

ISBN: 8147–4552–0

Manufactured in the United States of America

This book is dedicated to

CARL AND OLIVE KORTEPETER

and

FREDERICK AND EDNA KING

and
to the Memory of

ISFENDIYAR ALPAOUTI BEY OF SHUSHA

"Masters of the Old Ways and Harbingers of the New."

New York University Studies in Near Eastern Civilization

The participation of the New York University Press in the University's new commitment to Near Eastern Studies—building on a tradition of well over a century—will provide Americans and others with new opportunities for understanding the Near East. Concerned with those various peoples of the Near East who, throughout the centuries, have dramatically shaped many of mankind's most fundamental concepts and who have always had high importance in practical affairs, this series, New York University Studies in Near Eastern Civilization, seeks to publish important works in this vital area. The purview will be broad, open to varied approaches and historical periods. It will, however, be particularly receptive to work in two aspects of near Eastern civilization that may have received insufficient attention elsewhere but which do reflect particular interests at New York University. These are literature and art. Furthermore, taking a stand that may be more utilitarian than that of other publications, the series will welcome both translations of important Near Eastern literature of imagination, and of significant scholarly works written in Near Eastern languages. In this way, a larger audience, unacquainted with these languages, will be able to deepen its knowledge of the cultural achievements of Near Eastern peoples.

R. Bayly Winder
Richard Ettinghausen
General Editors

Preface

I

An imperial system stands at one end of the political spectrum and an integrated nation-state stands at the other. But neither system can long remain in a state of equilibrium, and in fact, the disintegration of the one system may eventually lead to the formation of the other.

The imperialist system, almost from its inception, is ruled by an ethnic core group to which other ethnic elements have access in more or less clearly defined career lines. Such a system, however, accepts and respects, on principle, the existence of diversity within its borders and devises political institutions which are responsive to diverse legal, religious and ethnic traditions. Such a state was the Ottoman Empire.

The nation-state, by contrast, whatever its form of government, remains basically intolerant of ethnic diversity and thus attempts to discourage "national" differences by requiring its citizens to use one language and to conform to one set of national laws. Religious diversity is tolerated only so long as the given "church" supports the nation-state and severs its political ties with extra-national bodies—hence the importance of the principle of secularism to the modern nation-state.

Both political systems, in their purest form, render a high degree of peace, security and the "good life" to their citizenry. It is ironic, however, that excessive desire to acquire control of new territories and peoples or zeal to promote a particular political or religious philosophy on the part of the ruling elites in either system may start a process of decay within the given system. The Ottoman Turks continued to add new ethnic units to the empire until, toward the end of the sixteenth century, they passed the point where they could remain administratively sensitive to the grievances of the various units of the Ottoman Empire. This inability to respond to administrative "feed-back" accelerated over the centuries until the various national units broke away from the empire. The net result was that the Turks in the twentieth century were forced to divest themselves of Empire and to create a nation-state.

In contrast, the United States, as a nation-state, by assuming too great an interest in affairs beyond its borders, has neglected the grievances of its own citizenry and thus has undermined the confidence of its citizenry in the principle of equality before the law. By so doing, it has awakened among those citizens who have subordinated their linguistic, ethnic and religious ties the desire to seek once again ethnic and religious privileges. The United States, thus, has set in motion certain trends which could lead to the establishment of an imperial form of political organization.

II

There are still many gaps in our knowledge about the Ottoman Turks who first came into prominence in world history in the early years of the fourteenth century. For seven centuries, until 1918, the Ottoman Turks remained on center stage as both a European and an Asian power. To understand the modern history of the Middle East, the role played in that region by the Turks must be understood. One need only recall that more than twenty-two modern sovereign states were once within the borders of the Ottoman Empire.

The Ottoman Turks, after their appearance in Western Asia, quickly made their presence felt in the capitals of Europe and Asia. By the end of the fourteenth century, they had advanced northward to the line of the Danube. After the defeat of Hungary at Mohaćs in 1526, Sultan Sulayman the Magnificent lead his armies to the gates of Vienna in 1529. Henceforth, the Ottomans held all the Balkans until the nineteenth century. Meanwhile Damascus, Jerusalem and Cairo and the sacred cities of Mecca and Medina, virtually the whole of the Eastern Mediterranean, had fallen to the Turks in the years 1516 and 1517. Shortly thereafter, Baghdad and most of Mesopotamia were wrested from Safavid Persia. Soon the Ottomans laid claim to and held much of North Africa, the Ukraine and the Caucasus. In these years of energetic expansion the Ottoman Turks may have seemed unlikely partners to their European Christian allies. But the evidence is clear. Valois France and Jagellon Poland-Lithuania quite often found their Turkish allies a mainstay of their regimes. Nor was Tudor England averse to selling cannon, gunpowder, lead and woolens to the Ottomans. And far-off Sweden often sought Ottoman or Tatar support whenever she contemplated warfare against Muscovy. Basically, it was the Spanish and Austrian Habsburgs and the well-to-do Renaissance Papacy which sought to stop the Turks before they undermined the entire European system. The Turks, threatened by a crusade after the failure of the Fifth Lateran Council (1512–1517), not only took control of most of Southeast Europe, but aided and abetted the spread of the Protestant Reformation.

Ironically, while the Turks were making fantastic territorial gains and winning many converts to Islam at the expense of their European neighbors, they were, in their own heartlands of Asia Minor, losing the allegiance of thousands of their own people to the ideology of the Shiʿite state of Safavid Persia. The initial reaction of the Ottoman Turks was to bring fire and sword to whole provinces in Asia Minor and to reduce Persia temporarily to the status of a second class power. Persia, in reply, sought and received military aid and supplies from Muscovy, the Habsburgs and England.

III

The intellectual foundations of this study derive from four years of study and research at the School of Oriental and African Studies of London University and the British Museum, 1957–1961, under the auspices of the U.S. government "G.I. Bill" grants to veterans. I conducted my doctoral work under the direction of Professor Bernard Lewis. Head of the Department of Near and Middle East History at the School. His overall supervision of my training and of the doctoral dissertation, entitled "The Relations Between the Crimean Tatars and the Ottoman Empire," was the best available anywhere. A second and equally important mentor of those London days was Professor Paul Wittek, Professor of Turkish, who conducted two major seminars, "The History of the Ottoman Empire" and "Ottoman Historiography." In fact, the rigorous studies of Professor Wittek and some of his Turkish contemporaries laid the foundations for modern Ottoman studies. I wish also to recall here the multiple insights and kindnesses of Mr. Vernon Parry, who is currently Reader in Islamic History in London University. Mr. Parry came to Islamic History by way of Romance Languages at Oxford and an unexpected stint as a British officer in the Middle East theater during World War II. His keen sense of military history and his vast knowledge of the treasures of Islamic history hidden away in the British Museum greatly enriched my background for this study. One other colleague who has made ongoing contributions to my thinking either personally or in his scholarly writings is Professor Halil Inalcik, Professor of Ottoman History in Ankara University. He took an early interest in my work and thereby lent encouragement to it. The scholarly works and the personal insights of these four men have not only made possible this study but have inspired a whole generation of students in the field of Ottoman history.

IV

While any piece of scholarly work owes its origins to an intricate pattern of intellectual influences, equally important are the contributions made by many individuals toward the accomplishment of innumerable practical tasks.

In particular, I acknowledge with feelings of indebtedness and affection the unstinting assistance of three colleagues: Professor G. M. Wickens, formerly chairman of the Department of Islamic Studies, University of Toronto, Professor R. Bayly Winder, currently Dean of the Faculty and Director of the Near East Center at New York University, and Professor Norman Itzkowitz of Princeton University. Each in his own way and at a decisive moment administered a figurative "kick in the pants" which served as a catalyst for the completion, the rewriting and the publishing of this narrative.

Apart from the valuable assistance of the aforementioned scholars, I should like to mention the friendly assistance which I have received from many libraries: The British Museum, particularly the staffs of the North Library (Dr. Rhodes and colleagues) and the Oriental Reading Room (Dr. Meridith-Owens, Assistant Curator of the Turkish collection, and Mr. T. Eisenegger); The Library of the School of Oriental and African Studies (Dr. Pearson and Mrs. Brown); the Wimbledon Public Library; the Toronto University Library (Miss Felix and Miss Falconer); Firestone Library of Princeton University (Mr. Dix and Mrs. Chasko); and the Near East Library of New York University (Mrs. Sidholm and Mr. Ok).

During the year of my sabbatical leave in Turkey (1966–1967), I had the privilege of pursuing research in the Archives of the Prime Ministry which were under the direction of Dr. Midhat Sertoğlu and his able assistants, Dr. Rauf Tunçay and Mr. Turgut Işîksal. I gratefully acknowledge that research in the Turkish archives and libraries would have been impossible without a generous grant from the American Research Institute in Turkey, and the granting of leave from the University of Toronto.

I wish to thank also the staff of New York University Press for their unflappable competence and their unshakable good humor in face of the many technical problems which a manuscript such as this can provide.

I should particularly like to thank Mrs. Nina Fuller, Mrs. Gladys Freeland, and our secretaries, Mrs. Georgi Hopkins and Miss Kim Hetherington, for their steadfast help during the numerous retypings of the manuscript.

I am pleased also to acknowledge my gratitude to Mrs. Roman Holod for her assistance in the Polish translations and to John Ashby for his aid with some difficult Latin.

My thanks also go to the editors of the *Slavonic and East European Review* and the *Journal of the American Oriental Society* for permission to use portions of my articles which they had printed at an earlier date.

V

I reserve the highest praise for my wife, Cynthia, who has provided the unceasing logistical support, typing skills and calmness of personality which has made it possible for us to weather all crises. During the course of six years,

1961–1967, we changed our domicile four times, from England to Canada, then to Turkey and finally to the United States! In a very real sense, also, this study has been an important background theme in the early lives of our five children, all of whom have been nurtured during the typical "nomadic" years of an aspiring young academic.

Max Kortepeter
Belle Mead, N. J.

Note on Transliteration and Geographic Terms

The transcription of the Cyrillic alphabet conforms to the "British System" as reproduced by W. K. Matthews in "The Latinization of Cyrillic Characters," *Slavonic and East European Review* XXX (1951–1952), pp. 542–543. For the transcription of Ottoman Turkish words, the system as set forth in Volume One of the Turkish *Islam Ansiklopedisi* will be generally followed with two exceptions: in place of Modern Turkish *c* as the transcription of the English *j* sound, and the Ottoman, Persian and Arabic *jim* (ج), the normal English *j* will be used, and for the Ottoman (ژ)—a very rarely used letter—the English *j* with a circumflex (ĵ) will be substituted. With reference to modern Turkish spellings, the Turkish undotted *i* sound will be indicated by an *i* with two dots. thus (ï). The Turkish *ch* and *sh* sounds will be rendered in the official Turkish manner, *ç* and *ş*, respectively. A slight variation of the Turkish transcription will be used for Persian spellings. All long vowels in the Arabic script will be denoted by a short line over such vowels, thus (ā, ī, ū).

The geographic terminology, whenever possible, conforms to the spellings as given in the John Bartholomew edition of the *Times' Atlas of the World* in five volumes (London, 1955–1959). In Eastern Europe, where as many as four different place names may apply to one locality or town, alternate names will generally be indicated, contiguously, in the text.

Table of Contents

LIST OF CHARTS AND TABLES IN THE APPENDIX

MAPS

CHAPTER ONE
Introduction: The Ottoman Empire in Eastern Europe and the Caucasus

1 The Pattern of Alignments

In Eastern Europe in the second half of the sixteenth century, the pattern of political alignments depended to a large extent on the relationships formed by European states with the two principal contenders, the Habsburg and the Ottoman empires. As a counterweight to the Spanish and German Habsburgs encircling her, France had long maintained close ties with the Sultan. The Ottomans benefited from this arrangement, particularly through their trade with France. As a friendly power, France also aided the Ottomans by remaining aloof from the attempts of the Papacy to form a holy alliance. Similarly, the peace policy of the Jagellons with the Ottoman sultans, which was necessary in order to secure the Polish flank during her incessant wars with Muscovy, placed the Polish-Lithuanian Commonwealth precariously in the Ottoman camp. Poland and the Ottomans generally shared their hostility for the Habsburgs and Muscovy but the status of Moldavia and the incursion of the Crimean Tatars into Polish territory and of the Cossacks into the *Dār ül-Islām* (the Abode of Islam) remained bones of contention between them.[1] There were also ties between Valois France and the Jagellons as was demonstrated in 1573 when Henri de Valois, during the first Polish interregnum, was elected king.[2]

The Holy See, above all, looked to the Habsburgs as the defenders of Christianity and could be counted upon to support Habsburg ventures against the Turks with important contributions of men and money. Even the Tsars of Muscovy, particularly when they showed themselves amenable to a union of the Russian Orthodox Church with Rome, had ready access to the ear of the Pope.[3] The Russians also found in the German Habsburgs a ready ally who shared the Russian desire to reduce Polish influence on every front.

On the fringes of these core alignments, Sweden was not averse to joining with Poland to divide Muscovite territories, and England helped the Ottomans by supplying them with war material during the last decades of the century.[4] Safavid Persia only hesitatingly made ventures into relations with European powers in the sixteenth century, a factor which gave to the Ottomans numerous advantages in technology, commerce, and warfare. Venice, whom the Habsburgs had failed to assist after the fall of Cyprus in 1570, made a separate peace with the Sultan in 1573. This move spoiled the plans of Pope Gregory XIII to reconstitute the Holy League of his predecessor, Pius V, the members of which had produced the Ottoman naval disaster of Lepanto in 1571.[5] In fact, Venice had suffered such severe losses to the Ottomans, partly as a result of her fickle allies, that she maintained a precarious neutrality during the remaining years of the century. Finally, Western Europe was torn in the sixteenth century, by the bitter religious wars that followed the Protestant Reformation. The advantages that this strife gave to the Ottomans have been studied by Stephen A. Fischer-Galati, *Ottoman Imperialism and German Protestantism, 1521–1555*. This study, while extending and deepening the work of Fischer-Galati, places the political activities of Southeastern Europe and of the Caucasus in the context of the expanding Ottoman Empire.

The Ottoman Empire, a power of great consequence in Europe and Asia in the sixteenth century, maintained careful surveillance over its own interests throughout the area. Disturbances infringing on the *Pax Ottomanica* were limited, generally speaking, to the borderlands. At midcentury the northern periphery of the Ottoman Sultanate in Eastern Europe—apart from Central Hungary which had been annexed outright—consisted of four vassal states: the principality of Erdel (Transylvania) whose vassalage followed closely upon the Ottoman victory at Mohács (1526), the principalities of Wallachia and Moldavia, both of which had paid tribute since the days of Meḥemmed II (1451–1481), and the Crimean Khanate, over whose Khans the same Sultan had established the right of appointment and dismissal after 1475.[6] These states provided an effective buffer to the north of the Danube against the Habsburg Empire, Poland-Lithuania, and Muscovy. From the Danube River to the Armenian plateau, the European and Asian heartlands of the Ottoman Empire stretched between the Black Sea and the Mediterranean, a position reflected in the Sultan's title, "Sultan of the two continents and the two seas."[7] Even when some of the vital provinces of the realm were to break out into open revolt at the end of the century, Constantinople, the nerve center of the Empire, could still, thanks to a powerful navy, maintain rapid communication with all parts of the realm and generally ensure the flow of commerce.

2 The Black Sea Region and the Danube Basin

The Mediterranean and its projection, the Aegean Sea, constituted the highway of foreign commerce for the Empire. The Black Sea, on the contrary, became largely a private concern of the Ottomans after the Genoese lost their colonies, and its commerce was generally accessible only to traders within the Ottoman realm. Minerals and produce coming from its shores and its hinterland could be purchased at Constantinople whereto it was transported, in many cases, in vessels of the Ragusan merchant fleet.[8] Much of the silk deriving from Persia came to Aleppo; spices, cloth, and luxury items from the further Orient, which succeeded in passing through the Portuguese blockade, found their way to Syrian and Egyptian ports by means of caravans from the Persian Gulf and the Red Sea. The grain exported from Egypt to Western Europe annually provided the Sultan with a handsome income. Wheat, rice, and beans also came from Egypt to the Constantinople emporium.

The commercial products of the Black Sea area were absorbed, to a large extent, by the Ottoman heartlands and particularly by Constantinople.[9] To gain some idea of the rich resources of the Black Sea region is to go a long way toward explaining the power and tenacity of an Empire which, until the end of the eighteenth century, was able to keep the European powers out of its Balkan and Anatolian heartlands.

By acquiring undisputed control over the Black Sea and its adjacent regions, the Ottoman Empire had made itself heir to vast and complex economic resources and, at the same time, had restricted or eliminated altogether the political, economic, and cultural ties of that region with other leading powers. The Venetians and the Genoese, after the fall of Constantinople and Kaffa respectively, attempted to resume normal trade relations with the Ottomans. Venice, in particular, was forced to resort to open warfare with the Sultan (1463–1475, 1499–1502, 1537–1540, 1570–1573) in the attempt to maintain her declining position in the Levant. Great inroads into the Venetian spice trade had been made by Portugal after the circumnavigation of Africa in 1498. Moreover, the Ottoman conquest of Syria and Egypt in 1516 and 1517 had restricted Venetian trade possibilities even further.[10]

The Ottoman control of the Black Sea and of the Transdanubian lands also altered conditions north of the Danube. The already vulnerable political structure of Hungary was made even weaker as the Ottomans slowly began to strangle its commerce on the Danube and to threaten its agricultural economy through the periodic devastation of the Hungarian countryside.[11] In truth, Ottoman control of the shores of the Danube up to Belgrade was the prelude to the victory of Mohács. The Danube basin was in this sense an offshoot of the Black Sea. The three Hungaries—the sliver of Austrian Hungary in the northwest, the Ottoman provincial government at Buda which controlled the Danubian plain from Esztergom to Belgrade, and the Ottoman protectorate of Erdel (Transylvania)—each had their individual economic interests. The Hungarian plain, enriched frequently by spring and autumn rains, might have been a prosperous farming region. Indeed, the tracts of land administered as *haṣṣ*, that is, imperial domain, were quite productive. Life on the imperial estates was regulated in a manner advantageous to the peasantry. By contrast, peasants subject to the whims of *tīmār*-holders, or more particularly to the harshness of Hungarian feudal laws, fared much worse. The Danubian basin as well as Transylvania suffered from a scarcity of population, a scarcity closely connected to the harshness of the social system and the frequency of warfare. If one were so hapless as to live close to the border areas between Habsburg and Ottoman, apart from paying taxes to both imperial systems, one lived in terror of losing one's life. The lesser nobility fostered cattle grazing as a means of gaining hard currency. Exports of cattle and hides went to Italy, Austria, Bohemia, and Poland. Silver and other mining, particularly in Transylvania, attracted the interest of Ottoman and Habsburg alike. As a general rule, periods of prosperity on the Danube were interrupted by periods of social unrest and war. Neither the Habsburgs nor the Ottomans in the sixteenth and seventeenth centuries were able to knock out the adversary and organize the region as an economic whole.

The proud Polish-Lithuanian monarchy, which had stretched from the Baltic Sea to the Black Sea in the fifteenth century, also saw its growth being stunted to the south as the Ottomans slowed down its lucrative trade on the Dnieper, Dniester, the Prut, and the famed "Tatar Way."[12] The Safavids in turn competed actively with the Ottomans for the material, human and spiritual resources of the Caucasus and Asia Minor, and they might have bested the Ottomans in the end had they possessed the ready access to seas and waterways and the consequent advantages of rapid (for the sixteenth century) communications, logistical support for their armies, and accessibility to abundant resources, new technology, and markets which gave their rivals such physical superiority. In short, the conquest of Constantinople had been the first step which led logically to the acquisition and control by the Ottomans of the Black Sea littoral, the wealth, quantity, and variety of whose resources had fostered the economic stability of Byzantium and had helped finance the building of magnificent cities in Renaissance Italy.

On the basis of regional specialization and social organization, the Black Sea littoral may be divided roughly into four separate regions: the Balkans; the Pontic Steppe and the Crimea; the Caucasus; and Asia Minor.[13]

3 The Balkan Region

One cannot, in the course of an introduction, produce economic details on the entire Balkan area, but it is important to have an idea, for the purposes of this study, of how the Ottoman economy functioned. By the beginning of the sixteenth century, the Bulgarian and Thracian regions, typical of productive regions elsewhere in the Balkan peninsula, had been incorporated into the Ottoman provincial system.[14] Most of the land was divided up according to the Ottoman military fief or *tīmār* system.[15] The peasantry or *Re'āyā* paid their dues, ranging from 10 to 50 per cent of their production per year, to their respective tīmār-holders (*Erbāb-i Tīmār*), tax farmers (*Mültezim*) of state lands, or intendants (*Mütevelli*) of *Waḳf* (piously endowed) property. The "dues" portion of the annual production, which was generally paid in kind in the form of grain or livestock, either served to nourish the households of the *tīmār*-holders and the dignitaries who received their "living" from the usufruct of state lands assigned to them, or it served to replenish the state granaries and pastures. Generally speaking, surpluses at all levels had to be sold at a fixed price to government agents such as the *jeleb*.[16] In spite of the strict surveillance of the government over prices and illegal sales, there were the usual abuses on the part of the state agents, the peasants, the *tīmār*-holders, and tax farmers. The peasants and *tīmār*-holders having access to caravan or water routes could sell off some of their produce at prices higher than the official rate. Tax farmers tended to take more tax than they were entitled to and government agents often bought at prices below the official rate.[17] Typical of some of the special economic groups in Bulgaria were the *Voynuks* (Bulgarian, *Voinitsi*)—Bulgarians, both Muslim and Christian, whose special duty it was to rear horses, tend the imperial stables, and perform similar functions. In exchange for their services, they were tax exempt.[18] Besides the production of the most common grains, rice growing was introduced for export to Istanbul in the Plovdiv and Pazarcïk (Pazarjik) regions during the fifteenth century. Leather, wax, wool, dried meat, and linen also were exported from Bulgaria, chiefly to Istanbul.[19]

Apart from agricultural, handicraft, and pastoral products, Bulgaria, like the adjacent regions of the Balkan peninsula, was important to the Ottoman economy for its mineral wealth. Its iron industry, for example, was concentrated at Chiprovits, Samakov, and Etropole. Copper and silver came from Chiprovits and Kratovo and were turned into copper and silver coins at the Ottoman mint of Kratovo.[20]

Documents and other evidence give clear testimony that the economic contributions of Bulgaria and Thrace to the Ottoman economy also included the production of wheat, the breeding of horses, and sheep raising.

Beyond the Danube in the principalities of Wallachia and Moldavia, the Ottomans were content, in the beginning, to exercise imperial control over foreign policy and trade, to exact special services in time of war, and to take a varying percentage of production in the form of an annual tribute. This meant that the traditional social structure—of *voivode* (~prince), *boyars* (notables with social ties and estates in the provinces), peasants (free and serf), and townsmen (artisans and traders)—was left largely intact; yet it did not mean of course that the machinery of the autonomous states was permitted to function in a traditional manner. Increasingly the position of voivode, which formerly had been filled by election from among the leading boyars, was subject to the will of the sultan. Ambitious boyars, by ingratiating themselves with the sultan and his confidants, could obtain the voivodeship for a few years until they were outbid by a rival. This new state of affairs placed the independent peasantry, who formerly could expect redress from the voivode, at the mercy of the boyar class. The privileged position which the Ottoman sultans accorded to the Millet-i Rum,[21] or the politico-religious community headed by the Greek Orthodox patriarch, also brought about changes in the artisan and merchant classes of the towns and cities. According to Stoianovich, the Ottoman conquest produced three basic stimuli that awakened the nascent commercial instincts of the Orthodox merchant community:

(*a*) The Ottoman encouragement of trade with the West and the freedom to expand commercial enterprise within the Ottoman realm (in the sixteenth century);

(*b*) The exclusion of non-Ottoman ships from the Black Sea;

(*c*) The building of new and the revival of declining Balkan towns and the capital, Constantinople.[22]

Stoianovich rightly points out that the establishment of the Empire and the resurgence of Constantinople as the emporium of the eastern Mediterranean forced Ottoman officialdom to seek out dependable markets and to find reliable traders and contractors as middlemen within the Empire. As the Jewish, Muslim, Greek, Ragusan, and other merchants took over these functions, the Black Sea in the sixteenth century was progressively closed to the Genoese and Venetians. Henceforth the merchants of the various non-Turkish ethnic groups extended their state functions to include tax farming and banking.[23]

These developments help explain the gradual takeover by the Greek Orthodox of the merchant-middleman function in the tributary principalities of Wallachia and Moldavia. Already by the end of the sixteenth century a rather ugly pattern of Christian exploiting Christian in the name of the Ottoman state had begun to sow seeds of deep animosity between peasant, middleman-merchant, and the Ottoman Muslim military or bureaucratic functionaries.

Thanks to the efforts of a number of Roumanian scholars, the economic history of Roumania and particularly of Moldavia has been closely examined. As Nistor has indicated, the Danubian principalities in the fifteenth century were located between two principal regions of manufacturing, the Genoese-Venetian sphere on the Black Sea and the Transylvanian sphere of central Europe. The principalities had served these two areas as a great reservoir of natural resources. The land produced a variety of grains, livestock, timber, and other goods. Moreover, the political organization of these countries served trade by protecting the merchant and his goods.[24] The Ottoman elimination of the Genoese factories and seizure of the ports of Kilia and Akkerman forced the reorientation of part of the Wallachian and Moldavian trade toward Istanbul and the Levant.[25] The principalities still managed, however, to keep intact their trade with Transylvania and Poland, particularly in produce such as swine and oxen, which was of secondary interest to the Ottomans.[26] As the ports were closed to all but the state-controlled ships of Ragusans, Muslims, and Greeks, much clandestine trade—for example, in grain—had to be routed to ports on the Aegean.[27] Such enterprises beyond the boundaries of the principalities appear to have placed the profit in other than Wallachian and Moldavian hands. By the mid-sixteenth century, when the Ottomans became much more concerned about provisioning their armed forces and the large cities, they introduced a system of state controls on prices and thereafter livestock and grain were supposed to be offered to the state buyers. About this time also the practice of farming out customs collections was being introduced. As this system in the principalities fell into the hands of the Greeks, they in turn imported their own relatives and friends to operate it. From such beginnings Greek influence grew in the principalities until even the princes themselves were chosen from the Greek aristocracy of Istanbul after 1711. If forced sales hurt the Wallachians and Moldavians, it appears at least that the letter of the law was difficult to enforce.[28]

In summary then, the chief exports from the principalities entering the sphere of Black Sea commerce included grain, livestock (chiefly sheep), horses (chiefly draft horses, *bārgīr*, for pulling cannon), fish, and timber. Mining was relatively unimportant. Silver and copper were imported from Transylvania and to a lesser extent from Poland, as was metalware. Some manufactured items also came from Istanbul and other Levantine centers.[29] Apart from controlling trade, the Ottomans required the voivode to pay the annual tribute in ducats at the current rate and to furnish the sultan with horses and carters [*'arābajīs* (Wallachia) and *Voynuk* (Moldavia)] and light cavalry in time of war.[30]

4 **The Crimea and the Kipchak Steppe**

The social structure of the Crimean Khanate might best be described as federated tribalism. Originally the tribes forming its nucleus were closely related to the tribal structure of the Golden Horde. During the fifteenth century as the Horde broke up, successor Khanates formed under the leadership of one of the many direct descendants of Jenghiz Khan. Thus in the Crimea, the Girāy ("Girey" as a variant) dynasty traced its descent from Urang-Tīmūr, great-grandson of Jenghiz. When the Ottomans established their suzerainty over the Crimean Khanate between 1575 and 1578, they assumed the right of appointing and dismissing the Girāy Khans, generally speaking in consultation with the chief dignitaries or *mīrzās* of the Khanate. The *mīrzās*, in turn, were the leaders of the various Crimean Tatar tribes which held winter and summer grazing and agricultural rights in the peninsula. The southern littoral of the Crimea, which had formerly been leased to the Genoese by the Khans of the Golden Horde, had been incorporated after 1475 into the Ottoman state as a *sanjāḳ* or province. Beyond the confines of the Crimean peninsula, the Crimean Khans exerted their authority over the Nogay Tatar tribes which grazed their herds of horses and flocks of sheep between the Dnieper and the Don rivers.[31] They also considered themselves the protectors and overlords of the Besleni Circassians who dwelt in the Caucasus region close to the Crimea. Each year the Circassians were expected to render tribute to the Khan in the form of the much-sought-after Circassian youths, who were in turn sent to the sultan or other dignitaries in Istanbul to curry their favor.[32] The Khans further inherited from the Khans of the Golden Horde pretensions to the overlordship of the steppe. In the name of the Golden Horde they periodically sought "gift" payments (*Ṭiyiş*) from Moldavia, Poland-Lithuania, and Muscovy in exchange for Tatar good will in peacetime and Tatar assistance in time of war.

The steppe served as a great natural barrier between the Ottoman Empire and Muscovy. Moreover, the products deriving from the steppe or its rivers provided valuable resources for the Empire. The slaves, which were acquired in raids upon the settled periphery of the steppe and the Caucasus, helped replenish the slave markets of Kaffa and Istanbul at a time when the *Devşirme* or draft of Christian youth had ceased to fill all vacancies in the palace service and the Janissary Corps.[33] As troops requiring little logistical support, the Tatars served well as light cavalry and raiders, inflicting much damage with their accurate bows and their "scorched earth" tactics. They further guarded the steppe approaches to the Black Sea and were sometimes called upon to quell revolts in the Christian principalities of Moldavia, Wallachia, and Transylvania.

One should not conclude, however, that the Tatars had to make war on their neighbors because of the absence of any agricultural activity in their own territories.[34] There is good evidence that the Crimean Tatar *begs* (variant of modern title, *Bey*) and *mīrzās* produced quantities of wheat and millet on their agricultural tracts with serf labor.[35] In exchange for pastoral products, the Crimean Tatars and Nogays also acquired grain and horses from Circassia, Abkhazia, and Moldavia. The Nogays, in addition to slaves, sold large quantities of butter and furs to the Armenian and Turkish merchants from whom the Nogays preferred to receive cotton twill or drapery trousers instead of money.[36] Fletcher estimated that thirty to forty thousand Tatar horses were sold in Moscow each year. Doubtless the Ottomans bought as many more.[37]

Besides their horses, the steppe dwellers kept large herds of cattle and flocks of black sheep. The natural deposits of salt and the abundance of fish also made the Crimea an important center for the export of dried and salted fish. Moreover, fish producing caviar and botango (mullet roe) were plentiful in the streams flowing off the steppe.[38] The southern littoral of the Crimea produced an abundance of fruit, olive oil, vegetables, and some wine. Crimean honey was famous in many parts of the Near East.[39] In short, the portion of the Kipchak steppe under Ottoman jurisdiction made an important contribution to the effective operation of the Empire. Moreover, the neighboring regions of Poland were known to be rich in deposits of saltpeter, an important component of gunpowder.[40]

5 The Caucasus

The peoples dwelling in the Caucasus, the region bordering the eastern shores of the Black Sea, had shared the culture of the successive peoples and empires which had held sway on the Black Sea. While often occupied or controlled at its shoreline by garrisoned fortresses, Abkhazia had maintained a certain autonomy, owing to the protection afforded to its people by her dense forests and difficult terrain. It was from these forests that the Abkhazian King, David II, had emerged in the twelfth century to unite the Georgian lands. By the sixteenth century, regionalism had become so strong that Abkhazia and Mingrelia represented little more than a series of feudal states and warring tribes whom the Ottomans occasionally assisted against attacks from Circassian or other mountain tribes. The Ottomans appear to have established permanent garrisons in Imereti only in the seventeenth century. The constant feudal warfare and miserable life of the serfs on the individual estates served the interests of the slave traders so well that the population of the entire region was greatly reduced by the eighteenth century to the benefit of the rival Russian, Safavid, and Ottoman states.[41]

Apart from the slave trade, one may catch glimpses of the economic potential of the area which was doubtless never fully realized in Ottoman times owing to lack of both manpower and diligence. The Venetian Contarini, who visited Mingrelia toward the end of the fifteenth century, found stone quarries and a little grain and grape growing. Canvas and wax were produced in small quantities.[42] Evliya Çelebi, that inveterate Ottoman traveler of the midseventeenth century, makes observations both similar to and differing from those of the earlier travelers. Thus he noted that many of the villagers lived in the mountains beyond the control of the Ottoman soldiers; he mentions also that the Circassians were often given rights of free passage so that they might bring beeswax and slaves through Abkhazian territory to the seacoast. But of Abkhazia in general he stated, "In this region there are never such things as markets, bazaars, inns, bath houses and shops."[43] Even the old traveler and his companions found the slaves so tempting that they bartered clothing, rugs, coats, and cloth to obtain a few. As he descended to the region of Mingrelia and Imereti, however, he found a prosperous land with well-built storehouses and an abundance of millet and wheat. Upon reaching the Sanjāḳ of Batum, he observed the local inhabitants trading salt, iron, and weaponry across the Mingrelian frontier in exchange for boxwood, wax, and slaves.[44]

These reports correlate well with other information about the Caucasus in the sixteenth century gleaned from a number of sources. The Circassians, from ancient times, had grown grain and raised livestock. The excellence of their sheep and horses was well known. They also followed occupations in mining, fishing, and beekeeping. The mountain ranges, which cut across portions of Circassia, Abkhazia, Mingrelia, Imereti, and Samtzkhé on the eastern littoral of the Black Sea, yielded iron, silver, gold, antimony, and lead. The Ottomans doubtless profited as much as they could from the mines but, as available sources indicate, they did not begin to exploit the mineral wealth of this region to any great extent before the seventeenth century.

The most distinctive exports of the Abkhazians, who were a people closely related to the Circassians, were falcons and wax. All of the Adighe (Circassian) peoples were noted for their fine metalwork. Butter and uncured ox and cow hides from Mingrelia also flooded the markets of Constantinople.[45] The boxwood and other forest resources were exploited for ships' timber and constituted a valuable strategic reserve. In spite of the mineral wealth of these regions, the inhabitants appear to have understated its extent in order to avoid complete occupation by the Ottomans.

The Transcaucasian hinterland—particularly Dagestan, Kakheti, and Shirvan—produced raw silk and saffian (saffron). Even the petroleum of Baku was exploited for combustible materials, heating, and medicinal uses.[46] The wealth of the region was already well attested in a thirteenth-century Armenian account:

> *Situated among the towering mountains of the Caucasus, the land of Albania is fair and alluring, with many natural advantages. The great Kur flows gently through it bearing fish great and small, and it throws itself into the Caspian Sea. In the plains round about there is to be found much bread and wine, naphtha and salt, silk and cotton, and innumerable olive trees. Gold, silver, copper and ochre are found in the mountains.*[47]

The wealth of the natural and human resources of the Caucasus and the weakness of the political organization of the region were facts well known to the Ottomans and these considerations must have exerted considerable influence on their decision to occupy part of the region in the late sixteenth century. Even in the time of Evliya Çelebi, however, the Ottomans had great respect for the ferocity of the peoples of the Caucasian mountains and only disturbed them when necessary. As Evliya Efendi once admitted when discussing Anapa, the seat of the *Sanjāḳ* of Taman, "The people of Shefaki, which is the name of the inhabitants, only pay their tithes at the point of the halberd, and are three hundred rebellious subjects."[48]

6 Asia Minor

The upland plateau of Asia Minor had been noted since ancient times for its production of grain and livestock. A series of mountain chains bordering the plateau hinder the easy transition from hinterland to coastal plain. On the Black Sea periphery of Asia Minor it is chiefly the river valleys which facilitate commerce and communications with the interior. Moreover, if one moves in an easterly direction toward Persia on the upland plateau, one encounters the characteristic topography of eastern Asia Minor, high mountains and upland valleys phasing into the Armenian, Georgian, and Caucasian Chains. Typically, the plateau, the coastal plains, and the river valleys, with their easy access to the main currents of Ottoman life, interest us here. There is, however, a secondary but very important theme to Ottoman culture in Asia Minor, a theme closely connected to the mountain refuge areas and the symbiotic relationship between the tribal-pastoral and the town-agricultural peoples dwelling in those regions and having only limited access to Islamic-Ottoman civilization. One need only follow the progression of Evliya Çelebi across Asia Minor, read the accounts of the Jelālī rebellion, review the role of tribal military units in Ottoman armies as related by Koçu Bey, or study mystical and folk poetry of the sixteenth century to catch a glimpse of that unofficial Ottoman world which still awaits systematic description.[49]

The social organization and the political cross currents of Asia Minor deserve full consideration in any detailed treatment of the Ottoman economy. In a survey of this nature, however, one must take it for granted that a great deal of regional commerce of the type described by Evliya Efendi took place and confine one's self to the enumeration of produce and craft goods of ready access to the merchants of the Black Sea region.

In contrast to the social structures of the Danubian principalities, the Crimean Khanate, and the fractious feudal and tribal areas of the Caucasus region, no precise description of a social structure may be applied to the Black Sea periphery of Asia Minor as a whole. As in the case of Thrace and Bulgaria, however, Asia Minor belonged to those heartlands of the Empire where the countryside, generally speaking, was organized on the basis of the *tīmār* system and the cities relied upon the corporate structure of the guild system to provide for the orderly production of craft goods for local consumption and export.[50] In those localities where mining and smelting were the chief occupations, the mines were customarily leased to an entrepreneur who, in turn, had to pay the state a percentage of his profit each year in accordance with the Islamic tax on booty or treasure trove. Strictly speaking, this amounted to 20 per cent or the *khums* or *penjiḳ* of Islamic law. The town-dwelling *Re'āyā*, who worked in the mines, were relieved of their tax obligations. As elsewhere in the Empire, the state licensed Christians and Muslims to procure the items of commerce at a price fixed by market and state controls. The traders attempted, naturally, to buy up goods in the interior at prices below the *narḥ*, or official rate.[51]

One may gain some idea from Evliya Çelebi of the nature of the transition from the Caucasus region to Asia Minor. The old traveler has indicated that the Batum *Sanjāḳ* (~district) of the Trabzon *Eyaleti* (province of Trebizond), which was situated on the Mingrelian border, consisted of thirteen *zi'āmets* (military fiefs larger than *tīmārs*) and fifty-three *tīmārs*. When this district was called on campaign it was required, in theory, to furnish 800 mounted warriors (*jebelū*) and 300 troops for the pasha of the province. As the Laz and Mingrelians were very turbulent, however, these troops were never sent on campaign; moreover, a detachment of 800 Janissaries was assigned to the district to help garrison the fortress on the shores of the Çoruh river.[52]

The region from Geresun to Sinope was known in Byzantine times as "the orchard of Constantinople." The skills of the gardener and fruit grower in this region have persisted in Ottoman times and even to the present day.[53] From Geresun (Cerasus), that legendary city of the first cherry trees, came, of course, cherries and from the reticulated and irrigated gardens (*müşebbek bostānlarï*) of Amasya, only a two-days' journey from the coast, derived barley, *noḫūd* (chick peas), choice apples, grapes, and unstrained grape juice (*şīre*). Practically the entire shoreline produced hazelnuts. The *nardenk* or pomegranate juice and dried fish of Sinope were widely acclaimed as were the pears and pickles of Samsun. The camelot or Angora goat hides and rice coming from the interior were also exported from Sinope.[54]

Trebizond exported such important items as raw silk, olives, pears, wine and grapes, *kermés* or crimson, linen, wool, and silk cloth, *basma* (cotton prints), and hides. From the general region of Lazistan was also exported wheat, cotton thread, and the skins of martins and wolves. Honey and wax were important export commodities, as was the case in the Caucasus.[55]

Further down the coast the port of Ünye (Honio) was noted for tallow and also served as the closest outlet for the *basma*, *bokhayrani* (cotton tissue), carpets, and other exports of Tokat.[56] Amasya and Tokat, both important centers of cloth and carpet weaving, doubtless vied for the export market. Apart from this similarity, however, each of these cities on the Yeşilïrmak river went their own separate ways. Amasya, richly endowed with *medreses*, remained an intellectual center of the Ottoman empire for centuries and also took pride in its horse trading, while Tokat earned acclaim as an important caravan crossroads.[57]

In the sixteenth century, the Ottoman state never suffered from lack of naval stores on the Black Sea. While much construction timber and firewood derived from the Balkans, the coast of Asia Minor and particularly the region between Sinope and Istanbul abounded in construction materials of the finest sort, including boxwood, fir, oak, walnut, and plane. Timber in the region from Sinope to the capital was so visibly plentiful that the Venetian baili reflected their envy and concern in numerous reports to the Venetian Senate and the Turks dubbed the region around the Sakarya river as *Ağaç Denizi* or "Sea of Trees."

This same abundance was reflected in the mineral wealth within easy access of Black Sea ports. Evliya Efendi blandly mentioned in one of his reports that the Sultan possessed seventy silver mines within his dominions.[58] While in no sense exhausting the evidence at hand, one may easily grasp the importance of mining to the ecomony of Asia Minor and to the Empire. The Armenian highlands were particularly important for their wealth in copper, silver, lead, iron, arsenic, gold, alum, and mercury. Again one cannot emphasize too much the importance of access to minerals as a part of Ottoman strategy on the Persian frontier. [59] These mines had also been known to the Venetians and Genoese. Near Tokat and Amasya the Genoese and Venetians had exploited extremely productive silver mines, as did the Ottomans at Gümüşhane and Gümüş Hajji Köy where Ottoman mints were also located.[60] To the West, in the Isfendiyar range between Sinope and Kastamonu, rich copper mines kept the furnaces of Kastamonu blazing and the pure metal was exported from the port of Inebolu (Zinopoli).[61] The renowned iron mines of Paphlagonia, the region of which Kastamonu was the capital, also contributed to the wealth of the empire and the smelting industry of the area.[62]

The importance of mining and smelting in this part of Asia Minor was further attested by the secondary industry observed by Evliya Efendi. He praised the fine cutlery in the town of Kerde near Bolu and went on to acclaim the goldsmiths and hatchet makers of Trebizond as the best in the world.[63] Thus, in spite of the strong attraction that Constantinople held for the artisan classes, as witnessed by the detailed account of its guilds given by Evliya Çelebi, the provincial centers mentioned herein still appear to have been thriving up to the mid-seventeenth century.[64]

7 The Political Structure of the Crimean Khanate

At the base of Crimean society, as has been noted, were a number of seminomadic Turkic tribes, many of which traced their origins to the Golden Horde.[65] Their leaders, called "mīrzās," were chosen from certain hereditary noble families of their respective tribes. Tradition had determined that the mīrzās of four specific tribes, the Şīrīn, Argīn, Barīn, and Ḳipçāk (Kipchak), stood above the other mīrzās and were known as the "*dört Karaçi beği*" (the four Karaçi begs).[66] These four leaders effectively controlled all of the tribes by reason of their senior position to the other mīrzās. The mīrzā of the Şīrīn tribe, moreover, was recognized as the *bāş beg* or chief beg of all the mīrzā aristocracy and in this role he wielded great authority. Of his own volition he could call a *kurultāy* (general assembly) of all the tribal dignitaries in times of crisis. Generally also, he kept close contact with the ruling circles of Constantinople through channels independent of the khan, and thus could exert pressure in favor or to the detriment of the khan. The khan, of course, had to have the support of the mīrzās in order to raise an army among their respective tribes.

The Crimean khans, who were descendants of Jenghiz Khan, bore the family name Girāy.[67] Until the khanate came under the protection of the Ottomans in 1475, the leading contenders of the Girāy line for the post of khan made alliances with the principal Crimean Tatar tribes, and often also sought support from the Nogay tribes on the Kipchak steppe, or from the Circassians.[68] It was also not unusual for pretenders to be sponsored by Poland-Lithuania, Muscovy, or the Genoese.

The ancestors of the Girāys had taken refuge in Poland-Lithuania during the first decades of the fifteenth century when they had been driven out of their *ulus* or hereditary appanage by Jenghizids of other lines. During the formative years of the Girāy dynasty in the Crimea, it is not unfair to consider the Crimean khans as near vassals of the Polish crown. When Menglī Girāy became khan in 1466, he weakened the ancient tie with Poland-Lithuania by forming alliances with the Ottoman Turks and with Muscovy. It was owing to the intrigues of the Genoese, then in possession of the southern shores of the Crimea, that the Ottomans were persuaded by the Şirīn Beg to intervene. This intervention led to the establishment by the Ottomans of the right of the Sultan to appoint and dismiss the Crimean khans.[69]

By establishing their right to appoint and dismiss the khans, the Ottomans gradually increased the respect for the office of khan and also introduced a considerable amount of stability for the khanate itself. Nevertheless, throughout the sixteenth century the tribal aristocracy split roughly into two factions, one pro-Ottoman and the other traditionalist, the latter advocating election of the khan in the traditional manner and a closer adherence to the *Yāsāḳ*, the collection of regulations and restrictions promulgated by Jenghiz Khan which was based on the traditions of the Mongols and other steppe peoples.[70] The Ottomans supported their choice for khan by providing him with funds, over and above his yearly income, to establish his own household troops. This payment, the so-called *sekbān aḳçesi*, was instituted upon the forcible installation of Ṣāḥib Girāy, the pro-Ottoman candidate, in 1534.

The khan, within the dictates of custom, controlled appointments for his administration. He first appointed his *veli'ahd* or heir apparent, who was known by the title *Ḳalġay*. The khans jealously guarded this privilege as one of the few means by which they could influence the choice of their successor, usually appointing a younger brother or a son to this post. Meḥemmed Girāy II, when his brother and Ḳalġay, 'Ādil Girāy, was murdered in Persia, wished to appoint his son Sa'adet as Ḳalġay but, upon the objections of his brother Alp Girāy, was forced to appoint the latter to this rank. Khan Meḥemmed, however, according to tradition, then created the office of *Nūr ed Dīn*, or second in succession to the khanship, to which he appointed his son. He was able to gain the Sultan's approval for this innovation because Tatar troops were badly needed in Persia.[71]

Apart from the Crimean peninsula, over which the khan had jurisdiction except for the *sanjaḳ* (later, *eyalet*) of Kaffa (Feodosiya) and the garrison towns of Gözlev (Evpatoriya) and Kerch, the khan also controlled most of the Kipchak steppe from the Dniester to the Don and portions of the Kuban River basin and the surrounding steppe. These regions were predominantly occupied by Nogay Tatars and Circassians. To act as agents of the khan and as commanders of the military contingents in these regions outside the Crimean peninsula, the khan customarily appointed three other officials, the so-called *ser'asker sulṭāns*, who controlled the districts known as the Bujak, Yedisan, and Kuban.[72] The khan, moreover, appointed the *Or beği* or commander of the fortress at Orkapï (Perekop). This office was ordinarily the prerogative of the Şīrīn beg. Among other important posts, the khan also appointed the *muftī*, the *ulūġ-agā* (the vezir), the *ḳażī'asker*, the *hazīnedār başï*, and the *defterdār*.[73]

The khan wielded his power with the aid of these dignitaries. The checks upon his authority could originate with the Ottoman Sultan, the Grand Vezir, the Crimean Tatar tribal aristocracy, the muftī, or the defterdār. To a certain extent, the khan was restricted by the *Yāsāḳ* and other customary law as well as those acts coming within the jurisdiction of the *Şerī'at*. Throughout the sixteenth century there is an imperceptible assimilation by the Crimean Tatars of many aspects of the Ottoman way of life. The khans, however, retained one important privilege, their right to have separate coinage (*Sikke*), throughout the existence of the khanate. Islam Girāy (1584–1588), the immediate predecessor of Ġāzī Girāy, acquiesced in the loss of a second great privilege of independent Muslim rulers, the right of being first mentioned in the Friday prayers (*Ḫuṭbe*).[74]

8 The Politics of the Steppe and Their Significance for the Great Powers

At midcentury, apart from the doomed khanates of Kazan and Astrakhan, four distinct loci of power survived on the steppe, each possessing a certain amount of freedom of action: the Crimean Tatars, the Circassians, the Cossacks, and the Nogay Tatars. The power of the Crimean Tatars centered in the Crimean peninsula but radiated to the Beslenī Circassians in the Northern Caucasus and to those Tatars, Nogay and others, who wandered between Azak (Azov) and the Bujak (Bessarabia). Traditionally an ill-defined suzerainty even extended over the Beştepe[75] and Kabardinian Circassians. The firmness of the Crimean Tatar hold over the Circassians depended largely on the personal effectiveness of any given khan in exerting his authority in that region. These considerations, however, did not keep the Circassians from arranging separate alliances with the Don Cossacks, the Tsar of Muscovy, the Şamẖal of Tarku, or the Ottoman Sultan, nor from repulsing an overzealous Crimean khan.

The Cossacks of the Dnieper and Don rivers, in the main, were Christians of Slavic origin. Although they cooperated with their Muslim neighbors on occasion, they were, culturally speaking, an extension into the steppe of the Polish-Lithuanian and Muscovite powers. In defense of the agricultural side of their economy, as well as their homes and villages, they frequently but not always assisted the Christian powers at the expense of the Muslims. For the period of this study, the two Cossack settlements will be considered as independent of each other. The Don Cossacks had their center on the Don River near Voronezh and by the end of the century their settlements had moved downstream toward Azov and through various portages to the Donets. The Dnieper Cossacks or the Zaporozhians, as these names imply, had their stronghold "beyond the rapids" on an island in the Dnieper river. By mid-century, these two vanguards of Slavic civilization on the steppe had firmly established themselves. As the century advanced, the Don Cossacks, who frequently married their Circassian captives,[76] served the interests of Muscovy in its expansion down the Volga and into the Northern Caucasus. The Zaporozhians, moreover, were frequently encouraged by the Tsar of Muscovy to raid the Crimean Tatars either across the steppe or by sea. Also these Dnieper Cossacks frequently assisted or embarrassed the Polish kings by their bold attacks on Ottoman territory. The Nogay Tatars, the Turkic group on the western steppe which was most strongly committed to a nomadic way of life, traditionally had its center near the well-watered deltas of the Volga (Itīl) and Ural (Yā'iḳ) rivers and had long been closely associated with the Khanate of Astrakhan.

The early decades of the sixteenth century were critical for determining the direction of the steppe's future development. At that time, a long struggle commenced for the control of the sparsely populated and ill-defined territories between the Ottoman and Muscovite states. During this period the Ottoman Empire had to face formidable enemies to the west, south, and east and was therefore content, in general, to leave the problems of the steppe to the Crimean khans. But, much to the consternation of the Sublime Porte, Meḥemmed Girāy Khan I (1514–1523) and Ṣāḥib Girāy Khan I (1534–1551), at the height of their power as khans, succeeded in reestablishing some of the prerogatives of the Golden Horde, thus offering a threat to Ottoman domination of the northern shores of the Black Sea.[77] Meḥemmed Girāy had extended his sway over Kazan, Astrakhan, and much of the Northern Caucasus, and at the same time had managed to extract large tributes from Moscow. At one point, Ṣāḥib Girāy had been almost equally successful. Both died violent deaths: the former at the hands of the Nogays, who resented too much control by the Crimean Tatars; the latter in the struggle to retain control of the Khanate after the Sultan had appointed Devlet Girāy to succeed him. Meḥemmed Girāy had been a traditionalist and hence a strong supporter of the Yāsāḳ prescriptions; Ṣāḥib Girāy made every effort to introduce Ottoman institutions into the Crimea. Both khans, however, had dared to oppose the Ottoman hierarchy at critical stages. It is little wonder, then, that the Ottomans initially paid limited attention to Muscovy except as a potential ally who could be called upon to clip the wings of their Crimean vassal.[78]

The fall of Kazan and Astrakhan alarmed the Porte, particularly as the Beştepe (Pyatigorsk) Circassians sought Muscovite protection against the Crimean Tatars in 1552. The Kalmucks and Kabardinians followed suit in 1557.[79] The Muslim dam had broken and a flood of Christian Slavs began to pour into the Volga-Kama basin.

What had become apparent in a few years on the political level had been developing for decades on a social and economic plane. Generally speaking, Muscovite merchants, dealing in metalwares, firearms, cloth, and grain, had more to offer to the steppe dwellers than did the Crimean Tatars. The longstanding trade relations of Muscovy with the Hanseatic League and other Western European states were to be enhanced by direct trade with England after the opening of the Northern Route to St. Nicholas (later, Archangelsk) by Richard Chancellor in 1553,[80] and by direct contact with Safavid Persia across the Caspian Sea after 1556. An agrarian economy possessing skilled, town-dwelling craftsmen and a society based on a pastoral economy could work out in the short run a symbiotic relationship profitable to both, but the Crimean Tatars, on their own, could not compete economically with Moscow, either as grain growers or craftsmen. Only Ottoman traders could have filled the economic gap, but the Crimean Tatars, by continuing the fiction of the Golden Horde prerogatives and by putting obstacles in the way of smooth relations with the Ottomans, may have alienated the steppe market and also the Ottoman traders.[81] Furthermore, trade in human beings instead of trade along craft or agricultural lines continued to bring the best profits to the Tatars. With the growing advantages of the settled populations over the nomadic, as a result of technological advances, the settled people began to dominate the nomads more than had previously been possible. Muscovite control of the Volga also checked the flow of Tatar manpower into the western steppe at a time when pressure from the eastern steppe, notably from the Kazaks, was tending to force the Nogays westward out of their traditional pasturage in Western Siberia.

The Cossacks, in particular, by means of their *tābūrs*[82] or armed wagon trains, their *şayḳas*, or light seacraft armed with small cannon, and their increasingly effective use of firearms, developed techniques for moving about the steppe and rivers in relative safety. Such innovations as these, combined with factional rifts among the tribal leaders over what measures they might take to preserve their way of life, helped bring about a great split in the Nogay *ulūs* during the khanship of Ṣāḥib Girāy.[83] As the tribes had to acquire such necessities as grain and firearms, they were forced to choose between the Ottomans and the Muscovites, the two principal powers in this region that could provide such items. Insofar as technical skill was required to handle new weapons, the provision of technicians also played a part.[84] The Nogays also found a more accessible market for their horses in Moscow than in Constantinople.[85] Finally, it seems that the Ottomans, in leaving Nogay affairs largely in the hands of the Crimean Tatars, had taken for granted that the Nogays would continue to support their coreligionists against the *Dār ül-Harb*, i.e., the non-Muslim enemy countries. Moscow, on the contrary, sent to the Nogays skilled diplomats such as the Maltsevs, who could speak the Nogay-Tatar dialect with ease.[86] By midcentury the so-called Ulūġ or Great Nogays, under the leadership of Ismā'īl Mīrzā, a descendant of Edigū, left the Volga section of the steppe and entered the Crimean-Ottoman sphere of influence by settling between the Dnieper and the Kuban rivers.[87] These movements and alignments during the later years of Ṣāḥib Girāy's reign did not constitute a blessing for the Crimean Tatars or their steppe policy. On the one hand, the Ulūġ Nogays, by supporting Muscovy, played a vital role in the subsequent loss of Kazan and Astrakhan to Muscovy. The Kiçī Nogays, far from helping the Crimean Tatars stem the tide, actually threatened the existence of the Khanate. Only after they were brought to obedience in 1546 could Ṣāḥib Girāy again take measures against the Moscow State.[88]

These fundamental economic and political moves enabled Moscow, in the absence of active opposition on the part of the Ottomans, to divide the steppe into two parts and to establish a foothold on the Caspian Sea. The Tsar could now control the movements of the tribes and the east-west flow of trade.

NOTES

1. Vaughan, *Europe and the Turk: A Pattern of Alliances 1350–1700*, pp. 104–186.
2. Ibid.; also Skwarczynski, "The *Decretum Electionis* of Henry of Valois," *S.E.E.R.*, XXXVII (Dec. 1958), 113–130; Karttunen, "Die Königswahl in Polen, 1575," *Suomalaisen Tiedeakatemian toimituksia*, Ser. B., Vol. 12, No. 4.
3. Novak, "The Interregna and Stéphan Bathory, 1572–1586," in *Cambridge History of Poland to 1696*, pp. 384–385.
4. Parry, "Barūd," *E.I.*², I, 1061–1066.

5. L. von Pastor, *History of the Popes from the Close of the Middle Ages,* XIX, 332, 338.
6. Inalcïk, "Yeni Vesikalara göre Kïrïm Hanlïğïnïn Osmanlï Tabiliğine Girmesi ve Ahitname Meselesi," *Belleten 8,* No. 30 (1944), 185–229.
7. Dunlop, "Baḥr-i Rūm," *E.I.*[2], I, 936.
8. Braudel, *La Méditerranée et le Monde Méditerranéen à la Epoque de Philippe II,* pp. 79–81.
9. Andrea Badoaro, the envoy sent to the Porte in 1573 to confirm the treaty of peace, wrote, ". . . tutto (di vettovaglie) e somministrato dal Mar Maggiore d'onde continuamente trae pane, carne e pesce." Alberi, ed., *Relazioni degli Ambasciatori,* Ser. III, Vol. I, 353.
10. Between 1454 and 1463, Venetians farmed the copper and alum mines and took charge of the Ottoman mints and customs. A good account of their subsequent vicissitudes is found in Heyd, *Histoire du commerce,* II, 315–328, 508–552.

For an interesting account of the ups and downs of Venetian and Ragusan trading activities in the 16th century, see Mirkovich, "Ragusa and the Portuguese Spice Trade," *S.E.E.R.*, XXI/1 (March 1943), 174–187. Most significant for the purpose of this study is the following quotation:

> *Most harmful to* [*Venetian*] *trade was . . .* [*the war*] *fought with Turkey 1537–1540. For long periods she was excluded from the ports of the Ottoman Empire. The decline of her shipbuilding was also a very important factor in the rise of her rival Ragusa . . . .*

While Venice was able to maintain a foothold in the Levantine trade by going along with Ottoman policy in the late 16th century, Genoa became wedded to Habsburg fortunes and in 1566 lost even the island of Chios to the Ottomans. See Pàstine, *Genova e l'Impero Ottomano nel Secolo XVII,* especially pp. 5–7. For an account of Venetian-Ragusan clashes at the close of the 16th century in connection with Venetian-Balkan trade via Spalato, see Braudel, *Le Méditerranée,* pp. 247–248.
11. A number of writers have singled out the decline of the monarchy and the increased influence of the magnates as important factors in the success of the Ottoman expansion into Hungary. W. H. McNeill, in his recent study *Europe's Steppe Frontier 1500–1800,* has traced this development and associated it with the increase in wheat cultivation on the Danube, in the Ukraine, and in Poland as suggested earlier by Braudel, p. 642, and by Blum, "The Rise of Serfdom in Eastern Europe," *Am. Hist. Rev.*, LXII/4 (July 1957), 807–836. See also Salamon, *Ungarn im Zeitalter der Türkenherrschaft, passim.*
12. Rutkowski, *Histoire économique de la Pologne avant les partages,* pp. 186–197, and Nistor, *Handel und Wandel in der Moldau bis zum Ende des 16. Jahrhunderts,* especially pp. 11–19.
13. See the author's article, "Ottoman Imperial Policy and the Economy of the Black Sea Region in the Sixteenth Century," *J.A.O.S.*, 86 (Apr.-June 1966), 86–113.
14. For details on the Ottoman system, see Gibb and Bowen, *Islamic Society and the West,* Vol. I, *Islamic Society in the Eighteenth Century,* and Inalcïk, "Ottoman Methods of Conquest," *Studia Islamica,* II (1954), 103–129. Among the standard works on Ottoman administration in Bulgaria is the study by Refik, *Türk Idaresinde Bulgaristan,* which is basically a document collection.
15. For details, see Gibb and Bowen, I, Pt. 1, 235 ff., and Sakazov, *Bulgarische Wirtschaftsgeschichte,* pp. 172 ff. See also Inalcïk's valuable survey, "Bulgaria," *E.I.*[2], I, 1302–1304.
16. The best article on the subject of Ottoman price and produce controls is by Hahn, "Die Verpflegung Konstantinopels durch staatliche Zwangswirtschaft . . ." *Vierteljahrschr. für Sozial- und Wirtschaftsgeschichte,* VIII, 1–22, and 45 documents, pp. 23–64. Hahn shows that, contrary to the Byzantine practice of squeezing both the producer and the consumer for the benefit of the emperor and the court, the Ottomans squeezed the producers (i.e., the peasants) and the merchants to the benefit of the urban consumer (and presumably the army). The Ottomans were more interested, in Hahn's opinion, in placing military restraints on their vassal states than in forging commercial ties; in tribute, rather than commercial profits. Thus rather than rely on the forces of the market, the Ottomans built up a kind of police state to ensure that produce would be brought to the capital. Among the root causes for these attitudes, Hahn notes the following:

(a) Islamic concern for the poor and the weak (but famine in the province was more acceptable than famine in the city);

(b) Ottoman distrust of the Greek, Italian, Jewish, and Armenian merchant classes;

(c) Istanbul, as a city, developing few trade ties with the immediate countryside beyond its walls (i.e., organically disconnected from the hinterland);

(d) Limitations placed on free trade which led to illegal trade and subsequent repressive measures.

17. Güçer, "Le Commerce intérieur des céréales dans l'empire Ottoman . . . du xvi siècle," *Ikt. Fak. Mec.,* XI, Suppl., 166–168; and Stoianovich, "The Conquering Balkan Orthodox Merchant," *J. of Econ. Hist.,* XX (1960), 241–243.

18. For further details, see Gibb and Bowen I, Pt. 1, 54, 249; and Dorev, ed., *Dokumenti za Bulgarskata Istoriya,* III/I *Dokumenti iz Turskite Derzhavni Arkhivi, passim.*

19. MacDermott, *A History of Bulgaria 1393–1885,* pp. 34–35.

20. *Ibid.* Consult also the excellent survey of Ottoman mining by Âfet Inan in *Aperçu général sur l'histoire economique de l'Empire Turc-Ottoman,* Türk Tarih K. Seri VIII/6, 40–42, and p. 68 where it is noted that there were 17 ironworks in Samakov and that some 8000 cartloads of iron products left Samakov via Salonika each year as late as the mid-17th century.

21. See Nistor, *Handel and Wandel,* pp. 50–54; Inalcïk, "Boghdan," *E.I.*², I, 1252–1253; and Beldiceanu, "Eflāḳ," *E.I.*², II, 687–689. On the millet system, see Gibb and Bowen, I/2, 207–261.

22. Stoianovich, "Balkan Merchant," *J. of Econ. Hist.* XX, 235.

23. *Ibid.,* pp. 238–241. One may conclude that Professor Stoianovich overrates the extent of the commercial monopoly of the Greeks and Slavs in the 16th century if some attention is given to Iorga, *Les Voyageurs français dans l'Orient européen,* who quotes Pierre Belon du Mans [*Les Observations de plusieurs singularités et choses memorables trouvés en Grèce . . .*, II, f. 181] thus: "Quant aux Juifs, ils sont 'cauteleux plus que nulle autre nation' et ils ont 'tellement embrassé tout le traffic de la marchandise de Turquie que la richesse et revenu du Turc est entre leur main.' " The same author, citing the account of Pierre Lescalopier, notes: "Sofia lui apparoît avec ses marchands turcs, juifs et ragusans." Doubtless we are confronted here with the question of the generations, with first and second generation "Ottomans" securing the family fortune while third generation "Ottomans" served as diplomats, bureau secretaries, interpreters, and tax farmers. See further on this subject Gottwald, "Phanariotische Studien," *Leipziger Vierteljahrsschrift für Südosteuropa, V,* 1–57; Roth, *The House of Nasi: Doña Gracia, passim*; and Lewis, *Notes and Documents from the Turkish Archives,* pp. 28–34.

24. Nistor, *Handel und Wandel,* pp. 1–3.

25. *Ibid.,* pp. 8–9; Inalcïk, "Boghdan" *loc. cit.* A plan on the part of Poland and Ottoman Turkey to dredge the Dniester to improve navigation in the late 16th century failed (Nistor, pp. 31–32).

26. See Nistor (p. 160) on the importance of beech forests (Buchovina) for fattening pigs. A notable success for Wallachian commerce was the conclusion of an agreement in 1588 to export livestock to Poland for transshipment to England. See Nistor, p. 12, and Podea, "A Contribution to the Study of Queen Elizabeth's Eastern Policy, 1590–1593," *Mélanges d'histoire générale,* p. 54.

27. Nistor, p. 9, and Güçer, "Le Commerce intérieur des céréales," *Ikt. Fak. Mec.,* XI, Suppl., 168.

28. See Nistor, pp. 9–11, and the series of 16th-century documents in Hahn, "Die Verpflegung Konstantinopels," *Beiheft* VIII, 23–64.

29. Nistor, pp. 157–167.

30. Inalcïk, "Boghdan," and Peçewī, *Tārīh-i Peçewī,* II, 152 ff.

31. For further details see Inalcïk, "Giray," *I.A.,* IV, 783–789; the same author's "Osmanlï Tabiliğine," 88; and the article by Kortepeter, "Ġāzī Girāy II, Khan of the Crimea, and Ottoman Policy in Eastern Europe and the Caucasus, 1588–1594," *S.E.E.R.,* 44 (1966), 139–166.

32. Belokurov, *Snosheniya Rossii s Kavkazom, 1578–1613, passim,* and the more recent Kusheva, *Narodny Severno-Kavkaza i ix Svazi c Rossiey v xvi–xvii vv.* The Ottoman and Crimean Tatar pressure

on the northern Caucasus in the 16th century is made quite clear in a number of the documents published under the editorship of Kumykov and Kusheva, *Kabardino-Russkie Otnosheniya,* I, xvi–xvii vv., and the article by Namitok, "The 'Voluntary' Adherence of Kabarda (Eastern Circassia) to Russia," *Caucasian Review,* 2 (Munich, 1956), 17–33, which tempers considerably the purely Russian point of view.

33. Ayalon, "The European-Asiatic Steppes: A Major Reservoir of Power for the Islamic World," (Trudy) *Proceedings of the 25th International Congress of Orientalists,* II, 47–52.

34. Novosel'skiy, in his important study *Bor'ba Moskovskogo Gosudarstva s Tatarami v pervoy polovine xvii veka,* rather oversimplifies the operation of the Tatar economy and too readily concludes that the Tatars were "unproductive," see particularly, his conclusions, pp. 416 ff.

35. Da Lucca, "Relation des Tatars . . . ," in *Relation de Divers Voyages Curieux,* I, 15; and John Smith, *Travels in Europe, Asia, Africa and America,* pp. 23–28, where this famous soldier of fortune describes his own temporary enserfment on a Crimean Tatar estate.

36. Da Lucca, pp. 18–20.

37. Fletcher, *Of the Russe Common Wealth,* pp. 91–92. As to the place of origin and the prices received for various breeds of horses available in Moscow at the end of the 16th century, see Margèrét, *Estat de l'Empire de Russie,* pp. 26 recto and verso. The significance of the horse on the steppe, even at this late date, is best interpreted by Creel, "The Role of the Horse in Chinese History," *The Am. Hist. Rev.*, LXX/3 (April 1965), 647–672.

38. Fletcher, pp. 91–92; and Braudel, pp. 79–81.

39. Samoylovich, "Beiträge zur Bienenzucht in der Krim im 14.–17. Jahrhundert," *Festschrift Georg Jacob,* pp. 270–275.

40. Chirovsky, *Old Ukraine,* pp. 174 f.

41. Allen, *A History of the Georgian People,* pp. 265, 282–288.

42. Allen, p. 341.

43. Evliya Çelebi, *Seyāhatnāme,* II, 96–97, 104–107.

44. *Ibid.,* p. 96.

45. Lamberti, *Relatione della Cholchide Hoggi Detta Mengrellia,* pp. 229–232; Alberi, ed., "Relazione . . . di Marino Cavalli (1560)," in *Relazioni degli Ambasciatori,* Ser. III, Vol. I, 278–279; and Tavernier, *Les Six Voyages . . . ,* 325, where the author remarks, "J'ay remarque ailleurs que la plus grande partie du fer qui se consomme en Turquie vient de Mingrelie." Da Lucca (p. 15) and Braudel (pp. 79–81) also add interesting observations to this general picture.

46. Marco Polo, *Marco Polo de Venice sia de la meranegliose cose del Mundo,* pp. (a^8) verso–(b^1) recto. For details of Caucasian silk, see Heyd, *Histoire du commerce,* II, 670–674.

47. Dowsett, tr., *The History of the Caucasian Albanians of Movsès Dasxuranci,* p. 5.

48. Evliya (Hammer tr.), II, p. 59.

49. See Evliya, *Seyāhatnāme,* III, *passim*; Akdağ, "Celâlî Isyanlarïnïn Başlamasï," *Ankara Üniversitesi Dil ve Tarih-Coğrafya Fakültesi Dergisi,* IV, 23–50; Refik, *Anadoluda Türk Aşiretleri, passim*; the summary of Koçu Bey's *Risâle* by Behrnauer, "Kogâbeg's Abhandlung über den Verfall des osmanischen Staatsgebäudes seit Sultan Suleiman dem Grossen," *Z.D.M.G.,* XV (1861), especially pp. 279 ff., and 307 ff.; and the historical introduction to and the poetry of Karacaoğlan prepared by Öztelli, *Karacaoğlan, Hayatï, Sanatï, Şiirleri* [*Türk Klâsikleri*: 1]. Recently Cengiz Orhonlu has made an important contribution to the history of the tribes in his *Osmanlï imparatorluğunda aşiretleri iskân teşebbüsü* (*1691–1696*) (Istanbul, 1963).

50. Gibb and Bowen I/2, *passim*; Mantran, *Istanbul dans le deuxième moitié du xviie siècle,* pp. 349–394; and Taeschner, "Das Bosnische Zunftwesen zur Türkenzeit (1463–1878)," *Byzantinische Zeitschrift,* 44 (1951), 551–559. See also Lewis, "The Islamic Guilds," *Econ. Hist. Rev.*, VIII/I. (Nov. 1937), 20–37. See Anhegger, *Beiträge zur Geschichte des Bergbaus im Osmanischen Reich,* 2 vols. (Istanbul, 1943–45); and Beldiceanu, *Les Actes des Premiers Sultans,* I, 151–153, for documents setting forth policies for the Ottoman customs officials and Vol. II for details of Ottoman mining operations.

51. For a description of the economic structure of the city, see Gibb and Bowen, I/1, 276–313,

and of price fixing by the Grand Vezir, Mantran, *Istanbul dans la deuxième moitié du xviie siècle*, pp. 125–126, 323 ff.
52. Evliya, *Seyāhatnāme*, II, 95–96. The Laz are considered to be a branch of the Georgian peoples speaking a tongue closely related to Mingrelian. See Minorsky, "Laz," *E.I.*[1], III, 20–22.
53. Primaudaie, *Histoire du commerce de la Mer Noire*, pp. 257–259; and Taeschner, "Anadolu," *E.I.*[2], I, 476–477.
54. Evliya, *Seyāhatnāme*, III, 203–204; Primaudaie, pp. 180–191.
55. Primaudaie, pp. 248–254. That these exports persisted is clear from the report of Evliya (Hammer tr.) II, 44–47 in which he details the class structure of Trebizond.
56. Primaudaie, pp. 254–256.
57. Evliya, *Seyāhatnāme*, III, 204; Primaudaie, pp. 254–259. In the mid-17th century the population of Amasya was estimated at 25,000 to 30,000. See Darkot, "Amasya," *I.A.* I, 393–394; also, Hüseyin Husameddin, *Amasya Tarihi*, especially vol. II.
58. Evliya (Hammer tr.) II, 47–48, 92; Primaudaie, *passim*. Sinope and other Black Sea ports also contained shipyards, and as Evliya Çelebi noted, one guild in Trebizond was famous for its mother of pearl and inlaid woodwork. Alberi, ed., *Relazioni degli Ambasciatori*, III/3, 353. As noted by Inan (*Aperçu général*, p. 52), the income from certain of these forests was assigned to the Admiralty.
59. Streck and Inanç, "Ermeniye," *I.A.*, IV, 324.
60. Primaudaie, p. 179, citing Minas, p. 489; see also Taeschner, "Anadolu," 476–477.
61. Kritouvoulos, *History of Mehmed the Conqueror*, p. 166; Primaudaie, p. 180, citing Chalcondyle IX, 202, 261–261; Darkot, "Kastamonu," *I.A.* VI, 401; and Taeschner, *loc. cit.*
62. Hammer, *Histoire de l'Empire Ottoman*, III, 74–75, citing Chalcondyle X, 154. It is thus no surprise that the German-inspired Karabük and the American-inspired Ereğli steel complexes are located in the same region in modern Turkey.
63. Evliya (Hammer tr.) II, pp. 47–48, 93.
64. Decei, "Karadeniz," *I.A.* VI, 245.
65. Togan, *Umumî Türk Tarihine Giris*, I, 241–346.
66. Inalcïk, "Kïrïm," *I.A.*, VI, 753.
67. It is generally agreed that they descended from the Toḳay Tīmūr (Tuḳa Tīmūr) line of Juchi. Togan, *Umumi Türk Tarihi, loc. cit.*, and Inalcïk, "Giray," *I.A.*, IV, 783–789.
68. Prof. Inalcïk, following Nemeth Gyula [*Hong-foglalo Magyarsag Kialakula-sa* (Budapest, 1930), pp. 265–268], associates the name "Giray" with the name of the Mongol tribal confederation of Keraits.
69. For a fuller consideration of this portion of the early history of Crimean Tartary, see the monographic article by Inalcïk, "Yeni Vesikalara göre Kïrïm Hanlïgï . . ." *Belleten*, VIII 30 (1944), 349–402, and his article, "Haci Giray" *I.A.*, V, 25–27.
70. Vernadsky, *A History of Russia*, III, *The Mongols and Russia*, 99–109.
71. For further details, see Inalcïk, "Ḳalġay," *I.A.*, VI, 131–132.
72. These positions were generally filled, in fact, by sons of the khan, who were referred to either as *Ḫānzādes* or *sulṭāns*. Inalcïk, "Kïrïm," p. 755. *Bujak*, a Turkish word meaning "corner," presumably referred to the corner of the steppe or much of the region known today as Bessarabia. Inalcïk, "Budjak," *E.I.*[2], I, 1285–1286. The *ser'asker sulṭān* in charge of that district presumably had charge of the Tatars living in the Bujak, between the Danube and the Dniester. The region known as Yedisan appears to have included the portion of the steppe between the Dniester and the Dnieper (Shepherd, *Historical Atlas*, p. 139). The Kuban district encompassed the steppeland between Azak (Azov) and the Kuban river. According to Lykhachev, *Puteshestviya Russkikh Poslov*, p. 385, note 67, the Besleni (Beslani) Circassians lived between the Kuban and Laba rivers. These presumably came under the jurisdiction of the ser'asker of the Kuban. The remaining Crimean Tatar territory between the Dnieper and the Don seems to have been the preserve of the *Or Begi* (beg of Perekop). The *Tiyiş* registers in Velyaminov-Zernov, *Materiali dlya Istorii Kryjmskaġo*

Khanstva. The account by Giovanni da Lucca, (*Voyages curieux*) also confirms these details.
73. Inalcïk, "Kïrïm"; Gibb and Bowen, I/i, 166–168, and *passim* for a general explanation of these terms.
74. Almost since the time of the submission of the khans to the Ottomans, the khans had regularly been confirmed in office by the reception of standards (*tūġ*), literally, horsetails; robes of honor ((*ḫil'āt*), and written patents (*ḫaṭṭ*) from the Sultan. Inalcïk, "Kïrïm".
75. In Russian, Pyatigorsk; Howorth, *History of the Mongols*, II, 489, calls them "Beshtav"; Peçewī, II, 77, refers to the region as "Beş Depe."
76. Belokurov, *Snosheniya Rossii s Kavkazom*, pp. xxxii–xxxiii.
77. Inalcïk, "Don-Volga Kanalï Teşebbüsü . . ." *Belleten*, No. 46 (1948), pp. 355–364; and Spuler, "Astrakhan," *E.I.*², I, 271–272.
78. Inalcïk, "Don-Volga Kanalï Teşebbüsü . . . ," *loc. cit.*
79. Howorth, p. 489; Belokurov, p. xxxv.
80. See the description of this event in R. Hakluyt, *The Principal Navigations*, II, 239 ff.
81. It is interesting to note that the Ottomans sold a great deal of cloth of all kinds, leather goods, precious metals and stone, candles, and even weapons to Muscovy in the 16th century. Fekhner, "Torgovlya Russkogo Gosudarstva so Stranami Vostoka v xvi veka," *Trudy Gosud. Istorich. Muzeya*, No. XXI, table on p. 118.
82. Németh, "Neuere Untersuchungen über das Wort *Tabor* 'Lager,'" *Acta Linguistica*, III, 431–446.
83. Inalcïk, "Don-Volga Kanalï Teşebbüsü . . . ," pp. 359–360.
84. The Ottomans, for example, had provided the Uzbegs (Uzbeks) of Central Asia with gunners and hand guns during the reign of Sulaymān the Magnificent. See the translation by Vambery, *The Travels and Adventures of the Turkish Admiral Sidi Ali Reis in India, Afghanistan, Central Asia, and Persia during the years 1553–1556*, of the work by Sīdī 'Alī Re'īs (Kātib-i Rūmī), *Mir'at al Memālik*, pp. 68–78 and *passim*. Margèrét (p. 27) also describes how the Tsar of Muscovy provided arms to the Cossacks.
85. Margèrét, pp. 18 ff.
86. Sadikov, "Pokhod Tatar i Turok na Astrakhan' v 1569 g.," *Istoricheskie Zapiski*, XXII, 132–166.
87. The vacating of the Don Volga region opened it to Don Cossack settlement. Inalcïk, "Don-Volga Teşebbüsü . . . ," citing Togan, *Bugünkü Türkistan ve Yakïn Mazisi*, pp. 110–115.
88. Inalcïk, "Don-Volga Teşebbüsü . . . ," pp. 110–115.

CHAPTER TWO
Crimean Tatar Affairs and the Early Years of Ġāzī Girāy, 1554–1578

1 The Education of a Ḫānzāde

Ġāzī Girāy, son of Devlet Girāy Khan (1551–1577), began his life in 1554.[1] In the same year, Astrakhan fell to Muscovy. In 1555, the Ottomans made peace with Safavid Persia at Amasya at the same time that the Protestant and Catholic parties in the Holy Roman Empire signed the Peace of Augsburg, ending the first phase of the Wars of Religion. Two years later in 1557 the Livonian War began. These were among the momentous events that set the stage for the next half century of history, a stage on which the newly born *ḫānzāde* was to play a considerable role.

The sources give us few details of the birth of Ġāzī Girāy; nevertheless, as his father was at the time Khan of the Crimean Tatars, he was probably born in Bāġçesarāy (Russian; Bakhchisaray), the palace begun in 1503 by his grandfather, Menglī Girāy Khan (d. 1515).[2] Apart from the fanfare that must have accompanied the birth of a *ḫānzāde* and the public rejoicing that took place after his circumcision—usually at the age of five or six—the most important event in the life of a young Crimean Tatar *sulṭān* (~prince) was the appointment of his *lālā* or *atābeg*.[3] The *atābeg* (lit., father *beg*) assumed control of the affairs of the young prince during the khan's pleasure. This important post ordinarily devolved upon an elder of a powerful family in whom the khan had full confidence. Rather than a tutor, the atābeg corresponded to the position of a counselor and regent. He was chiefly a political adviser and, during the minority of the prince, a protector. The atābeg at various stages in the development of his charge could and usually did call in various learned men of the '*Ulemā*' class to instruct the youth in the Islamic sciences.

To this extent the practice of *aṭālīḳ* among the Crimean Tatars corresponded to the general Islamic pattern. Princes and sons of dignitaries also were subjected to rigorous military training. For the sons of the Crimean Tatars, however, a special institution existed which the Crimean khans had inherited from the Golden Horde. A tribe of the Circassians, the Besleni (Russian, Besleney), apart from their normal economic activities, had the special function of training the h̲ānzādes in horsemanship, use of weapons, and military exercises.[4] It was customary for each prince to receive a different atābeg in order to avoid any strife that might occur among the princely rivals as they reached maturity.[5]

These young sulṭāns, Ġāzī Girāy and the other alert, able-bodied ones, received a good education and training based on Ottoman standards.[6] The impression that both Ġāzī Girāy and his elder brother 'Ādil Girāy made upon their peers in the Safavid Court during their captivity provides some indication of their upbringing according to the best Islamic practices of the times.[7]

The return of the h̲ānzāde from his period of training among the Besleni Circassians provided the occasion for a celebration that commenced when the sulṭān was met on the shore near Kerch by the khan and the chief dignitaries of the Khanate.[8] On that occasion, those princes who had demonstrated their fitness for leadership received appointments to positions of authority in the Khanate. The most senior of the h̲ānzādes were appointed to posts of ser'asker of the Bujak, Yedisan, and Ḳuban, respectively. Henceforth, the sulṭāns, although generally speaking still under the supervision of their atābegs, could begin to attract personal followers to their standards. The relatives of the h̲ānzādes, out of regard for their station, were also assigned appanages.[9]

By the time of the Ottoman expedition to Astrakhan in 1569, Ġāzī Girāy had reached the age of sixteen. It is not known what position he held, if any, in the governmental hierarchy of the Khanate at the time. At least one contemporary source, however, reveals that the young prince went on the Astrakhan campaign with his older brothers, Meḥemmed Girāy, the Ḳalġay, and 'Ādil Girāy.[10] This was doubtless the first major campaign in which Ġāzī Girāy participated.

2 The Astrakhan Campaign and Muscovite Aspirations in the Northern Caucasus

In the light of the numerous wars that have taken place between the Russian and Ottoman Empires, this affair has attracted the interest of Soviet and Turkish scholars because it was the first hostile encounter between these states.

The incident was the attempt by the Ottoman and Tatar forces to re-take Astrakhan from Muscovy in 1569 as part of a project to open up a water route between the Black Sea and the Caspian to counter the growing influence of Muscovy and Safavid Persia in the Caucasus.[11] The Ottomans, faced with more formidable enemies on the borders of their western European and Asian empire, were content to consider steppe politics as a prerogative of the Crimean Khans. The Khanate, however, was split dangerously into pro- and anti-Ottoman factions during much of the sixteenth century. This internecine warfare greatly weakened the Crimean Tatars at a time when the tsars were gradually making encroachments in the Volga-Kama basin at the expense of the Khanates of Kazan and Astrakhan.[12] The Nogays—heretofore a kind of buffer for the Crimean Tatars against Muscovy—also had become alienated from the Crimean Tatars by the attempts of the latter to dominate them. After the Nogays actually split into two groups in the 1540s, Kazan became more isolated than previously from her Crimean Tatar and Astrakhan allies to the south. The Khanate of Astrakhan, this previously rich emporium of the north-south, east-west trade routes, had also been weakened by almost continual internal and external disturbances among the Nogays, the Crimean Tatars, and the Cossacks.[13] After the breakaway and subsequent immigration of the so-called Little Nogays from the middle Volga, the Don Cossacks commenced filling up the vacated portion of the steppe. While these events were taking place, Kazan fell to Moscow in 1552 and Astrakhan in 1554.[14]

The people to the immediate south and east of Astrakhan viewed this new proximity of a relatively strong state with mixed feelings. Some looked upon Muscovy with mistrust; others welcomed the opportunity, as had the Great Nogays, to escape from Crimean Tatar domination. Initially at least this feeling appears to have predominated among the Kabarda Circassians of the Northern Caucasus.[15] The Beştepe (Pyatigorsk) Circassians, probably because of their proximity to Crimean Tatar home territories, sought Muscovite protection as early as 1552. The Kabardinians followed in 1557.[16] The Kalmucks (Ḳalmīḳ), a nomadic people dwelling on the steppe between the Terek and Astrakhan, submitted to Moscow in the same year. The seriousness of Muscovite intentions became quite clear when Ivan IV married the daughter of a leading Kabardinian prince, Temruk, in 1561.[17] The Tsar was quick to help his new Circassian relatives. In 1563, at the request of his father-in-law, Temruk, he caused fortifications to be built in Kabardinian tribal territory.[18]

According to the Russian accounts, the Ottomans and Tatars were now prodded into action against Moscow upon the appearance of petitions from Circassians, Tatars of Astrakhan and Kazan, Nogays, Turkman (Tyurmen), and the Krym-Şamẖals (*Krym-Shevkalov*)—petitions which came from refugees or secret delegations to the Porte and to Bakhchisaray.[19]

In actuality, in spite of the diplomatic successes of Moscow in the

Caucasus, there were already signs that the position of Muscovy on the steppe, upon which the successes depended, was slowly deteriorating. Ismā'īl, Khan of the Great Nogays, who had been friendly to Muscovy, died in 1563 and was succeeded by Tīn Aḥmed, a brother-in-law of Ivan IV through his marriage to another daughter of Temruk. The Tsar's envoy to the Crimea in 1565, Afanasiy Nagoy, received information that diplomatic exchanges were taking place between the Great Nogays and the Crimean Khan.

During the sixties, moreover, Muscovy became increasingly involved in the Livonian War. The Crimean Tatars, in alliance with the Polish King Sigismund August, had carried out diversionary raids on Riazan in 1564 and besieged the city of Volkov in October 1565 with guns that they had carted to the site on wagons.[20]

The Tsar, who during the course of 1564 had unleashed a terrible vengeance on his boyars, the so-called *oprichnina* reform,[21] had greatly reduced their power; he thus wanted no major conflict on his southern borders. In a move to ease the mounting tension, he agreed to negotiate with the Crimean Khan on the question of the annual gifts, offering to pay the subsidies as agreed during the reign of Ṣāḥib Girāy.[22]

It appears that a Russian town with an *Ostrog* (~fort) was erected by Muscovy early in 1567 on the right bank of the Terek river at the mouth of the Sunzhu.[23] To show his displeasure with this kind of effrontery, Devlet Girāy took part in raids on Muscovite territory every year between 1567 and 1574.[24] One of these "raids" was the Astrakhan campaign of 1569.

The continuation of the Hungarian War after the death of Sultan Sulaymān before the walls of Szigetvar in 1566[25] postponed the projected Ottoman campaign on the steppe until a peace was concluded with the Emperor in 1568. At the same time, existing agreements with Poland and Safavid Persia were renewed.

By 1569, the long-discussed plans for the Astrakhan campaign were put into effect. Ṣoḳōllū Meḥemmed Pasha, the Grand Vezir, had entrusted the command to Ḳāsim Pasha, the Kaffa Sanjāḳ Bey of Circassian origin. The final plan called for the digging of a canal between the Don and the Volga rivers, as the Tsar was told later, to facilitate trade with Moscow! At Astrakhan, should it prove impossible to dislodge the Tsar in the first year of the campaign, the Serdār (commander-in-chief) was commanded to erect a fortress that would prove to the Tsar the power of his Turkish adversary.

Although Astrakhan was the tactical objective, considerations had been given from a strategic standpoint to the security of the northern trade routes along which passed the caravans of commerce and the annual pilgrimage. Moreover, the Ottomans wanted to frustrate a possible Muscovite-Safavid alliance and at the same time to establish another route by which to conduct war against the Safavids.[26] Two further problems doubtless received attention in the prior deliberations. Communications with the anti-Safavid Uzbegs [modern, Uzbek] in Central Asia had been greatly hampered by the Muscovite seizure of Astrakhan. Moreover, the sea routes from the Persian Gulf and the Red Sea to India had almost entirely been blocked by the Portuguese at the time. Sīdī ʿAlī Reʾīs, an Ottoman naval commander, had fought the Portuguese in the early fifties and had only managed to avoid capture after a skirmish by leaving his vessels in Gujarat and by proceeding overland to Constantinople across Central Asia. The account of his journey and the information it provided about the warfare of his day on the Indian Ocean and in Central Asia may have influenced the thinking of the Ottoman leaders in the sixties a great deal.[27]

The campaign commenced in the spring of 1569 despite the Khan's pessimistic excuses about the severity of the weather, the dangers of changing the water level of the Sea of Azov, and the threat of attack from Moscow by means of the canal once it was constructed.[28] The digging did not progress as rapidly as had been expected.[29] Thus, Ḳāsim Pasha, aware of the approach of autumn and encouraged by a delegation of Nogays to march on Astrakhan, left the heavy guns on the Don and marched upon Astrakhan overland before the season had advanced too far. Upon facing the island stronghold that Moscow had built in the early sixties, the army began to lose its morale. Both the captured Russian envoy Simeon Maltsev, and the Crimean Khan were later to take credit for discouraging the Ottomans. Maltsev, in his *Rechi* or Memoir on the campaign, described the rumors in the camp about the shortage of food and the coldness of the steppe winter.[30] The Crimean Tatars were restive. They had been subjected to rumors, said to have originated with the Khan, that the Sultan planned to occupy the Crimea. The Khan certainly appeared to do all he could to hinder the success of the campaign. In May 1569, the Tsar actually had sent the officer, Khoznikov, to the court of the Shah to enlist his support.[31]

Attempts to take the fortress by storm proved hopeless without the support of the siege guns. Ḳāsim Pasha now prepared to winter in the old quarter of the city. Under pressure from the rank-and-file, however, he was forced to order a withdrawal on September 20th. Karamsin goes so far as to suggest that the Khan led the troops back over a desert route, exposing them to the hazards of the weather and the raids of Circassian bandits.[32] The withdrawal became a rout of troops strung out from Astrakhan to Azov. In this way, a large Ottoman force demonstrated the weakness of its discipline and consequently suffered a disaster of considerable magnitude. Many perished on the steppe from a shortage of food and water. As a crowning blow to all who had supported the Grand Vezir in this venture, goods and equipment sufficient for a three-year campaign, which had been stockpiled at Azov, caught fire either through the negligence or the deliberate activity of the disgruntled soldiery. Not for some time was the Empire to attempt another northern campaign. Ṣoḳollū's prestige had been damaged; Devlet Girāy was no longer trusted. In the words of Kâtib Çelebi, "One does not leave important matters to lesser officials."[33]

Although information about the actual part played by the Tatar princes in the Astrakhan campaign is extremely fragmentary, it is probable that they were wing commanders in the military formations of the Khan, which are said to have numbered 15,000.[34] Ġāzī Girāy, however, remained with his father's retinue.[35] One incident is worthy of mention. It illustrates the sort of pressure that Moscow could bring to bear on the sophisticated members of the Tatar community. Karamsin reported a conversation between the Tatar princes and the captured Russian envoy, Maltsev, who had been conscripted to serve in a galley on the campaign. As Maltsev spoke the Tatar tongue, the h̲ānzādes questioned him freely about his homeland. The envoy invited the princes to join the service of the Tsar saying, "Your father has a numerous family. He will send you hither and yon. Your position is not what it ought to be because you wander as nomads from steppe to steppe. In Moscow, on the contrary, you will find honour, riches, and even your father will envy your lot."[36] That Ġāzī Girāy was impressed by what he heard and saw, there is little doubt. The Russian envoy, Vasil'chikov, who was sent to Persia on a mission in 1589, reported a conversation that he had with a certain Ferhād Beg, the governor of Isfahan (*Spagan*). The governor, while discussing the Muscovite army with the envoy, made the remark, "Our Shah held captive the Crimean Prince, Ġāzī Girāy, but he was in my charge; and the prince, Ġāzī Girāy related to me that he was privileged to wage war upon your sovereign and that he saw your ruler's army penetrate the great Turkish army. . . ."[37]

The Tatars had proved fickle allies. Sultan Sulaymān had maintained reservations about the effectiveness of Tatar troops after the Moldavian Campaign of 1538. Ṣāḥib Girāy was supposed to have expressed contempt for his own warriors thus:

> *The Tatars, the wretched fellows, are incapable of carrying out distant or difficult campaigns, and the equipping of a detachment of select brave men, in relation to its numbers, would cost the Sultan very dearly and would amount to a useless expenditure.*[38]

Sultan Sulaymān had trusted Ṣāhib Girāy, but apparently did not feel the same way about Devlet Girāy and had little to do with the Crimea after Ṣāḥib Girāy's death.[39]

Devlet Girāy had not helped wreck the Astrakhan Campaign without reason. He now wrote to Ivan IV demanding that he return Astrakhan and Kazan to Tatar rule. Tsar Ivan, fearing further Ottoman action against his domain, tactfully refused the Khan's proposal, but stated he would negotiate on the question of *Ṭiyiş* (tribute) payments at the rate agreed upon in the reign of Meḥemmed Girāy I.[40] Furthermore, the Tsar, not wishing to rely solely on Devlet Khan, sent his envoy Novosil'tsev to Sultan Selim II in 1570 to proffer congratulations for his accession—four years after the event—and to strengthen the ties of peace and friendship between their respective states at a time when the Livonian War had taken a turn against Muscovy.

The Sultan requested redress of four outstanding issues:

1. The opening of the trade and pilgrimage routes through Astrakhan;
2. The destruction of the Russian fortress in the Kabarda;
3. The security of travelers passing to and from the Ottoman state;
4. The return of the Khan's envoy, Yambuldu, who was being detained in Moscow.[41]

As no specific claims to Kazan or Astrakhan were put forward at the time, it was apparent that the Sultan did not intend to contest further the conquests of the Tsar for the present.

Although the Ottomans had failed in their objectives of connecting the Don and the Volga and seizing Astrakhan, the mere presence of a sizable Ottoman army on the steppe had, nevertheless, produced some favorable results. The lesson was obvious: If the Ottomans so desired, they could always send another army to the steppe. An important portion of the Great Nogays had shown themselves willing to cooperate with the Ottomans during the campaign. In 1571, they moved into the steppe closest to the Crimea and gave over the command of their forces to Devlet Girāy. These changing fortunes of the Tsar on the steppe were not missed by the Khan. He sent his sons to the Kabarda in 1570 where they soundly defeated the forces of Temruk Mīrzā. This stroke had the effect of purging the Kabarda of Muscovite presence and, at the same time, of eliminating the threat of a flank attack during the Moscow campaign of the following year.[42]

Muscovy, somewhat overextended in the Caucasus and fully engrossed in the Livonian conflict, was caught off balance by Devlet Girāy in 1571. The Khan routed the Muscovite forces defending the Oka river line south of Moscow and then swept to Moscow almost unopposed. The Tatars fired the suburbs, but the inner city, owing to a strong wind, also caught fire and was almost completely destroyed.[43] No act was calculated to bring more immediate renown to the Crimean Khan, to whom the Tatars now gave the title *Daġtī Alġān* (*Tahtï Alan*, or "Taker of the Capital").[44]

While this event was taking place, the Tsar's envoy, Kusminskiy, had made his way to Istanbul and presented a letter to the Sultan in which all of his previous proposals were accepted.[45] In view of the way everything was turning against Muscovy, the Sultan was no longer satisfied with just the settlement of his previous grievances. Now the Sultan, in a return letter, demanded the surrender of Astrakhan and Kazan and even called for the submission of the Tsar. Thus, at a time when Ivan IV would have liked to make an alliance with the Sultan, hard pressed as he was from all sides, his envoys were ill-received and even subjected to mild humiliation.[46]

The Tsar succeeded in checking a further attack by the Khan in 1572.

Thereafter, years of famine and plague, coupled with Cossack attacks and troubles with the Nogays, kept the Tatars actively engaged closer to home.[47] In 1574, the Nogays and Crimean Tatars made a successful raid into the Muscovite province of Ryazan, but these allies soon fell out again, partly over old grievances, partly over new ones. The Nogays under the leadership of Tīn Aḥmed consequently moved across the Don and again accepted the overlordship of Moscow.[48]

The facts show that the Astrakhan campaign had complex origins and that some of the results of this show of force, combined with other developments in Eastern Europe, tended to ease tensions for the Ottomans and Crimean Tatars on the steppe. Insofar as the position of Muscovy had deteriorated in the Caucasus, the Ottomans had succeeded also in lessening the likelihood of a Muscovite-Safavid rapprochement. Yet one basic purpose of the campaign—the opening of a water route to the Caspian for the purpose of improving logistics in any future clash of the Ottomans with the Safavids—had failed, and it failed because a fundamental premise was false. In the words of Peçewī,

> *Some experts said,* "*The* distance is small *between the Don river which flows into the Black Sea and the Volga river which flows into the Caspian Sea. If the Sultan would take the trouble,* it would be easy to join them together."[49]

3 The Crimean Khanate in Troubled Times, 1574–1578

In the absence of specific information one can only speculate that Ġāzī Girāy took an active part in the various campaigns and raids of the Crimean Tatars which took place between 1569 and 1578. This presumption would mean that Ġāzī Girāy accompanied his brothers on the campaign into the Kabarda in 1570 and that he was most likely before the walls of Moscow in 1571. Thereafter only minor skirmishes took place between the Muscovites and Tatars for some years. In 1574, following the revolt against the Sultan by Ivan Ivonia, Hospodar of Moldavia (1572–1574), which had been supported by some Polish grandees and the Zaporozhian Cossacks,[50] the Crimean Tatars received orders from the Sultan to attack the Cossacks.[51] According to Urechi, the Tatars, under the direction of ʿĀdil Girāy, actually took part in the campaign to crush the Moldavian revolt.[52] Ġāzī Girāy doubtless also took part in this campaign. Only in 1575, however, is Ġāzī Girāy specifically mentioned in the sources as having led a contingent of 10,000 Tatars in the company of his brothers, ʿĀdil Girāy and Alp Girāy, and his nephew, Saʿādet Girāy, son of Meḥemmed Girāy, the Ḳalġay.[53] This expedition into Podolia, and other eastern provinces of Poland-Lithuania during September 1575 brought terrible destruction and many inhabitants were carried off as captives by the Tatars. According to one Polish historian this action helped to hasten the selection of Stephan Báthory as King of Poland.[54] The new Hospodar of Moldavia, Peter (1575–1579 and 1583–1590), son of the Hospodar Mircea of Wallachia, had given the Tatars permission to cross his territory in exchange for a share of the booty.[55] Clashes between the Crimean Tatars and Zaporozhian Cossacks continued between 1575 and 1578 with the tacit support of the Cossacks by Poland and of the Tatars by the Ottoman state. Among some Polish magnates, who were supported by the Habsburgs, there had long been the desire to spark a conflict between Poland-Lithuania and the Ottoman Empire. The immediate object of such a venture would be to establish Polish hegemony once again over Moldavia and thus to acquire a direct outlet to the Black Sea.[56] Poland would again take up this struggle to regain a special position in the affairs of Moldavia during the long conflict between the Holy Roman Empire and the Ottoman state (1593–1606).

The Ottomans looked upon any interference in Moldavia as a threat to be met by strong measures; therefore, every encouragement was given by them to the Tatars to counteract the Cossack raids on Ottoman soil. The culmination of this phase of the border warfare came in 1577. In this year the Cossacks made severe attacks on Ochakov, Akkerman, and the Crimea. Behind these raids, in particular, the hand of Ivan IV also was detected. In supplying men and money to the Cossacks, he not only kept the Tatars from raiding his own territories, but also he must have hoped to start a major conflict between the Ottomans and Poland-Lithuania at a time when he had again taken the initiative in the Livonian War.[57] Fortunately, Stephan Báthory and his advisers realized the critical turn of events on the borders which had enabled Ivan Podkova and his Cossack followers to unseat the prince of Moldavia in 1577. Not until this adventurer was beheaded and apologies sent to the Sultan did the Ottomans renew their treaty of friendship with Poland. The signing of the peace left Poland free to settle the Danzig revolt and the Livonian War and the Ottomans and Crimean Tatars to prosecute the Persian War.

These events in the life of Ġāzī Girāy were but a prelude to the type of border warfare with which the young Khan would have to deal in the early years of his reign. Closer to home, the stresses on the ruling circles of famine, epidemics of plague, and continual raiding naturally led to quarrels over matters of policy for the Khanate. The rivalry between the eldest two sons of Devlet Girāy had become particularly acute during the last years of Devlet Girāy's life (d. 1577). Finally, 'Ādil Girāy, unable to reconcile himself with his brother and Ḳalġay, Meḥemmed Girāy, left the Crimea and caused a separate town to be built on the Kalmius river, which flows off the steppe into the Sea of Azov. This he called Bōlī Sarāy. Fortunately for the future survival of the Khanate, the brothers became reconciled just before the death of their father. Thus, the new Khan, Meḥemmed Girāy (1577–1584), appointed 'Ādil to the post of Ḳalġay and could then speak of the unity of the Crimea to the Muscovite ambassador.[58] Now the Crimean Tatars were in a better position than previously to assist the Sultan in the Persian campaign.

1. Meḥemmed Riżā, *Al Seb' es-Seyyār*, p. 111.
2. Spuler, "Bāġchesarāy," *E.I.*², I, 893–894.
3. Cahen, "Atabak (Atabeg)," *E.I.*², I, 731–732.
4. ". . . Altïn-Ordu devleti zamanïnda çerkesler bizzat ulu hanlara tabi ve Altïn-Ordu hanlarïnïn prenslerini terbiye ile mükellef mümtaz bir vilayet halinde idare edildi." (In the time of the Golden Horde state, the Circassians were subject personally to the great Khans and they were administered in the quality of a privileged province charged with training the princes of the Khan of the Golden Horde.) Bala, "Çerkesler," *I.A.*, III, 380. On the function of the Besleni Circassians within the Crimean Tatar system, see Belokurov, *Snosheniya*, p. xxxvii. For more information on the Circassians, see section A. Inalcïk, "Cherkes," *E.I.*², II, 21–25.
5. According to Bronowski, who observed this institution at first hand during his sojourn in the Crimea in 1578, the atābegs were court officials responsible to the khan not only for the training of the princes but also for the management of other matters that might be termed family affairs of the khan; Bronowski, "Collections out of Martin Broniovius," Purchas, *Purchas His Pilgrims*, XIII, 461–491; also, "Opisanie Kryma (Tartariae Descriptio)," the Russian version in the *Zapiski Odesskago Obshchestva Istorii i Drevnostey*, VI, 333–367.
6. To gain some idea of Ottoman standards of education for the dignitaries of the realm, see Miller, *The Palace School of Muhammed the Conqueror*.
7. The Turkish language, in one dialect or another, was a kind of *lingua franca* throughout the Ottoman, Safavid, and Uzbek territories of that day. It also had currency among the early Moghuls of India and throughout the Asian steppe. For a description of the way in which 'Ādil Girāy impressed the Persian court, see Ventura (?), *Thesoro Politico*, f. BBij verso.
8. Ḥalīm Girāy, *Gülbün-ü H̱ānān*, (London, B.M. Or. Ms. 11164) ff. 29b–30a.
9. Bronowski, Russian ed., *loc cit.*
10. Ivan Novosil'tsev, who was sent to the Porte in 1570, reported the following account: "Bylo dei pod Astarakhan'yu turskikh lyudey golova Kasim-beg Kafinskoy da vosm' sanchakov voevod, a s nimi tysyach poltret'yattsat' da krymskoy tsar', a s nim tri ego tsarevichi: bolshoy Magmed Kirey Kalga, drugoy Aldi-Girey tretei Kazy-Girey, a s nimi tatar bolshi pyatidesyat tysyach, . . ." (The head of the Turkish army Kasim, beg of Kaffa, and eight voivodes of the *ṣanjāḳs* were before Astrakhan, and with them were 25,000 men and the Crimean Khan, with whom were three of his sons: Big Meḥemmed Girāy, the Ḳalġay, another, 'Ādil Girāy, the third, Ġāzī Girāy, and with them more than 50,000 Tatars.) Lykhachev ed., *Puteshestviya Russkikh Poslov xvi–i xvii vv*, pp. 65 f.
11. Sadikov, "Pokhod Tatar i Turok na Astrakhan' v 1569 g.," *Istoricheskie Zapiski*, XXII (1947), 132–166; Inalcïk, "Osmanlï-Rus Rekabetinin Menşei ve Don-Volga Kanalï Teşebbüsü," *Belleten*, No. 46 (1948), pp. 349–402; and Kurat, "The Turkish Expedition to Astrakhan' in 1569 and the Don-Volga Canal," *S.E.E.R.*, XL (December 1961), 7–23. See also the recent studies of W. E. D. Allen, *Problems of Turkish Power in the Sixteenth Century*, pp. 22–28, and A. N. Kurat, *Türkiye ve İdil Boyu*.
12. Arat, "Kazan," *I.A.*, VII, 505–522.
13. Spuler "Astrakhān," *E.I.*², I, 721–722.
14. Arat, "Kazan." Astrakhan had to be reconquered by Muscovy in 1556.
15. Belokurov, *Snosheniya*, p. xxx.
16. It was through Cossack intermediaries that diplomatic relations between some Circassian

princes and Moscow commenced in the 1550s. *Ibid.*, pp. xxxii–xxxiii. The first documentation of the existence of Cossack settlements on the right bank of the Terek river dates from the early 1560s. See Kumykov and Kusheva, eds., *Kabardino-Russk. Otnosh.*, I, 398 n. 101; Belokurov, p. xxxv. In part, the eagerness of these principalities to come to terms with Moscow stemmed from the importance to their own economies of trading in the bazaars of Astrakhan. Karamsin, *Histoire de l'Empire de Russie*, VIII, p. 252.

17. Karamsin, IX, p. 41.

18. Belokurov, *Snosheniya*, p. lxxxv. The second marriage of Ivan IV to Maria Temrukovna (Christianized form) opened the way for Circassian nobles to marry into wealthy and important families in Moscow. In this way the Circassians strengthened their social position in the Caucasus. This orientation toward Moscow among the Kabardinian aristocracy thus seems to have become quite popular. Polievktov, "Iz perepiski severno-kavkazskikh feodalov xvii veka," XLV *Akademiku N. Ya. Marru* (Festschrift of N.Y. Marr), 745–756.

19. Belokurov, p. lxiv. It is not clear what Afanasiy Nagoy, whose dispatch Belokurov quotes, means when he refers to the *Krym-Shevkalov*. It is known that the line of the *Şamḫals* split after 1578 and each branch tended to side with whichever of the three powers—Muscovy, the Ottoman Empire, or the Safavid state—offered the most advantages. There is no doubt, however, that the Crimean Tatars had influence in Dagestan which may, at this time, have had the importance of a faction. Polievktov, pp. 748–749; Inalcïk, "Don-Volga Kanalï Teşebbüsü . . . ," pp. 383–384; and Belokurov, pp. lxiv–lxv.

20. Novosel'skiy, *Bor'ba*, p. 27; Karamsin, IX, 82–83, 136–137. The Polish king had sent the Khan a subsidy of 30,000 ducats.

21. Kluchevsky, *A History of Russia*, II, 74–90

22. The Tsar probably felt that he had to placate the Khan in the hope that he would oppose an Ottoman campaign on the steppe. Inalcïk, "Don-Volga Kanalï Teşebbüsü . . . ," pp. 367–368.

23. The Temruk faction of Kabardinians had used Muscovite and Cossack elements against the Beştepe Circassians the previous year. Now they asked the Tsar to build them a fortified town. Another strong faction opposed this measure but was crushed in the resulting struggle. Some 20,000 were reported killed. Belokurov, *Snosheniya*, pp. lxvi–lxxi. Referring to this new act of hostility, the Khan wrote to the Tsar ". . . If the tsar wishes to be [live] in friendship and brotherhood with me, then he would give me the gifts of [which were given in the time of] Meḥemmed Girāy (1) . . ." (*Ibid.*)

24. This new stage of Tatar warfare, which was generally coordinated with Poland-Lithuania, with whom the Khan was allied, came at a critical point in the Livonian War. These attacks made it necessary for the Tsar to revise the defense system on his southern borders. The new system, which called for the stationing of five regiments on the edge of the settled portion of the steppe, continued in force practically without alteration until the reign of Boris Godunov. For details of the regiments that were stationed generally in Serpukhov, Tarusa, Kaluga, Kolomna, and Kashira, see Novosel'skiy, *Bor'ba*, pp. 24–29.

25. In this year Meḥemmed Girāy, the Ḳalġay, had taken part in this campaign with a force estimated at 20,000 Tatars. Inalcïk, "Don-Volga Kanalï Teşebbüsü . . . ," pp. 267–268.

26. In the words of Marcantonio Barbaro (Alberi, Ser. III/I, 337): "Queste forze, e l'unione che ha col Persiano, siccome i Tartari l'hanno con i Turchi tentarono di far che con un taglio il fiume Volga entrasse nel fiume Tanai, per aprirsi la navigazione, come dicevano loro per comodita dei traffici di Moscovia cosa in vero che sarebbe stata di molto loro utile; ma piu veramente i Turchi si adoperavano per aprire la navigazione all'armata loro nel mar Caspio, atta a danneggiar gravemente tutta la Persia, liberandosi con questo modo de quelle incomodita suole apportar loro il lunghissimo viaggio di terra che loro convien fare quando hanno da andare contro il Sofi, l'armi del quale sous sopra modo ternute dei Turchi, si come or ora diro." The French envoy to the Porte at the time, M. de Grantrie de Granchamp, also emphasized the anti-Safavid nature of this expedition. He reported to his government that there was a ". . . projet de

la Porte pour la jonction du Volga a la mer Caspienne . . ." and that there were ". . . apprehensions de guerre avec la Perse . . . ," Charriere, *Négociations de la France,* III, 57 f.
27. A. Vambery, ed. and tr., *The Travels and Adventures of the Turkish Admiral . . . 1553–1556.*
28. Smirnov, *Krymskoe Khanstvo*, pp. 433–434. The fear of an attack by the Portuguese had been the excuse for abandoning the Ottoman Suez canal project earlier.
29. Kurat, "Turkish Expedition to Astrakhan," *S.E.E.R.*, XL, 17. Professor Kurat, in this article and in his book, *Türkiye ve İdil Boyu,* questions the Ottoman intentions to build a canal.
30. Sadikov. "Pokhod Tatar i Turok," *Istorich. Zapis.*, 22, 156 ff.
31. Karamsin, *Histoire de l'Empire de Russie,* IX, 163–165; Inalcïk (". . . Don-Volga Kanalï Teşebbüsü . . . ," pp. 367–368) states that it was I. P. Novosil'tsev who was sent to Persia.
32. Karamsin, *loc. cit.*
33. Inalcïk, "Don-Volga Kanalï Teşebbüsü . . . ," *loc. cit.*; Kurat (*Türkiye ve İdil Boyu,* p. 174) quoting the comment of Kâtib Çelebi from his *Tuhfet ül-Kibār*, p. 86.
34. Novosil'tsev, *Stateyniy Spisok*, in Lykhachev, ed., *Puteshestviya Russkikh Poslov*, p. 65 ff.
35. See also the mention of Ġāzī Girāy by Jedrzej Taranowski, an eye-witness, "Podrozei Poselstwa Polskie do Turcyi," in the *Biblioteka Polska*, Part 9, p. 54.
36. Karamsin, IX, p. 164.
37. Vesselovskiy, "Pamyat. Diplom. i Torgov. Snosh.," *Trudy Arkheolog. Obshchestva*, XX (1890), 75. From 1569 to 1589 there was no other direct contact between the forces of the Sultan and those of the Tsar. It is therefore most likely that the conversation mentioned by Ferhād Beg was in reference to the Astrakhan Campaign of 1569. Cf., Hammer, *Histoire de l'Empire Ottoman,* VI, 339.
38. Smirnov, *Krymskoe Khanstvo*, p. 425, citing Remmāl H̱ōja, f. 145.
39. *Ibid.*
40. Inalcïk, "Don-Volga Kanalï Teşebbüsü," p. 385. The tribute agreed upon at that time was known to be quite high.
41. *Ibid.*, pp. 385–388.
42. Inalcïk (*ibid.*) states that both sons of Temruk were killed in this battle. Belokurov (*Snosheniya,* pp. lxxvii–lxxviii), to the contrary, states that these sons, Mamstruk and Beberyuk, were captured by 'Ādil Girāy and taken to the Crimea and that Ivan IV, realizing their importance as political prisoners, offered a large ransom for them. When the Crimean Tatars learned that Ivan IV was responsible for the death of Mikhail, Temruk's third son, who was residing [as a hostage?] in Moscow, they made much of the affair to help reestablish their influence in Circassia.
43. Peçewī, I, 500, Cf. the references to the burning of Moscow and a general description of Muscovy during this period by A. Jenkinson in Hakluyt's *Principal Navigations*, III, 170–195. See also the account by Richard Uscombe, in Hakluyt, *ibid.*, p. 167.
44. 'Abd ul-Ġaffār, *'Umdet ül Ah̲bār, T.T.E.M.*, No. 85, p. 122.
45. The Tsar actually razed the fortress on the Terek. According to Belokurov, he did this not out of any fear of the Sultan, but as a sincere gesture of friendship. This view is not satisfactory. After the h̲ānzādes had defeated Temruk in 1570, it is highly doubtful that Muscovy enjoyed as much prestige among the Circassians as formerly. Moreover, after his defeat in Livonia and the burning of his capital, Ivan would have been foolish to continue stirring the already troubled waters in the South. Belokurov, *Snosheniya*, pp. lxxv–lxxvi.
46. Inalcïk, "Don-Volga Kanalï Teşebbüsü," pp. 389–390; and Hammer, *Histoire*, VI, p. 341.
47. *Ibid.*
48. Regardless of how often the Nogays assisted the Crimeans in their raids on Muscovy, the Nogays always received the brunt of Don Cossack and Zaporozhian attacks fostered by Moscow because of their exposed position on the steppe. Moreover, the old Crimean Tatar arrogance continued to offend the Nogays. Some Crimean Tatars also stole Nogay carts and livestock and even the Khan came under criticism for reserving the best grazing areas for the livestock of the Crimean Tatar dignitaries. Novosel'skiy, *Bor'ba*, p. 28.

49. Peçewī, I, p. 468.

50. The Porte had become annoyed by and suspicious of the connections that Bogdan IV (1568–1572), the former Hospodar, kept with Poland. He was deposed but, in the ensuing struggle, many Polish troops were put at the disposal of Bogdan. About this time (1572), Zygmunt August, King of Poland, died and the Poles were forced to return to their home territories, leaving the Turkish candidate, Ivan (the Cruel), in the office of Hospodar. The latter revolted against the Sultan in 1574 when the Sultan demanded tribute in excess of previous amounts. Hammer, *Histoire*, VI, pp. 440-444.

51. Novosel'skiy, *Bor'ba*, p. 30.

52. G. Urechi, *Chronique de Moldavie*, E. Picot, ed. and tr., pp. 499 ff.

53. Swietoslaw Orzelski, "Eight Books on the Interregnum," *Scriptores Rerum Polonicarum*, XXII, p. 362.

54. Novak, *Cambridge History of Poland*, p. 376. Contemporary evidence indicates that this devastating raid had economic, rather than political, origins. Gerlach, in an entry for 31 May, 1575 (p. 96), states simply: ". . . in der Tartarey sey grosser Hunger and Pest." See in this regard Karamsin, IX, p. 267.

55. Urechi, p. 511.

56. It is interesting to note that during the war between the Ottoman Empire and Venice (1570–1573), the spices, which formerly came from the Persian Gulf to Aleppo and then passed to Europe in Venetian vessels, began to pass from Persia to Constantinople and from there through Moldavia to Poland and Western Europe. Vincenzo Alessandri, "Relatione di Persia," in Alberi, Ser. III/II, p. 122. For further attempts by Poland to regain an outlet on the Black Sea, see Chapter VIII.

57. Novosel'skiy, *Bor'ba*, p. 30.

58. Novosel'skiy, *Bor'ba*, p. 33, citing *Krymskie Knigi*, No. 15, ff. 20–21. Doubtless also the Tatars, after a number of lean years, were anxious to take part in the Ottoman campaign.

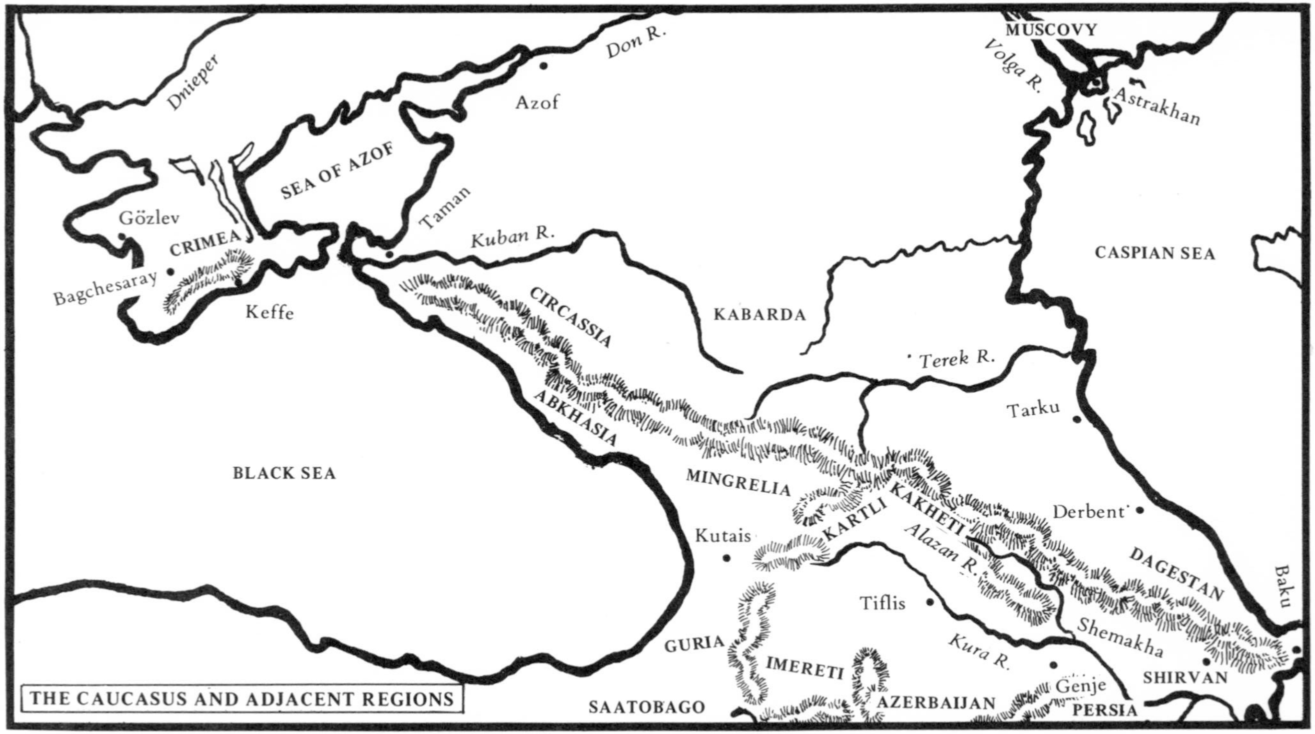
THE CAUCASUS AND ADJACENT REGIONS
MUSCOVY
Volga R.
Astrakhan
CASPIAN SEA
Dnieper
Don R.
Azof
SEA OF AZOF
Taman
Kuban R.
Gözlev
CRIMEA
Bagchesaray
Keffe
KABARDA
CIRCASSIA
Terek R.
Tarku
ABKHASIA
BLACK SEA
MINGRELIA
KARTLI
KAKHETI
Derbent
Kutais
Alazan R.
DAGESTAN
Baku
Tiflis
Shemakha
GURIA
Kura R.
IMERETI
Genje
SHIRVAN
SAATOBAGO
AZERBAIJAN
PERSIA

CHAPTER THREE
Ottoman-Safavid Rivalry and the Struggle for Transcaucasia

1 Shah Tahmāsp and the Ottoman Wars to the Peace of Amasya (1555)

Tahmāsp I (1524–1576), successor of Shah Ismā'īl I (d. 1524), had to contend with the threat of a two-front war, internal rivalries of the Turkmān amirs (i.e., the leaders of the Ḳïzïlbāş),[1] and attempts of his brothers to usurp his throne.[2] Under these circumstances, Shah Tahmāsp, while pursuing a defensive policy vis-à-vis the Ottomans throughout most of his reign, took steps to weaken the power of the Turkish tribes by building up slave corps of Georgian, Armenian, and Circassian origin.[3]

Sultan Sulaymān (1520–1566) conducted three campaigns against Safavid Persia. During the first, 1534–1536, in which the Ottomans came into possession of Arab Iraq, the Grand Vezir, Ibrāhīm Pasha, occupied Tabriz for a time but refused to give it over to the troops to be sacked. In this campaign, the Shirvanshah and the Prince of Gilan sent envoys to offer their submission to the Sultan.[4] The brother of the Shah, Alḳas Mīrzā, defected to the Ottomans in 1547. It did not take much urging on his part to convince the Porte that the time was propitious for a new eastern campaign. In the same year, the Sultan signed a five-year truce with the Holy Roman Empire.[5]

During the second campaign, 1548–1549, Tabriz was again taken without a struggle and incursions were made into Georgia and into Persia as far as Isfahan. The Ottomans acquired additional territory in the important border areas of Armenia and Kurdistan.[6] A renewal of war preparations in central Europe prevented the Ottomans from following up this short campaign with another thrust into Persia the following year. As soon as the Ottomans became fully engaged in Europe, however, a Ḳïzïlbāş detachment, under the leadership of Ismā'īl, son of Shah Tahmāsp, made a successful thrust into Asia Minor in 1552 and even defeated the Pasha of Erzurum.[7] This event was the curtain raiser for another determined effort by Sultan Sulaymān to punish the Safavids in the campaign of 1554–1555. In 1554, the only year in which significant action took place, the provinces of Nakhichevan, Erevan, and Karabagh (Karabakh) suffered the worst exactions of a marauding soldiery.[8] The reluctance of the Ottomans to occupy territory in Azerbaijan and the unwillingness of the Safavid force to engage the Ottoman army led to the important Peace of Amasya concluded on May 29, 1555.[9] This first formal peace between the Ottomans and Safavids resulted in the recognition of the *status quo*. Although the Ottomans had shown themselves reluctant to undertake permanent conquests of Azerbaijan proper, they were clearly in a position, when they assembled an army for a campaign, to dominate the border areas of Armenia, Kurdistan, and Georgia.[10]

2 The Safavids and Transcaucasia

The Safavids, however, in spite of the military prowess of the Ottomans during the reign of Sulaymān the Magnificent, made every effort to dominate Transcaucasia.[11] The forces of Shah Tahmāsp undertook four campaigns into the Georgian principalities during which they carried off thousands of women and children into captivity. Nor did the Safavids hesitate to dethrone rulers. If, however, the Safavids, after the conclusion of peace with the Ottomans, became more involved in the politics of the Caucasus, the converse was also true: the Georgians, Circassians, and Dagestanians began also to play an important role in the intrigues at the Safavid court. In the days of Ismā'īl I and during the first thirty years of the reign of Shah Tahmāsp, the court was divided into two principal factions: the Ḳïzïlbāş (Turkish) and Tājik (Persian). With the increasing embroilment of the Safavids in the Caucasus, however, a third faction consisting mostly of Georgians and Dagestanians began making their influence felt. Relatives and friends of the ruling families of the Caucasus, who were in Safavid harems, high governmental posts, or military units, in alliance with one or more of the Ḳïzïlbāş tribes, could wield great influence.[12]

The Georgians had been united and powerful at various stages in their history; the last occasion was in the time of Alexander Bagrati (1413–1443), son of Giorgi, following the breakup of the empire of Tīmūrlang.[13] By the end of the reign of Shah Tahmāsp, Georgia had split up into three independent kingdoms and a number of smaller principalities.[14] The Bagrati line, descendants of Alexander, ruled the kingdoms of Kartli (Tiflis) and Kakheti, while a collateral branch, descended from an illegitimate line of Giorgi IX (1212–1223), reigned in Imereti (Kutaisi). The king of Kartli, Luarssab I, died in 1558, leaving as heirs his sons Simon and Davūd. Simon, the elder, a very capable man of the sword, became king. As he had refused to become a convert to Islam and to conform to other policies of the Shah after Safavid influence became dominant in his realm, he was imprisoned by the Safavids in 1569, and his brother, Davūd, a weakling and a convert to the Shi'ite faith, was put in his place. In 1578, when it was learned in Kazvin that King Davūd had left Tiflis to the Ottomans without a struggle, Simon, who had accepted Islam and subsequently had been released from a Safavid prison in 1576, was given the trappings of a king, sufficient funds and equipment, and all of the Georgian prisoners, upon condition that he would take arms against the Ottomans. From 1579 until his eventual capture in 1600, he harassed the Ottomans who were occupying his country, and almost succeeded in reuniting all Georgia.[15]

While Kartli throughout the sixteenth century involved itself in incessant quarrels with its neighbors and the two Great Powers, Kakheti, ruled by Levan II (1520–1574), enjoyed prosperity and relative peace. Alexander II, son of Levan (hence the Iskender Levendoğlu of Ottoman sources), succeeded to the throne in 1574 and by placating both Persian and Ottoman, much in the tradition of his father, he was able to reign until his death in 1605.[16]

The Imeretian king of the period, Giorgi IV (1548–1585), controlled most of Western Georgia as the neighboring princes of Guria and Mingrelia were his vassals. In Ottoman sources he was designated as *Bāş açūḳ* (bare-headed), apparently because the Imeretians and Mingrelians shaved their heads. The vassal state of Guria was ruled by the Wardanidze family residing at Ozurgeti, who were known by the designation "Gurieli."[17] Lastly, the Dadiani family, dwelling at Zugdidi, ruled Mingrelia.

Samtzkhé or Meskhia, the country occupying the upper Kura river basin, was wedged between Ottoman territory and the other Georgian kingdoms. Its rulers, the atābegs of the Jaqeli family, were rivals of the Bagratis.[18] Their capital was at Akhaltzikhe, the "Altūn Ḳal'e" (Fortress of Gold) of the Ottoman sources. Here Kai Khusrau II had died in 1575, leaving his strong-willed Queen, Dedis-Imédí, and three sons, Quarqare V (called Alexander in some sources), Manuchar II (who received the Muslim name Muṣṭafá), and Beka III. This principality, which bordered on the Ottoman Empire, to the West, became the first to capitulate and do homage to the Sultan after hostilities between the Ottomans and Persians began in 1578.

Northern Azerbaijan, Shirvan,[19] and Derbent[20] were under direct Safavid control. The rulers of Dagestan, however, who were designated by the title *Şamḫal*, maintained a precarious independence.[21] At the same time, through marriage alliances with the Safavid rulers, they enjoyed considerable influence at the court in Qazvin.[22]

3 The Death of Shah Tahmasp and the Ensuing Struggle for Power

As long as Shah Tahmāsp held the reins of government firmly, the bickering among the Ḳïzïlbāş amirs and the rivalry of the various parties at the court were held in check. However, when the Shah fell ill in November 1575, two principal factions began to form, each determined to place its own candidate on the throne. The offspring of three of the Shah's wives had prominent roles in the subsequent deliberations and plots. The Shah's Dagestanian wife, a sister of the Şamhal, had given birth to the clever and capable Parī H̱ān H̱ānum and the latter, through her influence over the Shah, had insinuated herself into an important position in state affairs. Prince Ḥaydar, offspring of the Shah's Georgian wife,[23] had become a favorite of Shah Tahmāsp in his later years and had been given administrative tasks by his father.[24] Hence Ḥaydār Mīrzā and his half sister were rivals for their father's favor. It was the Turkmān wife of Shah Tahmāsp, however, who had brought into the world the eldest two sons of the Shah, Moḥammad H̱odābanda and Ismā'īl.[25] Moḥammad H̱odābanda had been named crown prince, but later became afflicted by an ailment that rendered him almost blind, and because of this he received little consideration as a possible successor to the Shah during the deliberations of 1575.

Although Shah Tahmāsp recovered from his first illness, the basic alignments made at that time persisted until his death in the following year (May 14, 1576). Only two candidates received enough support for serious consideration, Ismā'īl and Ḥaydar. Generally speaking, the half-Georgian Ḥaydar Mīrzā drew upon his fellow Georgians for support. The strength of this faction was greatly augmented by the support of the Ūstājlū, the most influential of the Ḳïzïlbāş tribes at that time. Moreover, Ḥaydar had the support of the Şeyḫāvand and Taleş tribes and the majority of the Persian Shi'ite hierarchy.[26] Ismā'īl, who had been rotting in Ḳahḳahe prison since May of 1557, was championed primarily by the other Ḳïzïlbāş tribes, but he also had the support of the Kurds and the Dagestanian faction.[27] Thus, with the Ūstājlū excepted, the struggle assumed a kind of ethnic character: the Georgians and Persians against the Ḳïzïlbāş Turks and Dagestanians.

All would have gone well for Ḥaydar Mīrzā had he not been cut off from his Georgian supporters. A Dagestanian-led force, which had been let into the palace by Parī H̱ān H̱ānum through a secret gate, beheaded Ḥaydar Mīrzā. Now the Ḳïzïlbāş, who had earlier intercepted orders for Ismā'īl's execution, quickly consolidated their position and aided the accession of their candidate to the throne of Persia.[28] Shah Ismā'īl was crowned on August 22, 1576. Just over a year later (November 24, 1577), after a night of carousing, he was found by his Vezir, Selmān Khan, dying of poison. His demise was welcomed by the majority of his subjects. In his short reign he had succeeded in alienating much of the support that had been responsible for bringing him to power. He had rewarded the decisive support of his Dagestanian half-sister by seizing much of her wealth and divesting her of influence over the administration. He had played off the Ḳïzïlbāş and Tājik dignitaries one against the other. Moreover, step by step, he had eliminated all of his brothers and their offspring except his own half-blind brother, Moḥammad H̱odā-banda.[29] He lost the support of his subjects partly because he took no interest in the state administration but even more because he showed a preference for the tenets of Sunni Islam to those of Shi'ism.[30]

The Ḳïzïlbāş amirs gathered at the *Meydān-i Asp* in Qazvin on November 26, 1577, to decide on a successor. Mīrzā Selmān, recently appointed the vezir (*wazīr*) of Shah Ismā'īl II, presided over the assembly. Upon the suggestion of some of the other amirs, Amīr Khan Mōsellū, of the Turkmān tribe and Pirah Moḥammad Khan of Ūstājlū, on behalf of their followers, agreed to avoid strife. As these two tribes were the principal contenders, the others followed suit. Moḥammad H̱odābanda, the only surviving son of Shah Tahmāsp and the offspring of a Turkish mother, then became the choice of the majority of the Ḳïzïlbāş.[31]

After the death of Shah Ismā'īl II and during the interregnum, Parī H̱ān H̱ānum, with the aid of her influential uncle, the Şamẖal, who was *Muhurdār*, took over control of Qazvin over which she had presided in the days of Shah Tahmāsp. Selmān Khan, whom the princess had long held responsible for her fall from grace under Shah Ismā'īl, received word of a plot against him and hastily departed for Shiraz where Moḥammed H̱odābanda confirmed him in his office as vezir, an act that marked the end of Dagestanian influence in Qazvin. One of the first orders of the new Shah called for the execution of his half-sister.[32]

The Shah, before he entered Qazvin on February 13, 1578, had broken the power of his sister to resist him by appointing the Şamẖal governor of Shekki, a principality neighboring Shirvan, on condition that he depart with his retinue forthwith. Seeing the number of his former supporters who had rallied to the support of the Shah, the Şamẖal complied.[33]

Once more the Ḳïzïlbāş amirs appeared to be in complete ascendance. The Georgian and Persian factions had suffered a serious setback when they failed to seat Prince Ḥaydār on the throne. Now that the malevolent Parī H̱ān H̱ānum was dead and the Şamẖal relegated to a distant province—albeit near his homeland—the Dagestanian-Circassian influence at court which had survived the turbulent reign of Ismā'īl II was reduced to nil.[34]

4 The Accession of Shah Hodabanda and the Beginning of the Ottoman-Safavid War (1578)

Although the Ḳïzïlbāş amirs had buried their differences long enough to place a successor of Turkish descent on the throne, they had become quite unwilling to cooperate with each other in other respects. It soon became evident that the inner cohesion of the Safavid state was insufficient to withstand the shock of a foreign invasion. The half-blind Shah, moreover, could not be expected to reassert the central authority with sufficient effectiveness to discipline the Ḳïzïlbāş tribes and to resist the onslaught of the Ottomans.

The Shah, as the price of his accession (February, 1578), dispersed the treasury and parceled out the provincial governorships to the amirs as a means of gaining their support. Already the Kurds, upon the death of Ismā'īl, had made an unsuccessful attempt to seize the town of Khoy. Now, with the encouragement of H̱usrev Pasha, the Ottoman commander at Van, a Kurdish force had brought fire and sword to a large section of the region between Lake Urmia and the mountains of Kurdistan. The most dangerous rising took place while the newly appointed governor of Azerbaijan, Amīr Khan Mōsellū (Turkmān), was still in Qazvin. The Turkmān and Tekkelū tribes were ordered to pacify the Kurds in support of Ḥusayn Sulṭān Ṣōlāḳ (Tekkelū), the governor of Dinavar. Amīr Khan was also to send a detachment. The Kurds withdrew after their raids. The government army followed suit because it lacked provisions. Many peasants evacuated the area as the army had left more destruction in its wake than had the Kurds.[35]

This revolt only served to encourage other provinces on the western borders to rise against the Shah. The province of Shirvan, after it was sacked by an army of Tahmāsp in 1574, had received a tax exemption for some years. Nevertheless, in the spring of 1578, when the Shah's treasury was exhausted, the *Ḳurçū* (Ḳūrçī) a special, paid regiment of household troops—bodyguards of the Shah—were asked to collect their pay directly from Shirvan.[36] Abū Bekr Mīrzā, son of Borhān Mīrzā, who was in Dagestan at the time, took advantage of the unrest in his homeland caused by the rude incursion of the Ḳūrçū to gain the support of the Dagestanians and to lead a force of Lezghian and Karaburk tribesmen against the tax-gatherers.[37] As the peasants had either taken part in the revolt or had fled to the mountains, the Ḳïzïlbāş governor of the province, Aras Khan (Rūmlū) and his second-in-command, Ertoġdī H̱alīfe (Tekkelū) could do nothing to assist the Ḳūrçū. Meanwhile a delegation of notables from the province made its way to Istanbul to seek Ottoman assistance.

The Ottomans had decided, sometime in late 1577 after the death of Shah Ismā'īl II, to wage war on Persia. H̱usrev Pasha, *Beylerbey* of Van, who was in contact with the Kurdish leader Ġāzī Beg, a son of Şāh Ḳūlī Balīl (-ān), had closely followed the events after the death of Ismā'īl II and had reported them to the Porte, emphasizing the rightness of the time for gaining revenge for ancient grievances and taking booty from the enemy.[38]

This report and the succeeding revolts on the Persian borders were only incidental to the major reasons behind the decision of the Ottomans to fight a war against the Safavids. During recent decades, the power of Persia had been waning; the Ottomans had every reason for keeping the Safavids weak and what better way was there to do this than to rob them of the rich provinces, Shirvan and Azerbaijan? But the problem went deeper. The Safavids, about the time of the Peace of Amasya (1555), had begun the expansion of their trade relations with Muscovy and England through the Caucasus and across the Caspian Sea. The Ottomans quickly showed their interest in stopping this, to them, dangerous association by undertaking the Astrakhan campaign of 1569.[39] After the Ottomans gained control of most of the Caucasus between 1578 and 1590, they wasted no time in placing a naval force on the Caspian Sea.[40]

It was also important for the Ottomans to maintain communications with Central Asia and the further Orient. The Uzbegs, Sunni Muslims bordering the Safavids in Khorasan, shared the interest of the Ottomans in keeping the Shi'ite Persian state weak. Moreover, both of these powers would benefit from keeping the trade and pilgrimage routes open, particularly in the case of the Ottomans, since the Spanish and Portuguese, by the late sixteenth century, had blockaded much of the Ottoman Near Eastern trade with the Orient which had formerly passed through the Persian Gulf and the Red Sea. The Ottomans, of course, had their own cultural and economic interests in the Caucasus, a subject more carefully detailed in Chapter 2.

Apart from the questions of free access and communication and Ottoman competition with the Safavid state for the economic resources—mineral and manpower—of the lands from the Caucasus range to Mesopotamia, the Ottomans had long faced a threat to their internal security and cohesion posed by the spread in Asia Minor of Safavid-oriented Shi'ite doctrines. Sultan Selim I had found this threat so serious that he had struck against Shi'ite elements in Asia Minor prior to his well-known victory of Chaldiran in 1514. That the Shi'ite "fifth column" persisted in Asia Minor and contributed to the causes of the war of 1578–1590 has been well documented in a recent Turkish study.[41]

In their own minds, the Ottomans felt themselves fully justified in resorting to war in 1578. They had renewed existing treaties with Venice in 1575 and with Poland and the Habsburgs in 1577. In the deliberations preceding the campaign, however, Ṣoḳōllū Meḥemmed Pasha, the Grand Vezir, and an important figure who had held his high post since the days of Sulaymān, raised a word of caution. His long experience with Ottoman campaigns, east and west, placed him in a position to know the problems ahead even if the campaign were a success. He said to the Sultan, as quoted by Peçewī:

> *Those paid troops will get out of hand and the trimonthly* [mevâjib] *salary obligations and other expenses will increase. The peasants will be oppressed by taxes* [tekâlif] *and the incursions of the army, and even if Persia is conquered, its peasantry will not accept becoming subjected to our rule. As to the expenses of the campaign, the collection of revenue from the provinces will not be sufficient. What difficulties even your illustrious grandfather, the late exalted Sultan Sulaymān,*

> *experienced! And when peace between the two parties was concluded, what indignation and what anxiety he suffered. Those who put forth this [project] are those who do not know the Persian campaign, [and] who, leaving aside horses and pack animals, do not [even] ride oxen.*[42]

NOTES

1. The Turkish-speaking followers of the Shahs of Persia (who, in Safavid times, were not only heads of state but also the heads of a Shi'ite religious sect) distinguished themselves from other subjects of the Shah by wearing a headdress of red cloth consisting of twelve folds. Both the color and the number of the folds (representing the 12 Imams) symbolized the Shi'ite faith which the Ḳïzïlbāş (lit., red heads) professed. Only some details are known about the origin of the various Turcoman groups represented in the Safavid order. The *Rūmlū*, believed to be the oldest followers, were supposed to have derived from the descendants of the prisoners of war Tīmūrlang brought with him after defeating Yïldïrïm Bāyazīd in 1402. The *Şāmlü* rose to prominence during the Sheikhdom of Ḥaydar, as did the *Ūstājlū*. The name Şam (Syria) points to the possible geographic origin of the *Şāmlu* and there is some evidence that the *Ūstājlū* are a branch of the *Şāmlu.* At the same time (under Ḥaydār) the *Ḳajars* appear, but their origin is unknown. Somewhat later but before 1500, i.e., when Shah Ismā'īl commenced his rise to power, the Ḳaramanlū and the Ẕū'l-Ḳadr are mentioned. The remaining Ḳïzïlbāş tribes, of which the *Tekkelū* from a region of that name in Southern Anatolia and the *Afşar* from the region around Lake Urmia are the most important, appear during the reign of Ismā'īl I (1501–1524). Hinz, *Irans Aufstieg zum Nationalstaat im Fünfzehnten Jahrhundert*, pp. 78–80.
2. Alḳas Mīrza, brother of Shah Tahmāsp, who was appointed governor of Shirvan, crossed the Kipchak Steppe and took refuge at the court of Sultan Sulaymān. During the Ottoman campaign against Persia, 1548–1549, the Sultan supplied this prince with funds to undertake a sortie deep into Persian territory. Although successful in this undertaking, Alḳas Mīrzā was subsequently captured by another brother, who turned him over to Shah Tahmāsp. Hammer, *Histoire de L'Empire Ottoman*, VI, pp. 11–14.
3. The most important single source for this area in Safavid history is the V. Minorsky edition and notes of the *Tadhkirat al-Mulūk*, Gibb Memorial Series, N.S. XVI, especially pp. 43–45, 112–113, and 164–170 where the jurisdiction of the "Border amirs" and *beylerbeys* is discussed. For details of the life of Shah Ismā'īl, see the study by W. Hinz, "Schah Esmā'īl II. Ein Beitrag zur Geschichte der Safaviden," *Mitteilungen des Seminars für orientalische Sprachen*, Vol. 36, Pt. II, 19–100.
4. Hammer, *Histoire*, V, 210 ff. Partly as a result of this hasty action, Shirvan became a province instead of a tributary of the Safavid State.
5. *Ibid.*
6. *Ibid.*, VI, 10–15.
7. For details of this battle, see Hinz, "Schah Esmā'īl II," pp. 29–32.
8. As a result of this pillage, the Shah, in a letter to the Sultan, implied that the Ottomans took refuge behind their firearms. To this the Grand Vezir replied that the Ottomans would gladly lay aside their firearms for a chance to have combat with the Persians. Hammer, *Histoire*, VI, 64–65.
9. Among the stipulations of the agreement, which took the form of an exchange of letters with the Shah, the Ottomans agreed to show tolerance of Shi'ism, with certain reservations. The frontier commanders were urged to avoid issues which might lead to conflict and to protect pilgrims who were proceeding to Mecca and Medina. *Ibid.*, p. 70. A letter relating to this treaty appears in Peçewī I, 337–340.

10. Apart from the rigors of moving men and equipment over the Armenian mountains, it became particularly difficult, once a large army was in Azerbaijan, to maintain communications with, and bring in supplies from, the Ottoman hinterland. The Safavids, knowing this, destroyed all foodstuffs as they retreated and urged their supporters among the Kurds, Armenians, and Georgians, to harass the supply lines.

11. This tendency was no doubt necessitated—at least in part—by the close proximity of the Ottomans to the Caucasus and their own increased pressure on this region. The Ottomans quite clearly supported the Dadian of Mingrelia in his wars with the Abkhazians and largely dominated the entire Black Sea Coast. See Alberi, ed., "Relazione . . . di Marino Cavalli" (1560), III/I, 278–280. Cavalli reported that the Georgians preferred the Persians as did the Armenians, but that the Mingrelians called upon the Ottomans for assistance against the Circassians.

12. Hinz, "Schah Esmā'īl II . . . ," pp. 46–49.

13. Allen, *A History of the Georgian People*, p. 126.

14. W. E. D. Allen has prepared a succinct summary of the Georgian dynasties in this period in his "Notes on Don Juan of Persia's Account of Georgia," *B.S.O.S.*, VI, 179–186.

15. Allen, *History*, pp. 155–160.

16. *Ibid.*

17. According to Ulug Beg, Yusūf, son of Gori, joined the Ottomans and became a Muslim. Cf. G. Le Strange, ed. and tr., *Don Juan of Persia*, pp. 139 ff. Allen ("Don Juan of Persia," *B.S.O.S.*, VI, pp. 182–186) states that Giorgi II ruled in Gurieli at the time of the Ottoman invasion, and that he died in 1600. He spent an exile of four years (1583–1587) in Constantinople and was succeeded by his son, Mamia II, who may have had the Muslim name "Yusūf."

18. An atābeg of Meskhia had earlier usurped the throne and henceforth the line of succession remained in his family; hence the term "Sa-Atobago" [Georgian, 'Land of the Atabegs'] is found in some chronicles. Allen, "Don Juan of Persia," pp. 182–186. See also Cahen, "Atabak (Atabeg)," *E.I.*², I, 731–732.

19. Shirvan was made a province of Persia in 1536. Thereafter, various attempts were made by the descendants of the Shirvanshahs to reestablish themselves in the kingdom. In 1547 when Alḳas Mīrzā, brother of Shah Tahmāsp and at that time governor of Shirvan, defected to the Ottomans, Ismā'īl Mirza, the fourteen-year-old son of Tahmāsp, was appointed to the post, accompanied by his *lālā* or *atābeg*, Gōkça Solṭān of the Ḳājār tribe. Borhān 'Alī Mīrzā, son of the deceased Shirvanshah H̱alīl, made an unsuccessful attempt to regain his father's heritage but was repulsed by the forces of Ismā'īl. The following year when Shirvan, as a result of the Ottoman campaign, became devoid of Safavid troops, the same Borhān 'Alī successfully established himself in Shirvan until he was driven out after the Ottoman withdrawal. See Hinz, "Schah Esmā'īl II, pp. 26–28.

20. Shah Ismā'īl I conquered Derbent in 1509; thereafter, the governor of Derbent was appointed by the Shah of Persia. Barthold, "Derbend," *I.A.*, III, 537.

21. Şamẖal Çūbān, a Kumuck (Ḳūmūḳ) who controlled most of the region from the Terek river to Kaytaq (Kaya dağ or Kayakent [?]; [See *The Times' Atlas of the World*, II, Pl. 44]), and from the Avar country (*ibid.*, the branch of the river Sulak called "Avarskoye Koysu") to the Caspian Sea, died in 1578 at Buynak. According to Barthold ("Dağistan," p. 454), Çūbān died in 986/1578–1579. He left four sons—Andiy, Gerey, El'dar, and Magomet—by his Kaytak (Ḳaytaḳ) wife. They divided up the realm of their father among themselves and thereafter elected the Şamẖal (Şāh Ba'l) in turn from the four houses. A fifth son of Çūbān, But (*sic*), because he was born to a daughter of a Circassian concubine, was excluded from the original division of the Dagestan lands and only later, by force, won himself an appanage between the Sulak and Terek rivers. Following Çūbān as Şamẖal, were Andiy, Gerey, and El'dar, respectively. Such a system led to a number of internal clashes. See Polievktov, "Iz Perepiski Severno-Kavkazskikh Feodalov XVII veka," *XLV Akademiku N. Ya. Marru*, ed., I. I. Meshchaninov, pp. 745–755.

22. The Şamẖal, presumably Şamẖal Çūbān (see note 21), held the position of *Muhurdār*

(~sealbearer) under Shah Tahmāsp and Shah Ismā'īl (Roemer, *Der Niedergang Irans*, pp. 14–16). His sister, a wife of Shah Tahmāsp, had given birth to the *Sultana* (~princess) Parī H̱ān H̱ānum and *Sultan* (~prince) Sulaymān (*ibid.*; also Hinz, "Schah Esmā'īl," p. 47). Moreover, the Şamẖal's daughter, who was the mistress of Levan of Kakheti, had given him a daughter who became the wife of Simon of Kartli (Allen, *History*, p. 140).

23. The Georgian wife of Shah Tahmāsp was the daughter of Othar Shalikashvili, a powerful noble of Samtzkhé. Her brother, Waraza, was the lover of Dedis-Imédí, queen of Samtzkhé. In 1574, Shah Tahmāsp, suspecting Levan of Kakheti of negotiating with the Turks, moved an army to Genje. King Levan averted disaster by casting suspicion on Waraza in a communication to Dedis-Imédí. The queen had her lover executed. Now the Persian army, to avenge the death of Waraza, sacked Samtzkhé. *Ibid.*, p. 153.

24. Hinz, "Schah Esmā'īl II, pp. 40–41.

25. The mother of Moḥammad H̱odābanda and Ismā'īl was the daughter of the Amir, Mūsā Sulṭān Mōsellū of the Turkmān tribe. Roemẹr, p. 5.

26. The Ūstājlū occupied most of the important posts of the Safavid state under Shah Tahmāsp. If Ḥaydar became the new Shah, they might expect to retain this position; under Ismā'īl they could expect only his bitter enmity. Hinz, "Schah Esmā'īl, pp. 46–50.

27. Ismā'īl Mīrzā, who had rendered so much service to his father during the wars with the Ottomans, seems to have looked upon the Peace of Amasya (1555) with disfavor; he broke completely with his father shortly afterwards. He was appointed governor of the province of Khurasan in 1556, but the Shah became suspicious of his son's independent activities and had him imprisoned the following year. In prison Ismā'īl lived a life of debauchery which seriously affected his health and his mind. *Ibid.*, pp. 33–39, 47.

28. *Ibid.*, pp. 50–60.

29. *Ibid.*, pp. 69–92 and *passim*. At the time of his death Shah Ismā'īl had seen to the execution of Ḥasan, son of Moḥammad H̱odābanda. Also orders had been sent for the murder of 'Abbās.

30. Quite clearly the leading Shi'ites had opposed his accession to the throne. Hinz, "Schah Esmā'īl II, pp. 69–92, *passim*.

31. Roemer, pp.3–5.

32. *Ibid.*, pp. 13–17, 25–26.

33. *Ibid.*, pp. 19–20.

34. The subcurrents of life at the Persian court in this area have received detailed treatment by R. M. Savory. "The Significance of the Political Murder of Mīrzā Salmān," *Islamic Studies* III/2 (Karachi, June, 1964) pp. 181–191.

35. Roemer, pp. 28–29.

36. Savory, "The Principal Offices of the Safavid State During the Reign of Shah Tahmāsp I (930–984/1524–1576)," *B.S.O.A.S.*, XXIV/I (1961), 65–85.

37. The Lezghians and the Karaburks were smaller, less civilized tribal entities, living in the Caucasus mountain chain north of Shirvan.

38. Peçewī, II, 36, 54; Roemer, pp. 26–30.

39. Further details of this campaign appear in Chapter 2. There is no doubt whatever that the Astrakhan campaign was undertaken partly to prevent the Persians from receiving succor, and particularly military supplies, from Muscovite and Western European sources. The Ottoman merchants in Persia in 1562, the year Anthony Jenkinson arrived in Qazvin, made representations to the Shah by way of an Ottoman ambassador to the effect that ". . . [the Franks] coming thither would in great part destroy their trade, and that it should be good for [the ambassador] to persuade the Sophy not to favour the Frank, as his Highnesse meant to observe the league and friendship with the great Turke his master . . . " Jenkinson, "A compendious and brief declaration of the journey of M. Anth. Jenkinson," R. Hakluyt, ed., *The Principal Navigations* . . . . III, p. 29. According to the account of Vincenzo Alessandri, a Venetian Legate to the court of Shah Tahmāsp, the Persians were importing gold, silver, and copper from Turkey at great profit. See

Document No. XXVI (*Relazione* of Sept. 24, 1572) in G. Berchet, *La Repubblica di Venezia e la Persia*, pp. 179–180.

40. Vesselovskiy, *Trudy Vostoch. Otdel. Imper. Russk. Arkheolog. Obshch.* XX, 106–108.

41. For details of the ideological origins of the war, see Kütükoğlu, *Osmanlï-Iran Siyasî Münâsebetleri I, 1578–1590*, especially pp. 1–21.

42. Peçewī, II, 36–37.

ABBREVIATED GENEOLOGY OF THE SAFAVIDS

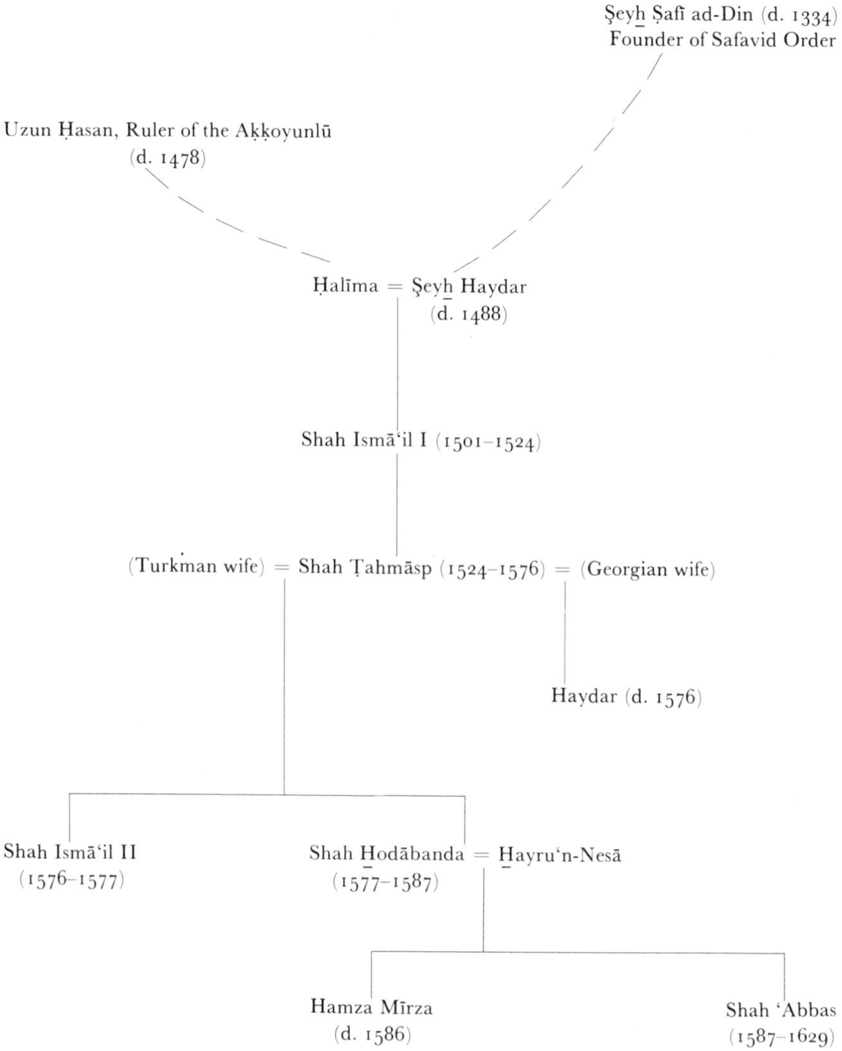

CHAPTER FOUR
The Crimean Tatars and the Persian War

1 The Conquest of Georgia and Shirvan (1578)

Once the Ottoman dignitaries had decided in consultation with the Sultan to open hostilities with Persia, it remained for the Grand Vezir, Ṣoḳōllū Meḥemmed Pasha, who was the most important link between the present regime and that of Sulaymān the Magnificent, to choose an appropriate commander (serdār) of the eastern campaign. This proved to be no easy task. The vezirs Lālā Muṣṭafā Pasha and Kōjā Sinān Pasha, two field commanders who had gained distinction in their respective campaigns of Cyprus and the Yemen, had defended a war policy before the Sultan and they now competed actively for the new post.[1] The Grand Vezir, seeking to maintain a balance between these aggressive subordinates, at first planned to assign to each of them a sector of the Persian frontier and an appropriate complement of troops. Sinān Pasha would receive the Baghdad sector and Muṣṭafā Pasha that of Eastern Anatolia. Immediately, however, Sinān Pasha, whom Peçewī describes as "obstinate and given to perverse contentions," complained to the Sultan that under the proposed arrangement he would receive inferior troops. In the end, Sinān Pasha became so disturbed and unmanageable that Ṣoḳōllū Meḥemmed urged the Sultan to appoint Muṣṭafā Pasha the serdār; that is, the sole commander of the force to be sent to Persia. This he did on 22 Şevāl 985/2 January 1578.[2]

Muṣṭafā Pasha, an experienced campaigner in the Ottoman tradition, immediately began preparations for the war. Nor did he neglect the opportunity to gain be peaceful means what might have cost much in terms of men and material. Understanding well the disarray of his enemy, he directed his *kātib*, 'Alī Efendi—an important chronicler of these events—to dispatch letters to Şāhruh̲ Mīrzā, descendant of the rulers of Shirvan;[3] the Şamh̲al, ruler of the Kumucks (Ḳumuḳ) and Ḳaytaḳs of Northern Dagestan; Ġāzī Sāliḥ, the ruler of Tabaseran (Southern Dagestan); and Tūçe Lāv Beg, the ruler of the Avars, inviting their aid and support in this "righteous" Ottoman cause.[4] Although these rulers controlled populations that lay outside the normal Ottoman political sphere, most of them were known to have Ottoman sympathies because of their affiliations with Sunni Islam or because of their political position vis-à-vis the Safavids. Similar letters were sent to all of the petty Georgian princes, some of whom were openly friendly with the Ottomans while others had close ties with the Safavid court.[5] Finally, Muṣṭafā Pasha called upon the newly appointed Crimean Khan, Meḥemmed Girāy, to lead his forces against the Safavids as "serdār of Shirvan."[6]

The army, led by Muṣṭafā Pasha, left Constantinople in April for the long march across Asia Minor. Many of the provisions were sent by sea to Trebizond and from there overland to Erzurum.[7] The Janissaries went by way of Bolu, while the serdār took the longer way over Konya to collect his troops. At the Sivas station Muṣṭafā Pasha received letters of submission from the princes of Guria and Mingrelia.[8] The Serdār assembled his troops at Erzurum in July. At about this time, letters of submission also arrived from the Şamh̲al, from the rulers of Tabaseran and Avaria, from Mīrzā Şahruh̲, and from Prince Gregor (Giorgi II) of Imereti.[9] Thus, before any conflict had taken place, the conciliatory measures of Muṣṭafā Pasha had proved at least nominally effective; of the Transcaucasian lands, only Kartli, Meskhia, and Kakheti had failea to respond.

When in early August the army camped at Ardahan, "the gateway to Georgia," some recently captured prisoners revealed that Ṭoḳmaḳ Khan, governor of Erevan, planned to cut the communications of Muṣṭafā Pasha and attack him from the rear.[10] On 5 Jumāda II 986/August 9, 1578, the Ottoman army left Ardahan and crossed the borders of Meskhia.[11] Soon contact took place between the two armies on the elevated plain of Childir. According to Minadoi, Ṭoḳmaḳ Khan, through a miscalculation based on false intelligence, committed his main body against the Ottoman advance guard. The latter was badly mauled, but the Ḳïzïlbāş, thus caught off balance, were put to rout when they were attacked by the Ottoman main body. The losses amounted to thousands on either side.[12] Throughout the battle rain had fallen so heavily that neither handgun nor cannon could be fired, a factor that weakened the technical superiority of the Ottomans.[13]

In actuality both combatants had reason to bemoan the results. On the Ottoman side a muster after the conflict revealed that many men had not even taken part in the battle.[14] On the Persian side, before the Battle of Childir, Imām Ḳūlī Khan (Ḳājār) and Amīr Khan (Turkmān), the governors of Genje and Barda'a (east of Genje) respectively, had been ordered by the Shah to join Ṭoḳmaḳ Khan but, because of the discord between the Turkmān and Ustājlū tribes, only Imām Ḳūlī Khan had joined his troops to those of Ṭoḳmaḳ Khan.[15]

Some weeks before the Battle of Childir the Serdār, Muṣṭafā Pasha, had sent a letter to Manuchar, the youngest of the princes of Meskhia, urging him and his family to renounce whatever connections they might have with the Shah and submit themselves to Ottoman rule. Now Manuchar appeared in person before Muṣṭafā Pasha to offer his submission. In recompense, he sought a diploma guaranteeing his sovereignty over the lands of his father. The Ottoman commander did not miss the point that Manuchar had waited until Ottoman arms had proved victorious at Childir. In fact, the psychological effect of Childir on the people in the Safavid sphere of influence greatly outweighed its actual military importance. However, not wishing to alienate a newly professed vassal entirely, and yet not feeling himself obliged to comply with the wishes of this now helpless prince, Muṣṭafā Pasha assigned to him an appropriate sanjāḳ and specific fiefs to other members of his family.[16]

Now the Ottomans, having accepted the submission of Meskhia, proceeded against Kartli.[17] Dāvud Khan, the ruling prince of this realm, who resided in Tiflis, had not answered the requests for submission addressed to him by Muṣṭafā Pasha. When the troops reached the city on August 24, 1578, they found it and the surrounding territory devastated and evacuated. Dāvud Khan and his subjects had withdrawn to the mountains.[18] During a pause of five days, Muṣṭafā Pasha appointed the *Sanjāḳ Bey* of Kastamonu, Meḥemmed Pasha, to the governorship of Tiflis. He received a contingent of Janissaries and other support troops totaling about 2,000 men and also supplies and cannon for the ramparts of the citadel.[19]

Three days march out of Tiflis, while making camp by a stream called Kapūr Ṣūyū, the Ottoman army received high dignitaries sent by Alexander, prince of Kakheti, who were escorted by a contingent of Georgian troops.[20] They showered rich gifts upon the serdār and his staff. Alexander now received the rank of *beylerbey* over his own domain.[21]

Ten days after leaving Tiflis, the army bivouacked on the peninsula formed by the confluence of the Alazan and the Kura rivers.[22] Meanwhile Ṭoḳmaḳ Khan, who had been routed at Childir, and a number of other regional commanders with their troops, were following the movements of the Ottoman army from the southern side of the Kura, hoping to take revenge at an opportune moment.[23] After the Ottomans had pitched camp on the Alazan, Ṭoḳmaḳ Khan devised a plan whereby he hoped to deprive the Ottomans of their mounts and supplies and then massacre them. Amīr Khan, governor of Tabriz, who had joined his forces to those of Ṭoḳmaḳ Khan and Imām Ḳūlī after Childir, secured the head of a ford across the Alazan which was called Ḳoyun Geçīdī ("sheep crossing"), so that other troops could pass over to the peninsula and separate the Ottomans from their camels and other animals grazing behind the camp. Muṣṭafā Pasha learned of this plan, however, and sent ʿOs̱mān Pasha, Meḥemmed Pasha, Beylerbey of Aleppo, and Muṣṭafā Pasha, Beylerbey of Ẕūʾl Ḳadr, with contingents to repulse the already attacking Ḳīzīlbāş. Amīr Khan's force, the first across, had succeeded in gaining a foothold on the peninsula, but he could not hold such an exposed position against the Ottoman onslaught. As the force at the head of the ford gave way, those troops already on the peninsula had to face enfilade fire as they attempted to withdraw again across the ford. Many were killed and many also drowned, for they missed the ford in the din and confusion.[24] About this time the governor of Shemakha, Aras Khan, and the governor of Shekki, Aḥmad Khan, approached the scene of battle with their own forces and, when they witnessed from afar the distress of the Ḳīzīlbāş forces, they urged their troops headlong into the fray. As they crowded over the only bridge leading from the Shirvan side onto the peninsula, the bridge, already under a strain from the swollen river, collapsed, sending many soldiers to their death. The other Shekki and Shirvan forces, witnessing this disaster, took it as a bad omen and withdrew.[25]

After the Battle of Alazan, which took place early in September 1578, the Ḳīzīlbāş commanders returned to their respective provincial capitals with the remnants of their troops. In the light of the information available it seems that the force actually confronting Muṣṭafā Pasha on the Alazan was not merely a few isolated provincial troops but an assemblage of all the provincial troops on the Persian northwest frontier. The reasons for the failure of what was probably a superior numerical force are apparent. The Ḳīzīlbāş attacked the Ottoman army on a peninsula where nature rendered to the latter every advantage. Once the Persian force lost the element of surprise, the Ottomans merely shot down the enemy as he attempted to recross the ford. On the other hand, Muṣṭafā Pasha, by coming to terms with Alexander of Kakheti, had already brought into some degree of control the most powerful forces of the area, namely the cavalry squadrons of Kakheti. Finally, it is difficult to say how eager the Armenian, Kurdish, and Shirvanian feudatories of the period were to aid their Safavid overlords. Only later, when the Turkoman forces of the Central Safavid government reached Shirvan, did the action turn against the Ottomans.

After this second major conflict with Safavid forces, Muṣṭafā Pasha experienced extreme difficulty urging his troops forward. In order to consolidate his victory he wanted to lead the army into actual Shirvan territory. This meant fording the swollen Alazan River. Had it not been for the lateness of the season and shortage of rations, perhaps this intention would have been accomplished much more easily. Finally, by making an example of himself and by offering special rewards to all who braved the stream, Muṣṭafā Pasha led his forces into Shirvan. Once across the river, the army proceeded unopposed to the city of Aresh on the Kura River.[26]

Owing to its strategic position, commanding the Persian approaches to

Derbent and Central Georgia, Aresh was to be much fought over before the war in Transcaucasia ended. The region around Aresh was relatively prosperous and hence the army was able to replenish its supplies and recuperate. Meanwhile, Muṣṭafā Pasha and his staff, concerned about winter's approach, hastily took measures to rebuild the bridge over the Alazan and to construct a citadel in Aresh. As these preparations reached completion, news arrived from Derbent that the inhabitants had killed their Persian governor, Nadan H̱alīfe, and that they now sought the appointment of an Ottoman governor in his stead.[27]

During his final Dīvān (staff meeting) before returning to Erzurum, the Serdār, Muṣṭafā Pasha, divided his conquests into four governorships: Shirvan, Tiflis (Kartli), Gurjistan (Kakheti), and Sukum (Abkhazia?). Muṣṭafā Pasha had considerable trouble persuading one of his staff to assume the duties of governor of Shirvan. This is quite easy to understand in the light of the existing circumstances, with winter approaching and no one able to predict how the local population or the Safavids might behave toward a relatively small occupying force. 'O̱smān Pasha, the hero of the two prior engagements of the army, was finally persuaded by his supporters to accept the post.[28] Then both Lālā Muṣṭafā and 'O̱smān Pasha used every means to encourage seasoned officers and troops to remain with the Shirvan force.[29] In terms of actual men and equipment, three thousand Janissaries, sixty cannon, and one hundred eighty boxes of ordnance supplies and equipment were allotted to 'O̱smān Pasha. The remainder of the force numbering about ten thousand was made up of Ottoman provincial troops and local volunteers. Ḳayṭās Pasha, Beylerbey of Erzurum, was appointed governor of Aresh with a force of five thousand.[30]

Muṣṭafā Pasha took care in appointing the *defterdār*, the *taḥrīr emīni*, and the various *ḳadīs*. Thus, Muṣṭafā Pasha set in motion in Shirvan the long-established administrative measures which the Ottomans considered necessary for the pacification of new territories and their incorporation into the structure of the Ottoman Empire.[31] In spite of all these administrative measures, Muṣṭafā Pasha must have realized that the loss of Shirvan would not be taken lightly by the Safavids, for the Shah's yearly income from the silk production, the salt works, the rice fields, and the petroleum of this province alone was estimated at 25,200,000 aspers, all of which might now go to the Sultan's coffers.[32] Therefore, the Serdār now sought to gain by conciliation what he had not as yet taken by force of arms. In a letter to Jamşīd Khan, the ruler of Gilan, Muṣṭafā Pasha urged that Gilan declare its submission to the Sultan; to the governor of Shemakha, Aras Khan, whose father had defected to the Safavids, he offered a pardon in return for recognition of the Sultan's authority. Both attempts at conciliation proved fruitless. It was still quite evident that it would be extremely difficult for 'O̱smān Pasha to conquer the rest of Shirvan with the small number of troops at his command;[33] consequently, Muṣṭafā Pasha continued to seek support from the Crimean Khan.[34]

Muṣṭafā Pasha departed from Aresh with the bulk of the Ottoman army on 6 Şa'bān 986/8 October 1578. Eight days after crossing the Alazan he was met by the Şamḫal who, after his submission, was assigned Shabiran (Apshiran?) as a Sanjāḳ.[35] In Tiflis from October 24 to 29 the army received its first taste of the Georgian winter when it was swept by high winds and a snowstorm. As the season advanced and as the sporadic attacks of small forces under Imām Ḳūlī Khan and Simon Luarssab[36] increased, the return of the army to winter quarters in Erzurum turned into a disorderly retreat during which the Ottomans suffered serious losses of men, animals, and equipment in the mountains.[37]

Muṣṭafā Pasha stopped in Akhaltsikhe long enough to pick up the two sons of Dedis Imédi, Manuchar and Alexander, whom he sent under escort to the Sultan.[38] The army reached Erzurum on 21 Ramażān 986/21 November 1578. The campaign had lasted eight months from its inception to its close. In terms of actual travel time, it is not surprising to learn that the army stopped at sixty-five overnight stations between Constantinople and Erzurum and that from Erzurum to Aresh and back, there were sixty-nine.[39] From the Bosphorus to Aresh alone the Ottoman troops had marched or ridden well over two thousand miles.

2 The Advent of the Crimean Tatars and the Death of 'Âdil Giray

The events described in the previous section constituted the effort of the main Ottoman army in the first year of the Ottoman-Safavid War. These events in themselves, however, only serve to introduce some of the *dramatis personae* and *dramatis loci* of a struggle which continued until 1590, a struggle which, in part, reflected a three-cornered competition of Muscovite, Safavid, and Ottoman for control of the vital trade, pilgrim, and communication routes of the Caucasus. In the case of the Ottoman-Safavid clash, if the Ottomans had succeeded in making the Peace of 1590 final, they would have been able, in league with their coreligionists, the Uzbegs of Central Asia, to reduce the Persian state to a third-rate power.

Only the Italian writers of the period—although their accounts are often confused in matters of detail—were able to remove themselves from the tactical situation and to provide future generations with a view of the over-all Ottoman plan for the conquest of the Caucasus. In the words of Minadoi:

> *The Turks in the present war have sought to occupy all four* [*regions of Georgia*] *simultaneously; by way of the Colchis* [*Mingrelia*] *sending an armada to the mouth of the river of Phasis* [*Rioni*], *by the shores of the Albanians* [*Dagestanians*] *leading 'Ādil Girāy, the Tatar, into Shirvan; and then through these* [*previously mentioned mountains of Georgia*] *two* [*mountain*] *passes the entire army moved into their regions as we shall describe . . . .* (p. 59)

Taking into consideration that Muṣṭafā Pasha most likely did send a detachment across the mountains to Tiflis by a route other than the one taken by the main body of his forces, this description adds two elements to the invasion plan of the year 1578: naval support and Crimean Tatar participation. The Ottoman navy was responsible, in fact, for making incursions into Mingrelia and Imereti by way of the "river of Phasis" (the Rioni River). The immediate objective, apart from a show of force, was apparently to seize the town of Kutaisi as the first stage toward opening communications to Tiflis by this short route. The first attempt was discouraged by the resistance of the local inhabitants, but the Ottomans succeeded in building a fortress on an island at the mouth of the river.[41] In the following year further incursions were made under the direction of the Ḳāpūdān Pasha.[42]

The participation of the Crimean Tatars in the Safavid campaign was not possible initially. Even in 1577, during the life of Devlet Girāy, the Sultan had informed the Khan that his services would be needed in case of a future conflict with Persia.[43] As an answer, however, to the activities of Cossacks, and urged on by subsidies from the Tsar, the Crimean Tatars perpetrated heavy raids on Poland in 1577 and 1578.[44] Only through the active intermediation of the Grand Vezir was peace between Poland and the Crimean Tatars concluded in September 1578.[45]

By 1578 unrest in Transcaucasia and the Crimea had its counterpart in the Northern Caucasus. The two Kabardinian princes, Kan (Khan?) Bulat and Mamstruk Temruk, petitioned Ivan IV to reestablish the fortress on the Terek River which had been destroyed around 1570 either by the Muscovites themselves or by the Crimean Tatars. The Kabardinians again sought the protection of Moscow, in particular against the Crimean Tatars and their Circassian allies.[46]

The ambassadorial reports of Luk'yan (or sometimes Luka) Novosil'tsev, on the occasion of his mission to the court of the Emperor Rudolph II in 1585, provide an eye-witness account of the Tatar expeditionary force. According to Novosil'tsev, who was *voivode* on the Terek in 1578, 'Ādil Girāy led a force of fifteen thousand Tatars past his fort (*gorod*) and crossed the Sunzhu river near Goryachaya Kolodez'.[47] At this time the Cossacks, under the command of the *voivode*, assisted the Tatar river crossing. When the Tatars returned after their defeat in Shirvan, they crossed the Sunzhu further upstream and got ten thousand men across the Terek before they were discovered by the Cossacks.[48] The implication here is that the defeat and dispersal of the Tatars in that year had made them wary of any potentially hostile force in the area. The Crimean Tatars en route to Shirvan reached the Sunzhu branch of the Terek River at the end of October 1578.[49] The contingent was led by 'Ādil Girāy, the Ḳalġay, who was accompanied by his brothers, Ġāzī and Mubārek, and the son of the Khan, Sa'ādet. Whether or not the Tatars had received further dispatches from 'O̱smān Pasha after the departure of the Ottomans from Aresh is not clear.[50]

While the Tatars were thus proceeding toward Transcaucasia, ‘Os̱mān Pasha and Ḳayṭās Beg had pacified much of Shirvan. As the shortage of food continued to create hardship among the troops, ‘Os̱mān Pasha led a very successful raid into the enemy territories of Genje and Karabaġ (Karabakh) across the Kura. Meanwhile word reached ‘Os̱mān Pasha that Aras Khan, who had retired across the Kura near the city of Sal‘yany in the face of the superior numbers of the army led by Muṣṭafā Pasha,[51] had again entered Shirvan and was marching on the capital, Shemakha, with fifteen thousand men.[52] ‘Os̱mān Pasha and Ḳayṭās Beg took up defensive positions near their respective strongholds of Shemakha and Aresh. Of the ten thousand troops allotted to him, ‘Os̱mān Pasha must have had about eight thousand with him.

The battle of Shemakha commenced on 9 Ramażān 986/9 November 1578. At about the same time, Imām Ḳūlī Khan, governor of Genje, and Amīr Khan, ruler of Gilan, attacked Aresh with a combined force of fifteen thousand. Ḳayṭās Beg sallied forth to meet the Safavid attack only to fall victim to an enemy sword. Soon his small garrison of troops was routed and the victorious Kïzïlbāş entered the city, bringing death or humiliation to leading Sunni Muslims and completely sacking entire districts.[53] The greatly outnumbered troops of ‘Os̱mān Pasha in Shemakha managed barely to hold their positions against the Safavid attack led by Aras Khan.

The second day of the battle proved to be as bloody as the first, but a certain ‘Abdī Çāvuş got through the Persian lines to bring the news that the Tatars were only one station away. By now the Ottoman lines were quite weakened but this news brought strength to all the troops.[54] The third day, as both armies had fought to near exhaustion, the intense fighting slowed down to an exchange of arrows and lead. Then at the time of the afternoon prayers, a numerous Tatar force appeared on the scene and, although they were doubtless weary from their long journey, they entered the melee and shortly broke the Persian resistance.[55] During the course of the battle Aras Khan was taken alive by Ġāzī Girāy's Mīrāẖōr (master of horse), who accomplished this feat by shooting down the successive mounts of the former governor and then wounding his sword arm. This unfortunate commander was shortly after put to death.[56]

When the conflict had subsided, the Tatar leaders and their troops were warmly thanked and greatly honored by the Ottomans for their timely arrival. Having considerable familiarity with the Tatar character, however, ‘Os̱mān mentioned to ‘Ādil Girāy and to his brothers and the other dignitaries in the Tatar camp that even in the war zone it had been Ottoman policy to protect the lives and property of the Muslim inhabitants. The Tatars replied that "for the Tatars, raiding was as necessary as worldly goods were for the repose of ordinary people" and they let it be known that they could not accept his restriction.[57]

Soon a fitting task for the Tatars diverted them from indiscriminate raiding. 'Os̱mān Pasha learned that many of the fleeing Safavid dignitaries, including a certain Ertoğdī Khan, had entrenched themselves with their retinues and households, and also with the worldly wealth of Aras Khan, across the Kura River near Sal'yany on their former camp site. In this same area, which was probably a staging area of long standing, there gathered a number of the Safavid troops who had fled from Shemakha. The trenchworks were defended by cannon, but the Tatars quickly overran the position and acquired more booty and slaves than they could carry off.[58] As a result, this generally mobile force incautiously loaded itself with an excess of pack animals.[59]

While the Tatars set out from Sal'yany to rejoin 'Os̱mān Pasha at Shemakha, the main Persian army, numbering thirty to forty thousand men,[60] the advance guard of which had so successfully sacked Aresh, now moved in the direction of Shemakha under the command of Selmān Khan, the Vezir of Shah H̱odābanda.[61] In the evening of 24 Ramażān 986/24 November 1578, the Kïzïlbaş army began its siege of Shemakha.[62] After surveying the situation, 'Os̱mān Pasha attempted to send word to the Tatars, but his Çāvuş was intercepted. Upon discovering the whereabouts of the Crimean Tatars, Selmān Khan, recalling the dire extremities in which he had found the Ottomans, left a containing force around the walls of Shemakha and led the bulk of his army against the Tatars.[63] On the last day of Ramażān 986/30 November 1578, the Tatars and Safavids clashed on the plain near Maḥmūdābād (Mollā Ḥasan).[64] Fierce fighting followed for three days between the Tatars and the numerically far superior Safavid forces. According to 'Alī, the Tatars had gained a considerable advantage over their adversary when a terrible rainstorm swept over the battlefield. This storm greatly hampered the Tatars, who relied heavily on their bows and arrows and the maneuverability of their mounts. The vanes or feathers of the bolts became soaked and the bows warped; thus, their accuracy was greatly impaired. Their horses, also, became mired in a sea of mud. The Tatars disengaged and retreated in the direction of Derbent; the Kïzïlbāş moved off toward the Kura River.[65]

Supplementing the material found in the *Nuṣratnāme* ('Alī) and the *Şeja'atnāme* of Aṣafī, the *Tārīẖ-i 'Ālam Arāye 'Abbāsī* indicated that 'Ādil Girāy became a prisoner of the Safavids during this struggle.[66] Moreover, the *Tārīẖ-i 'Ālām* gives further details concerning the strength of the Tatar forces at the time of the battle. When the latter reached Shirvan, they are said to have been 20,000 strong. In the clash with the forces of Selmān Khan in the Menlā Hasan (Mollā Ḥasan) district, the Tatars numbered twelve thousand but had additional support from four to five thousand Lezgians, Ḳaraburks, and Shirvan rebels.[67]

The Safavids conducted 'Ādil Girāy to Qazvin where he received particularly good treatment, thanks to the favor of the Shah's wife, the Begum H̠ayru'n-Nesā, who had accompanied the army in the recent campaign and who controlled the Safavid state because her son, Hamza, was still a youth and the Shah was nearly blind. Qazvin, during this troubled period, offered the young Tatar prince great opportunities for intrigue. It soon became rumored that the Tatar prince had entered into intimate relations with the Begum. He most certainly was under serious consideration as a suitable match for one of the *sultanas* (~princesses) providing the Tatar h̠ānzāde would help arrange closer political ties between the Crimean Tatars and Persia.[68] It is not clear how much 'Ādil Girāy felt it necessary to play this game in order to save his life. At any rate, in the end he apparently overplayed his hand, for it was not a grandiose scheme of Persian control of the Tatars but the liberties 'Ādil Girāy was alleged to have taken in the harem that outraged the court and the royal guard and led to the deaths of the Begum and 'Ādil Girāy.[69] One also must not forget the role that the Begum's domineering personality and the intrigues of the court played in this event.

Meanwhile, 'O̱smān Pasha, having heard the results of this latest clash, decided to withdraw from Shemakha to Derbent before Selmān Khan could regroup his forces around Shemakha. He had suffered severe losses against both Aras Khan and Selmān Khan and within his own ranks he had to fight the seditious activities of the Şamh̠al, who joined the Ottoman forces after the departure of Muṣṭafā Pasha.[70] A detachment of Tatars helped remove a part of the army supplies and equipment; the remainder was burned.

Under the circumstances, the fortress city of Derbent offered 'O̱smān Pasha the only refuge possible for so few regular troops.[71] 'O̱smān Pasha, upon his departure, dispatched a letter to the Serdār in Erzurum describing the recent events. In his letter he called upon the Serdār to inform the Sultan concerning the needs of the people of Shirvan who once again would be at the mercy of the Safavids. He also pleaded for reinforcements in addition to the Tatars.[72] The retreat over the mountains in the month of December proved disastrous. As Dal Meḥemmed wrote in the *Şejā'atnāme*, equipment, animal corpses, and human bodies left a gruesome trail in the snow from Shemakha to Derbent. Dal Meḥemmed, called Asafī, was assigned to the rear guard with Ġāzī Girāy. This body of men succeeded in rescuing much equipment and saving many lives.[73]

En route the rear of the column was harassed by Safavid detachments and the forward areas were subjected to attacks from some of the wild Dagestan tribes. Finally the army reached Derbent, where more than a foot of snow lay on the ground.[74]

As he approached Derbent, 'O̱smān Pasha sent his Keth̠udā forward to arrange for the arrival of his troops. However, as some of the Tatars fleeing from the previous battle had passed through Derbent bringing news of total defeat, the dignitaries who controlled the city were reluctant to yield to the

Ottoman army. ʿO̱smān Pasha thus had to gain access to the city by a show of force.[75]

This Ottoman "holding force" had barely escaped extermination in Shirvan. This would undoubtedly have been their fate had the Tatars not reinforced them. In spite of this assistance, they were cut off from further support and supplies from Ottoman territory by way of Tiflis and they now had to face a severe winter. This prompted the withdrawal to Derbent which was more easily defendable and which lay further from the Persian supply centers. Derbent also had the advantage of possessing an alternative overland connection with the Ottoman domain. In Derbent the Ottomans were reinforced by Nogay and Dagestan troops.[76] For the moment at least the Ottomans still had a foothold in the Caucasus.[77]

As a fitting close to this first year of the Caucasian War, it is instructive to recall the reasons Minadoi gave for the success of the Ottomans against the Persians.[78] He pointed to the rapid increase of Ottoman power in the sixteenth century on land and sea. As a counterweight to this foe on their borders, the Persians had not even fortified their cities. Therefore, when once the mounttains were crossed, there were no physical barriers to deter the Ottomans. Particularly advantageous for the Ottomans, he notes, is their "conquest of the arts." They learned Western skills from the conquest of Christian cities. The Ottoman used his newly acquired weapons better than his adversary and improved upon them. Finally, Minadoi contrasts the concord and celerity of the Ottomans with the discord and dissension of the Safavids.

Braudel in his study of the Mediterranean lands emphasizes the fundamental difficulties of the Caucasian campaign.[79] Largely he reflects the objections to the campaign attributed to Soḳōllū Meḥemmed Pasha: the tenacity of the adversary, the inconstancy of the local population, the great distances from Ottoman centers, and finally the difficulties of terrain and climate.

3 The Crimean Tatars in Shirvan (1579)

Although the first year of the Caucasian War had resembled in some respects previous Ottoman-Safavid encounters, new Ottoman goals had altered the situation considerably. In former wars with Persia, Ottoman armies had generally entered the eastern provinces of Persia only to withdraw upon the approach of winter. Thus, the campaigns of Sultan Sulaymān had ended in stalemate. Now, however, the Ottomans were making a concerted effort to occupy Transcaucasia permanently. Such a grand project became plausible only after the Ottomans had secured long-term peace treaties with their enemies in Western Europe.

The Russian occupation of Astrakhan had been the result of long-term Ottoman neglect of her northeastern frontier following her conquest of the

Genoese colonies in 1475. Russian acquisition of Astrakhan served further to emphasize to what extent the Ottoman east-west trade monopoly had been undermined by hostile powers. Earlier the Portuguese, by using the Cape route, had hindered the flow of goods to Persian Gulf and Red Sea ports. Now, Muscovy had severed an important link with the eastern trade routes that crossed Central Asia. Thus the Persian War became strategically important as a check to Muscovite and Safavid economic and political activities, as a move to maintain direct religious and economic ties with Central Asia and, lastly, as a confirmation of Ottoman rights on the shores of the Black Sea and in the Caucasus.[80] The discontent of the semi-independent Georgian, Shirvanian, and Dagestanian Emirates in the Caucasus and their bitter rivalries over the choice of a successor to the Persian throne after the death of Shah Tahmāsp had provided ample excuse and opportunity for the onset of hostilities.

The campaign of 1578 had shown that, with a sizable force, the Ottomans had been more than a match for the Persian provincial forces. Ṣoḳōllū Meḥemmed Pasha had already warned his countrymen about the pitfalls of climate and terrain and the stubbornness of the local inhabitants but, upon the withdrawal of the main army, had it not been for the stamina and courage of old campaigners like 'O̱smān Pasha and the timely arrival of Tatar reinforcements, the entire effort would have ended in failure the first year of the war. Moreover, with the appearance of Selmān Khan, the Persian Vezir, who was nominally under the command of the young Persian heir apparent, Hamza Mīrzā, came the best fighting forces of the Persian realm.[81]

Henceforth the war progressed on two largely uncoordinated fronts: in the western Caucasus the action developed around supply trains and fixed fortifications; to the east, raids, battles, and the gain and loss of territories continued.

At the beginning of 1579, 'O̱smān Pasha and his exhausted forces found themselves in Derbent, a region poorly provided with rations to feed even a small army. To all of the surrounding regions supply missions were sent. When peaceful requests produced no results from the Ġūrī tribe, 'O̱smān Pasha resorted to force. He did not, however, merely extract much-needed grain and livestock from this tribe; he reduced them to obedience by evacuating them from certain districts. In Tabaseran (region south of Derbent) the Ottoman supply mission was attacked and destroyed. This time a force led by Sīdī Ġāzī Beg brought fire and sword to the area and actually took charge of Mahariḳe, the principal town.[82]

Shortly after the basic needs of the army had been met by these two actions, Burhān Oġlū Abū Bekr Mīrzā conceived a plan for unseating the Persian commander, Moḥammed H̱alīfe, who had been left in charge of Shirvan upon the withdrawal to winter quarters of the main body of the Persian army. He reasoned that, because of his direct descent from the old ruling family, the inhabitants of Shirvan would flock to his banner.

'Os̱mān Pasha was taken in by this argument. Little did he realize that Abū Bekr Mīrzā intended to negotiate with the Safavids for a portion of Shirvan, for he had grown disillusioned with the Ottomans after being offered only a *zi'amet* or feudal estate by 'Os̱mān Pasha. Abū Bekr Mīrzā clashed with Moḥammed H̱alīfe at Tenk Boġazī (a mountain pass) but, as he shortly fled from the field, his small force was defeated and routed.[83]

'Os̱mān Pasha already had too few troops. He could little afford such adventures as this. After news of the defeat had circulated through the mountains, the Ḳaytaḳs, one of the strongest tribes in the region, revolted. 'Os̱mān Pasha personally led a punitive raid against them. Although they were not evacuated, as the Ġūrīs had been, the Ḳaytaḳs were effectively subdued and now many came to Derbent to serve under 'Os̱mān Pasha.[84]

Meanwhile Muṣṭafā Pasha had convinced the Porte of the necessity for building a series of permanent fortifications right across Georgia to Shirvan in order to hold permanently the recent conquests. In the spring of 1579 he set about this task by rebuilding the fortress at Kars which had formerly belonged to Meskhia or "Saatobago." Meanwhile, 'Os̱mān Pasha was left to make the most of a bad situation. Muṣṭafā Pasha doubtless counted on the Crimean Tatars to fill the gap.

From the military standpoint, it made sense to secure the Caucasian flank before undertaking any adventures on the Tabriz plain.[85] Thus, Muṣṭafā Pasha again moved his strong Ottoman force to the borders of Persia and Georgia in the summer of 1579. This action at least prevented the Safavids from deploying all of their provincial forces against Tiflis and other fixed positions held by the Ottomans. While the main army marked time at Kars, a strong Ottoman detachment raided the country around Erevan bringing back numerous prisoners. At the same time, one of the principal tasks of the army was to move supplies arriving at Erzurum up to the fortress in the Caucasus.[86]

Imām Ḳūlī and Simon Luarssab had besieged Tiflis for over four months with an army of 10,000. To relieve this hard-pressed, starving garrison, Meḥemmed Ḥasan Pasha, the son of Grand Vezir Ṣoḳōllū Meḥemmed Pasha, was sent with a relief force and supplies in Jumāda II, 987/July 1579. He accomplished this perilous task in sixteen days, but was harassed continually by Georgian irregulars led by Simon.[87]

The Serdār had counted on the Tatars to provide as much support for 'Os̱mān Pasha in 1579 as they had the previous year. He was not able to ensure this, however, without special concessions. First of all, the Khan was officially appointed commander-in-chief of the Ottoman army in Dagestan.[88] The letter to the Khan from Murād III, dated 987/1579, which is found in the Ferīdūn collection, clearly indicates how much discretionary power the Khans, at this time, still possessed. The Sultan hoped that the Khan would send as much assistance as in the previous year.[89] When once it became known that ʻĀdil Girāy had been captured by the Safavids, Meḥemmed Girāy faced the problem of choosing a new Ḳalġay acceptable to the Tatar Mīrzās and to the Sublime Porte. He preferred his own son, Sa'ādet Girāy but, as his brother Alp Girāy was the senior member of the family, the Khan was forced to appoint him to the post. Nevertheless, not wishing to eliminate his own son entirely from the prerogatives of high office, he proposed to the Porte that a second heir to the Khanship be designated who would be known as *Nūr ed-Dīn*. Relations being what they were between the Porte and Persia, the Ottomans needed Tatar forces and therefore accepted his suggestion.[90]

The Khan, long before his departure for Derbent from Bakhchisaray (Bāġçesarāy) on 1 Jumāda II 987/26 July 1579, had furnished Meḥemmed Bey, Sanjāḳ Bey of Azak (Azof), with 10,000 Tatars. This advance party and supply train reached Derbent in exactly 74 days. Thereupon ʻOs̱mān Pasha rewarded Meḥemmed Bey by giving him the honorary title of Kāpūdān ($\sim$ Grand Admiral) of the Caspian Sea (*Baḥr-i H̱azar*) with an annual income of 800,000 aḳçe. Shortly after the arrival of the advance party, ʻOs̱mān Pasha went forth from Derbent in person to receive the Khan.[91]

ʻOs̱mān Pasha and Meḥemmed Khan made a triumphal entry into Derbent together; the Tatars had completed the journey in thirty days.[92] Neither the Ottomans nor the Tatars remained in Derbent. They removed themselves to a prearranged headquarters about one league from the city. After the Tatars had feasted and rested several days the campaign commenced. From Şabiran (Apshiran Peninsula) a large force was detached and sent ahead. This army defeated Moḥammed H̱alīfe (Ẕu'l Ḳadr), the Persian general and governor of Shirvan, in two separate clashes, made him a prisoner, and sent the remainder of the Persian forces scurrying across the Kura river into Karabaġ (Karabakh) and Muġan. After Shirvan had once again been cleared of Persian troops, a force was sent against Baku.[93] Thereafter, the Tatars spread out and collected booty and slaves throughout the countryside.

All of these joint efforts by ʻOs̱mān Pasha and the Tatar Khan had been carried out in the full expectation of the early arrival of Muṣṭafā Pasha. Finally, however, a courier arrived from Kars bearing the news that Muṣṭafā Pasha would not return to Shirvan that year.[94] The Tatar Khan held council with his brothers and the other Tatar dignitaries and together they resolved to return to the Crimea. ʻOs̱mān Pasha was able to dissuade them from this action for a time by suggesting a raid into the provinces south of the Kura. The Khan and his horsemen thus crossed the river and concentrated on the province of Genje (district around modern Kirovabad) where still no trace of a Persian army was apparent. In fact, after gathering booty an entire month, the Tatars left that province in disarray. When these successes were announced to the Serdār in Kars, a return dispatch urged ʻOs̱mān Pasha and the Khan to attempt even the conquest of Ardabīl, the sacred city of the Safavids. Both

'Os̱mān Pasha and the Khan, however, recognized the folly of such an undertaking with so few forces. As winter was approaching and as the Serdār was withdrawing from Kars to Erzurum, the Tatars left Genje, rested a few days in Aresh, and then started for the Crimea.

Although the Khan was urged by 'Os̱mān Pasha to winter in Shirvan, he only consented to leave his brother Ġāzī Girāy and his son Sa'ādet Girāy in the Caucasus with a few thousand Tatars. He told 'Os̱mān Pasha that he considered himself an independent prince, not a bey subject to the Porte. It was just this uncompromising attitude that was ultimately to earn for Meḥemmed Girāy the distrust of the Sultan.[95]

When it was known for certain among the Ottomans that the Tatars were leaving, friendly relations ceased between 'Os̱mān Pasha and the Khan. The Ottoman troops, in most of the previous engagements, had had to stand by while the Tatars took the lion's share of the booty. They now realized that they had to garrison this frontier and to fight the Persian army while the Tatars returned to the safety of their homeland.[96] Although 'Os̱mān Pasha knew that the Tatars would never be reliable as garrison troops, he only partially succeeded in maintaining discipline among his own men after their departure. A group of two thousand Ottoman troops deserted the Shirvan force and started for Erzurum of their own volition. Only a third of them were destined to survive the attacks of the Georgian irregulars.

With only a handful of 3,000 to 4,000 Ottoman regulars, 'Os̱mān Pasha could not hope to hold Shirvan. To make things more difficult Meḥemmed Khan ordered his son, Sa'ādet Girāy, to return to the Crimea with his retinue. Thus, Ġāzī Girāy was left in command of a still smaller group of Tatars.[97]

Meanwhile, Selmān Khan was leading a large Persian force toward Shirvan. An advance contingent sent against Shemakha met with defeat at the hands of Dāl Meḥemmed, the author of the *Şejā'atnāme*, who was in charge of the Shemakha garrison. This gave 'Os̱mān Pasha time to make an orderly withdrawal to Derbent through Baku. 'Os̱mān Pasha was able to gain some local profit from the direct control of the Baku region by selling petroleum and silk products. Selmān, closely pressing 'Os̱mān Pasha, occupied Shemakha and the delta of the Kura.[98]

While preparations for further clashes were taking place on the Shirvan front, an assassin had killed the Grand Vezir Ṣoḳōllū Meḥemmed Pasha on 8 Şa'ban 987/30 September 1579. This event led to the appointment of Aḥmed Pasha, an Albanian by origin, to the grand vezirship.[99] The news reached Muṣṭafā Pasha on October 27,[100] and in the month of Şeval/November-December, Kōjā Sinān Pasha, the general who had contended for the command of the eastern front, replaced his old rival, Muṣṭafā Pasha. The latter returned to the Porte and assumed his place in the governmental hierarchy as second vezir.[101] He died during the following year while acting as *Ka'immaḳām* (deputy vezir) in Istanbul.[102]

4 Persian Internal Strife and Ottoman Consolidation of the Eastern Front

Why had the Safavids failed to oppose the Ottoman-Tatar invasion of their tributaries and territories in 1579? The period between the death of Shah Tahmāsp in 1576 and the accession of Shah 'Abbās in 1587 was one of virtual anarchy in Persia. The general reasons for this state of affairs were well known to contemporary observers. In his *Relazione* of 1592, Lorenzo Bernardo, the Venetian *bailo*, explained that the troubles of Persia could be attributed to intrinsic and extrinsic causes ("... une intrinseca, l'altra estrinseca....."). As intrinsic causes, he called attention to the incapacity of Shah Ḫodābanda, and to the discord which prevailed between the Shah and his sons, Hamza and 'Abbās, and between the Shah and the chief dignitaries (the "Sultani," or Ḳïzïlbāş aristocracy). As for the extrinsic causes of the difficulties in Persia, Bernardo called the attention of the Venetian Signoria to the struggle which Persia had to conduct against two strong enemies, the Ottoman Turks in Azerbaijan and the Uzbegs (Uzbeks) in Khurasan. Moreover, these powers were secretly in alliance ("... Usbech re de' Tartari ... il quale, sia per secreta intelligenze col Turco. ..."). Finally, Bernardo mentions the form of government, the quality of the army, and the lack of artillery as reasons for the weakness of Persia. Nor is the Kingdom of Persia centralized like that of France or the Ottoman Empire, he said, but more like Poland or Germany, for the power and the wealth is diffused among the "Sultani," the heads of the Turcoman tribes, each of which governs his own province as he chooses.[103]

After Selmān Khan had put the Tatars to flight at Mollā Ḥasan in November 1578, and had garrisoned Shemakha upon the withdrawal of 'Os̱mān Pasha to Derbent, he had returned with the army to Ḳara Aġaç where the Begum Ḫayru'n-Nesā' and her son, Hamza Mīrzā, had remained during the campaign.[104] The decision of Selmān Khan to return to winter quarters displeased the Begum. She had ordered that the Tatar ḫanzāde be sent to the court and that a winter campaign be launched against Derbent. But Selmān Khan was free of blame; internal dissension among the Ḳïzïlbāş amirs had made the extension of the campaign impossible.

The Begum was not to forget this act of disobedience. During the remaining months of her life, she took every occasion to humiliate the leading Ḳïzïlbāş families by exercising the prerogatives of the Shah without due regard for the real power still wielded by the tribal leaders. Two incidents in particular serve to illustrate the anti-Ḳïzïlbāş policy of the Begum, which brought about her own downfall and death.

In the early months of 1579 the Begum directed her attention to Māzandarān, her land of origin. Some years before, her father, the reigning prince of Māzandarān, had been murdered by the forebears of the then ruling prince, Mīrzā Khān. As the latter prince had failed to do homage to Shah

Ḫodābanda upon his accession, the Begum, in the spring of 1579, sent an army to besiege him. When, however, Mīrzā Khān obtained the sworn oaths of the leading Ḳïzïlbāş amirs and of Selmān Khan for his safe conduct, he agreed to make the required journey of homage to Qazvin. The Begum, however, disregarding the oaths of the leading personages in the realm, had him murdered as he approached the capital. Thereafter, Selmān Khan and several of the Ḳïzïlbāş amirs plotted the removal of the Begum from her seat of power.[105]

Another event, paralleling the previous one, began unfolding in Khorāsān early in 1579, thus further distracting the attention of the capital from the events in Shirvan and Genje. Imperceptibly at first, the old rivalries between the chief tribal protagonists, the Shāmlū-Ustājlū and the Turkmān-Tekkelū, began to revive. 'Abbās Mīrzā, the second son of Ḫayru'n-Nesā' and Shah Ḫodābenda, when only a child, had been sent, as governor of Khorāsān, to Harāt in the charge of his lālā (~guardian) 'Alī Ḳūlī Khan (Shāmlū). The Begum, considering the residence of her son outside the capital a threat to her own authority and to that of the *Velī Ahd* (~Heir Apparent), Ḥamza Mīrzā, ordered his return to the capital. The leaders of the Shāmlū Ustājlū rightly saw in this measure an attempt on the part of the Begum to reduce their influence; hence, they took measures to oppose her. 'Alī Ḳūlī opposed the request ostensibly on the grounds that, for the security of Persia, a member of the ruling family must remain in residence on the northeast frontier. Now the Begum ordered Ibrāhīm Beg (Turkmān), the governor of Qom, to bring 'Abbās Mīrzā to the capital. Murtażī Ḳūlī (Turkmān), governor of Meshhed, who heretofore had adhered to the party of 'Abbās Mīrzā merely to maintain the support of his local Begs, now joined with his kinsman to enforce the decrees of the central government. Meanwhile, the Begum attacked the powerful relatives of 'Alī Ḳūlī at court. Prominent among these was the father of 'Alī Ḳūlī, the governor of the capital. He journeyed to Herat in an attempt to dissuade his son from this treasonable activity but, when his mission failed, he was removed from high office.

As a result of these two important developments, Selmān Khan had lent his full support to the Ḳïzïlbāş intrigues against the Begum. The formation of this coalition against the Begum coincided with the return to the capital in late July of the disgruntled Ḳūrçū, who had been sent to Shirvan late in 1578 with a carte blanche to "collect" their pay.[106] It is believed that the ensuing rebellion of the Ḳūrcū was encouraged by the dissident amirs who, in order to inflame the hatred of these forces, accused the Begum of having intimacies with the Crimean Tatar Ḫānzāde, 'Ādil Girāy. Both, consequently, were brutally murdered.[107]

In spite of the discord in the capital and in Khurāsān, the Ḳïzïlbāş amirs still loyal to the Shah were able to assemble an army and march to Shirvan in the autumn of 1579. After the reoccupation of Shemakha, however, the unity of the force was threatened because of eternal bickering and Selmān Khan once again was forced to withdraw without engaging the meager forces under the command of 'O̱smān Pasha in a major battle.[108]

The following year (1580), the Shāmlū-Ustājlū faction defeated the Turkmān faction and gained control of Khorāsān, but this rebellious act in the province brought to an end the formidable influence of the Shāmlū-Ustājlū tribes at the court in Qazvin. Not until 1583, by strenuous efforts indeed, was the Shah able to bring the revolt in Khorāsān under control. Even then his vezir, Mīrzā Selmān, whose daughter was the wife of the heir apparent, Hamza Mīrzā, became the political sacrifice. He was blamed by the Ḳïzïlbāş amirs for stirring up trouble between the tribes and wrongly casting suspicion on the good intentions of 'Abbās Mīrzā. Subsequently he was executed. As a Persian, he had usurped military and political powers that had become the prerogative of the Ḳïzïlbāş Turkic elite.[109]

Ḳōjā Sinān Pasha took to the field in the spring of 1580. The Safavids grew alarmed at the new preparations.[110] In view of the Khurāsān rebellion it might have been better for the Persians to make small concessions for peace with the Ottomans than to risk the extension of the war to Southern Azerbaijan, where it was rumored Sinān Pasha would attack.[111] But Sinān Pasha showed himself more capable of talking about war than actually fighting it. During the months of the campaign season, he achieved only the provisioning of Tiflis and a show-of-strength in the form of a military review for the Persian ambassadors, which accomplished very little. What was more serious, the Ottomans, in spite of the absence of a serious battle, again suffered a great number of casualties at the hands of Georgian and Persian irregulars in the Georgian mountains.

In spite of his do-nothing policy, Ḳōjā Sinān Pasha became Grand Vezir during this campaign and, after spending the winter in Erzurum, he returned to the Porte in the summer of 1581. Peçewī characterized his services as worth . . . "a half-akçe tip. . . ."[112]

In the capital preparations were already under way for a sumptuous feast in honor of the circumcision of the Ottoman heir apparent, the future Meḥemmed III, on 6 Jumāda I 990/29 May 1582.[113] During the year 1581, as both the Safavids and Ottomans had shown themselves inclined toward peace, no campaign took place. Only in Shirvan, by a major effort against 'O̱smān Pasha, did the Ḳïzïlbāş appear to take advantage of the lull on their western borders in order to improve their bargaining position at the peace table.

At the end of August 1582, a convoy of supplies under the command of Meḥemmed Pasha, a nephew of Lalā Muṣṭafā, and the eunuch Ḥasan Pasha, *Beylerbey* of Diyarbakir, with the assistance of Muṣṭafā Bey (formerly the Georgian prince Manuchar), left Erzurum for Tiflis. Upon the suggestion of Muṣṭafā, the Georgian, they did not take the mountain route through

Dmanisi but followed the Kura River. Along the river route, Meḥemmed Pasha, confronted with a combined Persian and Georgian force under Simon Luarssab on the plain of Gori, sought to avoid combat but, in his flight toward Tiflis, lost the all-important baggage to the enemy and many of his troops were drowned at the crossing.[114] After making up the shortage for the garrison at Tiflis through purchases and gifts from Alexander Levend, Meḥemmed Pasha on his return journey planned to kill Muṣṭafā, the Georgian, partly because he suspected him of informing his father-in-law, Simon Luarssab, of the Ottoman troop movements, and partly to detract attention from his own negligence and dereliction of duty. Muṣṭafā (Manuchar), however, suspected a trap and escaped with his retinue. He now reverted to Christianity and joined the forces of Simon. Much of the blame for this debacle and for the utterly inadequate peace proposals put forward by the Persian ambassador fell upon the Grand Vezir. Sinān Pasha was now replaced by Siyāvüş Pasha on December 5, 1582.[115] Thereafter, Ferhād Pasha was appointed serdār and he departed for the Persian front in the spring of 1583.[116] This year marked the fall of Erevan. At the same time, strong detachments relieved the garrison at Tiflis and carried fire and sword to Meskhia, the homeland of Manuchar.[117]

During the celebrations of the previous year, ʿOs̱mān Pasha had sent a letter to the Porte depicting the dangerous state of affairs in Shirvan and describing Safavid treachery. It seems that a Persian commander in Shirvan had pretended that peace had been concluded between the Ottomans and the Persians. He then slaughtered an Ottoman force in his locality when the latter had ceased its vigilance. This occurrence had hastened the downfall of Sinān Pasha and had led to the humiliation of the Safavid ambassador, Ismāʿīl Khan.[118] But fortunately for the holding operation at Derbent, a strong contingent of troops, led by Jaʿfer Pasha, *Beylerbey* of Kaffa, went to the relief of the Ottoman force in the autumn of 1582 by way of the northern route through Circassia and Kabarda.[119]

In the spring of 1584, Ferhād Pasha had apparently planned to attack Nakhichevan, but, under orders from the Sultan, he directed his army to Georgia where he proceeded to complete the work of his predecessors by building additional or strengthening the existing fortresses between Kars and Tiflis. This great effort had the desired effect of pacifying the central provinces of Georgia. Now, with corresponding successes against the Persian forces in Shirvan, the northern flank had become reasonably stabilized. The revolt of the Ottoman troops against Riżvān Pasha and Ferhād Pasha at the end of the campaign of 1584 gave evidence of the harshness of the task.[120]

Fortunately for the Ottomans, the Safavids had their own acute internal problems which made it difficult for them to check the Ottoman plundering of their western provinces. Amīr Khan (Turkmān), governor of Tabriz, had failed to come to the relief of Erevan the preceding year and consequently, for this and other acts of disobedience, was blinded. The Turkmān tribe revolted.[121] The Shah and his son, Hamza Mīrzā, certainly had little cause for optimism when it was learned on the eve of the campaign of 1585 that 'Os̱mān Pasha, the newly appointed Grand Vezir, would personally lead the Ottoman troops to Tabriz.

5 Ġāzī Girāy in the Service of 'Os̱mān Pasha; The Battle of the Torches

Ġāzī Girāy had played an important part in the extremely fluid campaign which took place in Shirvan. He had led one wing of the Tatar forces under 'Ādil Girāy, which had saved 'Os̱mān Pasha and his Shirvan army from defeat in 1578. Also, according to the account of Munejjimbaşī, he was present at the defeat of Maḥmūdābād (Mollā Ḥasan) with 'Ādil Girāy.[122] When the latter fell captive to the Safavids in the same battle, Ġāzī Girāy became the senior Tatar commander in Shirvan. At the time, the H̱ānzāde was twenty-four, physically mature and on the threshold of gaining a wealth of political and military experience under the tutelage of the brilliant commander, 'Os̱mān Pasha.

The defeat of the Tatars had decided the fate of the Ottoman and Shirvanian troops who were besieged in Shemakha. In the hasty retreat that ensued, the Tatar forces, perhaps two thousand, over which Ġāzī Girāy had maintained control, and probably a small number of Lezghians, had the important role of acting as rear guard for the eight to ten thousand Ottoman and Shirvanian troops with their equipment.

In 1579, apart from the major raid across the Kura and the garrisoning of Shemakha and Baku after the Tatar Khan had come to Derbent in the summer, 'Os̱mān Pasha, with the aid of Ġāzī Girāy, had spent his time consolidating his position in Dagestan. Even the garrison at Shemakha had to withdraw when the Safavid army, or a portion of it, re-entered Shirvan in the late autumn.

But Shemakha remained the only advance position of the Safavids in the year 1580. There is even some question whether it was any longer garrisoned by either side. Christopher Burrough, an English merchant who traded in Shirvan and Daġestan that summer, reported that "Shamaky was wholly spoyled."[123] In this year of the 'do-nothing' campaign of Sinān Pasha and of peace overtures and tribal conflict in Persia, the Shirvan front remained relatively quiet. The visit of the English merchants to the Ottoman expeditionary force between late May and early October doubtless provided a pleasant interlude for 'Os̱mān Pasha and Ġāzī Girāy. The merchants anchored their vessel at a town called Bildih in the latitude 40° 25′, about six leagues from Baku.[124]

Burrough described the retinue of the Bey in charge of the strongly fortified town of Baku as wearing "... shirts of mail, and some of them had gauntlets of silver, others of steele, and very faire."[125] After they had exchanged gifts with the Bey and had sent word of their purpose to 'O̱smān Pasha, they were instructed to proceed to Derbent in their vessel in order to deal directly with him. An adverse wind made it necessary for one of the merchants, M. Turnbull, to journey overland to Derbent, with an escort provided by the Bey, where a royal reception awaited him:

> *then came forth noble men, captaines, and gentlemen, to receive them into the castle and towne. As they entred the castle, there was a shot of twentie pieces of great ordinance, & the Basha sent M. Turnbull a very faire horse with furniture to mount on, esteemed to be worth an hundred markes, and so they were conveyed to his* ['*O̱smān Pasha's*] *presence: ....*[126]

'O̱smān Pasha granted them trading privileges, but he urged them to concentrate their activities at Derbent, "... knowing the state of his country to be troublesome. ..."[127] From the Pasha they purchased one thousand batmans of raw silk. On all of their transactions the Pasha levied a duty of 4 per cent. Shortly before the merchants departed for Astrakhan, Burrough happened to witness the arrival of an Ottoman wagon train bringing the pay of the soldiers:

> *After being on shoore he saw there the coming in of the Turkes treasure, being accompanied with 200 souldiers, and one hundred pioneers, besides captaines and Gentlemen: .... Treasure was the chiefe thing they needed, for not long before the souldiers were readie to breake into the Court against the Basha for their pay: there was a great mutinie amongst them because hee had long differred and not payed them their due. The treasure came in seven wagons, and with it were brought tenne pieces of brasse* [*i.e., cannon*].[128]

The report of Christopher Burrough provides an intimate view of the small Ottoman holding force in the Caucasus during a period of relative calm. Without any prompting, the Bey of Baku made reference to the "mayden Queene" (Queen Elizabeth) and verified the home of the merchants as "Enghilterra." In summarizing the manner in which 'O̱smān Pasha had dealt with the merchants, Christopher Burrough notes, "His dealing with our Merchants as it was not with equitie in all points according to his bargaine, so it was not extreme ill."[129]

In early autumn, around the time the English merchants departed for Astrakhan (October 5, 1580), 'O̱smān Pasha learned from his spies that a large Safavid force under the leadership of the Vezir, Selmān Khan, had begun to concentrate on the Mugan Steppe. This locality was a most appropriate assembly area from which to launch an attack on the Ottoman-held strong points of Baku and Derbent.[130] Considering the formidable nature of the fortresses at Baku and Derbent and the severity of the winters in Dagestan, there is every reason to believe that the Ḳïzïlbāş army was actually going into winter quarters at the time in preparation for an offensive early in the spring of 1581. ʿOs̱mān Pasha, in anticipation of this plan, wintered in Baku from where he could maintain better surveillance of the enemy situation.[131]

In late November or December ʿOs̱mān Pasha and Ġāzī Girāy, who enjoyed the full confidence and intimate council of the Ottoman commander,[132] conceived a plan which would delay and harass the Safavid preparations for the expected offensive. A mixed force of Tatar and Ottoman cavalry was to be sent against the Safavid *Kïşlāḳ*, or winter quarters, in a night raid. In order to take the enemy by complete surprise, this force of two or three thousand would have to attack the position from an unexpected quarter. Ġāzī Girāy effectively carried out this raid with the assistance of his cousins Murād Girāy, and Ṣafā Girāy, sons of the Khan.[133] The Safavid camp was thrown into great disorder and Selmān Khan only barely managed to escape capture by galloping away on a draft horse.[134] Little news of the hard-pressed force in Shirvan reached the Porte, but somehow ʿOs̱mān Pasha got word through to the Sultan after his singular feat of bravery. Ġāzī Girāy received a personal commendation (*Hukm-i Şerif*) from the Sultan, dated 24 Muharrem 989/28 February 1581, in which the ha̱nzāde was informed of a 50,000 aḳçe increase in his annual subsidy.[135]

The Safavids lost little time over this setback. In the spring of 1581, Ġāzī Girāy and Dāl Meḥemmed, a cavalry commander and author of the *Şejaʿatnāme*, were decisively defeated before Shemakha, and the two commanders only just managed to escape.[136]

ʿOs̱mān Pasha now left a garrison at Baku and prudently withdrew to Derbent. A Persian force, led by Pīrī Moḥammed Beg, a notable Ustājlū commander, skirted the Baku strong point and harassed his withdrawal along the Caspian shore to within range of the guns on the ramparts of Derbent. This same force then occupied the seaport of Shābirān.[137] Furthermore, Baku was now besieged but in spite of inadequate supplies and munitions the defenders held out. Pīrī Moḥammed died shortly after this failure and with his death the Ustājlū-led force withdrew beyond the Kura.[138]

Now Imām Ḳūlī Khan (Ḳājār), who had long been in the forefront of those amirs who bore the brunt of the Ottoman invasion, took charge of the operations in the Caucasus and suggested to the Shah that Paykar Khan, a member of his own tribe (Ḳājār), be appointed governor of Shirvan. The Shah complied and furnished the latter with fifteen thousand troops.[139]

ʿOs̱mān Pasha, learning through spies of the intention of Paykar Khan (Ḳājār) to advance on the Ottoman strong points, again selected Ġāzī Girāy to lead a diversionary action against the advancing Safavid forces. With two or three thousand men the Tatar prince held up the Persian advance for one day at a point somewhere between Shemakha and Shābirān.[140] According to the Ottoman version, at the end of the first day the two forces disengaged and after posting a night watch, Ġāzī Girāy took his repose. During the night Abū

Bekr Mīrzā, who had taken part in this action on the Ottoman side, suddenly dashed off through the night with his Lezghian followers, scattering the Ottoman force. Taking advantage of the confusion, the Safavids moved into the melee. Ġāzī Girāy, whose mount was said to have struck a tree, fell into the hands of Paykar Khan. Later, he was brought in chains before Hamza Mīrzā and, because he betrayed the pride befitting his station when he was submitted to questioning, Ġāzī Girāy was sent to the Castle of Alamūt, former stronghold of the Ismā'īlī (Assassin) sect, where he languished in prison for much of the next four years.[141]

In the Persian version of this noteworthy encounter, word came to Imām Ḳūlī Khan that Ġāzī Girāy and Ṣafā Girāy had again entered Shirvan. Imām Ḳūlī, aiming to give the Tatars a proper reception, sent reinforcements to Baykar (*sic*!) Khan. 'Os̱mān Pasha also sent an Ottoman commander with many troops to the support of the Tatars. Ġāzī Girāy distinguished himself by his bravery and attracted attention to himself as he galloped about making repeated attacks. During one such sally he fell into the midst of a group of Ḳājār Turcomans who blocked his every mode of escape. In this manner, Ġāzī Girāy received his "divinely ordained" imprisonment in Alamūt.[142] The two versions of this important setback for the Ottoman cause in the Caucasus appear to be minor variations of a similar event. Each version gives additional details about the life of Ġāzī Girāy.

The position of the Ottomans in the Caucasus now reached its most critical stage. Dāl Meḥemmed, in another attempt to disrupt and harass the Safavid advance on Baku and Derbent, garrisoned a fortress known as Ḳabāle Kal'esi, probably located at a mountain pass or other strategic point.[143] Paykar Khan who boasted, in letters to 'Os̱mān Pasha, that he could now seize Baku and Derbent, deceived Dāl Meḥemmed by informing him that peace between the two powers had been signed in Istanbul. When the Ottomans abandoned the isolated stronghold to return to Derbent, the superior Persian force fell upon them and slaughtered great numbers. Dāl Meḥemmed also became a prisoner of the Safavids.[144] When the news of this treachery reached the Sublime Porte, it hastened the dismissal of Sinān Pasha and peace negotiations were broken off. Moreover, the tone of imminent disaster in a letter of 'Os̱mān Pasha prompted the immediate equipping and embarkation of a sizable army to Derbent by way of Kaffa and Circassia in the autumn of 1582.[145] Meanwhile, 'Os̱mān Pasha had not been idle. While most of the Persian army had been attempting to stamp out the Shāmlū-Ustājlū rebellion in Khurāsān during the summer of 1582, the Ottoman troops had again garrisoned Shemakha withdrawing in the fall.[146]

The Ottoman troops hardly reached Derbent in time to provide themselves with adequate shelter from the severity of the winter season. Food grew very scarce indeed.[147] The arrival of this strong Ottoman force was not overlooked by the local rulers or the Safavids. The incursion of a new force presenting so much diversity of dress and skill alarmed the Şamhal, the Georgian princes, and other local Beys to such an extent that they addressed letters to the Safavid commander, Imām Ḳūlī, requesting help, saying: ". . . Let us, allied with each other, quickly get rid of them [the Ottomans], or else, if things continue like this for one or two years longer, they will eliminate us."[148] It is interesting to note, in this regard, that the Ottomans had already arranged to have ships built on the Caspian Sea. The expeditionary force led by Ja'fer Pasha also contained consignments of men and equipment to help man and equip a Caspian naval force.[149]

When Imām Ḳūlī launched his offensive against 'Os̱mān Pasha in the spring of 1583, he could boast of an army numbering fifty thousand.[150] Near Shābirān, in a preliminary skirmish between a number of Ottoman troops and the Persian advance guard, the Ottomans were easily routed. Already Abū Bekr Mīrzā, the descendent of the Shirvan Shahs, had gone over to the Persians, and now many of the Georgians, who had wavered between joining the Ottomans or the Persians, went into the ensuing battle in the ranks of the latter.[151] The Safavid leader taunted 'Os̱mān Pasha for remaining in his fortress (Derbent) and accused him of sole responsibility for the blood bath of Shirvan. 'Os̱mān Pasha replied, "Let them not trouble themselves, I am coming."[152]

The Ottoman army left Derbent on 6 Rabī II 991/30 April 1583. Between the Samur River and Shābirān the two armies clashed and fought a four-day engagement (14–18 Rabī'II 991/7–11 May 1583) which became known as the "Meş'ale Ṣāvāşī" (The Battle of the Torches) because the armies were so intent on destroying each other that they fought at night, sword in one hand, torch in the other. The Ottomans routed the Persians but, as so often was the case in this war, the casualties were heavy on both sides. After the battle, various pockets of resistance were eliminated and new fortifications were built at Shemakha. The Georgian princes, meanwhile, hastened to show their loyalty to the Ottomans. In fact, this campaign proved to be the last major attempt to oust the Ottomans from Shirvan until the reign of Shah 'Abbās. As an example to the Safavids, the heads of their dead, some seventy-five hundred, were piled up into a pyramid.[153]

After spending Ramażān in Derbent, 'Os̱mān Pasha appointed Ja'fer Pasha acting governor of Shirvan and he departed for the Crimea by the northern route on 4 Şevāl 991/21 October 1583. While crossing the Sunzhu river, only a few stations from Dagestan, the Ottoman force of about four thousand veterans of the Shirvan campaign ran afoul of a Muscovite Cossack force stationed on the Terek. After a brisk encounter, which entailed pursuing the Cossacks through the dense forests of that region, the Ottomans besieged them in their *tābūr*.[154] The Ottomans quickly reduced the fort to ashes and, according to Munejjimbāşī, few escaped. The Ottomans then pushed on across the steppe to which the Cossacks had previously set fire, passed an

Ottoman relief force for Shirvan on the Kuban steppe, and reached Kaffa late in December 1583 or early in January 1584. The weather was so cold that the ice on the straits between the Taman peninsula and Kerch was frozen to a depth which supported the crossing of the Ottoman troops.[155]

By 1584 the Ottomans had largely stabilized their hold over Dagestan, Shirvan, and Georgia and had made important preparations for an all-out attack on Azerbaijan by occupying Erevan and the mountainous portions of Kurdistan. So far no commander on the eastern front had distinguished himself as much as had ʿOs̱mān Pasha in Shirvan and Dagestan. Ġāzī Girāy, until his capture by the Safavids, had served the great Ottoman commander with honor; as a reward, this young Tatar ẖānzāde, who had come to Shirvan at the age of twenty-four, gained a wealth of battle experience in a lean environment against great military odds. This experience would later serve him well as Khan of the Crimean Tatars.

NOTES

1. These generals had been bitter rivals since the time of the revolt in Yemen (1569–1570). See Hammer, *Histoire de l'Empire Ottoman*, VI, p. 368 ff.
2. Peçewī, *Tārīh*, II, p. 36 ff.
3. He was living in exile in Dagestan at this time.
4. ʿAlī, *Nuṣratnāme*, f. 19b.
5. ʿAlī, f. 20b. After the murder of Prince Haydar, the Georgian influence at court had of course been eclipsed. Nevertheless, the retinues of the dignitaries and the bodyguards of the Shahs consisted almost exclusively of Circassians, Armenians, and Georgians. Cf. M. Vincenzo degli Alessandri, "Relazione di Persia (1574)," Alberi, *Relazioni degli Ambasciatori*, III/II, p. 116 ff.
6. ʿAlī, ff. 15a–18a.
7. According to the report by Balbi, the Venetian Consul, at Aleppo, ". . . l'on mena en Alep seulement environ huict mille charges de froment, & par la voye de la mer Majeur on porta plusieurs desdites provisions, au port de Tresibonde (*sic*) . . . ." "Relatione de Perse," in the compilation *Le Trésor politique*, p. 187. This report and a similar one by ʿAlī (f. 40a) indicate that 1578 was a year of famine and drought.
8. ʿAlī, f. 37b.
9. ʿAlī, f. 42a, b.
10. Although the Turkish sources call him the governor of Erevan, in fact, Ṭoḳmaḳ Khan was the governor of the border province of Çohūr-i Sa'ad, the seat of which was Erevan. See Roemer, *Der Niedergang Irans*, p. 32, and V. Minorsky, ed., *Tadhkirat al-Mulūk*, pp. 165 f.
11. Peçewī II, pp. 38–39.
12. Cf. "Relatione de Perse," *Le Trésor Politique*, p. 188. Also, see Minadoi, *Historia della Guerra fra Turchi, et Persiani*, pp. 80 ff.
13. Peçewī, II, p. 40.
14. Minadoi, p. 81. The Ottomans had already started to have more than just technical difficulties on these campaigns. More and more of the *Sipahīyān* (feudal cavalry) were finding the distances from their land holdings to the frontiers quite excessive. It is not surprising that they no longer relished these campaigns. As compensation for their bravery and the costs of equipping themselves and their men-at-arms (*Jebelī*), they stood little chance of increasing their personal wealth or prestige owing to the paucity of booty and the nature of the warfare in the mountains of

Georgia or the swamps of Hungary. Concerning the loss of men and material, see the "Relazione" of Marco Venier, Alberi, III/II, pp. 297 ff.

15. Roemer, pp. 32–33.

16. 'Alī, f. 65a, b.

17. The main body of the Ottoman army followed the right bank of the Kura river from Ardahan to Akhaltsikhe and then to Tiflis, where the river was crossed (Peçewī, II, p. 43). En route, apart from the Battle of Childir in which much of the army participated, smaller detachments seized control of strong points such as Hertīz (Khertvisi) and Dāẖil Kelek (Akhalkalaki). (*Ibid*, p. 42.)

18. Peçewī, II, p. 42.

19. *Ibid.*, Minadoi, pp. 83–85.

20. For details regarding this prince, see Chapter III.

21. Peçewī, II, p. 43; Minadoi, pp. 85–87.

22. Allen, "Notes on Don Juan of Persia's Account of Georgia," *B.S.O.S.*, VI (1930–32), pp. 179–186, indicates that the river Alazan was known as the "Kanak" by Muslims.

23. Besides Ṭoḳmaḳ, there were Murād Khan, governor of Mugan, Şeref Khan, governor of Nakhichevan; Imām Kūlī Khan, governor of Genje; and Amīr Khan, governor of Tabriz, according to Peçewī, II, pp. 46–47.

24. Peçewī, II, pp. 46–47. Minadoi's account (pp. 86–92), preferred by Hammer (*Histoire*, VII, pp. 86–87), states that the Ottoman army was so short of rations when it reached the Alazan, that a body of 10,000 men was detached and sent to the peninsula which was known to have an abundance of grain still unharvested. The Persian force, led by the Khans Ṭoḳmaḳ, Imām Kūlī, and Amīr, fell upon the foragers and nearly exterminated them but were unable to beat a retreat before they were trapped on the peninsula, with their backs to the rivers, by Muṣṭafā Pasha's alerted main body. For a variation of the Minadoi account, cf. Roemer, p. 34.

25. Peçewī, II, pp. 46–47. The people of Shirvan, many of whom were Sunnite Muslims, were not, in general, loyal to the Safavids. The withdrawal of these forces may be best explained on this basis. Cf. also, Minorsky, "Shekki," *E.I.*[1], IV, pp. 346–348.

26. Allen, "Don Juan of Persia" *B.S.O.S.*, VI, pp. 179–80, considers that the city of Aresh must have been near the modern city of Jevat, situated on the Shirvan side of the junction of the Kura and Araxes rivers. The writer concurs in this conclusion, particularly as Jevat lies on a direct north-south route to Shamakha, is opposite the regions of Karabagh (Karabakh) and Mugan, and is a well-watered region much more capable of sustaining agriculture than the predominantly arid neighboring regions. Cf. Hellert, *Atlas de l'Empire Ottoman*, Pl. XX and XXI; Fillipov, *Geograficheskiy Atlas*, particularly pp. 104, 105. Most conclusive evidence is provided in the Persian history *Tārīh-e 'Alam Araye 'Abbāsī* by Iskandar Beg Turkmān (I, p. 237) who actually refers to the "Jevād Bridge." See also Minorsky, *Tadhkirat al-Mulūk*, p. 167.

27. Peçewī (II, p. 48) reports this incident. He states that the people rebelled against the Persian governor, Harag Ḫalīfe, killing him and a garrison of three hundred men. Abū Bakr Mīrzā entered Shirvan from Dagestan with three thousand followers. Roemer, p. 35.

28. Özdemīroġlū 'O̲smān Pasha, of Circassian origin, had distinguished himself in the reconquest of the Yemen before Sinān Pasha had removed him from his command. Muṣṭafā Pasha, who had helped bring 'O̲smān Pasha back into favor with the ruling circles, asked him to come on this campaign. In the battles of Childir and Alazan, this exceptional leader again distinguished himself. As governor of Shirvan, he proved his skill as a military leader time after time against the superior numbers of the Safavids. On the basis of this service and his suppression of the revolt of the Crimean Khan, Meḥemmed Girāy, he was appointed Grand Vezir. Cf. Hammer, *Histoire*, VI and VII, *passim*.

29. According to the version of 'Abd ur-Raḥmān Şeref, based on the *Şeja'atname* of Aṣafī ("'O̲smān Pasha" *T.O.E.M.*, IV/22, p. 1358), Lalā Muṣṭafā initially wanted to remain in Shirvan himself. Realizing that this would not be advisable, he appointed the Beylerbey of Aleppo, Meḥemmed Pasha, one of his relatives, to the governorship of Shirvan. The latter, however,

excused himself in a few days. Therefore, the post was offered to various members of the command. Even 'O̲smān Pasha, at first, refused the position.

30. Hammer, Histoire, VII, p. 89; Minadoi, pp. 97–99.

31. Peçewī, II, p. 49. For details on the successive stages of this process, see Inalcïk, "Ottoman Methods of Conquest," *Studia Islamica* II (1954), pp. 103–129.

32. Hammer, *Geschichte des Osmanischen Reiches*, IV, p. 71. For further comment on the resources of the Caucasus, see Chapter I of this book.

33. Ḥasanbeyzāde (*Tārīḫ-i Al-i 'O̲smān* (Istanbul, Nūr-u 'Osmaniyye Ms. No. 3105/06) f. 470a) estimated 'O̲smān Pasha's forces at 8,000 men. For details, see Munejjimbāşī, *Sahā'if al Aḫbār*, III, p. 541.

34. 'Alī, ff. 15a–18a.

35. Munejjimbāşī, *loc. cit.*; Peçewī, II, p. 50. The anonymous "Successi della Guerra" (1581) (in Alberi, III/II, p. 455), concurs with Peçewī insofar as it speaks of the Şamḫal's meeting Muṣṭafā Pasha on the Alazan, but Muṣṭafā Pasha is here given credit for striking a bargain with the Şamḫal: the latter was to provide 4,000–5,000 troops to help 'O̲smān Pasha and also was to give his daughter in marriage to 'O̲smān Pasha in exchange for the Sanjāḳ of Shabiran and further rewards from the Sultan. The marriage also served as a guarantee of the Şamḫal's loyalty.

36. As recorded in Chapter III, Simon, after his imprisonment by Shah Ṭahmāsp, had become a Shi'ite Muslim. He was released from prison during the reign of Ismā'īl II (1576–1577) and given men and arms to fight the Turks in 1578. Roemer, p. 36. Cf. "An anonymous report," Alberi, III/II, p. 456, and Allen, *History of the Georgian People*, pp. 55 f.

37. Peçewī, II, p. 51.

38. According to Minadoi (pp. 103–105), Manuchar, the younger, had accompanied Muṣṭafā Pasha on the campaign. In Constantinople he became a convert to Islam. As a reward he was made governor of his father's kingdom and became responsible also for his brother Alexander who refused to change his faith.

39. Hammer, *Histoire*, VII, pp. 92–93.

41. Lamberti, *Relatione della Cholchide*, pp. 230 ff.

42. According to Seyyid Luḳmān (*Mujmil at-Tūmār*, f. 185b) in Rabi 'I, 987/April—May 1579, the Ḳāpūdān Pasha with forty galleys sailed to the Black Sea and, from the Phasis River, undertook an expedition against the province of Imereti (Bāş Açūḳ), a principality of Georgia. (". . . Ḳāpūdān Pāşā ḳirḳ pare kadirge ile Ḳara Denïze vārūb Fāse ṣūyundan Gurjistān ḫiṣṣatïndan açūḳ bāş vilāyetine 'azm-i jihād eyledi . . .")

43. A. A. Novosel'skiy, *Bor'ba Moskovskogo Gosudarstva*, p. 31, citing *Krymskie Knigi*, No. 15, f. 30.

44. Novosel'skiy, p. 31. See also the correspondence of the Grand Vezir with Stephan Báthory, Hurmuzaki, *Documente privitóre*, III, pp. 14, 17, and 35, and Karamsin, Histoire de l'Empire de Russie, IX, pp. 351–354.

45. Novosel'skiy, p. 31; according to S. Juye, the French envoy at the Porte, ". . . les seigneurs du pays [Poland-Lithuania] se sont accordes avec le Tartari de luy payer sa pension ordinaire . . ." Charrière, *Négociations de la France dans le Levant*, III, p. 752.

Belokurov states that Kan Bulat and his family became Christians, and that the fortress was rebuilt and Luk'yan Novosil'tsev received the appointment as *voivode* with a strong contingent of troops (*Snosheniya Rossii s Kavkazom*, pp. lxxix, lxxxvii).

47. Hot well, or hot spring; probably near the locality today designated *Goryacheistochnenskaya.*

48. Kumykov and Kusheva, eds., *Kabardino-Russkie Otnosheniya*, I, pp. 46–48. On the basis of this account it is possible to conclude that the Crimean Tatars lost some 5,000 men in their clashes with the Persians.

49. The timing here depends upon the following facts: The Tatars reached Shemakha on November 11. In 1583 an Ottoman relief force, traveling from Kaffa to Derbent, a distance of about 800 miles, reached their destination in about 80 days. (Peçewī, II, p. 61.) On the other hand, a Tatar force made a similar journey during the year 1579 in 30 days (Şeref, *T.O.E.M.*, IV, p. 1422, and

Hammer, *Histoire*, VII, p. 98). This gives us the rough measure that the Ottomans, other conditions being equal, traveled about ten miles per day (probably drawing artillery and other heavy goods); the Tatars, thirty miles per day. As the distance between the Terek River and Shemakha is approximately 300 miles, the Tatars must have taken 10 to 12 days to reach their destination. Cf. J. Bartholomew, *The Times Atlas of the World*, II (1959), Pl. 44.

50. Minadoi (pp. 106–107) writes that Muṣṭafā Pasha ordered 'O̱smān Pasha to send further dispatches to the Crimean Tatars.

51. Roemer, p. 35.

52. 'Alī, ff. 134a and 134b; according to Munejjimbāşī (III, p. 542), 25,000.

53. 'Alī (f. 135a) speaks of Ḳayṭās as "devoid of caution and exceedingly vainglorious"; Cf. Peçewī, II, p. 53, and Munejjimbāşī, III, pp. 542–543.

54. Şeref, *T.O.E.M.*, IV pp. 1364–1365.

55. Peçewī, II, pp. 52–53, gives the figure of the Tatar forces as 40,000–50,000. In the light of succeeding events, this appears to be a gross exaggeration. Perhaps a figure of 15,000–20,000 would be more accurate. As Iskandar Beg (I, p. 236) described the demise of Aras Khan, ". . . From one side, the Ottoman soldiers, from another side, the Tatars, and from still another side, the Lezgīs, the Ḳarābūrks and the Shirvan rebels surrounded the Kïzïlbāş."

56. Şeref, *T.O.E.M.*, IV, p. 1365; 'Alī, f. 135b.

57. *Ibid.*, p. 1366.

58. *Ibid.*, Peçewī's description of this event (II, p. 54) is obviously taken from 'Alī, 163b and 164a.

59. Peçewī (II, p. 54) reports that the Tatars acquired 12,000 camels loaded with booty; Munejjimbāşī gives the more believable figure of 2,000 (III, p. 543).

60. Peçewī (II, pp. 54–55) names this figure; 'Alī (f. 164a) gives 50,000; Şeref (*T.O.E.M.*, IV, pp. 1366–1367) estimates 30,000.

61. In Qazvin the recent change of rulers had left the Safavid state devoid of firm leadership. A portion of the Turkoman tribes had been sent to quell the uprising of the Kurds. The forces on the northwestern frontier had been in contact with the Ottoman army. When the Ottomans had succeeded in penetrating into Shirvan, Selmān Khan was sent to bolster the troops already committed against the Ottomans with an army consisting of contingents from Iraq, Fars, and Kerman. Hamza Mīrzā, the young Crown Prince, and his mother, the Begum H̱ayru'n-Nesā', who was the real power in Persia after the accession of Shah H̱udābanda until her death in 1579, accompanied the army as far as Ḳara Aġāç, which the army reached about the 9th or 10th of November, 1578. Roemer, pp. 15, 36–38. See also, Munejjimbāşī, III, p. 543, where he refers to the Begum as ". . . the wife [of the Shah] who was exercising almost absolute dominion over his state . . . ." (. . . Devletine tesalluṭ uzere olan zevjesi . . . .)

62. Peçewī, II, pp. 54–55; 'Alī, f. 164a.

63. Şeref, *T.O.E.M.*, IV, pp. 1366–1367; Roemer, pp. 40–42.

64. The exact location of this battle is difficult to determine. Şeref (*T.O.E.M.* IV p. 1368) places it on the shore of the "Menlā Ḥasan" river. 'Alī (f. 164b) locates it near "Mahmūdābād." According to Roemer (*loc. cit.*), the district was called "Mollā Ḥasan" and the stream was the Aḳṣū (cf. the town of Aḳṣū south of Shemakha).

65. 'Alī, f. 164b. Munejjimbāşī, III, p. 543), provides additional information about this battle which helps account for the setback of the Tatars. After they had defeated the remnant of Aras Khan's army near Sal'yany and had seized the booty, ". . . 'Ādil Girāy and Ġāzī Girāy, together with fifteen thousand Tatars, remained with 'O̱smān Pasha; all of the others, including the Han vekili [vezir], Ḥajjī Muṣṭafā Beg and the H̱ānzāde, Mubarek Girāy, departed for their home province." Munejjimbāşī gives the figure 40,000 for the original number of Tatars thus only a fraction had remained to fight at Mahmūdābād (or Mollā Ḥasan).

66. Iskandar Beg, I, pp. 236–237.

67. *Ibid.* See also n. 65 above. The figures of Iskandar Beg appear to be more nearly accurate than those of Munejjimbāşī.

68. Peçewī, II, p. 59.
69. Cf. Minadoi, pp. 121–123; Iskandar Beg, I, pp. 237–239 and II, pp. 668–669. J. Malcolm, *The History of Persia*, I, p. 518, following the Persian history, *Zubdat at-Tevārīḫ*, states that "the leader ['Ādil Girāy] of the latter [the Tatars], who had attacked Gilan, was defeated, made prisoner, and afterwards murdered." Peçewī, II, p. 55, gives the impression that 'Ādil Girāy was not captured at all during the encounter at Mollā Ḥasan, but rather in a later skirmish after Hamza Mīrzā and Selmān Khan had regrouped in Karabaġ with possible intentions against Derbent. In this regard, cf. Kazimirski, "Précis de l'histoire des Khans de Crimée," *Journal Asiatique*, Serie 2/XII (1833), pp. 375–376. Peçewī gives details of the defilement of the Shah's harem and the ignominious murders of the Begum and 'Ādil Girāy by the *Kūrcū* or Imperial guard (II, pp. 59–61).
70. During the three-day intensive siege of Shemakha the odds in favor of the Persians must have been about 4 or 5 to 1. This greatly demoralized the Ottoman troops and the auxiliaries attached to them from Lesghia and Dagestan. All were considerably fatigued by the previous battles and the persistent shortage of rations. Encouraged by the Şamḫal of Tarku, several troops began showing signs of disaffection. 'Os̱mān Pasha immediately rebuked or punished the known dissenters and put the Şamḫal under arrest. Şeref, *T.O.E.M.*, IV, p. 1368.
71. Peçewī, II, pp. 54–55.
72. 'Alī, f. 165a.
73. Peçewī, II, pp. 54–55; I. H. Ertaylan, *Gazi Geray Han* (Istanbul, 1958), p. 14.
74. Selānīkī, *Tārīḫ-i Selānīkī*, p. 156.
75. *Ibid*; Kazimirski, "Précis," *J.A.*, Ser. 2/XII, p. 375, states that the Tatars were sent ahead.
76. Peçewī, II, p. 55.
77. 'Os̱mān Pasha now sent a long dispatch to the Sultan describing the entire action. This time, however, he sent his messenger to Istanbul across the Nogay Steppe north of the Caucasus range to Temruk and Kaffa instead of to his immediate superior in Erzurum. Peçewī (*ibid.*) considered this move a strong indication that 'Os̱mān Pasha had become estranged from Muṣṭafā Pasha owing to his lack of assistance during the recent events.
78. Minadoi, pp. 74–78.
79. Braudel, *La Mediteranée*, pp. 1011–1012.
80. Rights implicitly or explicitly granted in the Peace of Amasya of 1555 as well as the vague rights over the orthodox Muslim community assumed by the Ottoman Sultan in his role as Ḫādim al Ḥaremayn (Servitor of the Sacred Cities, i.e., Mecca and Medina). Cf. this writer's article, "Ottoman Imperial Policy and the Economy of the Black Sea Region" *J.A.O.S.*, 86/1 (April-June 1966), pp. 86–113.
81. Among the dignitaries in Hamza Mīrzā's retinue were the following: Mīrzā Selmān, the Vezir; the Head of the *Ḳūrçū*; Şahruḫ Khan, the Muhurdār; Moḥammed Khan (Turkmān); Pira Moḥammed Khan (*Ustājlū*); Sultan Ḥuseyn Khan, grandson of Durmīş Khan (Şāmlū); Veli Ḫalife (Şāmlū); Musi'Khan, Şeref ed-Dīn Oğlū (Tekkelū); Imām Ḳūlī Khan (Ḳājār) and Amīr Hamzah Khan, son of 'Abdullah Khan (Ustājlū). Cf. Iskandar Beg, I, p. 237. Here it is interesting to note the variety of tribal representation (in parentheses).
82. Şeref, IV, pp. 1418–1419. Mahariḳe is a town in Southern Dagestan.
83. Şeref, *T.O.E.M.*, IV, p. 1419. The location of this skirmish is unknown to the writer. Burhān Mīrzā is said to have had his center of operations at Ḫāḫamir (Kuba?). See Roemer, p. 78.
84. Şeref, *T.O.E.M.*, IV, p. 1420.
85. Minadoi, pp. 129–130.
86. Muṣṭafā Pasha left Erzurum on 18 Jumāda I, 987, and arrived in Kars on the 2nd Jumada II, (July 13–July 27, 1579), Şeref, *T.O.E.M.*, IV, p. 1420. The details of these events and the *Fetvas* applicable to the treatment of prisoners of war appear in Peçewi, II, pp. 56–58. See also Braudel, p. 1012.
87. Şeref, *T.O.E.M.*, IV, pp. 1420–1422; Peçewī, II, pp. 57–58; Munejjimbāşī, III, p. 547.

88. Hammer, *Geschichte des osmanischen Reiches,* IV, pp. 88–89, citing a diploma of *Die Briefsammlung der von Diez'schen Handschriften,* Nr. XLV, Bl. 60, of the Berlin State Library.
89. Ferīdūn, II, pp. 122–123. J. Rypka, *Festschrift Georg Jacob,* pp. 251–252, states that this dating of the letter comes into question because the capture of 'Ādil is not mentioned. According to Kütükoğlu, citing *Mühimme,* XXXVIII, 242, the Khan had good relations with the Safavids and had promised the release of 'Ādil Giray, news of his death reached the Tatars only after they arrived in Derbent ("Murad III," *I.A.*, VIII, p. 618).
90. For details see Smirnov, *Krymskoe Khanstvo,* pp. 439–440; Halim Giray, *Gülbün-ü Hānān,* p. 55; Inalcïk, "Giray," *I.A.*, IV, p. 786. The Khan also received general subsidies of money. Cf. Charrière, *Négociations de la France dans le Levant* II, pp. 789–793; Alberi, Ser. III/II, p. 462.
91. Peçewi, II, p. 61; according to at least one source (Kazimirski, "Précis," pp. 377–78), the Khan first sent his son Murad with a small force, but this did not satisfy the Sublime Porte. He then presumably followed the supply train after he had made preparations. Smirnov (*loc. cit.*), mentioning this campaign, gives us the information that the Khan was so fat he had to make the long journey in a wagon. Iskandar Beg (I, p. 253), emphasizes the revenge aspect of the Khan's campaign in Shirvan and Karabaġ (Karabakh).
92. Cf. Hammer's time table (*Histoire,* VII, p. 98) with that of Şeref, *T.O.E.M.*, IV, p. 1422. Apparently the time table of Şeref, who used Peçewī for supplementary material in his treatment of Özdemiroğlu 'Os̱mān Pasha's life, confused the 74 days' journey of the supply train with the much more rapid transit of the Tatar main body. Cf. Peçewī, II, p. 61.
93. Şeref (*T.O.E.M.*, IV, pp. 1422–23) states that 'Os̱mān Pasha instigated this move while the Anonymous Chronicle of Kazimirski ("Précis", pp. 377–78), stated that the Khan sent his son to conquer Baku; Munejjimbāsī (II, p. 547) mentions that a "contingent of Tatars" was sent to Baku.
94. Şeref, *loc. cit.*
95. Şeref, *T.O.E.M.* IV, p. 1424; Peçewī, II, pp. 61–62; there is an unconfirmed report that Alexander of Kakheti was also disciplined for refusing to send supplies to 'Os̱mān Pasha (Alberi, Ser. III/II, pp. 464–465.) Cf. Kazimirski, "Précis", pp. 377–378.
96. Şeref, *loc. cit.*
97. *Ibid.*, pp. 1425–1426.
98. *Ibid.*, pp. 1426 ff.
99. Hammer, *Histoire,* VII, p. 99.
100. Peçewī, II, p. 62.
101. It is interesting to note that, while Ṣoḳōllū and his Serdār were Bosniaks, the new Grand Vezir, Aḥmed Pasha, an Albanian, selected Kōjā Sinān Pasha, another Albanian, as Serdār (Peçewi, II, pp. 62–63). A small body of men who had managed to escape the defeat of Ḳayṭās Beg at Aresh had succeeded in reaching Erzurum and in spreading the word about the insufficient measures taken by Muṣṭafā Pasha to strengthen the Shirvan garrison. These and other reports helped bring about the demise of Muṣṭafā Pasha. See Selānīkī, *Tārīḫ,* p. 157.
102. This title was given to the Pasha who was left in charge of affairs at the capital during the absence of the Grand Vezir.
103. "Perche consiste tutta la forza, la milizia, e la ricchezza di esso nelli sultani, cioe principi, ognuno de' quali e padrone di qualche provincia, e la regge e governa a modo suo . . ." Alberi, Ser. III/II, pp. 391–392.
104. Roemer, p. 38. Ḳarā Aġaç was the traditional winter quarters of the Persian army.
105. For further details of this episode, see Roemer, pp. 44–50.
106. Roemer, pp. 51–58. The Ḳïzïlbāş saw in the Begum, who was a Tājik (Persian), a definite threat to all Ḳïzïlbāş power. Selmān Khan also met his end partly for the same reason.
107. Roemer, pp. 58–59. Uluġ Beg (Le Strange, *Don Juan of Persia,* p. 153) considered the charge a fabrication. Peçewī (II, p. 59) blames the begum and the sultana for throwing themselves at the H̱ānzāde. He also discloses that all three were killed.

108. Peçewī, II, p. 78.
109. *Ibid.*, pp. 84–86; "Relatione de Perse", *Trésor Politique*, pp. 197–198, and R. M. Savory, "The Significance of the Political Murder of Mīrzā Salmân", *Islamic Studies*, III/2 (June, 1964), pp. 181–191.
110. Peçewī, II, p. 64.
111. Hammer, *Histoire*, VII, pp. 101–103. Two different ambassadors sent by the Shah to Sinān Pasha during the year 1580 showed themselves willing to make minor concessions at the expense of Georgian territory.
112. As the Serdār Muṣṭafā Pasha is known to have gone to Tiflis by way of Tomānij (Dmanisi), there is every reason to believe that some relief trains to Tiflis took this much shorter but more hazardous route over the Malyy Kavkaz range from Childir. The Safavids are known to have brought their troops as close as the Arpa river in that year. See Peçewī, II, pp. 64–70. According to the "Relatione de Perse" (*Trésor Politique*, p. 193), the forces of the Shah waited in Ḳarā Aġaç for an Ottoman attack but Ṭoḳmāḳ Khan and Imān Ḳūlī were detached to harass the Ottoman lines.
113. Munejjimbāşī, III, p. 549.
114. Simon Luarssab, who in the previous year had proposed to Sinān Pasha that he be given the province of Tiflis as a Sanjāk in return for a generous tax, apparently now sought to avenge his rebuff. Hammer, *Histoire*, VII, pp. 104–107.
115. Hammer, *Histoire*, VII, pp. 104–107; see also, "Relatione de Perse," *Trésor Politique*, pp. 195–197. Sinān Pasha had actually boasted that he had "made peace" with Persia, according to Peçewī (II, p. 86). Sinān Pasha was banished and many of his followers were consigned to the galleys (Peçewī II, p. 75). Paolo Contarini, in his report to the Senate, described the crisis in the Ottoman army brought about by the slaughter of the cavalry on the eastern front (Alberi, Ser. IV/III, p. 230). According to a French report, the Shah in 1582 was willing to cede the province of Shirvan to the Sultan. Cf. Charrière, IV, p. 128.
116. Peçewī, II, pp. 75. The same author (p. 86) states that Siyāvuş Pasha, fearing he would be sent to the eastern front as serdār, quickly promoted Ferhād Pasha, *Beylerbey* of Rum, to the rank of vezir in order that he would qualify for the difficult eastern assignment. Later, Ferhād Pasha, as the senior commander on the eastern front, appointed Jigālazāde Sinān Pasha as governor of Erevan. Peçewī ironically points out how this was a sign of the times. Jigālazāde, a product of the palace school, was high in the favor of Sulaymān the Magnificent. Ferhād Pasha, on the contrary, had formerly been a member of the kitchen staff of Sultan Selīm II (*ibid.*, p. 87). See also Parry, "Čighalazade Yusuf Sinān Pasha," *E.I.*[2], II, pp. 33–34.
117. "Relatione de Perse," *Trésor Politique*, pp. 199–201; Hammer, *Histoire*, VII, pp. 109–110, Peçewī, II, pp. 86–87. The defection of Manuchar was not confirmed until he had murdered the *ḉāvuş* and the *kāpūjī* whom Ferhād Pasha had sent to him.
118. Peçewī, II, p. 75; Munejjimbāşī, III, p. 549.
119. *Ibid.*
120. The troops, both Janissaries and Sipāhīs, objected to becoming "masons and dabbers." On the return march to Erzurum the tent ropes of the Serdār were cut, his baggage carried off, and his harem assaulted and dispersed (Peçewī, II, p. 88; Minadoi, pp. 250–255; Hammer, *Histoire*, VII, pp. 110–111). According to Leunclavius (*Neue Chronika türkischer Nation*, pp. 127–128), there developed a great outcry in Istanbul against Ferhād Pasha when it was rumored that he had sold the provisions of the Army for his own profit.
121. Minadoi, pp. 259–261.
122. See note 65.
123. See Christopher Burrough, "Advertisements and Reports of the 6(th) voyage into the parts of Persia and Media, for the company of English Merchants for the discoverie of new trades, in the yeeres 1579, 1580 and 1581 . . . ," Hakluyt, ed., *The Principal Navigations, Voyages, Traffiques and Discoveries of the English Nation*, III, p. 224.

124. They therefore landed on the Apsheron Peninsula east of the present city of Mashtagi.
125. Burrough, *Principal Navigations*, III, p. 225.
126. *Ibid.*, pp. 228–229.
127. *Ibid.*
128. *Ibid.*, III, p. 234. To my knowledge there is no report of this supply train in Ottoman or Russian sources; therefore, it is quite difficult to determine exactly by which route it came. Given the difficulties of passing through the Georgian irregulars and the rugged terrain, it seems most likely that such a small force could expect to reach its destination only by the northern route through Circassia.
129. *Ibid.*, pp. 226 and 234.
130. Şeref, *T.O.E.M.* IV, p. 1426.
131. *Ibid.*
132. Ertaylan, *Gâzi Geray Han*, p. 15.
133. Şeref, *T.O.E.M.* IV, pp. 1427–1429. Smirnov (*Krymskoe Khanstvo*, p. 441) calls Ṣafā Girāy the son of Meḥemmed Giray.
134. Şeref, *loc. cit.* This sudden attack caused sufficient stir in the *Ḳīzīlbāş* camp to warrant mention in the Safavid histories. See Iskandar Beg, I, p. 262.
135. For a copy of the *Ḥukm-u Şerif* (citation of honor) to Ġāzī Girāy, dated 24 Muḥarrem 989/28 February 1581, see Şeref, *loc cit.*
136. Şeref, *T.O.E.M.* IV, p. 1430.
137. This town, apparently no longer in existence, was probably the one designated by William of Rubruck as Samaron, located at about 41° of latitude. See W. R. Shepherd, *Historical Atlas*, p. 102. Cf. the description of "Shavaran," described as 4 days' journey from Shemakha, in the account of the Muscovy Company trading expedition of the years 1568 to 1574 in Hakluyt, *Principal Navigations*, III, pp. 151, 154. It is also close in spelling to Apshiron, the peninsula on which Baku is located.
138. Şeref, *T.O.E.M.*, IV, p. 1430.
139. *Ibid.*
140. See above note 137; also Iskander Beg, I, p. 270.
141. Şeref, *T.O.E.M.*, pp.1431–1432; Iskander Beg, I, p. 270.
142. *Ibid.*, pp. 270–271.
143. The exact location of this fortress is not known. Most likely, however, it is situated somewhere between Shemakha and Derbent.
144. Şeref, *T.O.E.M.*, IV, pp. 1432–1433.
145. Peçewī, II, pp. 75–79. The forces, under the leadership of Ja'fer Pasha, beylerbey of Kaffa, consisted of 3,000 Janissaries, the *Silāḥdār* units, the left and right wings of the Rūmīlī (Rumeli) forces, and the *erbāb-i tīmār* and the *zu'umā'* of the Sanjāḳs of Kustindīl, Silistre, and Nikboli. The combined force left Kaffa on Şa'ban 7/August 27 and reached Derbent 80 days later, on Şewal 27 990/November 24 1582. The route of march took the Ottomans across the straits of Kerch to Temruk, across the Kuban River on Circassian rafts, across the wasteland known as Hayhat to Beştepe (Pyatigorsk), and on to Derbent through the Kabarda. Munejjimbāşī (III, p. 550) mentions, in particular, the friendly reception of the Ottomans in the Kabarda (Kabartāy). This was doubtless a conciliatory move in view of the size of the relief force.
146. Iskander Beg, I, p. 271.
147. Peçewī, II, pp. 75–79.
148. ". . . Hemān ittifaḳ iyle būnlarī ōrtadan ġōtūrelim y̱oẖsa bir īkī yīl daẖā bōyle ġiderse ānlar bizī ġotūrūrler." Peçewī, II, p. 79.
149. Safvet Bey, "H̱azer Denizinde 'Osmānlī Ṣanjāğī," *T.O.E.M.*, III (No. 14), pp. 859–861.
150. Peçewī, *loc. cit.* The Ottoman army probably amounted to about half this number.
151. Şeref, *T.O.E.M.*, IV, pp. 1438–1440. According to Peçewī (II, pp. 80–81), a detachment of Rūm Īlī troops, while grazing horses near Shābirān, suffered this defeat.

152. "Zaḥmet etmesinler, ben geliyorum." Şeref, *Ibid.*
153. Peçewī, II, pp. 80–83; Şeref, *T.O.E.M.*, IV, pp. 1441–1443. The encounter took place in a locality called "Beşdepe."
154. This *tābūr* is probably the fort that the Kabardian princes in 1578 had requested the Tsar of Muscovy to build.
155. Peçewī, II, pp. 84–86; Munejjimbāşī, III, p. 553; Şeref (*T.O.E.M.*, IV, pp. 1481–1484) states that after this encounter some of the Kabardinian Beys met with 'O̱smān Pasha and that one of them was a close relative of the Ottoman general. Peçewī (II, pp. 84–86), in attempting to assess the motives for the Cossack attack, states that they had foreknowledge of the treasure shipment that 'O̱smān Pasha soon encountered on the steppe before he reached Temruk. Although the Ottomans continued to use this route as long as Dagestan and Shirvan remained in their hands, they also continued to be harassed by Cossacks who had direct contact with Moscow. See, for example, a copy in Russian of the letter sent in 1583 by Murād III to Ivan IV, complaining about the seizure of Ottoman ambassadors and messengers by Cossacks on the Terek River. Kumykov and Kusheva, eds., *Kabardino-Russkie Otnosheniya v xvi-xviii. vv.*, I, p. 35.

CHAPTER FIVE
The Tatar Revolt and the End of the Persian War

1 The Revolt of Mehemmed Giray Khan

ʿOsmān Pasha, after having informed the Porte of his signal victory over the Safavids in Shirvan, received an order from the Sultan to proceed to Istanbul and, en route, to put an end to the rule of Meḥemmed Girāy Khan.[1] Since his personal participation in the campaign of 1579, the Crimean Khan had only aided the war effort in Shirvan with a detachment of two or three thousand Tatars under the leadership of Ġāzī Girāy. After the latter had been captured, the Khan was reluctant to provide further aid. Booty and slaves, which ordinarily served as an incentive for the Tatars, had largely been carried off or scattered after the first two years of the war. In spite of the repeated insistence of the Sultan, Meḥemmed Girāy had made excuses for not participating in the campaign.[2] By 1583 the Sultan, who had meanwhile permitted the Khan to name his son as second heir to the khanship,[3] had increased his subsidies to the Khan and had sent to him a great quantity of military equipment and supplies. Thereafter, when support failed to materialize, the Sultan no longer trusted the Khan and sought his dismissal.

The Khan was most certainly guilty of disobeying his overlord. It is wrong, however, to judge the Khan exclusively on the basis of the Ottoman chronicles which, with the exception of Selānīkī, place most of the blame on the Khan. The Crimean Khan never made any decisions without the concurrence of his principal advisers, the leaders of the Crimean Tatar tribes.[4] Moreover, Meḥemmed Girāy, like all the Crimean Khans, had to wrestle continually with enduring problems threatening his state: (*a*) internally, because of insufficient production of foodstuffs, and (*b*) externally, because of the proximity of powerful neighbors. In 1581 the Khan sent his vezir to the

Porte to declare that he would go on campaign if the revenues of Moldavia and Kaffa were given to him and his son, respectively. The Sultan refused to consider this extreme request at all.[5]

It is important to remember that at this time the Livonian War was entering its final stages and Muscovy was being defeated. The Crimean Tatars, who were traditional allies of Poland, quite naturally wished to participate in the spoils, perhaps even to the extent of regaining control of Kazan and Astrakhan. Both the Crimean Tatars and the Nogays maintained steady pressure on the southern regions of Muscovy during 1580 and 1581, and the Crimean Khan was at least partly responsible for instigating a revolt in Kazan.[6] For a time, during the year 1582, it appeared as if the Crimean Khan would go to the aid of ʻOs̱mān Pasha on condition that the Sultan would provide him with sufficient weapons, armament, and money. When the Sultan met these conditions, Meḥemmed Girāy actually started out as if he were going on campaign, but he soon returned to his capital. He excused his action this time by blaming (*a*) the advanced season, (*b*) the anxiety he felt about his sons, some of whom had fled to the Porte,[7] and (*c*) the Cossacks, who were planning to attack the Crimea in his absence.[8]

These excuses, which were received with so much skepticism at the Porte, may have had some validity. It is known, for example, that in 1582 the Russian ambassador, Vasiliy Mossalskiy, succeeded in concluding a five-year truce with the Crimean Tatars.[9] Such an agreement did not, however, keep the Crimean Khan from supporting a general revolt of the Cheremiss in 1583[10]—but such a treaty most certainly disturbed Poland. Perhaps news of the Russian treaty was behind the Polish decision to withhold the subsidy that the Poles had been paying the Khan during the Livonian War.[11] At any rate, in 1583 the peace measures between the Ottoman Empire and Poland-Lithuania, which had been worked out in 1578, now once again broke down. The Cossacks made a devastating attack on Bender and other of the Ottoman and Crimean Tatar settlements, according to one account, just at the time Meḥemmed Girāy had started for Derbent.[12] The Sultan made strong protests to Stephan Báthory and the latter, not wishing to incense the Sultan, had the Cossack leaders who were responsible beheaded.[13] The Sultan, on his part, forestalled a clash between Polish forces and the Crimean Tatars over the issues of tribute and the Cossack raids by agreeing that the Crimean Khan should no longer demand tribute or violate the Polish frontier. The Sultan, in turn, compensated the Crimean Khan for his loss of tribute in the hope that his aid would be forthcoming.[14]

After these most involved events and negotiations, the patience of the Sultan came to an end. Perhaps the Khan had secretly been bribed by agents of the Shah.[15] In any case, ʻOs̱mān Pasha received the order to depose the Khan. These two cunning leaders, Meḥemmed Girāy and ʻOs̱mān Pasha, each sought to sap the strength of the other by a series of strategems. Initially,

'Os̱mān Pasha, who had proceeded to Kaffa, counseled the Porte to mask its intentions with conciliatory letters for, he cautioned, much trouble could develop here at a time when the outcome in Persia was not yet conclusive.[16] The Khan, on his part professing friendship for his former comrade-in-arms, invited the Pasha to come to Baġçesarāy (Bakhchisaray). When the Khan learned that he had been dismissed by the Sultan and that his brother, Islām Girāy, had been appointed in his stead, he besieged Kaffa in the spring of 1584 with a large body of his followers and personal retinue.[17]

Awaiting the arrival of the Ottoman fleet, which was bringing the new Khan to the Crimea, 'Os̱mān Pasha had to withstand a siege of thirty-seven days. During this time, however, he was not idle. Apart from spreading the news of the Khan's dismissal, he invited the 'Ulemā' and other dignitaries to come over to the side of the new Khan.[18] Behind him, as everyone knew, lay the power of the Ottoman Empire. Meḥemmed Girāy now even sought to justify his revolt by asking the Muftī of Kaffa for a *fetvā*, or legal decision, on the rightness of his cause. The judgment went against the Khan.[19] After the new Khan arrived, the Tatars, at first one by one and then in whole groups, went over to Islām Girāy.[20] Prominent among the leaders of the defection were Alp Girāy, the *Kalġay*, and 'Alī Bey, head of the powerful Shīrīn tribe and the son-in-law of Meḥemmed Girāy. Soon only the household troops of the Khan, said to have numbered 7,000 and all of Circassian stock, remained loyal. The Khan and his dwindling retinue now hastened to take refuge beyond Perekop on the steppe with the Great Nogays, but their escape was blocked by the *Kalġay* who had his brother strangled forthwith "with his own bow-string."[21]

'Os̱mān Pasha had put an end to this dangerous revolt, but the opposition to the Ottomans in the Crimea, to which Meḥemmed Girāy had given voice, was later effectively carried on by his sons with the assistance of Muscovy. 'Os̱mān Pasha, thus delayed, now made his triumphal entry into Istanbul accompanied by the veterans who had shared in and had managed to survive the long ordeal in the Caucasus.

2 'Osmān Pasha as Grand Vezir and the Escape of Ġāzī Girāy

When 'Os̱mān Pasha sailed into the Golden Horn at the beginning of Rejeb 992/early July, 1584, his prestige had reached its highest point.[22] This was never more clear than during the personal interviews which Sultan Murād III held with 'Os̱mān Pasha. There were several small-minded men among the dignitaries, however, chief of whom was the Grand Vezir, Siyāvüş Pasha. The latter begrudged 'Os̱mān Pasha his hard-won prestige and had sought means of undermining his position long before the hero had reached Istanbul. Thanks to the evidence provided by his friend, the Bōstānjī Bāşī, 'Os̱mān Pasha was able to show that Siyāvüş Pasha had conspired with the Crimean

Khan to do him harm.[24] The continued attempts of Siyāvüş Pasha and his accomplices to defame ʻO̱smān Pasha came to the attention of the Sultan in a different manner. The Grand Vezir, in the Imperial Dīvān, had not approved of the pay increases and promotions with which ʻO̱smān Pasha had rewarded his troops on battlefields from Shemakha to Kaffa. These troops, most of whom were members of the Silāḥdār regiment, had returned with their pasha to the Porte. When they learned of the decision of the Imperial Dīvān, they marched on the palace and caused a great disturbance. This led to the dismissal of Siyāvüş Pasha, who was replaced by ʻO̱smān Pasha on 20 Rejeb 992/27 July 1584. Ironically Siyāvüş was accused of exacting heavy taxation which had obviously become necessary owing to the war and ʻO̱sman Pasha's liberality![25]

The new Grand Vezir was not destined to have a few months of well-deserved rest. In Ramażān 992/September–October 1584, news reached the Porte that the sons of Meḥemmed Girāy Khan, Murād Girāy and Saʻādet Girāy, leading a strong force of Nogays, Cossacks, and dissident Tatars, had sacked the Crimean capital and routed Islām Girāy Khan, forcing him to take refuge in Kaffa.[26] Upon hearing this news ʻO̱smān Pasha immediately assembled an army and left Istanbul on 10 Şevāl 992/15 October 1584 for Kastamonu, where he made his winter quarters. From there an army could easily be dispatched either to the Crimea from the port of Sinop, about one hundred and twenty miles further to the east, or to the eastern front. At first, ʻO̱smān Pasha had resolved to settle the Crimean affair in person, but upon his arrival in Kastamonu, he sent Ferhād Pasha, who had recently been dismissed from his post as Beylerbey of Bosnia. Before the latter had reached Kaffa, however, Islām Girāy, with the aid of the existing Beylerbey of Kaffa, had driven out the invaders.[27]

At least three factors had helped bring about this revolt against the new Khan. In the first place, Murād and Saʻādet Girāy, like their father, had given vent to anti-Ottoman feelings still harbored by the more conservative elements of the Crimean Khanate. Doubtless most of the Crimean Tatar leaders realized that, without the Ottomans, they would go the way of Kazan and Astrakhan; yet, they could not accept certain aspects of Ottoman domination, such as the appointment of Khans and their enforced participation in unremunerative campaigns. Secondly, Islām Girāy—who had been turned over as a hostage (*rehīn*) to the Ottomans early in the reign of his father, Devlet Girāy—had become Ottoman in taste, speech, and habit and, moreover, had spent the last few years living the life of a Mevlevi dervish in Konya.[28] In short, in most respects, the new Khan preferred things Ottoman. He proved this early in his reign when he "voluntarily" gave up the time-honored privilege of *ḫuṭbe* (having his name mentioned first in the Friday prayer). Naturally a Khan in such a position did not enjoy the full support of his people.[29] A third element was the unrest on the steppe, particularly among the Great Nogays, as the threat of Muscovy and the pressure of the Cossacks became more apparent. As Sa'ādet Girāy had married the daughter of a mīrzā of the Great Nogays, it was natural that he should seek refuge with his father-in-law and also that he should be able to count on Nogay support in an attempt to establish himself in the Crimea as Khan.[30] The unrest of the Nogays at this time expressed itself along traditional lines: they sought a union with the Crimean Tatars and they also ardently sought the protection of the Ottoman Sultan. Moscow, by supporting the invasion of the Crimea and by harboring the rival Khans, actually weakened the Crimea and the position of the Nogays.[31] Apparently a second attack was made on the Crimea by Sa'ādet Girāy in the early part of 1585, but this attack was repulsed by the Ḳalġay, Alp Girāy.[32]

In the spring of 1585, when the outcome of the Crimean uprising became known, 'Os̱mān Pasha led the army to the eastern front. Prior to his departure, he received the Muscovite ambassador to whom he complained about the Terek Cossacks and the question of religious freedom in Kazan and Astrakhan.[33] During his sojourn in Istanbul the Grand Vezir had not felt well.[34] Apparently his physical condition became progressively worse as he approached Persia. In Erzurum he found a severe food shortage. 'Os̱mān Pasha, in spite of his infirmity, let it be rumored that he planned an attack on Nakhichevan. This rumor served to split the Safavid forces between Hamza Mīrzā in the North and 'Alī Ḳūlī, governor of Tabriz.[35]

Before 'Os̱mān Pasha left Erzurum for Persia an event took place that brought great joy to him. Ġāzī Girāy, who had become such a favorite of the Pasha before his capture in Shirvan during the spring of 1581, appeared suddenly in Erzurum after escaping from his Persian confinement. The sources are about evenly divided on the question of whether he spent four years in the prison of Ḳahḳahe or the prison of Alamūt.[36] The story of the escape of the h̲ānzāde is directly connected with the events described in the paragraph above. When Hamza Mīrzā learned from the Şamh̲al, that the Tatars had revolted against the Ottomans, he suggested to his father, the Shah, that they curry favor with the Tatars by releasing Ġāzī Girāy. If he was found to be sufficiently obedient, he could be made a son-in-law by arranging a marriage between him and a sultāna. Finally, he could be given troops and appointed Khan of Shirvan. Ġāzī Girāy, seeing an opportunity to escape, played along with this scheme and was released from prison. He became a close and trusted associate of Hamza Mīrzā, who took his Tatar charge with him to Tabriz.[37] From Tabriz, Ġāzī Girāy escaped across the border dressed as a dervish. He took refuge in Van and from there was sent to Erzurum by Çiġālazāde Sinān Pasha, the Beylerbey of Van.

After mutual rejoicing, 'Os̱mān Pasha gave Ġāzī Girāy the command over all of the Tatar and Circassian troops in his army and ordered the advance on Tabriz. The physical condition of the Pasha had meanwhile deteriorated to such an extent that he had to be carried in a litter. The Ottomans had a particularly bloody encounter with Hamza Mīrzā at Sufian, a town to the west of Tabriz, from which Çiġālazāde emerged the hero. Now the path to Tabriz was open. The army entered the city on 28 Ramażān 993/23 September 1585. ʿO̱smān Pasha ordered the construction of a fortress in the midst of the city. Upon its completion Jaʿfer Pasha was put in charge of a garrison numbering 12,000. Thereafter the army withdrew.[39] In the city some incidental killings of Ottoman troops had sparked a general massacre of the local population. Moreover, Çiġālazāde, who was accompanied by Ġāzī Girāy and Dāl Mehemmed during a battle outside the city, had let himself be tricked by a feigned withdrawal of the enemy and, against the advice of his companions, had involved his troops in a severe conflict. It is possible that Çiġālazāde may have henceforth held a grudge against the ẖānzāde which would come to light in 1596, when Çiġālazāde became Grand Vezir.[40]

Hamza Mīrzā, who by this time had gained a great reputation for bravery among the Ottomans, harassed the Ottoman withdrawal mercilessly. ʿO̱smān Pasha, upon whose presence and reputation the discipline of the army depended, died shortly after the army had left Tabriz. Çiġālazāde, who had been appointed *serdār* by O̱smān Pasha in anticipation of his death, remained commander of the rear guard in the attempt to hide this news from the Ottomans and Persians alike. But for this and other measures of Çiġālazāde, the withdrawal might have turned into a major disaster.[41] On 8 Ẕiʿl Hijje 993/December 1 1585, the eunuch Mesīh Pasha became the Grand Vezir and Çiġālazāde was confirmed as *serdār* of the Eastern Front, only to be transferred to Baghdad a few months later.[42]

3 The Close of the Persian War

With the conquest of Tabriz, the Persian War entered its second and final stage. The conquests of the previous seven years had shorn the Safavids of their borderland tributaries; this new thrust into the rich heartlands of Azerbaijan was designed to bring the Safavid state speedily to its knees. The move had the desired effect, but the Ottomans left nothing to chance. Apart from the annual convoys for reinforcing their garrisons and provisioning them, they completed the conquest of Northern Azerbaijan by seizing Genje in 1588 and Nakhichevan in 1589. Çiġālazāde, at the same time, marched on Hamadan from Baghdad. Ferhād Pasha, who had been responsible for the last major conquests in Azerbaijan, made a triumphal entry into Istanbul in the following year, bringing with him the Persian plenipotentiary and a royal hostage.[43]

Another development hastened the signing of peace in 1590. ʿO̱smān Pasha, in the early years of the war, had sought diligently to establish Ottoman naval supremacy on the Caspian Sea as a means of blocking any relief measures that Moscow might attempt, and also as a means of establishing liaison with the friendly Uzbeg power in Central Asia. There is at least some evidence that, by the accession of Shah 'Abbās in 1587, the Ottomans had established a measure of naval power on the Caspian.[44] The liaison, which now developed between the Ottomans and Uzbegs, enabled the latter power to open a second front against the Safavids in Khorāsān in 1588.

While these events were taking place, Hamza Mīrzā was assassinated in 1586. His murder, although a great loss to Persia, eliminated the division of the population into two hostile camps, one supporting Hamza Mīrzā as successor to the throne, and the other, 'Abbās Mīrzā. In a decisive battle that took place early in 1587 between the Shāmlū, the tribe that had heretofore protected 'Abbās, and the Ustājlū, the Ustājlū won the day, deposed the half-blind Shah Muhammad Ḫodābanda, and placed 'Abbās Mīrzā on the throne.[45] The young Shah solemnly resolved to reconquer what the Ottomans had taken but, this resolve, for a time, remained only a wish. He was forced to ratify the humiliating peace of 1590 which was based on the *status quo*. Now much of Georgia, Shirvan, Derbent, Azerbaijan, and Kurdistan passed into the hands of the Ottomans.[46]

As a result of the Persian War, 1578–1590, the Ottoman state came into possession of much of the Caucasus. Viewed in historical perspective, the outcome proved to be a Pyrrhic victory. No empire could withstand a war lasting thirteen years without sacrifices of men and material and without altering some of the institutions and goals of its society. These considerations, although extremely important, are beyond the scope of this study.[47] In the short run, the Ottomans had upset the balance of power in the Caucasus and Central Asia. Safavid Persia appeared to be well on the way toward becoming a second-rate power. Even before the war had officially ended, all of the states and principalities that had relations, to a greater or lesser degree, with either of these powers had begun coming to terms with the new equilibrium in western Asia. On the one hand, some of the smaller political entities of the Caucasus tended to band together and to cast about for allies in order to offset the dominating influence of the Ottoman Empire. Alexander of Kakheti, for example, followed an equivocal policy. He paid a generous tribute to the Ottomans and thus avoided the establishment of a direct Ottoman administration on his home soil. At the same time, however, between the years 1586 and 1588 he established close diplomatic ties with Muscovy.[48] On the other hand, some political entities such as the Nogays, the Kumucks and Kaytaks of Dagestan, the Uzbegs of Central Asia, and the people of Shirvan who, geographically speaking, had been isolated from the main centers of Ottoman control and yet shared common cultural, political, or economic aims with the Ottomans, generally welcomed the new state of affairs. This tendency was particularly true in those cases, represented by the Nogays and Shirvanians, where the nearest great power actually pursued a policy of complete domination over them.

Muscovy, in view of the new situation in the Caucasus, had become more cautious in Circassia. After 'O̱smān Pasha had destroyed the fort on the Sunzhu in 1583, no further direct contact with the Kabardinians was accomplished until 1587 and 1588. During the course of 1588, a new fort was built on the Terek, but this time it was situated at the mouth of the river (the Staryy Terek branch) far from the normal Ottoman supply lines. This fort and the town that grew up around it soon became the center of Muscovite trade and political activities with the peoples of the Northern Caucasus, Dagestan and Kakheti.[49]

During the eventful years of the Persian War, Ġāzī Girāy had matured. He had gained, by the accident of circumstances, firsthand knowledge of all of the traditional adversaries of his ancestors. As a youth he had joined in the Astrakhan campaign and had accompanied or led raids into Poland, Russia, and the Caucasus. During the Persian war he had served 'O̱smān Pasha, one of the greatest of Ottoman commanders, in Shirvan and Dagestan. Later, he had observed the Safavid society at first hand during his captivity. After the death of 'O̱smān Pasha, he spent some time in Istanbul and then settled into a quiet life on one of the Tatar estates that were maintained for Crimean Tatar princes near the capital. The young ẖānzāde had now ended his long apprenticeship; in the future, he would carry the burdens and responsibilities for which his earlier experiences had trained him.[50]

While the Persian War affected its contemporaries in different ways, the campaign of 1578–1590, in the judgment of one thoughtful student of Ottoman history, marks a critical stage in the modern history of the Islamic Middle East; hereafter, economic stability in the Ottoman Empire was never again regained.[51]

NOTES

1. Hammer, *Histoire de l'Empire Ottoman*, VII, p. 118; Ḥasanbeyzade, *Tārīẖ-i Al-i 'O̱smān*, f. 478a.
2. See the letter to the Khan from Sultan Murād in the year 1580, Ferīdūn Bey, *Münşe'āt es-Selāṭīn*, II, pp. 123–126. In a letter of De Germigny to Henri III there is a description of the rich gifts sent to Meḥemmed Girāy in 1580, E. de Hurmuzaki, ed., *Documente privitóre la Istoria Romanilor*, Suppl. I/I, p. 51.
3. See above Chap. 4, note 90.
4. Novosel'skiy, *Bor'ba*, pp. 33–34.
5. De Germigny to Henri III (April 15, 1581), Hurmuzaki, Suppl. I/I, p. 56. For a similar report, see Zinsendorf to the Emperor, (April 15, 1581) in Hurmuzaki, III, p. 61. Some reports even say that the Khan also desired the possession of Derbent. *Ibid.* IX, p. 108.
6. Karamsin, *Histoire de l'Empire de Russie*, IX, p. 393, discloses that the Tsar had to garrison heavily the line of the Oka River in anticipation of Tatar attacks during 1580. Novosel'skiy, *Bor'ba*, pp. 31–33, states that although the role of Poland and Sweden in the Livonian War is well

known, no study has yet been made of the serious effect of the Tatar and Nogay attacks. In fact, Ivan IV could do little to quell a revolt in Kazan until peace was concluded with Poland in 1582.

7. In a dispatch from Cobham to Walsingham it is stated that these errant sons were returned to the Khan, *Calendar of State Papers*, Foreign Series XVII (January–June, 1583), pp. 185–186.

8. Leunclavius, *Neue Chronika*, pp. 109–110. In a letter from Stephan Báthory to the Grand Vezir, Sinān Pasha, mention is made of the flight of the brothers of the Khan to Poland (Hurmuzaki, III, p. 68; XI, p. 671; see also Şeref, *T.O.E.M.*, IV, pp. 1487–1491).

9. Karamsin, IX, pp. 454–455.

10. *Ibid.*, p. 529.

11. See *C.S.P.*, Foreign XVIII (January–June, 1583).

12. It is certain that a terrible raid took place against Moldavia and Bender in May or June of 1583. Apparently, however, the Khan was not "on campaign," but had sent Tatars to the assistance of the garrison at Bender. The Cossacks, by their adroit use of cannon, held the Tatars at bay until the arrival of the Janissaries. See the reports of Preyner to the Emperor, Hurmuzaki, XI, pp. 665–666.

13. Hrushevsky, *History of the Ukraine*, p. 180; and Harbonne to Walsingham, *C.S.P.* Foreign XIX (August 1584–August 1585), pp. 65–67.

14. Harbonne to Walsingham, *C.S.P.* Foreign XVIII (January–June 1583), pp. 185–186, 397. In spite of this subsidy, the Khan nonetheless seems to have conducted a raid. In this regard, see Eyzing to the Kaiser, Hurmuzaki, XI, pp. 682–683.

15. Only the French ambassador, De Germigny, in a dispatch to Henri III, mentions that the Khan had had contact with the Shah. See Charrière, *Négociations*, IV, pp. 284–285. Considering the attempts the Safavids made to gain support among the Crimean Tatars by giving reasonable treatment to such prisoners as 'Ādil Girāy and Ġāzī Girāy, this disclosure does not seem surprising.

16. Peçewī, II, pp. 90–91.

17. As an interim measure, 'O̱smān Pasha is supposed to have announced that Alp Girāy was the new Khan. To this the Khan is supposed to have replied, "While I am an absolute sovereign, possessor of the right to have my name on the coinage and foremost in the Friday prayer, who is able to dismiss or to oppose me?" (Ben sāḥib-i sikke ve ẖuṭbe pādişāh īken, beni 'azl ve naṣbe kim ḳāder ōlūr.) *Ibid.*

18. Munejjimbāşī, *Ṣaḥā'if al-Aẖbār*, III, p. 553; Selānīkī, *Tārīḫ-i Selānīkī*, pp. 177–178, recalls that 'O̱smān Pasha had nursed a grudge against the Khan since 1579. The Khan really did not want to revolt and it was only his careless speech, enlarged upon by informers, which had brought about such extreme measures. As the 'Ulemā,' largely derived from appointments made in Istanbul, they probably followed the bidding of 'O̱smān Pasha.

19. Munejjimbāşī, III, p. 553.

20. Peçewī, II, p. 91.

21. *Ibid.*; Munejjimbāşī, III, p. 553; Kazimirski, "Précis," *J.A.*, Ser. II/XII, p. 380; Smirnov, *Krymskoe Khanstvo*, p. 441.

22. Peçewī, II, p. 91; Selānīkī, pp. 178–179.

23. For details see Peçewī, II, p. 91; Selānīkī, pp. 178–179; and Munejjimbāşī, III, p. 554.

24. *C.S.P.*, Foreign XIX (August 1584–August 1585) pp. 44–46; Minadoi, *Historia della guerra*, pp. 272–275.

25. Selānīkī, p. 180; Munejjimbāşī, III, p. 554. 'O̱smān Pasha was known to be a lover of wine and the question of his drinking was closely scrutinized before he received the appointment. Peçewī, II, pp. 93–95.

26. Selānīkī, p. 183.

27. Peçewī, II, p. 96. The invaders had seized the Khan's treasure and many slaves. Now Sa'ādet and Murād sought the protection of the Tsar. Sa'ādet was permitted to lead a nomadic life with the Nogays and Murād Girāy lived in Astrakhan. For details, see Chapter VI.

28. Halīm Girāy, *Gülbün-ü H̱ānān*, p. 57.

29. Novosel'skiy, *Bor'ba*, p. 34, Inalcïk, "Girāy," *I.A.*, IV, p. 786.
30. Leunclavius, *Neue Chronika*, p. 113. Among the Crimean Tatars it was customary for the leading families to make marriage ties with prominent Nogay or Circassian families. This practice often had the effect of increasing the influence of any given ẖānzāde in the affairs of the Khanate.
31. Novosel'skiy (*Bor'ba*, p. 35) points out that the Muscovite policy of carefully planned campaigns followed by the building of forts to hold ground soon convinced Urus Khan of the folly of attempting to establish an independent power on the lower Volga.
32. Ḥalīm Girāy, pp. 57–58; *C.S.P.* Foreign XIX (August 1584–August 1585), pp. 313–314; Kazimirski, "Précis," *J.A.*, Ser. II/XII, p. 379. For further details on these events, see Smirnov, *Krymskoe Khanstvo*, pp. 442–443, and Howorth, *History of the Mongols*, II, pp. 520 ff.
33. The Muscovite ambassador, Boris Blagov, conferred with Islām Girāy, 'O̱smān Pasha, and the Sultan. The Sultan also requested the return of messengers and envoys who had been captured on the Terek. Belokurov, *Snosheniya*, pp. lxxxix–xcvi. Blagov had been sent to the Porte to announce the accession of Tsar Fyodor. In his conversation with 'O̱smān Pasha in Kastamonu, he was struck by Ottoman concern over Muscovite-Safavid relations and the threat this might offer to Ottoman communications in the Northern Caucasus, Kumykov and Kusheva, eds., *Kabardino-Russkie Otnosheniya*, I, pp. 36–46.
34. Peçewī, II, pp. 96–99; Morosini reported to the Venetian Senate in 1585 that although 'O̱smān Pasha, whom he estimated to be 60 years of age, had volunteered to take command of the Eastern front, he had hoped the Sultan would refuse in view of 'O̱smān Pasha's long service in Shirvan. This was unfortunately not the case; Alberi, Ser. III/III, pp. 285, 305.
35. "Relatione de Perse" *Trésor Politique*, pp. 201–214.
36. The Persian sources and the best informed Ottoman sources say Alamūt. See also Munejjimbāşī, II, p. 703 and Halīm Girāy, p. 54.
37. Şeref, *T.O.E.M.*, IV, pp. 1499–1500. It is interesting that Dāl Meḥemmed, the former companion of the Khan of Shirvan, had also been sent to Alamūt. When Ġāzī Girāy needed a scribe to answer the letters of the Shah, he was able to obtain the release of Dāl Meḥemmed for the purpose. Later at the time of the escape of Ġāzī Girāy, Dāl Meḥemmed also managed to escape by a different route. He reached Erzurum about the same time as did Ġāzī Girāy (*Ibid.*). According to the above account, Ġāzī Girāy must have been released from prison during the time of the revolt of Meḥemmed Girāy.
38. Selānīkī, pp. 241–242, Şeref, *T.O.E.M.*, IV, pp. 1499–1500.
39. The withdrawal started on 4 Ẕi'l Ka'de, 993/28 October 1585. In Tabriz, during the feast that followed Ramazan, 'O̱smān Pasha, for perhaps the last time before his death, confided in Ġāzī Girāy and Dāl Meḥemmed. He told them that the only satisfactory means of holding the possessions newly acquired from Persia was to gain the full support and assistance of the Crimean Khan. He also expressed his desire to have Ġāzī Girāy appointed Khan and to have Dāl Meḥemmed made the Beylerbey of Kaffa. Şeref, *T.O.E.M.*, IV, pp. 1502–1505. See also Peçewī, II, pp. 97–101, for details of the occupation of Tabriz.
40. Şeref, *T.O.E.M.*, IV, pp. 1503–1504.
41. Peçewī, II, pp. 101–102; Munejjimbāşī, III, pp. 559–560; "Relatione de Perse," *Trésor Politique*, p. 204.
42. Peçewī, II, p. 107. After 6 months Mesīḥ Pasha was deposed and Siyāvüş Pasha was named Grand Vezir for the second time. In April 1589, he was replaced by Ḳōja Sinān Pasha (Hammer, VII, p. 226.).
43. Munejjimbāşī, III, pp. 560–563; Selānīkī, pp. 204–250, *passim.*; Peçewī, II, pp. 107–113.
44. Selānīkī (pp. 225–226, 236) states that an ambassador arrived at the Porte from Abdullah II, Khan of the Uzbegs, in 1587. By the years 1588 to 1589, the Ottomans were able to stop and search vessels on the Caspian Sea. A merchant of Gilan was questioned about the Russian ambassador who had gone to Persia and then was robbed. Cf. Vesselovskiy, ed., "Pamyatniki Diplomaticheskikh i Torgovykh Snosheniy Moskovskoy Rusi s Persiey," *Trudy Vostochnago*

Otdeleniya Imperatorskago Russkago Arkheologicheskago Obshchestva, XX, pp. 106–108.
45. See Savory, "Abbās I," *E.I.*[2], I, pp. 7–8.
46. Selānïkï, pp. 236 ff.; "Relatione de Perse," *Trésor Politique,* pp. 204–206; "M. de Maissé to Henri III," Charrière, IV, pp. 578–585; for further details, see Hammer, *Histoire,* VII, pp. 222–228; Savory, "'Abbās I," *E.I.*[2], I, pp. 7–8. At one stage, before Shah 'Abbās made peace with the Ottomans (ca. 1588), he promised to give Derbent and Baku to the Tsar of Muscovy if he took action against the Sultan. The Muscovite Ambassador to Persia, G. Vasil'chikov, claimed that his Government had already intervened on the Shah's behalf when it had constructed the fort on the Terek and had intercepted the Crimean Tatars and Ottomans. Belokurov, *Snosheniya,* p. xcviii; for documents on the Vasil'chikov mission, see Vesselovskiy, "Pamyatniki Dipl. i Torgov. Snosh." *Trudy . . . Arkheolog. Obshch.,* XX, pp. 53–54 and *passim.*
47. The European sources provide a considerable amount of insight into the economic and social aspects of the war. See, for example, the French report of ". . . pertes croissantes des Turcs dans la Guerre de Perse . . . ." (Charrière, IV, pp. 436 ff.). Leunclavius (*Neue Chronika,* pp. 133–134) explains the uprising in Istanbul of June 1589 in terms of the arrears in the pay of the soldiers and the falsification of the gold content in newly minted ducats. Giovanni Moro, Bailo, reported to the Venetian Senate (1590) how seriously the authority of the Grand Vezir had been undermined by court favorites during the last years of the war (Alberi, Ser. III/III, p. 366). Gianfrancesco Morosini, Bailo, likewise reported in 1585 (*Ibid.,* pp. 301 ff.), "Questa guerra da turchi e grandemente abborita, e stimate fastidiosissima; perche fra li confini de turchi e il paese abitato da persiani si ritrove una interposizione di molti terreni sterili e disabitati che non possono servire per sostenter gli eserciti di maniera che e necessario portarsi dietro tutti i viveri . . . ." This bailo then takes up the problems of the great losses of men and the complete disability and infirmity of those who manage to survive the long journey and the scarcity of food.
48. Belokurov, *Snosheniya,* pp. xciii–xcv. Danilov had gone to Kakheti in 1586, and when he returned he brought with him an ambassador of Alexander Levend. The negotiations that followed led to the acceptance by Kakheti of an ill-defined Muscovite overlordship. This was, at the time, only a means of putting pressure on the Ottomans. Meanwhile, the Ottomans continued to collect their *h̲arāj* (Peçewī, II, p. 109).
49. The princes Mamstruk and Kudensk, in the name of Prince Kanbulat, petitioned the Tsar to set up a city on the Terek and to protect the Kabardinians from the Crimean Tatars, the Ottomans, and the Şamh̲al (Kumykov and Kusheva, eds., *Kabardino-Russkie Otnosheniya,* I, pp. 50–51, and notes p. 399). See also Belokurov, *Snosheniya,* pp. xcvi–xcvii. A German embassy returning from Persia in 1604 stopped at a Muscovite settlement on the Terek (see Georg Tectander, *Iter Persicum,* pp. 127 ff.).
50. Selānīkī, pp. 241–242.
51. See J. R. Walsh, "Giovanni Tomasso Minadoi's History of the Turco-Persian Wars of the Reign of Murad III," in *Proceedings of the 25th International Congress of Orientalists* (*Trudy*), II, pp. 448–449.

CHAPTER SIX
Ġāzī Girāy Khan and his Relations with the Steppe Powers, 1588–1594

1 The Legacy of Meḥemmed Giray Khan

The Crimean Khans, in their eagerness to assert claims to leadership on the steppe—claims based on their direct descent from Jenghiz Khan—alienated some of their own dependencies, notably the Nogay Tatars and the Circassians, and the supporters of the Crimean Tatars in the Khanates of Kazan and Astrakhan. As a result, they caused both the Nogays and the Circassians to split into pro- and anti-Crimean factions and also weakened their support elsewhere.[1] This situation had prepared the way for the seizure of Kazan and Astrakhan by Tsar Ivan IV, a calamity which ended forever Crimean pretentions to exclusive leadership on the steppe. In one fell swoop, Moscow extended her frontiers to the Ottoman outposts in the northern Caucasus and to Persia by way of the Caspian. The English, moreover, after opening up a northern route to Muscovy in 1553, were quick to develop commercial ties with Moscow and Persia. It must be emphasized, however, that the loss of the Volga to Moscow, important as it was in the long run, did not at first alter appreciably the importance of the Crimean Khanate either as a buffer state for the Ottomans or as a force to be reckoned with on the steppe.

If the chief concern of the Tatar khans in the first half of the century had been to maintain their position on the steppe, subsequent events tended more and more to draw the Tatars into the service of the Ottomans. There were a number of precedents for this. In 1484, Menglī Girāy Khan had assisted Sultan Bāyezīd II during the Moldavian campaign. The same khan, by lending Tatar support to his son-in-law Selīm Çelebi, son of Sultan Bāyezīd, helped to seat Selīm on the Ottoman throne in 1512. The Tatar khans, in the years 1538, 1543, and 1566, had accompanied or sent Tatar contingents to the Balkans in support of Sultan Sulaymān. The Tatars, as already noted, had also reluctantly joined in the ill-fated Ottoman attempt to wrest Astrakhan from Muscovite control in 1569—a move considered by Devlet Girāy, the then reigning khan, as excessive intermeddling of the Sultan in Crimean affairs. But it was particularly during the two long wars of the Ottomans, the first with Safavid Persia (1578–1590) and the second with the Habsburgs (1593–1606), that the Crimean Tatars began to make regular contributions to the Ottoman campaigns.[2]

At this period in the history of eastern Europe, the khan of the Crimean Tatars was generally left a free hand in his dealings with the Tsar of Muscovy, but in matters concerning Poland-Lithuania he was required to coordinate his policies with those of the sultan. The possessions claimed by the khan included much of the Kipchak Steppe (Deşt-i Kipçak) from the Dniester to the Don, that is, the region that became known as the Ukraine in Slavic countries. This region was occupied by the nomadic Little Nogay Tatars, Crimean Tatar tribes, and tribal elements taking refuge from other areas such as Kazan. In the Crimean peninsula, the khan could draw upon the services of Ottoman, Cossack, and Circassian warriors, merchants, bureaucrats and "Ulemā" as well as the special skills of Jews, Greeks, Armenians, and Genoese, ethnic groups that had long maintained their colonies there.

Meḥemmed Girāy Khan (1577–1584), continued in the tradition of his father, Devlet Girāy Khan (1551–1577), firmly defended the semi-independent position of the Khanate, not only against outside encroachments, but also against the encroachments of the Ottoman state. Yet, paradoxically, it was during his reign and the reigns of his immediate successors that pressure on the steppe portion of the Khanate from the adjoining lands of Muscovy and Poland-Lithuania reached such proportions that more reliance on the might of the Ottoman Empire became inevitable. In the time of Meḥemmed Girāy, as on previous occasions, a clear conflict of interest developed between the Khan, representing traditionalist sentiment in the Crimea, and the Ottoman Sultan. While Meḥemmed Girāy was willing to supply the Sultan with a limited numbers of Tatars for the Persian War—particularly from among the supporters of his rival brothers (hence the initial participation of Ġāzī Girāy and ʿĀdil Girāy in the Caucasus campaign)—he wished to keep his main forces at home, available for the protection of the Khanate. Meḥemmed Girāy also wished to perpetuate the khanship in his own immediate family, a dynastic goal that would have undermined the sultan's prerogatives of appointing and dismissing the khans. As these policies ran counter to the interests of the Sultan, they led eventually to the deposition and death of the Khan. Nevertheless, the sons of Meḥemmed Girāy, Saʿādet Girāy and Murād Girāy, were able to disrupt the rule of their father's successors by drawing support for themselves from the same traditionalist, basically anti-Ottoman faction in the Khanate that had supported the father.[3]

After the revolt of Meḥemmed Girāy in 1583 and its suppression and the execution of the Khan in 1584, Islām Girāy was appointed khan (1584–1588). This inexperienced khan, who had spent most of his life in Istanbul and in other parts of the Empire, was alien to the ways of his countrymen.[4] As he did not enjoy the full support of his subjects he had to rely upon the Beylerbey (governor) of Kaffa and an Ottoman garrison in Bakhchisaray (Baġçesarāy) to maintain himself in power.[5] Even then he was driven from his capital on two occasions, in 1584 and 1585, by the pretender to the khanship, Sa'ādet Girāy, who was assisted by his brothers, Murād Girāy and Safā Girāy, and by the Great Nogays and the Don Cossacks.[6]

After their expulsion from the Crimea in 1585, Sa'ādet Girāy and Safā Girāy sought refuge, first among the Kumucks of Dagestan, then with the Great Nogays to whom Sa'ādet Girāy was related by marriage. Murād Girāy took refuge in Astrakhan and from there was summoned to Moscow where he had an audience with the Tsar. Soon (c. 1586) he returned to Astrakhan as the nominal governor of that province, a position in which he served as the puppet of Moscow until his mysterious death about 1590.[7] The incursions into the Crimea by Sa'ādet Girāy and his supporters had left the Khanate in disarray and the treasury empty, and had greatly increased the concern of the Tatars for their northeastern flank, exposed as it was to hostile attacks, particularly from the Don Cossacks. Moreover, when Stephan Báthory, King of Poland, died in December 1586, and Poland entered its third interregnum in a period of only fifteen years, the ensuing breakdown of discipline within the Polish-Lithuanian state was of particular importance for the Crimean Tatars. After the death of Báthory, the Zaporozhian Cossacks lost no time in carrying out a series of raids on the Danubian principalities, the Ottoman towns on the Dniester and the Dnieper, and the Crimean Khanate.

Now the Khanate faced threats from both flanks of the steppe adjacent to the Crimea. Islām Girāy made every effort to hold the hostile forces at bay. His Tatars raided the borderlands of Muscovy in 1586 and 1587 and the latter raid was followed by a foray into Circassia.[8] During the same year, some of the Khan's Nogay subjects dwelling in the Bujāḳ region (Bessarabia) were deemed responsible for an attack on Moldavia. This unauthorized raid upon the possessions of the Sultan led to strong protests from the Porte and a demand by the Sultan for the Khan to facilitate the return of all property and prisoners immediately. The affair serves to illustrate the poor state of order within the Crimean Khanate in the time of Islām Girāy Khan. These events accentuated the reliance of the Khan on the Porte and led to further humiliation for Islām Girāy. As proof of his loyalty, the Khan either felt it necessary or was forced to give up an important Islamic mark of sovereignty, the right of *ḥuṭbe*, the mentioning of his name first in the Friday prayers. Henceforth the name of the Ottoman sultan preceded that of the khan. The degree of control the Ottoman state exercised in the Crimean Khanate was definitely on the increase.[9]

Meanwhile, the Zaporozhian Cossacks were capturing Tatars and driving off Tatar livestock. In retaliation, the Crimean Tatars are reported to have invaded the Polish-Lithuanian borderlands in 1587, the same year in which Maximilian of Austria was attempting to make good his claim to the Polish throne by an attack on Poland through Silesia.[10] The Cossacks answered this raid with an attack on Ochakov, Bender, and the coast of the Crimea. Islām Girāy had just commenced a counterraid in the spring of 1588 when he died.[11] The new Khan, Ġāzī Girāy, inherited the task of pacifying the Zaporozhians. The time had come to deliver a blow to their increasing audacity. Not only did they hamper the passage of merchants and embassies across the steppe between the Ottoman-Crimean possessions and Poland-Lithuania or Moscow, but they also maintained their *Sich*, or island stronghold, on the lower stretches of the Dnieper, within easy striking distance of the Principalities, of the Ottoman border districts of Akkerman and Bender, and of the possessions of the Crimean Khan.[12] These seemingly insignificant raids and counterraids on the borderlands of the Ottoman and Polish states led to a serious crisis between the two powers in 1589 and 1590.

Moreover, before the advent of Ġāzī Girāy the stage was set for a Muscovite seizure of the Crimea on the Don-Volga side of the steppe through the exploitation by Moscow of the equivocal position of Murād Girāy. Tsar Fyodor and his advisers had seen in the rebellion of Meḥemmed Girāy Khan and the unpopular rule of Islām Girāy a chance for Moscow to establish a puppet ruler in the Crimea as Ivan IV had done in Kazan and Astrakhan prior to the Muscovite conquest of those khanates. In the dispossessed sons of Meḥemmed Girāy—Sa'ādet, Murād, and Safā—the Tsar had placed his hopes. In addition, these H̱ānzādes (sons of the Khan) could be used as figureheads in an attempt to create factions among the Nogays who revolted against Moscow.[13] This twofold intention of the Tsar was brought to the attention of the Sultan by Uzbeg and Little Nogay ambassadors in Şevval 995/ September 1587. They urged that a campaign be launched against Astrakhan immediately. The Sultan now ordered the preparation of a campaign against Astrakhan in the following year.[14]

As soon as the Tsar received word of the Sultan's intentions, he sent an ambassador to the Crimea to assure the Khan that he would not permit the sons of Meḥemmed Girāy to attack the Crimea on three conditions: if the Khan would not attack the lands of Moscow, if the Khan would dissuade the Sultan from attacking Astrakhan, and if the Khan would send information to Moscow about the plans of the Ottomans.[15]

It is not entirely clear why the plans for an attack on Astrakhan evaporated in the following year. As the war in Persia had not yet ended and the interregnum in Poland still continued, it is little wonder that the Ottomans hesitated to launch a costly campaign on the lower Volga, particularly after the death of Islām Girāy early in 1588. Professor Inalcïk suggests that the Crimean Tatars, fearing a flank attack from Poland or Muscovy while they were marching on Astrakhan, preferred a direct attack on Moscow and refused to support the Ottomans.[16] Doubtless the lessening of tension following the accession of Ġāzī Girāy contributed much toward establishing a new equilibrium on the steppe. Furthermore, by 1588 the Sultan would have heard of the capitulation of the Great Nogays to Moscow, a factor that may have discouraged the Ottomans from intervention since such a move would perforce have to be planned on the scale of a major campaign. Ġāzī Girāy wrote to the Tsar that he had persuaded the Sultan to give up his claim to Astrakhan. The Khan also sought a treaty of alliance with Moscow. All these considerations doubtless played their part in the decision of the Porte not to wage a campaign against Astrakhan. One thing is certain: although Moscow suffered serious defeats from the armies of Poland and Sweden in the Livonian War, she nevertheless continued her pressure on the Caucasus and the steppe.[17]

2 The Accession of Ġāzī Girāy Khan and the Nogay Question

Upon the death of Islām Girāy Khan, Ġāzī Girāy was designated the new Khan of the Crimea. He had returned to Istanbul after the Persian campaign of 'Os̱mān Pasha in 1585 and henceforth had led a comparatively quiet existence in Yanbolu, a place of residence for members of the Girāy dynasty in Thrace. It was here that Crimean Tatar h̠ānzādes—some exiles, others hostages—were detained at the sultan's pleasure. The chronicler Selānīkī states that Ġāzī Girāy received the news of his appointment with considerable surprise, for he had spent his time in the interim in the company of learned men and actually contemplated a life dedicated to letters.[18]

The Tatar dignitaries meanwhile elevated Alp Girāy, the *Ḳalġay* and senior surviving son of Devlet Girāy, to the position of khan and sought the approval of the Sultan; however, their petition was ignored.[19] Ġāzī Girāy Khan, after the customary ceremony of investiture at the Porte, departed for Kaffa on April 18, 1588. To the posts of *Ḳalġay* and *Nūr ed-Dīn* he appointed his brother, Fetḥ Girāy, and the son of 'Ādil Girāy, Bah̠t Girāy, respectively.[20] Alp Girāy and Şaḳay Mubārek Girāy, after an abortive attempt to maintain themselves in power, fled, the former to Istanbul and the latter to Circassia.[21]

From the time of his accession to the beginning of Crimean Tatar participation in the long Ottoman-Habsburg War in Hungary (1593–1606), Ġāzī Girāy had to face a series of external threats to the Khanate. The first, an attempt to place a Moscow puppet regime in Bağçesaray, was already far advanced. In the view of Moscow, the realization of this scheme depended on two factors: the maintenance of internal strife in the Crimea, and the pacification of the Great Nogays—who acted as a kind of buffer between the Muscovite strip of territory along the Volga and the Crimean lands.

The new Khan, instead of merely reacting to events in the manner of his predecessor, devised a stratagem that checked the machinations of Moscow and eventually brought considerable stability to his regime. He understood that the external difficulties of the Khanate in part derived from internal strife during the reign and after the murder of Meḥemmed Girāy Khan. Saʿādet Girāy, the eldest son of Meḥemmed Girāy, was related by marriage to Urus Khan, the titular head of the Great Nogays, and therefore was assured of refuge with the Nogays for himself, his brothers, and their supporters. This faction, with the support of the Don Cossacks, had been chiefly responsible for the sack of the Crimea in 1584 and 1585. The Tsar set up the puppet regime of Murād Girāy in Astrakhan only after the sons of Meḥemmed Girāy had failed to establish themselves permanently in the Crimea. Ġāzī Girāy took a long step toward resolving the grievances of this faction by announcing, with the support of the Sultan, a general amnesty and by appointing Safā Girāy, a son of Meḥemmed Girāy, as *Nūr ed-Dīn* in place of Baẖt Girāy. This policy of reconciliation proved so successful that even Murād Girāy, who was little more than a tool of Moscow, expressed the desire to return to the Crimea. He died of poisoning in Astrakhan about 1590; thereafter the Tatars and the Russians accused each other of murdering him.[22]

Ġāzī Girāy had thus in one bold move brought back to the Crimean fold a number of influential relatives and dignitaries with their followers. He next attempted to win support and cooperation for his regime among the Great Nogays themselves. Under Ismāʿīl Khan the Great Nogays had accepted the overlordship of Muscovy. Upon his death in 1563, his eldest son and successor, Tīn Aḥmed Khan (1563–1578), initially vacillated in his relations with Moscow, but later sought to re-establish the lost independence and former influence of his people on the lower Volga in league with the Crimean Tatars. The attempt at cooperation with the Tatars failed, but the Great Nogays continued to fight against the encroachments of Muscovy and the Don Cossacks. Urus Khan (1578–1590), another son of Ismāʿīl Khan, succeeded Tīn Aḥmed. Although he was a bitter opponent of Moscow, he was forced, through the traitorous offices of Murād Girāy, to accept an uneasy truce with the Russians even before the accession of Ġāzī Girāy. But the disunited Nogays were proving no match for the single-minded policy of repression fostered by Moscow. The Don Cossacks and the Muscovite troops, armed with hand guns and cannon, pushed across the steppe toward the traditional strongholds of the Nogays and built a series of fortifications as they progressed.[23]

When Ġāzī Girāy declared his amnesty and appealed to the former supporters of the Crimean Tatars among the Nogay Mīrzās, a number of the most anti-Moscow elements, including Urus Kḫan, left the vicinity of Astrakhan and moved to the shores of the Don. These dignitaries, however, were not yet prepared to put themselves at the mercy of the Crimean Tatars from whose hands their people had suffered in the past. They petitioned the Sultan, seeking permission to reside in the vicinity of Boli Saray at the mouth of the Kalmius. The Sultan, however, appeared unwilling to meddle in affairs which by tradition were dealt with by the Khan and the petition was not successful. A further hindrance to the settlement of large numbers of Great Nogays in the Khanate now became apparent. The Little Nogays, who had since midcentury formed part of the Crimean Khanate, showed themselves quite unwilling to share their pasturage and water supplies with an enemy whom they considered largely responsible for the extension of Muscovite power to the lower Volga, Don, and Yaik (Ural), the traditional grazing lands of the Nogays. A bitter struggle took place on the shores of the Don between the Great and Little Nogays during the winter of 1588–1589, immediately following the accession of Ġāzī Girāy. This enmity upset his plan to bring all the Nogays into the Ottoman-Crimean sphere of influence. Urus Khan was killed in 1590 during a clash between Great and Little Nogays.

Ġāzī Girāy had clearly demonstrated how ephemeral the hold of Moscow was on the Nogays. In the ensuing years this became more apparent; nevertheless, neither the Ottomans nor the Crimean Tatars, in view of their commitments to the war in Hungary, were able to assist the Great Nogays at a time when they were being beaten into submission for lack of modern equipment and tactics and of internal unity. The sons of Tīn Aḥmed, Ur Meḥmet and Tīn Meḥmet, successively occupied the khanship of the Great Nogays in the 1590s. Throughout this period the Tīn Aḥmed faction had to face the opposition of the Urus Khan faction. At the end of the century the latter group, led by Yanārāslān Mīrzā, appears to have dominated the tribe. Such a situation clearly pointed to the election of Yanārāslān Mīrzā as khan in 1600, but the strength of the Muscovite support for Işterek Mīrzā, another son of Tīn Aḥmed, made possible the manipulation of the election in his favor. Henceforth, the leaders and supporters of the sons of Urus Khan were hunted down, imprisoned, banished, and even exterminated by the sons of Tīn Aḥmed and their Muscovite allies. Yanārāslān himself was captured in 1604 and taken to Moscow as a hostage.[24]

Viewed in the light of this perspective, the internal policy of Ġāzī Girāy at the beginning of his reign was only partially successful. He eliminated the threat to the Crimea presented by the sons of Meḥemmed Girāy and supported by Moscow, but he failed to augment appreciably the number of his followers from the ranks of the Great Nogays. The Ottoman Sultan and the Crimean Khan, by not coming to the aid of their coreligionists, left to the Muscovite state the Volga basin and, ultimately, control of the steppe.

3 The Ottoman-Crimean Crisis with Poland-Lithuania

Upon the death of Stephan Báthory in December 1586, the ancient treaty of peace and friendship between the Ottoman and Polish states became subject to renewal by his successor. This fact was acknowledged in an exchange of letters between Murād III and King Sigismund Vasa late in the year 1587. The letter of the Sultan referred specifically to Islām Girāy thus: "Our letters are also directed unto the most excellent Tatar Prince Isbam [*sic*] Gerai (whom God bless) straitly charging and commanding him not to make or suffer any incursion to be made into the borders of Polonia."[25] As already mentioned, the Zaporozhians had for some time been causing havoc on Crimean Tatar soil. The death of Stephan Báthory had relaxed the hold of the central government on the border areas, which were populated by the Cossacks. Moreover, pay for the registered Cossacks was grossly in arrears.[26] But an affair that had commenced as a series of raids for local advantage was quickly seized upon by the Polish state, then under the tutelage of the Grand Chancellor, Jan Zamoyski, as an opportunity to remove some of the more objectionable clauses of the traditional treaty of peace and friendship between the Ottoman and Polish states. The Ottomans, however, who were satisfied with the *status quo*, viewed any changes on the part of Poland as a threat to their hold on the Principalities and, ultimately, their preserve on the Black Sea.[27] The raids of the Zaporozhians increased in ferocity after the accession of Ġāzī Girāy. The English representative at the Porte, William Harborne, in a dispatch dated June 26, 1588, quoted excerpts from a letter the Sultan had recently sent to the Polish King. In this document the Sultan warned that the Cossacks must be held in check for, according to information that he had received from the Crimean Khan, the Cossacks were continuing their attacks; when the Tatars gave chase ". . . the Cossacks . . . by flight do succour themselves in the Polish castles Bar, Vintis, Braslow, Nestbosa and Camanets . . ."[28]

Two raids in particular brought the Ottoman state to the brink of war with Poland. It was customary for the Ottomans, in exchange for similar forbearance on the part of neighboring powers, to overlook small-scale raids. The Cossacks, however, according to a dispatch received by the Austrian Emperor, in the spring of 1588 raided the Ottoman sanjāḳ (district) of Bender (Tehine) and destroyed thirteen villages. This attack led to the mobilization of the provincial forces in the Ottoman territories south of Poland.[29] The new threat caused the Sultan to order the construction of a fort at the usual crossing place of the Cossacks on the Dnieper, and furthermore to demand that the Polish King send an ambassador to renew the ancient agreement between the two powers. The continuing turbulence of the steppe bordering the sanjāḳ of Bender prompted the Sultan to combine the sanjāḳs Özü, Bender, and Akkerman into one large sanjāḳ, thus providing additional administrative and military resources for the preservation of order on the borderlands of the Empire.[30]

It is not clear to what extent the devastation wrought by the Cossacks in 1588 and the subsequent raid on the Crimea in 1589 can be traced to attempts on the part of Poland to improve her bargaining position with the Ottomans before negotiations. It is known, for example, that the Polish-Lithuanian state had failed to pay the registered Cossacks.[31] Their dearth of funds may have encouraged them to raid the Ottoman and Tatar settlements. For some years, particularly since the Livonian wars, Poland had also defaulted on her annual "gift" payments to the Sultan and the Khan. There is no doubt that the Polish state desired to eliminate the "gift" payments from the traditional peace arrangements between the two states. The Sultan, however, was under pressure from Ġāzī Girāy to force Poland to pay the tribute alleged to be seven years in arrears.[32]

The Khan had his own economic problems, for he had inherited an empty treasury from his predecessor. Both the Polish and the Ottoman states had ample reasons for a shortage of silver in this period, owing to the cost of Muscovite and Persian wars. It is highly probable, moreover, that their currency problems were related to the monetary crisis in western Europe, which had been aggravated by the influx of New World silver.[33]

In the spring of 1589 a raid of considerable proportions was directed against the Crimea by the Zaporozhian Cossacks. Led by the Ataman Kulaga, they attacked the city of Gözlev (Yevpatoriya) after having slipped a flotilla of *shaykas* past the Ottoman fortress of Ochakov at the mouth of the Dnieper.[34] According to the sources, a trade fair was in progress at Gözlev at the time of the attack. When word reached the Khan of the approach of the Cossacks, he assembled his forces and rode to intercept them. Before the Khan arrived, however, the Cossacks had already penetrated the city and robbed the shops of their finery. They killed some Turks and Jews and took many prisoners but they were suddenly attacked by the Ḳalġay, Fetḥ Girāy, and a general struggle ensued. After thirty Zaporozhians had fallen prisoner and their leader, Kulaga, had met his death, they withdrew. While these events were taking place at Gözlev, other, presumably Don, Cossacks raided the environs of Azov. These actions prompted the Sultan to send five galleys (*kadīrgā*) to the mouth of the Dnieper and three to the Crimea, equipped with cannon and filled with troops. He now ordered the Khan to attack Poland. Ġāzī Girāy, following the bidding of the Sultan, conducted a counterraid into Podolia.[35]

At this point, diplomatic relations between the Ottoman and Polish states almost broke down. The Sultan assembled a sizable force on the Polish frontier and ordered the Khan to encamp with his Tatars on the shores of the Dnieper, close to the Lithuanian border. Ġāzī Girāy, while complying with the order, sought to turn this to his own advantage. He sent word to the Tsar of the forthcoming action and suggested that he support the move with appropriate gifts of money. At the same time, the Khan, testing the friendly overtures of the Tsar, requested that Murād Girāy be released to him. The

Tsar, however, neither sent money nor released his puppet governor.[36]

A revolt of the Janissaries in 1589 brought about a significant new development at the Porte. The Sultan dismissed the Grand Vezir, Siyāvūş Pasha, and on 17 Jumadi I 997/3 April 1589 appointed in his place the old "war horse," Kōjā Sinān Pasha.[37] Furthermore, as the war in Persia was drawing to a close, a large number of troops would soon be again at the disposal of the Porte. The Grand Vezir appeared ready to open hostilities and the insolence of Poland, as well as her apparent internal troubles, made her a likely target. One dignitary, possibly Sinān Pasha, is reported to have argued that Poland had defaulted on her tribute and interfered in the affairs of the Principalities, and that a victory over Poland would provide an easy access to the Habsburg state, to the unruly Cossacks, and to Muscovy. He also argued that there was internal dissension (i.e., an Austrian invasion supported by the Zborowski faction) and that the Poles were known to have little skill in military matters. Had not even King Stephan Báthory relied heavily on Hungarian (Transylvanian) mercenaries for his successes against Moscow?[38]

While the Ottoman and Tatar forces continued to make sorties into Polish territory, Poland made an inauspicious attempt to re-establish amicable relations. A Polish ambassador arrived at the Porte on April 12, 1589. He quickly undermined the precarious position of Poland by declaring that his master neither could nor would continue to pay tribute. The unfortunate ambassador, whether through mistreatment or other mishap, died shortly thereafter.[39] The bellicose Chancellor Zamoyski reacted to these events with a fiery speech to the Polish Senate proposing an attack on the Tatars and the occupation and fortification of Moldavia on the line of the Danube.[40]

By the end of the year, reason seems to have gained the upper hand. The new Polish ambassador reported to Zamoyski that the chief cause of the recent troubles, from the point of view of the Ottomans, was the unprovoked raids of the Cossacks on Bender (Tehine), Ochakov, and Gözlev (Yevpatoriya). The Grand Vezir had laid down the terms upon which he was prepared to make peace. In particular, Poland would have to renew the annual gifts, and moreover, no resident ambassador from Poland would be acceptable.[41] The ambassador also informed the Grand Chancellor that gifts of fur and English dogs to the Beylerbey of Rumeli, who commanded the Ottoman and Tatar forces on the border, would encourage him to restrain his forces from raiding Podolia and Pocoutia (Pokutia) during the negotiations.[42] Apparently the wrath of Poland had turned to peaceful considerations when the outcome of the Persian War became generally known in the course of 1589. The Sultan even boasted of his acquisitions in a letter to King Sigismund and threatened him with total war, but, upon the mediation of the English ambassador, Edward Barton, and the Hospodar of Moldavia, Bogdan, the Sultan consented to accept a peaceful solution. A preliminary agreement was signed on May 15, 1590 and confirmed in the following year.[43] Now the Ottomans could turn their full attention to the border disturbances in Hungary, while Poland could take measures to control the turbulent Cossacks, who had been mainly responsible for the recent crisis. The settlement of the tension between Poland and the Ottoman Empire also gave to Ġāzī Girāy an opportunity to settle grievances with Moscow.[44]

4 The Attack on Moscow and the Crimean-Muscovite Settlement of 1594

Ġāzī Girāy had taken effective measures toward establishing his position in the Crimean Khanate by patching up a family feud; he had also strengthened his position on the frontiers of the Khanate by regaining the allegiance of some Nogays and by helping the Sultan to re-establish peace with Poland. The Great Nogays, through their struggle against Muscovite domination, tended to keep Don Cossack pressure off the Khanate. But the Nogay question and the attempt to establish a puppet regime in the Crimea were just two phases of a concerted attempt by Moscow to consolidate her position on the Lower Volga and to aggrandize herself at the expense of her southern neighbors who were much weaker and more politically divided than were her enemies to the west, Poland and Sweden.

While Moscow successfully contained the Nogays within a ring of fortifications, she made her next move in the direction of the Caucasus. The Persian War did not officially end until 1590. Between 1588 and 1590 considerable diplomatic activity took place between Moscow and Persia. On the one hand, the Shah sought to bring the Tsar into the conflict on his own side by promising to compensate him with territories in the Caucasus over which Persia no longer had control. On the other hand, the Tsar could not view with equanimity Ottoman political control of the Caucasus and naval control of the Caspian. The distinguished Ottoman commander in the Caucasus, 'Os̱mān Pasha, had already destroyed a Muscovite fort on the Terek in 1583. Now the Tsar, in answer to petitions from a pro-Moscow faction of the Circassians, built another fort on the Terek. Moscow also established diplomatic and trade relations with the Georgian principality of Kakheti.[45] After the accession of Shah 'Abbās I in 1587, Persia sought an overt military commitment from the Tsar, but the Muscovite ambassador to the Shah equivocated by calling attention to the inconvenience the Tsar had already caused the Sultan through his intervention in the affairs of Circassia and Kakheti. When Ferhād Bey, the governor of Isfahan, asked the Russian ambassador if the Circassians, the Şamẖal of Tarku (virtual ruler of Dagestan), and Alexander of Kakheti would make common cause with Moscow and Persia against the Turks and Tatars, the ambassador replied that pressure had been brought to bear on them to this end through the offices of Murād Girāy in Astrakhan, but that the Circassians and the Şamḫal would keep faith with the Sultan.[46] The diplomatic exchanges between Persia and Moscow bore fruit, however, in the form of a trade agreement by which Moscow undertook to provide the Shah with arquebuses and up-to-date war materials in exchange for silk and other commodities.[47]

Meanwhile the youthful Shah 'Abbās, confronted by a war on two fronts[48] and by internal dissension among the Ḳïzïlbāş amīrs, continued to seek satisfactory terms from the Ottomans. When negotiations broke down between his representative and the Ottoman Serdār, Ferhād Pasha, in 1588, the Shah wrote to the Crimean Tatar Khan, Ġāzī Girāy, asking him to act as mediator for a peace settlement between the Persian and Ottoman states. Ġāzī Girāy brought this matter to the attention of the Porte, but the Sultan declined the offer.[49]

Moscow had shown herself reluctant to provoke the Ottomans excessively during the Persian War, but she did not abandon her interest in the northern Caucasus. In fact, before the ink of the Ottoman-Persian treaty of 1590 had dried, the Muscovites made provision for the rebuilding of their fort at the mouth of the Sunzhu (1590) and initiated plans for a march against the Şamḫal, whose territories blocked their own access to Kakheti. Alexander of Kakheti, traditionally an enemy of the Şamḫal, lent strong encouragement and support to this enterprise.[50] At this time the intention of Boris Godunov, the influential brother-in-law of the Tsar, to establish a kind of hegemony over a considerable portion of the northern Caucasus and its approaches became apparent. The Ottomans were quick to recognize the threat that this policy offered to their line of communications with Dagestan across the Kuban and Terek river valleys. Thus Ġāzī Girāy had no sooner checked the strategy of Moscow on the steppe than he was forced to deal with this new threat to the Crimean-Ottoman position in the Caucasus.

In the years 1590 and 1591, the Muscovite *voyevoda* (voivode) on the Terek, Gregory Zasekin, attacked the Şamḫal and succeeded in occupying territory up to the mouth of the Koysa (Sulak). As a result of this new aggression and the construction of *ostrogs* (forts) along the Terek, both the Khan and the Sultan must have become convinced that nothing short of a campaign would serve to check the Tsar.[51] Even though the attack on the Şamḫal had been on a small scale, as an attack on their vassal, it represented a clear affront to the Ottoman Sultan and the Crimean Khan. The affront, moreover, assumes greater proportions when it is placed in the context of Crimean-Muscovite diplomacy of the period. Ġāzī Girāy commenced his reign with an expression of good will toward the Tsar. The Tsar returned this cordiality, stating that only because Ġāzī Girāy had replaced the perfidious Islām Girāy had the Crimea been spared further attacks by the Zaporozhian and Don Cossacks. Beneath this verbiage, however, as the historian Solov'ëv has indicated, the Tsar revealed in several ways the growing contempt of Moscow for the power of the Khanate. The Tsar now addressed the Khan with *poklon* (bow, salute) and not *chelobit'ye* (petition, homage) and the Khan addressed Boris Godunov as "our brother"; the value of the gifts that were customarily sent to the khan and the leading dignitaries of the khanate diminished; the customary subsistence allowance that the tsars provided for bona fide diplomatic personnel of the khan and their retinues had recently been limited to thirty individuals.[52]

Ġāzī Girāy had other grievances which he brought to the attention of the Tsar. The Sultan had complained to him about the periodic attacks of the Don Cossacks on the environs of Azov, the Ottoman outpost at the mouth of the Don. The Terek Cossacks also were harassing Ottoman troops as they passed to and from Azov and Derbent across the northern Caucasus. Moreover, the Don Cossacks had driven off Tatar cattle and horses. The Khan warned the Tsar that the Sultan would not tolerate such activity and that the Ottomans would again demolish the fort on the Terek and wage war against Moscow. But all attempts to gain material or diplomatic satisfaction from the Tsar ended in failure. Moscow, to the end of the century, continued to deny that there was any connection between the Don Cossack encroachments and the Muscovite state.[53]

Apart from the displeasure of the Sultan over Muscovite pretensions in the northern Caucasus, certain vital interests of the Crimean Khan were disturbed by the presence of Muscovy in the Kabarda. The sons of the khans dating back to the days of the Golden Horde, were customarily trained by atābegs (preceptors) from among the Besleni Circassians, a confederation of the westernmost Circassian tribes which were generally vassals of the Crimean khan. Certain of the khans also recruited their bodyguards from the Circassians and exacted a tribute in slaves, particularly from the more distant (i.e., eastern) tribes. Such slaves were frequently used to curry the favor of the Sultan or other Ottoman dignitaries. It is little wonder that the Kabardinians, an eastern Circassian tribal confederation, were forced to seek accommodation with Muscovy during the latter part of the sixteenth century. The independence of the region was threatened from the west by the Ottomans and their Crimean vassals and from the east by the Safavids and their fickle vassal, the Şamẖal of Tarku, overlord of Dagestan.[54]

Against this complex background, the mysterious death of Murād Girāy in 1590,[55] the reconstruction of the Muscovite outpost in the Kabarda, and the Muscovite-fostered attack on the Şamẖal in 1590 precipitated a crisis in the relations between Moscow and the Crimea.[56] Moreover, there were numerous precedents for an attack on the Muscovite capital.[57] Nevertheless, even if local events favored a major effort against Moscow, Ġāzī Girāy would most likely not have launched a campaign into the heart of the Muscovite state in 1591 without some prospect of assistance. The renewed outbreak of war between Moscow and Sweden in 1589 provided the Khan with a reasonable assurance that he would not have to face the entire Muscovite army. Upon the resumption of hostilities, the Swedish King dispatched an ambassador to the Crimea with promises of rich gifts and subsidies and with assurances that the presence of Swedish forces in the north would draw off the main Muscovite army from the vicinity of the capital.[58] Preparations for the Tatar campaign against Moscow began, therefore, in the winter of 1590–1591.[59]

The conflict between Moscow and Sweden had its immediate background in the Livonian War. The collapse of the political power of the Livonian Knights in the 1550s had provided the occasion for the Baltic powers—Denmark, Sweden, Poland-Lithuania and Muscovy—to lay claim to portions of the Baltic littoral. Poland seized Livonia and forced Moscow to accept this new state of affairs in the peace of 1582. Sweden, moreover, by 1581 had made good her claims to all of Estonia; thus she hoped to control the western European trade of Moscow which had formerly passed through the port of Narva. A peace treaty recognizing this gain was concluded with Moscow in 1583. By reopening hostilities in 1589, Moscow intended to contest Swedish control of Estonia and the port of Narva. The Crimean Khan was doubtless aware of the implications of the Muscovite-Swedish war. The Khan most certainly was as much interested as Poland and Sweden in blocking the flow of military supplies to Moscow.[60]

Moscow, upon hearing of the negotiations between Sweden and the Crimea, attempted at the end of 1590 to forestall any hostilities from the Khan by dispatching a courier, Bibikov, to Bağçesaray. Unfortunately for Moscow, such a last-minute bid for the favor of the Khan could not gloss over her aggressive acts on the steppe and in the Caucasus. The Khan, after receiving the gifts and the compliments of the Tsar Fyodor and Boris Godunov, failed to answer this courtesy with suitable respect. On January 11, 1591, Aḥmed Aġā, the Vezir of the Khan, came to Kyrkor, the Jewish village in which the Muscovite courier was permitted to reside, and in the name of the Khan confiscated all his property, ostensibly because he had not sent an adequate gift of furs to the Khan and because he had contacted the Mullah, the chief religious dignitary of the Crimea, against the wishes of the Khan. On May 5 the Khan informed Bibikov that the Tatars were preparing a campaign against Lithuania, not against the borderlands of Muscovy. Only late in June did official circles in Moscow learn that the attack would fall on their own domain.[61]

On July 5 the Russian *voyevody* (military governors) and their troops, situated on the banks of the Oka south of Moscow and in the border forts on the steppe, were ordered to assemble at Serpukhov under the boyar, prince Fyodor Ivanovich Mstislavsky, but, when it was learned that the Khan appeared to be advancing on the capital and would avoid the concentration of troops at Serpukhov, the boyars and *voyevody* were ordered to withdraw to the capital to take up new positions. On the morning of July 13, a Sunday,

Ġāzī Girāy Khan took up a position opposite Kolomenskoye and ordered an attack on the Muscovites. The Muscovite cavalry, consisting of Lithuanian and German mercenary troops in support of the Russian forces, met the onslaught and fought bitterly the entire day without any decisive result. That night the Khan, doubtless realizing the folly of attacking such a well-defended city without siege weapons, ordered a withdrawal. Nothing more was heard of the Tatars save for a small rearguard action below Tula. Toward the end of July the Ḳalġay, Fetẖ Girāy, reached the Crimea with a contingent of Tatars. Not until the night of August 9, however, did the Khan, riding in a wagon, reach his capital. He had apparently injured his hand before Moscow.[62]

In an audience with the Khan at the end of August, Bibikov, the Muscovite courier, was kindly received and was invited to dine with the Khan. Ġāzī Girāy explained to him that the Tatar attack on Moscow had been long overdue. One of the Tatar dignitaries present then asked Bibikov why the Tsar was establishing towns on the Terek, the Volga, and the Don. Bibikov replied that the peoples of Muscovy had multiplied and were cramped and, as the Tsar was powerful, he built new towns. The Khan then referred to what must have been known among the Tatars as a classic example of Muscovite perfidy: "Your ruler thus wishes to do as he did with Kazan: at first he established a town close by, then afterwards seized Kazan; but the Crimea is not Kazan, in the Crimea there are many hands and eyes; it will be necessary for your ruler to go beyond the towns to the very heart (of the Crimea)."[63]

In the fall the Khan sent a diplomatic mission to Moscow. Upon being questioned about the motives of his recent attack, the envoys replied that their Khan no longer asked for the return of Astrakhan or Kazan but only for the traditional tribute, as provided in previous agreements. The boyars then stated that it was the Khan, a ruler little to be trusted, who should be sending the "gifts" and that Moscow was accustomed to sending gifts in return for friendship, which the Khan had not shown towards Moscow.[64]

In May 1592, Fetẖ Girāy, the Ḳalġay, suddenly fell upon the Ryazan, Kashir, and Tula regions of the Muscovite frontier area. This raid came at a time when the Muscovite troops were concentrated in the region below Viburg, northwest of Moscow, in preparation for further conflict with Sweden.[65] The Tatars killed many people, burned villages and towns, and carried off a number of local dignitaries and their families who, not suspecting an attack, had not left their estates to take refuge in fortified towns. Afterwards the Khan told the Muscovite envoy, Bezobrazov, who had been sent in all haste to him, that the Tatars were amazed at the absence of resistance to their intrusion and that they were able to drive off the captives with lashes. The envoy then answered feebly that the Tsar had not prepared for the attack because he believed in the friendly overtures of the Khan of the previous year. In truth, however, the Tsar had been giving all his attention to the prosecution of the war against Sweden.

The Tsar had provided his envoy with sufficient funds in gold coin to make gifts to the Khan and to the chief dignitaries of the Khanate and also to purchase the freedom of the important personages who had recently been captured. Finally, the envoy received detailed instructions from the Tsar to prepare the way for serious negotiations between the Crimea and Moscow. A tentative meeting place was even suggested, the town of Livny on the Sosna, which marked the border between the territories claimed by the Tsar and the Khan.[66]

In May 1593, before sending an embassy to represent him in negotiations, Ġāzī Girāy first sent another courier, Yamgurçi Atālik, to the Tsar for preliminary bargaining. The courier requested that the Khan be sent 30,000 rubles (Novgorodok) for the construction of a fortress on the Dnieper above the rapids at the ford known as Kashkina or Dobryy, and that the widow of the deceased Murād Girāy be released to the Crimea. The reaction of court circles to the first request was understandably cautious. One *d'yak* or highly-placed scribe remarked that the "Turks" wrote many things and he wondered how their intentions could be trusted. Upon probing the courier further, the officials of the Tsar became even more baffled. Had the Khan quarreled with the Sultan? Two clues provided by the courier suggested this. In the first place, he informed the Tsar that, with regard to the removal of forts on the Terek, the Tsar need not disturb his Cossacks there, but that he should inform the Khan officially that he had evacuated the forts so that the Sultan would no longer require the Crimean Tatars to wage a campaign in that direction. In the second place, when questioned about the purpose the Khan had in building a fortress on the Dnieper, the courier gave the surprising reply that the Khan planned to abandon his seat of power in the Crimea and to establish himself on the Dnieper as a support of the Muscovite state, presumably against Poland-Lithuania and the Ottoman Empire on the pattern of the Tatars of Kasimov.[67] In truth, after the hapless attack of the Khan on Moscow, the Sultan apparently considered removing Ġāzī Girāy from the khanship. Perhaps the Khan would have been dismissed if war had not then been threatening the Ottoman Empire on its Hungarian borders.[68]

The Tsar, on the basis of these preliminary conversations, decided, after the negotiations at Livny, to send Prince Shcherbatov on to the Crimea, with gifts as in former times, valued at 40,000 rubles, consisting partly of coin and partly of furs. He also decided to release the widow of Murād Girāy to the Khan. Thus, in October 1593, Prince Shcherbatov, accompanied by the boyar, Prince Fyodor Khvorostinin, and the sword-bearer, Bogdan Bel'sky, proceeded to Livny.[69] After a preliminary disagreement over whose tent and which bank of the Sosna should serve as the point for negotiations, Prince Khvorostinin agreed with Aḥmed Pasha (Aḥmed Aġā, the Khan's Vezir), the plenipotentiary of the Khan, to hold the discussions on a bridge connecting the two shores.[70] Aḥmed Pasha swore on behalf of the Khan and his heirs to be in sincere friendship and brotherhood with the Tsar. Khvorostinin promised that if the Khan, the Ḳalġay, and all of the hānzādes stood by their word and did not attack the borderlands of Muscovy in the summer of 1594, the Tsar would send his ambassadors in the autumn with the other half of the bargain (*zapros*). Shcherbatov would deliver the first portion of this "gift."[71] Henceforth gifts would be sent each year. Furthermore, Aḥmed Pasha stated that the Tsar should order the removal of the Cossacks from the Don and the evacuation of the route leading to Derbent and Shemakha. Khvorostinin, as regards the Don Cossacks, gave the traditional answer that these people were fugitives from Moscow and that they acted contrary to the wishes of the Tsar, but since the Khan was now establishing peaceful relations with the Tsar, the latter would send his troops to remove the Cossacks from the Don. ! As for the Terek, the Tsar would send strict orders to his *voyevoda* that Ottoman troops should not be inconvenienced in any way.

In spite of the large measure of agreement between Ḳhvorostinin and Aḥmed Pasha, all was not sweetness and light when Prince Shcherbatov arrived in the Crimea with his gifts. Of the gifts, whose total value had been estimated at 40,000 rubles, the Khan received 10,000 rubles. Immediately after the distribution of this largesse, those who had not been favored by a special gift, or those who felt their portion to be inadequate, commenced to quarrel among themselves or to complain to the ambassador. In private, the Ḳalġay, Fetḥ Girāy, became particularly incensed over his portion and quarreled with the Khan, his brother: "You received much money, you alone received all, and now you go to Hungary, but I shall remain in the Crimea and I shall attack the borders of Moscow."[72]

The Khan now hesitated to give his oath, and at an audience with the ambassador he asked that the Tsar should send every year to himself and to his brother 10,000 rubles. Shcherbatov quickly parried this suggestion, however, saying that if the Khan went to Hungary without giving the oath, the Tsar would make an alliance with the King of Poland and no one would receive anything in the future. Finally, after considering the problem carefully, and doubtless recalling also that he was under pressure from the Sultan to lead troops to Hungary, Ġāzī Girāy Khan gave the oath, agreed to write the full title of the Tsar on the sworn document, and to affix his own seal to it, an official act customarily reserved for correspondence with the Ottoman Sultan only. When the ambassador suggested that a mutual exchange of prisoners might take place, Ġāzī Giray declared that it was not for the Khan to worry about such matters. If any exchanges were to be arranged, they would have to be worked out with the ẖānzādes and mīrzās directly concerned.[73]

While these negotiations were taking place with the Crimean Khan, Moscow was also making overtures to Istanbul. The envoy Nashchokin left

Moscow in April 1592. After many difficulties, Nashchokin reached Istanbul and carried out his mission. He expressed to the Sultan the desire of the Tsar for amicable ties with the Ottoman state. During his stay in the Ottoman capital, however, news arrived that the Don Cossacks had taken captive one hundred thirty men of Azov and that the Tsar had built four new forts on the Don and the Terek. Once again the dignitaries at the Porte found it necessary to threaten Moscow with the combined might of the Ottoman army, the Crimean Tatars, and the Nogays. When news of the recent attacks reached the Tsar, he threatened to fortify the Don with his own troops and to drive away the Cossacks if they continued to undermine Moscow's relations with the Sultan. The Ottoman *çāvūş* (envoy), Riżvān, who returned with Nashchokin to Moscow, repeated the complaints that the Muscovite envoy had heard in Istanbul regarding the problems arising out of conflicts with the Cossacks of the Don and the Terek. As for the Don Cossacks, the answer of the Tsar was the same, that they were merely fugitive peoples and robbers. When the new Russian ambassador Islenyev reached the Porte in July 1594, he gave a new turn to the problems of the Terek region. In justifying the construction of forts and the attacks on the Şamḫal, the Tsar now claimed that the Circassians and the peoples of Dagestan were peoples of his realm who had long ago fled to the northern Caucasus.[74]

5 Tatar-Ottoman Relations on the Eve of the Hungarian War

Prior to the years under consideration here, the Ottoman Empire had risen to the heights of its prestige and power under the illustrious Sultan Sulaymān (1520–1566), a period of great expansion during which the Ottoman frontiers had been pushed uncomfortably close to Vienna. The war with Safavid Persia (1578–1590) must be considered a continuation of that period of expansion, for Persia lost to the Sultan her influence over much of Transcaucasia including the buffer areas of Kurdistan, Georgia, and Shirvan and the outpost of Derbent in Dagestan. The twelve-year conflict, which took place on extremely difficult terrain, took its toll of the manpower, the physical resources, and the institutions of the Empire. If under Sultan Sulaymān the limits of expansion to the west had been reached, in terms of the capabilities of mobilization and logistics, the pashas of Sultan Murād III (1574–1595) doubtless overstepped that limit in the east in the long Persian War, as subsequent events were to demonstrate.

To the north of the Black Sea the Crimean Khanate, apart from rendering assistance in the expansion and defense of the Empire, attempted to keep its own buffer elements in line, whether Nogay or Circassian, and to maintain surveillance for the Ottomans over the vast expanse of steppe from Bessarabia to the Caucasus. How well the Tatars performed these tasks depended partly on the attitude of the khans towards Ottoman power and partly on how much the khans were involved with their own internal and external problems. Meḥemmed Girāy Khan guarded his own prerogatives jealously and, fearful of Cossack attacks at a time when the Ottomans were heavily committed in Persia, refused aid to the Sultan. Ġāzī Girāy Khan, who had served with the Ottomans in Persia and was therefore more aware of Ottoman capabilities than his predecessors, welcomed Ottoman assistance against his enemies and, in turn, provided almost continual Tatar support for the Ottoman armies in the Hungarian War (1593–1606).

It would appear, however, that the Ottomans relied too heavily on the Crimean khans to police the steppe in the sixteenth century, perhaps because of their enormous commitments elsewhere. They may have, thereby, missed opportunities to keep in touch with Russian methods of conquest and developments in technology—albeit often borrowed from western Europe—which helped to turn the tide against the Muslims on the steppe. The Mongol-Tatar methods of controlling the steppe through tribal loyalties and well-disciplined mobile horsemen diminished in importance in the sixteenth century as the settled peoples on the periphery of the steppe developed hand guns that could compete with the accurate Tatar bow, improved their techniques of gun foundry, built fortifications of stone, and perfected methods of moving across the steppe and down the rivers in armored wagons and boats. These were the developments that lay behind the destruction of the Nogay power at the end of the sixteenth century and also helped to make it less and less profitable for the Crimean Tatars to enrich their own marginal pastoral and agricultural economy by raids on border settlements for slaves and booty.[75]

The Polish bid in 1589 for more equitable terms with the Ottoman Empire was poorly timed. The Ottomans had just reduced their chief rival, Safavid Persia, to a second-rate power—if only for a short time—and were in no mood to tolerate Cossack attacks or changes in the *status quo* with a Poland which was deeply divided internally after three consecutive *interregna*, and which continued to face the threat of a two-front war with the Austrian Emperor and the Tsar.

In the relations between Muscovy and the Crimean Khanate, the peace agreement of 1594 provided a welcome breathing spell for these traditional rivals. Henceforth, Ġāzī Girāy Khan would be occupied with his role in the Hungarian War. As for the three-sided rivalry in the Caucasus among the Tsar, the Shah, and the Sultan, the bilateral exchanges of envoys between the Porte and Moscow had produced little of substance. At best, there existed among the three states an armed truce which soon worked out to the advantage of Persia under the able leadership of Shah'Abbās, for Muscovy was entering her "Time of Troubles," and the Ottomans and Crimean Tatars were fully occupied with internal strife and the Hungarian War.

NOTES

1. These problems are discussed by H. Inalcïk, "Osmanlï-Rus Rekabetinin Menşei ve Don-Volga Kanalï Teşebbüsü (1569)," *Belleten*, XII/46 (1948), pp. 349–402; A. A. Novosel'skiy, *Bor'ba Moskovskogo Gosudarstva s Tatarami v pervoy polovine xvii veka*; and V. D. Smirnov, *Krymskoe Khanstvo pod verkhovenstvom otomanskoy Porti do nachala xviii veka.*

2. For an early but creditable treatment of Crimean Tatar history in this period, see H. Howorth, *History of the Mongols*, Part II, pp. 448–538. See also Inalcïk, "Ġāzī Girāy," and "Girāy," *I.A.*, IV, pp. 734–736, 783–789.

3. *Ibid.*; Inalcïk, "Osmanlï-Rus Rekabeti . . . ," *Belleten* XII (1948), *passim.*

4. Islām Girāy had been a *rehin* or hostage. Traditionally the sultan detained certain members of the ruling khan's family in the environs of Istanbul, both to ensure that the will of the sultan would be obeyed and also to protect any given branch of the ruling family from extermination at the hands of a vengeful relative. See Inalcïk, "Girāy," *loc. cit.*

5. Solov'ëv, *Istoriya Rossii*, VII, p. 259, citing archive *Krymskie Dela*, Nos. 16–21; for a full explanation of Ottoman terminology, consult Gibb and Bowen, *Islamic Society and the West*, I/1 and 2.

6. The Nogays, a tribal confederation dating back to the days of the Golden Horde, had pastured their livestock traditionally on the steppe in the Don-Volga-Ural (Yaik) basin. Their khans had long played a role in the affairs of the Khanate of Astrakhan which was overthrown by Muscovy in 1556. After Russian penetration of the area, a polarization developed among the Nogays. The *Ulu* or Great Nogays partly drifted and partly were forced into the Muscovite orbit while the *Kiçi* (rump) or Little Nogays (called Kazi- [Kassai] oğullarï, "sons of Kazi or Kassai") entered the Ottoman-Crimean sphere. See Howorth, pp. 1033–1043 and 1050–1053; Inalcïk, "Osmanlï-Rus Rekabeti . . . ," *Belleten*, XII (1948), p. 362; Spuler, "Astrakhan," *E.I.*², I, pp. 721–722.

7. Novosel'skiy, pp. 35 ff.

8. See Inalcïk, "Islām Girāy," *I.A.*, V, p. 1105; Howorth, II/1, pp. 515–523; Kazimirski, "Précis de l'histoire des Khans de Crimée," *Journal Asiatique*, Ser. 2, XII (Paris, 1833), p. 380. M. Karamsin, in his *Histoire de l'Empire de Russie*, X, pp. 76–77, states that the Russian towns of Belėv and Kozelsk were attacked and that Krapivna was seized.

9. See H. Girāy, *Gülbün-ü Ḫānān*, p. 58; also Inalcïk, "Islām Girāy," *loc. cit.*

10. Solov'ëv, *loc. cit.*; Barton to Walsingham, *Calendar of State Papers*, XXIII, p. 134; Braudet, "Les Origines de la candidature de Sigismund Vasa au trône de Pologne en 1587," *Annales Academiae Scientiarum Fennicae*, Ser. B, II/10, pp. 1–82.

11. Cf. letter of Jan Zamoyski to the Sultan (April 22, 1588) in Hurmuzaki, ed., *Documente privitóre la Istoria Romanilor*, Suppl. II/I, p. 295, with Selānīkī, *Tārīḫ-i Selānīkī*, pp. 241–242.

12. Solov'ëv, VII, p. 28; Soranzo, *L'Ottomano*, pp. 52ʳ–53ᵛ. For a description of the Cossacks, see Vernadsky, *Russia at the Dawn of the Modern Age*, pp. 249–268.

13. As puppet governor of Astrakhan, Murād Girāy helped the Tsar reduce the Great Nogays to obedience. Nevertheless, from beginning to end the puppet was never trusted. Whether he was negotiating, praying in the mosque, or decorating various tribesmen for special services, he was always under the close supervision of the real authorities, R. M. Pivov and M. I. Burtsov. See Novosel'skiy, p. 35.

14. Selānīkī, pp. 229–230. The Muscovites had expected some kind of Ottoman action against them in 1586. Murād Girāy had told the Tsar that he expected the Ottomans to build a fortified town on the Terek. See Belokurov, *Snosheniya Rossii s Kavkazom, 1578–1613*, p. xcvii. It is more likely that the Ottomans, rather than build a town, continued to rely on amicable relations with the local peoples, relations that were overshadowed, of course, by the grandeur and might of the Ottomans.

15. Solov'ëv, VII, pp. 259–260.

16. Contrary to a report that Islām Girāy was about to attack Moscow (Inalcïk, Osmanli-Rus Rekabeti . . . ," *Belleten*, XII, p. 395), which is based on the Selānīkī report (Selānīkī, p. 242),

it would appear that the Khan contemplated an attack on the Polish-Lithuanian borders. He died on April 1, 1588, at Tehine, according to a Polish account. Cf. Zamoyski to Radziwill (April 24, 1588), *Archivum Jana Zamoyskiego*, IV, pp. 198–199. It was believed that the Khan had been poisoned, according to J. von Hammer, *Histoire de l'Empire Ottoman*, VII, p. 207.

17. Karamsin, X, p. 144, citing archive *Krymskiye Dela*, 17, Moscow; Selānīkī, pp. 241–242; Inalcïk, "Osmanlï-Rus Rekabeti . . . ," *Belleten*, XII, p. 394. For a reference to the financial aid that Moscow managed to give Kakheti and Persia at the close of the Ottoman-Persian War, see the account of Jerome Horsey in Fletcher, *Russe Commonwealth*, extra ser., Hakluyt Society ed., pp. 223–224.

18. Selānīki, p. 242; 'Abd al Ġaffār, *Umdet ül-Aḫbār*, (N. Asim ed.) *T.T.E.M.* (and before 1920 *T.O.E.M.*), No. 85, Suppl. 2, p. 115. Edward Barton, the English ambassador, implied to the contrary, that Ġāzī Girāy sought the appointment from the Sultan (*C.S.P.*, Foreign, XXII, p. 174).

19. Selānīkī, p. 242; Howorth, II, pp. 523–524. Cf. M. de Lancosme to Henri III in Charrière, ed., *Négociations de la France dans le Levant*, IV, pp. 662–663, and Jan Zamoyski to the Sultan in Hurmuzaki, *loc. cit.*

20. Charrière, *loc. cit.* To the post of Ḳalġay or next in succession to the khanship, the reigning khan, by custom, usually appointed an able younger brother; to the post of Nūr ed-Dīn or third in the line of succession, the khan often appointed his eldest son. For further details, see Inalcïk, "Ḳalġay," *I.A.*., VI, pp. 131–132.

21. Meḥemmed Riżā, *Es-Seb' es-Seyyār*, pp. 107–108. On the basis of numismatic evidence, it would seem that Ġāzī Girāy first established his court and coined money at Gözlev (Yevpatoriya), perhaps because of local resistance in the interior. See O. Retovskiy, "Moneti Gazi-Geraya Khana II ben Devlet," (*Izvestiya Tavricheskoy Uchonoy Arkhivnoy Kommissii*, 8 (Sebastopol, 1889), pp. 90–98).

22. Cf. Novosel'skiy, pp. 33–37, and Inalcïk, "Osmanlï-Rus Rekabeti . . . ," *Belleten*, XII, p. 395 and Pl. VII. Inalcïk states that the initiative came from the fugitive ẖānzādes. Murād Girāy had secretly informed the Sultan of his intention to escape from Astrakhan and to cooperate with his uncle, Ġāzi Girāy (Mühimme Defterleri, 64/262 [996/1588]).

23. Forts were built at Ufa and Samara in 1586, at Tsaritsyn in 1589, and at Saratov in 1590, according to Novosel'skiy, pp. 28, 34–36, 40. See also the conversation of the Russian ambassador Vasilchikov and the Khan of Gilan (October, 1588) in Vesselovskiy, ed., "Pamyatniki Diplomaticheskikh i Torgovlennykh Snosheniy Moskovskoy Rusi s Persiey," *Trudy Vostoch. Otdel. Imperat. Russk. Arkheolog. Obshch.*, XX, pp. 52–53.

24. Novosel'skiy, pp. 35–37. These two protagonists within the Great Nogay Horde fought over the right of succession to the khanship during the 1590s and the early years of the 17th century; the Tīn Aḥmed faction upheld the principle of the seniority of the Tīn Aḥmed line while the Urus faction supported the principle of the seniority of age—Yanārāslān Mīrzā being older than his cousins. These considerations apart, Urus Khan was an outspoken enemy of Moscow and advocate of an independent Nogay confederation which would presumably maintain traditional ties with its Muslim neighbors. This accounts for the policy of repression that Moscow relentlessly pursued against the Urus Khan faction from 1590 until their power of resistance was broken. The rigged election of Işterek Mīrzā as khan in 1600 marked the ascendancy of Moscow over the Great Nogays.

25. R. Knolles, *General Historie of the Turkes from the first beginning of that Nation*, p. 1004.

26. Solov'ëv, VII, p. 260; the registered Cossacks were those enrolled by the Polish state to protect the frontiers.

27. Knolles, p. 1013. Poland was particularly interested in regaining free access to the Black Sea, as subsequent events were to indicate.

28. *C.S.P.*, XXI, p. 650. See also letter of Murād III to Queen Elizabeth (June 1590), tr. by B. Lewis in "The Ottoman Archives, a Source for European History," *Report on Current Research*,

pp. 23–25.

29. *Ibid.*; also Pezzen to the Emperor (November 30, 1588), Hurmuzaki, Suppl. I, p. 714, and Mühimme 64/247 (996/1588).

30. Barton to Walsingham (?), (October 25, 1588), *C.S.P.*, Foreign, XXII, pp. 281–282; Pezzen to the Emperor (November 30, 1588) and Pezzen to Archduke Ernst (June 21, 1589), Hurmuzaki, ed., Suppl. I, pp. 719, 725–726. See also Mühimme 64/365 (Zi'l-Hijje 996/Nov. 1588).

31. Hrushevskiy, *Istoriya Ukrayni-Rusi*, VII, p. 172.

32. Knolles, p. 1013; dispatch of Barton to London (August 15, 1588), *C.S.P.*, Foreign, XXII, p. 139. For a summary of the agreement made in 1578, see Hammer, *Histoire*, VII, p. 45. According to Soranzo, *L'Ottomano*, pp. 36[v]–37[r], Poland at this time was supposed to pay the Ottomans an annual tribute in furs valued at 25,000 crowns.

33. Cf. Spooner, *L'Economie Mondiale et les Frappes Monétaires en France, 1493–1680*, pp. 19–35, 319–331 and *passim*; Lewis, *The Emergence of Modern Turkey*, pp. 27–30; and Beldiceanu, "La crise monetaire ottomane au XVIe siècle et son influence sur les principautés roumaines," [*Südost-Forschungen*, XVI (Munich, 1957), pp. 70–86].

34. For a discussion of Cossack terminology in this period of history see O. Pritsak, "Das erste türkische-ukrainische Bündnis (1648)," *Oriens*, VI (Leiden, 1953), pp. 266–298.

35. Details of this raid are found in *Vraye Relation de la Route et Deffaicte des Tartares et Turcs* and in Solov'ëv, VII, pp. 261–262. The sources concerning this raid and particularly the ensuing clash are rather contradictory. Kazimirski (*Précis*, p. 428) reports that the Tatar counterraid brought in rich booty. Sagredo, in *Histoire de l'Empire Ottoman*, IV, p. 352, mentions that the Sultan rewarded Gāzī Girāy with a jeweled sword for his services on this occasion. Selānīkī (p. 257) confirms this report. In a dispatch to Archduke Ernst (August 18, 1589), the Habsburg ambassador Pezzen reports that 7,000 Tatars lay dead in Podolia (Hurmuzaki, Suppl. I, p. 728). The account *Vraye Relation* extols the deeds of the Poles. Quite obviously both sides claimed a victory.

36. Solov'ëv, *loc. cit.* Hammer (*Histoire*, VII, p. 253) states that the Porte was chagrined at the Poles—among other reasons, for having released their Habsburg captive, Archduke Maximilian. The Zborowski family had struggled unsuccessfully with the Zamoyskis to place the Habsburg candidate on the throne, a move which the Sultan had opposed. Cf. on this subject Caro, *Das Interregnum Polens im Jahre 1587*; Novak, "The Interregna and Stephan Báthory, 1572–1586," *Cambridge History of Poland to 1696*, pp. 369–391; and Halecki, *A History of Poland*, pp. 135–137.

37. See Hammer, *Histoire*, VII, p. 237.

38. Knolles, p. 1013.

39. Polish ambassador to Zamoyski, December 28, 1589, Hurmuzaki, ed., Suppl. II/i, p. 305; Hammer, *Histoire*, VII, pp. 253–254.

40. Zamoyski to the Senate, October 16, 1589, Hurmuzaki, ed., Suppl. II/i, p. 302.

41. The Ottomans allowed only those countries with whom they had capitulation agreements to maintain resident representatives.

42. Cf. Polish ambassador to Zamoyski, December 28, 1589, Hurmuzaki, Suppl. II/i, p. 305; von Hallegk to Archduke Karl (Carol), January 12, 1590, *Ibid.*, XI, p. 211; and the letter of the Beylerbey of Rumeli to Zamoyski, *Vraye Relation*, pp. 14–15.

43. Hammer, *Histoire*, VII, p. 254. Hrushevsky (*A History of the Ukraine*, p. 181) gives the false impression that the Ottomans were forced to make peace because of the Cossack raids. See also, in this regard, the letter of Murād III to Queen Elizabeth cited in note 28 above. For partial texts of the negotiations and the treaties, see Abrahamowicz, *Katalog Rekopisow Orientalnych Za Zbiorow Polskich, I: Katalog Dokumentow Tureckich . . . 1455–1672*, pp. 224–227. England was interested particularly in the movement of Moldavian cattle to England via Poland. Cf. Braudel, *La Méditerrané et le Monde Méditerranéen à la Epoque de Philippe II*, p. 149.

44. See Velyaminov-Zernov, *Materiali dlya Istorii Ḳrymskago Khanstva*, pp. 9–12, for a copy of the offensive and defensive understanding made between the Khan and the King of Poland in the spring of 1592.

45. According to Allen, *History of the Georgian People*, p. 164, the first contacts between Moscow and Kakheti took place at the Cossack fort of Terki, at the mouth of the Terek in 1586.
46. Vesselovskiy, ed., pp. 53–54 and 91. The Ottomans maintained sizable army units at several points in the Caucasus at this time.
47. Sagredo, IV, pp. 371–372.
48. Herat had fallen to the forces of Abdullah Khan, ruler of the Uzbegs, in 1588 (Bellan, *Chah 'Abbas I*, pp. 24 ff.).
49. Sagredo, IV, p. 347. Ġāzī Girāy, a captive of the Persians from 1581 to 1585, was well known to the Persian court. For an account of Persian attempts to woo the Crimean Tatars, see Roemer, *Der Niedergang Irans*, pp. 51 ff.
50. See the important letter of the Tsar to Mamstryuk Temryuk in Kumykov and Kusheva, eds., *Kabardino-Russkiye Otnosheniya v xvi–xvii vv*, I, p. 65 and n. 141; see also Novosel'skiy, p. 41. The Shah's envoy had urged the Tsar to put pressure on the Terek supply route of the Ottomans (Vesselovskiy, XXI, pp. 5–6). For the Georgian side, see Allen, *History of the Georgian People*, pp. 152, 164.
51. The attack on the Şamẖal was renewed in the years 1593 and 1594, but after initial successes, including the sack of Tarku, the Muscovite forces under A. Khvorstinin sustained heavy losses and were forced to withdraw. See Kumykov and Kusheva, *loc. cit.*, and Solov'ëv, VII, pp. 278–279, 291.
52. Ġāzī Girāy was informed of this latter restriction early in his reign. See Solov'ëv, VII, pp. 260–261.
53. *Ibid.*, p. 262.
54. Cahen "Atabak (Atabeg)" *E.I.*, I, pp. 731–732; Belokurov, *Snosheniya*, p. xxxvii; Bala, "Çerkesler," *I.A.*, III, p. 380; and M. A. Polievktov, "Iz perepiski severno-kavkazskikh feodalov xvii veka," *XLV Akademiku N. Ya. Marru*, pp. 745–756.
55. From the account of the death of Murād Girāy found in M. A. Obolenskiy's edition of the *Novyy Letopisets*, pp. 30–31, one is tempted to conclude that the cause of his death was bloodletting and not poison administered by members of the Little Nogay (Kazioğlu) faction. Cf. Novosel'skiy, pp. 33–36.
56. Kumykov and Kusheva, I, p. 401. For further interesting details regarding Circassia, see Namitok, "The 'Voluntary' Adherence of Kabarda to Russia," *Caucasian Review*, 2 (Munich, 1956), pp. 20–22.
57. For example, Devlet Girāy Khan had burned Moscow in 1571.
58. Information regarding negotiations between the Swedish envoys and the Crimean Tatars is to be found in Novosel'skiy, p. 41, citing archive *Krymske Knigi*, Moscow, No. 19, ff. 109, secure unchallenged access to the Arctic Sea across the Finnish wastes, enabling Sweden to interfere for mention of a Swedish mission to the Crimea. Unfortunately, before the year 1637, no Swedish archival material relating to the Crimean Tatars appears to have survived. Cf. Zettersteen, *Türkische, Tatarische und Persische Urkunden im Schwedischen Reichsarchiv*, p. xiii.
59. The treaty between Moscow and Sweden was due to expire on January 1, (OS) 1590. The Polish interregnum and the subsequent clash with the Habsburgs had at this time conveniently distracted the attention of Poland-Lithuania from her eastern borders. Nevertheless, Moscow went out of its way to assure Poland that there would be no violation of her border. Cf. Karamsin, X, pp. 144–156, 195–197; J. von Pastor, *History of the Popes from the Close of the Middle Ages*, XXII, pp. 162–163; and Solov'ëv, VII, pp. 262–263.
60. One very important objective of Sweden in the war beginning in 1589 was apparently to secure unchallenged access to the Artic Sea across the Finnish wastes, enabling Sweden to interfere with the trade between Moscow and England through St. Nicholas (near Archangelsk). Sweden, for a time, realized her goal in the Peace of Täysinä of 1595, the agreement that officially ended the conflict of Sweden with Moscow. See Roberts, *Gustavus Adolphus, A History of Sweden, 1611–1632*, I, pp. 11–13.
61. Cf. Obolensky, ed., *Novy Letopisets*, pp. 36–37, and Solov'ëv, VII, p. 263. Karamsin (X,

pp. 198–203) gives an excellent account of the improvisations that the Muscovites undertook prior to the Tatar onslaught.

62. Karamsin (X, p. 204) calls particular attention to the effective use the defenders made of arquebuses. The Russian version attributes the sudden Tatar withdrawal to the news, which Ġāzī Girāy acquired from prisoners, that the main Muscovite army fighting the Swedes in the north was coming to the aid of Moscow. These events are detailed in the Mühimme Defterleri, 67/429 (29 Zi'l-Ka'de 999/18 Sept. 1591) and 68/61 (9 Şeval 999/31 July 1591).

63. Solov'ëv, VII, pp. 264–265. According to Karamsin (X, p. 230), Ġāzī Girāy received a sharp reproach from Sultan Murād for having taken flight from Moscow. The implication was that he had dishonored the accompanying Ottoman troops. The Khan had another reason to rue his sudden withdrawal from Moscow. When his envoy, a certain Çerkes Anton, was sent to Sweden in the following year to collect the gold that had been promised, King John put him off with the words, "Gold is ready for the victor," (Karamsin, X, pp. 224–225; citing archive *Krymskie Dela*, No. 19). The "Relazione . . . di Lorenzo Bernardo" (1592) in Alberi, ed., *Le Relazioni degli Ambasciatori Veneti al Senato durante il secolo decimosesto*, Ser. III/II, p. 386, confirms Karamsin's report. The Porte considered that the Tatars had behaved in cowardly fashion. Bernardo, in passing, also mentioned what good arquebuses and artillery the Muscovites possessed. For a more specific reference to Ottoman troops from Azov and Akkerman who took part in this campaign, see Karamsin, X, p. 197.

64. Here it appears that the Khan was simply trying to renew previous remunerative agreements with the Muscovite state and, at the same time, to set forth other grievances. Cf. Solov'ëv, VII, pp. 265–271.

65. Obolensky, ed., p. 39.

66. Solov'ëv, VII, pp. 265–271.

67. For a copy of the actual document, see Lashkov, *Pamyatniki Diplomaticheskikh Snosheniy Krymskago Khanstva s Moskovskim Gosudarstvom v xvi i xvii vv.*, No. 27 (May 1593), pp. 29–31. In place of 30,000 rubles, the figure of Solov'ëv (*loc. cit.*), the document mentions 30,000 "novgorodok," the Russian feminine plural form of "novgorodka," a coin that was highly prized for its silver content in the late 15th and early 16th centuries, but which was debased thereafter. Cf. art. "Novgorodka," E. Andreyevsky, ed., *Entsiklopedicheskiy Slovar*, XXI, p. 235.

68. In the view of Karamsin (X, pp. 231 ff.), this was simply another attempt on the part of Ġāzī Girāy to deceive the Tsar. But there were always factions at the Ottoman court putting pressure on the sultan to remove any given khan. Typical of this sort of intrigue is the attempt by Mubārek Girāy, the former Nūr ed-Dīn of Islām Girāy Khan, to have his brother, Alp Girāy, named Khan and himself Ḳalġay. (Mubārek Girāy, it is to be recalled, fled to the Caucasus when his brother, Ġāzī Girāy, became Khan.) When his designs on the position of Ġāzī Girāy failed to find favor at the Porte, he then requested troops, money, and equipment to embark on a campaign to seize control of the Muscovite positions in the northern Caucasus. This project appealed to the Sultan and plans were well advanced when Mubārek suddenly died (c. autumn 1592). Now the pro-Ottoman faction of the Circassians petitioned the Sultan to equip them with arms and provisions to drive out the Muscovites. For details of these developments, see the dispatch of G. A. Nashchokin to the Tsar, in Kumykov and Kusheva, I, pp. 68–69.

69. For an interesting discussion of this question, see Solov'ëv, VII, p. 268.

70. The text of this agreement, concluded on November 9, 1593, near Livny, may be found in Lashkov, No. 30, pp. 35–36.

71. Prince Shcherbatov actually delivered a letter to the Khan from the Tsar accepting, in principle, the secret proposals placed before him regarding the establishment of the Khan on the Dnieper in a position to be independent of the support of the Sultan. See Lashkov, No. 28 (October 1593), pp. 31–34. The conclusion of the Livny agreement is also mentioned in the chronicle of Ivan Timofeyev (Derzhavin, ed., *Vremennik Ivana Timofeyeva*, pp. 224–225).

72. Shcherbatov heard about this quarrel from an old Russian captive who lived among the

millers of a certain mīrzā (Solov'ëv, VII, pp. 269–270).

73. This document also appears in Lashkov, No. 31, pp. 36-40. According to Novosel'skiy (pp. 41–42), this agreement was signed on April 14, 1594. The Khan, however, assumed no responsibility for the actions of the Little Nogays (Kazīoğlu) or the Azov garrison of the Ottomans.

74. Islenyev brought a letter from the Tsar in which the latter agreed to restrain the Cossacks in order to permit the free passage of Ottomans to and from Derbent if the Sultan would restrain Ġāzī Girāy. The Tsar also took upon himself the task of quieting the inhabitants of the Circassian mountains whom he claimed "were our ancient inhabitants of Ryazan." (!) See Karamsin, X, pp. 235–236.

75. See Kerner, *The Urge to the Sea*, *passim*; Lattimore, "Inner Asian Frontiers," *J. of Econ. Hist.*, VII, (May 1, 1947), pp. 24–52; and the conclusion of Novosel'skiy, pp. 416–422.

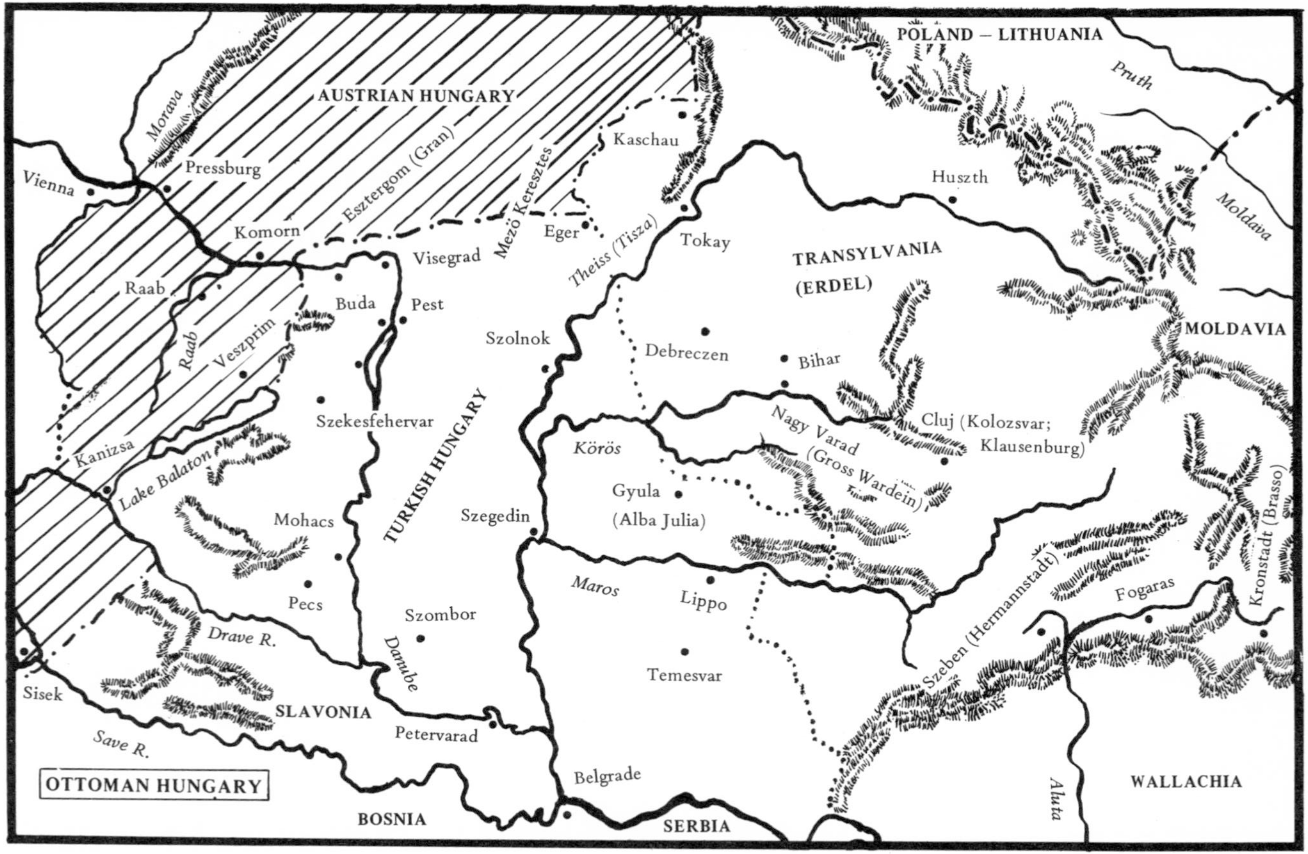

OTTOMAN HUNGARY
AUSTRIAN HUNGARY
POLAND – LITHUANIA
TRANSYLVANIA
(ERDEL)
MOLDAVIA
WALLACHIA
TURKISH HUNGARY
SLAVONIA
BOSNIA
SERBIA
Vienna
Pressburg
Morava
Komorn
Raab
Raab
Veszprim
Esztergom (Gran)
Visegrad
Buda
Pest
Mezö Keresztes
Eger
Kaschau
Tokay
Theiss (Tisza)
Szolnok
Debreczen
Bihar
Huszth
Pruth
Moldava
Szekesfehervar
Kanizsa
Lake Balaton
Mohacs
Pecs
Drave R.
Sisek
Save R.
Szombor
Danube
Petervarad
Belgrade
Szegedin
Körös
Gyula
(Alba Julia)
Nagy Varad
(Gross Wardein)
Cluj (Kolozsvar;
Klausenburg)
Maros
Lippo
Temesvar
Szeben (Hermannstadt)
Fogaras
Kronstadt (Brasso)
Aluta

CHAPTER SEVEN
Social and Political Unrest in Eastern Europe and the First Years of the Hungarian War (1593–1596)

1 The Background

By the end of the fifteenth century Ottoman power had increased decisively in the Balkan peninsula. This fact was soon to become apparent as the Ottoman Empire rolled back the buffer zones and occupied central Hungary. The three main centers of Christian resistance in Eastern Europe—Albania, Poland, and finally the Kingdom of Hungary—came to realize the futility of resisting Muslim arms and were forced to make accommodations favorable to the Turks. The resistance of the Albanian tribes, which was financed by the Papacy, had collapsed after the death of their famed leader Skanderbeg (d. 1467).[1] Jagellon Poland, which had earlier worked out a political union with Lithuania, was considered the chief power on the northern shores of the Black Sea almost to the end of the fifteenth century. Before the Genoese were eliminated as a separate power on the Black Sea by Sultan Meḥemmed II (1451–1481), they had cooperated with Poland in the economic domination of such states as Moldavia and the Crimean Khanate. While the Ottomans continued to recognize a kind of special position for Poland in Moldavia in exchange for Polish and Moldavian tribute, any thoughts of a Polish hegemony on the Black Sea were eliminated with the capture of Genoese Kaffa in 1475, the submission of the Crimean Tatars to the Ottomans in 1478, and a series of Ottoman-Polish clashes in the 1490s.

The third traditional center of resistance to the Ottoman advance was the Hungary of John Hunyadi (d. 1456) and his son, King Matthias Corvinus (d. 1490). But the erosion of royal power by the so-called magnate class began to weaken the throne in Hungary as it had in Poland. In fact after 1490 the Hungarian magnates placed a Polish Jagellon on the Hungarian throne but, contrary to what one might expect, the family ties between the monarchs of Hungary and Poland produced no visible strengthening of frontiers against Ottoman encroachments. One by one the border states of Serbia, Wallachia, and Moldavia were wrenched from Budapest or Cracow and added to the Ottoman sphere. Once the Ottomans had defeated decisively their eastern rival, Safavid Persia, at Chaldiran in 1514, and annexed the Mamluk Kingdom in 1517, they were in a good position to deal with problems as they arose on their Balkan frontiers.[2]

The ultimate destruction and occupation of much of the Kingdom of Hungary by the Ottomans took place during the Sultanate of Sulaymān the Magnificent (1520–1566). Moreover, the fall of Hungary was closely linked to the Renaissance and Reformation politics of central Europe. The church had made a serious attempt to reform itself with the Fifth Lateran Council (1512–1517) which was instigated by Pope Julius II. Upon the death of Pope Julius, the less reform-minded and more militaristic Giovanni de Medici was elected Pope Leo X. Thereafter, the reforming elements of the Council, and principally the German bishops, were neutralized and the Council ended its deliberations in 1517, not by treating the internal ills of Christendom, but by humiliating France and calling for a new crusade against the Turks. Ironically, in the years ahead the alliance of France with Ottoman Turkey, the reform movement in Germany begun by Martin Luther at Wittenberg in 1517, and Ottoman measures against the "Crusade Mentality" of the Papacy and the Habsburgs brought about important changes in the power relationships of all western Europe and spelled the end of independent Hungary.[3]

Locally the internal instability of Hungary had become fully apparent when the Voivode of Transylvania, John Zápolyai, was called upon by King Vladislav of Hungary to suppress the Dosza peasant revolt of 1514. Vladislav's successor, King Louis II (1516–1526), showed his utter disregard for Ottoman sensibilities or power by having a Turkish envoy murdered. Understandably the Ottomans reacted sharply when measures for a Crusade came under discussion in Rome in 1517.[4] Sultan Sulaymān began to put pressure on his western borders by seizing Belgrade in 1521, the Island of Rhodes in 1522, and Szaboc in 1524. After quelling a revolt in Egypt, the Ottomans destroyed King Louis and his army on the Plains of Mohács in 1526. Meanwhile, the Voivode of Transylvania craftily kept his forces out of the foray.

Even at this late date, it is clear that the Sultan would have been content to permit a neutral Hungarian Kingdom to exist on his borders if only the Papacy and the Habsburgs had foregone the temptation to place a Habsburg on the Hungarian throne, but the Habsburgs were impatient in the sixteenth century; thus they were forced to learn some harsh political lessons from the Ottomans. Emperor Charles V (1519–1556) had purchased his election as Holy Roman Emperor of the German Nation with Fugger money in competition with Francis I, King of France. Before the Protestant Reformation got out of hand, he sought to increase his possessions in Italy, again at the expense of France. But his Italian adventures were checked when the Imperial Diet refused to vote either funds or feudal troop levies. Furthermore, a growing number of German princes had joined the reform movement of the monk, Martin Luther, hence revealing clearly the deep-seated grievances of the German laity and clergy against Roman clerical and Habsburg imperial policies. The collapse at Mohács precipitated a serious political crisis for central Europe which the Habsburgs, supported by the Papacy, attempted to exploit by bidding for the Hungarian crown.

2 The Social Climate of Hungary in the Sixteenth Century

The allocation of power among nations is very seldom, if ever, altered peacefully, nor does one state forget easily a position of eminence previously attained. Moreover, downtrodden classes retain in their collective memory recollections of former persecutors whose deeds are avenged overtly or covertly, depending upon the relative peacefulness of any age.

The Papacy and the Habsburgs could not forget that prior to 1517 and 1526 there had been a veneer of spiritual unity and political hegemony emanating from Rome and Prague. Memories of the grandeur of the Hungarian monarchy in the days of the Hunyadis also lived on at the court of the princes of Transylvania whether at Lippa or Alba Julia. Transylvania, the only part of the former Hungarian Kingdom permitted a precarious independence under Ottoman protection, consisted of three legal estates: the Magyar nobility, the impoverished Szekelys (who traced their position as elite border guards back to the time of the Mongol invasion), and the German-speaking Saxons, who controlled much of the commerce and industry and were the farmers par excellence of the Transylvanian plains.

After the bloody suppression by John Zápolyai and his fellow magnates of the Dosza peasant revolt, the polarization of classes received added impetus. This result became readily apparent from the anti-peasant enactments of the "Savage Diet" and from the *Tripartitum*, the codification of the Hungarian customary law.[5] The nobility was split into "magnate" and "petty" categories, but most noblemen sought distinctions for themselves at the expense of their hapless serfs. Moreover, the semi-peasant Szekelys (Szeklers) were beginning to lose their ancient privileges. The Vlachs dwelling largely in the Transylvanian alpine regions had no status at all. One may not push these distinctions too far, but it is such dreams of grandeur and such class rivalries that lie behind the complex events which unfold in Hungary at the end of the sixteenth century when Emperor Rudolph II (1576–1608), who was personally preoccupied by astrology and fears for his life, prosecuted a "holy war" against the Turks and anyone in Hungary who dared abandon the true faith for some Lutheran or Calvinist substitute.

While it would be an oversimplification to state that Ottoman successes derived only from the dreams of grandeur and the perpetuation of social injustice on the part of Habsburg and Hungarian grandees, an understanding of the social history of Greater Hungary in the sixteenth century is an essential element. In particular, the rapidity with which the Reformation propaganda took root in Hungary serves as a register of social and class grievances. The sons of Magyar noblemen or of Saxon burghers, who had studied at German universities—notably Wittenberg—vied with merchants in the spreading of Reformation ideas in Hungary. The Saxons were early attracted to the new ideas; the Magyars, suffering from an understandable Germanophobia, absorbed the revolutionary doctrines somewhat more cautiously until the Turks actually assumed control over Hungarian affairs after the death of John Zápolyai.

A few landmarks of the Reformation in Transylvania serve to illustrate why the principality became an important target of the Counter Reformation after the Peace of Augsburg (1555). Already in the year 1542 the wealth of the Catholic bishopric of Transylvania had been secularized. Ironically, however, the wealth went to the grandees of the principality, not to the Protestant churches. In 1550, a full five years before the Peace of Augsburg, Lutheranism became a "tolerated," indeed, the dominant faith of Transylvania. At about the same time Debreczen became the center of the Calvinist movement in Hungary. In 1559, the clergy of Kolozsvar (Cluj, Klausenburg) opted for Calvinism which quickly became known as the "Hungarian" religion to distinguish it from the "German" religion or Lutheranism, the sect of Protestantism adopted by the Transylvanian Saxons. A final separation of the two sects took place in Transylvania in 1564, at which time all three "faiths" were recognized by the Transylvanian Diet. This show of tolerance was short-lived. The year 1566 saw the banishment of Catholic priests from the principality; in 1572 extremist Unitarians were outlawed. During the sixties the final phase of the Reformation fever produced the Unitarian and Sabbatarian sects. All sects but the extreme Unitarians or Sabbatarians received official sanction in 1572.[6]

In many respects, Transylvania serves as the "hot house" of Hungarian political and social development in the sixteenth century. With the tripartite division of Hungary after the death of John Zápolyai in 1541, the Habsburgs controlled the narrow northwestern borders of Hungary where Catholicism, protected by the weight of the Habsburg state, retained all of its prerogatives. In central Hungary, the Ottoman *beylerbeylik* of Buda, the cities tended toward Calvinism while the countryside gave up the old faith more reluctantly, following the lead of the magnates.[7]

The Ottomans appear to have paid little attention to such matters, but they were always attentive to the building of mosques and the spreading of Islam. In Transylvania, by contrast, the various Protestant sects enjoyed almost complete freedom to develop. At first, after the death of the elder Zápolyai in 1541, the affairs of state rested with the monk George Martinuzzi, the nominal State Treasurer. Until his death he managed to keep on good terms with the Ottomans while protecting, when possible, Catholic and Habsburg interests in Transylvania. With the murder of Martinuzzi in 1551, Isabella, the widow of John Zápolyai, served as the regent for her son, John Sigismund. She died in 1559 at the age of forty, leaving her twenty-year-old son as the ineffectual tool of court factions until his death in 1571. It was during his voivodeship—the Prince favored Unitarians—that Protestant sectarianism enjoyed its heyday.

Underneath the surface of Transylvanian court life, however, developments were taking place that would shape the destiny of Transylvania at the end of the century. Already in the 1540s, members of a number of Western Hungarian families, which had been prominent in regions occupied by the Turks, appeared in Transylvania and were given important posts at court in Alba Julia. Such a migration thus accounts for the reinforcement of the Piast or protonationalist feeling of the Hungarians in Transylvania in the sixteenth century. The Transylvanian Diet also continued to serve as an institution for nominating and confirming the voivode and as a sounding board for the local grievances of the three privileged estates.

Every voivode of Transylvania was forced to walk a tight rope between Ottoman and Habsburg interests externally and the interests of their respective factions within the country. Moreover, the Ottomans had made it very clear to the Habsburgs that any attempt on their part to control Transylvania directly would lead to war. A case in point was the Accord of Szatmar, forced upon John Sigismund on March 13, 1565, by the Emperor Maximilian II. In this document, the voivode agreed: (*a*) to retaining control of Transylvania and the fortress of Varad only (formerly the Prince of Transylvania had also controlled the so-called *Partium*, between the Tisza and the Danube); (*b*) to renounce the title of king; (*c*) to promise fidelity to Emperor Maximilian II who would become the brother-in-law of John Sigismund after the latter's marriage to a Habsburg princess; (*d*) if the voivode were to die without issue, Transylvania was to be again attached to the rest of Habsburg Hungary. When news of this deliberate encroachment on Ottoman prerogatives reached Sultan Sulaymān, he made preparations for his final campaign to Szigetvar in 1566. Meanwhile the Sultan assured John Sigismund of his support with the usual *Ahitname* (*'ahidnâme*), stating that (*a*) he would protect the Voivode and his land; (*b*) should the Voivode die without heir, the Porte would permit an election providing the annual tribute of 10,000 gold pieces was continued; (*c*) the Sultan also would meet John Sigismund in Hungary in 1566.[8]

In short, the lesson that might have been learned by the rulers of Transylvania was the following: the Prince or Voivode of Transylvania had to satisfy Habsburg claims to the crown of united Hungary by giving formal acknowledgment of Habsburg suzerainty. To the Ottomans, the Voivode also had to make an equally convincing acknowledgement of Turkish overlordship, together with the payment of an annual tribute. This delicate balance only broke down whenever the Habsburgs attempted to turn their *theoretical* control into reality, because the Ottoman state, in that era, held the preponderance of power.

John Sigismund died in 1571 without an heir. The vacancy provided the Ottomans with the opportunity of putting up their candidate, Stephan Báthory, for the voivodeship. The Báthory brothers, Andras, Stephan, and Christopher, were the sons of Stephan Báthory (d. 1534) who had served as the voivode of Transylvania during the reign of King John Zápolyai. The young Báthorys first came to the court in Alba Julia during the regency of Isabella. Stephan Báthory, in particular, had risen to political prominence as the most effective military leader during the voivodeship of John Sigismund. Shortly after his election as voivode, Stephan Báthory crushed an uprising of the Szekelys which had received encouragement from Caspar Bekes, the Habsburg candidate for the voivodeship.

The accession of Stephan Báthory, a devout Catholic, and the suppression of the Szekelys once again projected into high relief the social problems besetting Transylvania and to some extent all of Hungary. Without carrying the analysis too far, one can see a rough correlation among social status, ethnic ties, and religious proclivities.

By the end of the sixteenth century, the Saxon burghers and farmers had largely left military activities to the Magyar nobles and peasants whom they trusted to protect their political liberties in exchange for financial support. They fortified their towns and hired Szekelys or Vlach mercenaries as defense forces whenever the need arose. The majority were Lutheran and hence somewhat equivocally lent support to the pro-Habsburg faction because the towns were prosperous under Ottoman hegemony.

A large section of the nobility, whose interests other than war and politics seem to have centered on the rearing of cattle on their estates, went over to Calvinism, the "Hungarian religion." They were joined by a number of serfs and Szekelys. Much of the grass-roots support for Hungarian national leaders came from this element.

The bourgeoisie of Hungarian and Transylvanian towns and whole regions of the Szekelys embraced Unitarianism, the former because of intellectual inclination, the latter often as a social protest. The social misfits among the lesser nobility and the humiliated and disenfranchised Szekelys often joined the irregular bands of marauders and freebooters known as the Haiduks. These social outcasts, together with the largely Greek Orthodox Vlachs, fell in easily with the Turks, Roumanians, Tatars, or any other invader willing to bid for their services.[9]

Relatively few Roman Catholics remained; chiefly certain magnate families and their serfs. Stephan Báthory and his successors, in a quiet way, once again began building up Catholic institutions. In 1579, for example, Christopher Báthory installed the Jesuits in Kolozsvar and built an academy for them.

In the explosive and competitive religious climate of the sixteenth century, such a move would eventually lead to disastrous consequences. While social unrest could be controlled by a strong ruler like Stephan Báthory, the whole fabric of Transylvanian society was torn apart during the voivodeship of Stephan's nephew, Sigismund (1581–1602), who permitted a pro-Habsburg and largely Catholic entourage at Alba Julia to convince him that an anti-Turkish alliance would free him from Ottoman control.

Stephan Báthory had just established his position in Transylvania when he became a candidate for the throne of Poland, which had become vacant in 1572 after the death of Sigismund August, the last Jagellon. Henry, of the ruling house of Valois, had come from France in 1573 to occupy the throne, but shortly was called home to be King of France. After his sudden departure from Poland, Báthory, who had built a great reputation for himself as a general and as Prince of Transylvania, then became the candidate of the Piast or native Polish party. With the support of the Sultan, Báthory was elected King and moved to Poland in 1576. In Transylvania he arranged for the election of his brother Christopher to the post of voivode (1576–1581) and also had the Transylvanian army swear allegiance to Christopher and to Christopher's son Sigismund, who became Prince of Transylvania after his father's death in 1581. It is no secret, however, that the affairs of Transylvania were managed in the Transylvanian chancery of Cracow until the death of Stephan Báthory at the end of 1586. The Polish chancery in Báthory's day was staffed by a number of high functionaries known as the "Paduan Turkophiles," the doyen of whom was the chancellor, Jan Zamoyski. These functionaries, including Zamoyski, were graduated from the University of Padua, a dependency of Venice at the time, where a pro-Turkish atmosphere prevailed. They advised Báthory on a policy of fraternization with the Ottomans at least until Muscovy could be neutralized. Stephan Báthory generally followed this advice throughout his reign, successfully drawing upon Transylvanian and Ottoman resources to bolster the power of Poland.[10]

Báthory, realizing that his death was near, had attempted to extend the influence of his family. He obtained the Cardinalship of Poland for Andras, the son of his brother Andras. He also arranged a marriage between Griseldis, the sister of Sigismund, and the Polish Chancellor, Jan Zamoyski. But already before his death, King Stephan was running afoul of his own counter-Reformation policy in Transylvania. No sooner had the King died than the Transylvanian Diet, fearing Jesuit influence over the Voivode Sigismund, banished the Order from the province in 1588. Only one Spanish Jesuit, Alphonse Carillo remained to influence the unstable prince. Balthazar, brother of Cardinal Andras Báthory, inherited the rich domain of Fogaras; another brother, Stephan, was given command of the key fortress of Varad (Grosswardein). But the young Sigismund distrusted his cousins. Listening to the counsel of his mother, Elizabeth Báthory née Bocskay, he dismissed Stephan from Vārād and turned the fortress and the command of his army over to his uncle, Stephan Bocskay. Ironically, in the light of later developments, it was the combination of the Jesuit Carillo and the pro-Catholic influence of the Bocskays that turned the prince to an alliance with the Habsburgs against the advice of the more popular humanist and neutralist Transylvanian party which, before their execution, was led by the cousins of the Voivode, Stephan and Balthazar Báthory.[11]

3 Events Leading to the Long War

At this point, while keeping in mind the peculiar social background of Hungary and Transylvania in the sixteenth century, we shall re-emphasize the important political events that preceded the outbreak of the long war (1593–1606). After the Battle of Mohács, John Zápolyai, the Voivode of Transylvania and the so-called "National" candidate, was elevated to the Hungarian throne in 1526. But the Archduke Ferdinand, the brother of Emperor Charles V and of Mary, the widow of the fallen King Louis, became the "German" or "court" candidate for the Hungarian crown. With the aid of the Habsburg army, he succeeded in driving Zápolyai to the Polish border and in having himself declared king at Stuhlweissenburg [Istolni-Belgrad (Slav.); Székesfehérvár (Hung.)] in 1527. Now Zápolyai had no choice but to turn to the Sultan for support. The Ottomans re-established Zápolyai control over Hungary and emphasized their position as "protector" with a campaign that took them to the gates of Vienna in 1529. Thereafter, Zápolyai, ruling from Buda, served as the vassal of the Sultan until his death in 1540.

Archduke Ferdinand was left in control of a narrow band of Hungarian territory to the west and north of Lake Balaton. In 1538, John Zápolyai and the Archduke Ferdinand reached a secret agreement (Treay of Varad): each was to bear the title of "King" over the portion of Hungary that he then held. On the death of Zápolyai his lands would fall to the Archduke. Should Zápolyai marry—as indeed he did in 1539 (Isabella of the Polish House of Jagellon)—adequate provision was to be made for his widow and heirs. John Zápolai died in 1540 shortly after the birth of a son. The anti-Habsburg faction, whose leadership was assumed by Martinuzzi, the bishop of Grosswardein (Nagyvarad), called upon the Sultan to aid Hungary against the anticipated attempt by the Archduke Ferdinand to put into effect the agreement of 1538. This Habsburg threat gave to the Sultan an opportunity to make of central Hungary an Ottoman province. Queen Isabella and her son, John Sigismund, were moved to Lippa in 1541, from which place they ruled Transylvania as Ottoman vassals. The limits of the new Ottoman *beylerbeylik* extended north from the Drava and the Sava rivers, skirted the western shores of Balaton and encompassed Stuhlweissenburg (Székesféhervár, Istolni-Belgrad) and Gran (Esztergom) on the upper Danube. From there, the boundary of the new province curved eastward until, above Szolnok, it extended to the river Theiss (Tisza), which formed the eastern border of the province and which in turned joined itself with the Danube to the south. Buda became the seat of the pasha who controlled this new Ottoman province. Thus began the threefold division of Hungary, the Austrian-controlled portion in the extreme north and west, Transylvania, an Ottoman protectorate east of the Theiss, and between them, the territory now occupied by the Ottomans.[12]

Opposing the Ottoman strongholds of Belgrad, Temesvar, Stuhlweissenburg (Székesfehérvár), Buda, and Gran (Esztergom), the Habsburgs developed such strongpoints as Wihitsch, Kanizsa, Raab (Györ, Yānik), Komorn (Ḳōmurān), and Erlau (Eger, Egri). The Archduke Ferdinand, who served as Holy Roman Emperor of the German Nation from 1556 to 1564, and his successor, Maximilian II, attempted to unseat John Sigismund (Zápolyai) and his mother, but the truce of 1547, whereby Ferdinand was forced to pay a tribute of 30,000 Hungarian ducats annually to the Sultan for his control of the northwestern fragment of Hungary, became the basis of a semi-permanent truce between the Ottomans and Habsburgs. It was essentially this peace which was renewed in 1562 and 1568. Sulaymān the Magnificent died in 1566 while defending his "Hungarian system" and was succeeded by his son Selim II (1566–1574) and by Murād III (1574–1595). The Emperor Maximilian II (1564–1576) was unable to alter appreciably the *status quo* in Hungary. After the death of Selim II, Maximilian managed to have the truce renewed with Sultan Murād III in 1575. His death in the following year made it necessary for Rudolph II (1576–1608), his son and successor, to enter into fresh negotiations with the Porte. The Ottomans at this time were already far advanced in their preparations for the Persian War which began in earnest in 1578. Emperor Rudolph II, more devoted to astrology and alchemy than to the administration of an empire, held his court at Prague, leaving the government of Upper and Lower Austria to the Archduke Ernst (d. 1595) and the administration of the military border to the Archduke Karl (d. 1590).[13] After the Archdukes Karl and Ernst died, the Archduke Matthias and his brother, Maximilian, took an ever-increasing part in administering Upper and Lower

Austria, in attending to the affairs of the military border and in prosecuting the Long War (1593–1606). The Emperor Rudolph continued making foolish decisions concerning the war until he was finally forced by his brothers to give up much of his authority in 1605. In 1608 a further limitation was placed on the power of the Emperor. Henceforth he retained control in Bohemia only, leaving Matthias in charge of the Austrian, Moravian, and Hungarian parts of the realm.[14]

While the Ottomans were fighting Persia between 1578 and 1590, significant developments took place along the borders between the Ottoman and Habsburg possessions, which provided the *casus belli* for the Ottoman-Habsburg conflict beginning in 1593. In each of the treaties that had been concluded between the Emperor and the Sultan, special clauses dealt with the raids and counterraids of the borderers.[15] Each power maintained a series of lesser fortifications in the actual border areas (*palankas*) to maintain a modicum of control over the mutual raids of such border marauders as the Christian Uscocs and the Muslim Ġāzīs.[16]

The border raids continued in spite of the peace treaties signed on successive occasions. Neither Emperor Maximilian II nor his successor Rudolph wished to aggravate the Ottomans unnecessarily, but they also felt that they must improve their border defenses. A factor of great importance was their constant lack of funds to organize, staff, and equip the border defenses properly. It was also not clear which political body should be responsible for the organization of the border defenses. Should it be the responsibility of Inner Austria, with its greater efficiency and financial resources, or was it to be left to the Ban of Croatia or to the often rebellious Hungarian and Slavonian magnates? The latter of course feared that the Habsburgs might take away their local autonomy should Austria assume control of the borders.

In September 1577 the Austrian government had its way; Archduke Karl was placed in command of the military border that stretched from the Adriatic to the Sava.[17] Shortly thereafter a reform of the administration of the Croatian and Slavonian borders was instituted, which actually put the borders under the direction of Inner Austria. Now important measures were taken to strengthen the garrisons and to improve the conditions of the frontier fortifications. During the 1580s, however, interest in the border waned. One result of this neglect was that the Uscocs and the other borderers received their pay and allowances only intermittently, if at all. They tended, therefore, to have recourse to brigandage as a means of subsistence. Particularly irksome to the Ottomans and to the Venetians at this time were the Uscocs of Zengg (Seġna) who had turned to piracy on the Adriatic. The Uscocs of Zengg and other border elements had disturbed the Ottoman borders and sea lanes to such an extent during the course of the Ottoman-Persian conflict that, upon the conclusion of that war in 1590, a number of influential officials at the Porte viewed with approval the retaliatory raids of Hasan Pasha, the Bey of Bosnia, into Croatia and Slavonia.[18] In 1591 and 1592 the border forts of the Habsburgs on the Kulpa, Unna, and Sava rivers were systematically attacked. After the fall of Wihitsh to the Ottomans, the key city in the defense system of Archduke Karl, the Habsburgs mustered a strong force and engaged Hasan Pasha in June of 1593, while he was laying siege to Sissek (Sīsḳe). The Ottomans were pushed back toward the Kulpa, a large number of them being either slain or drowned in the river. This disaster, in which eight to ten thousand Ottoman troops are reputed to have perished, could not be overlooked.[19] War quickly followed. Von Kreckwitz, the ambassador of the Emperor, who at the time had just arrived in Istanbul with the annual "gift" to the Porte, was thrown into prison together with his retinue. Sinān Pasha, the octogenarian Grand Vezir, marched to Belgrade and carried out a campaign in the same year (1593).

4 Politicking Among the Border States

Each power now began maneuvering to gain, through diplomacy, tactical and strategic advantages over its adversary. Pope Clement VIII (1592–1605) promised and supplied the Emperor with funds and troops; moreover, he sent diplomatic missions to the Balkans, to Russia, and to Persia. The mission of Alexander Komulovič, rector of the South Slav church of San Girolamo in Rome, laid much of the groundwork initially. In 1593 he visited Sigismund Báthory, Prince of Transylvania, and the Voivodes of Wallachia and Moldavia, then he called upon the King of Poland, the leaders of the Zaporozhian Cossacks, and Tsar Fyodor of Muscovy.[20] The Emperor also sent his own emissaries to the Polish king, to the Cossacks, and to the Tsar. In the year 1594, the Emperor's envoy, Mikolay Varkach, was told by the Tsar that Muscovite representations to the Khan of the Crimea on behalf of Emperor Rudolph had kept the Khan at home.[21] The mission of Varkach did not result in an overt alliance but the Tsar assisted the Emperor with a gift of furs in 1595 which was valued at 400,000 rubles.[22]

The aim of these diplomatic efforts, first of all, was to form an anti-Ottoman league. This project met with only a limited success. The stronger states—Venice, Spain, Poland, and Moscow—remained aloof, but the endeavor to incite Transylvania, the Danubian Principalities, and the Zaporozhian Cossacks to revolt against the Ottomans and the Tatars proved to be more rewarding.

On the second visit of Komulovič to Transylvania in January 1594, the young prince Sigismund Báthory, under the influence of Stephan Bocskay, agreed to make a secret pact with the Emperor. He signed an offensive and defensive alliance at Prague on January 28, 1595. In this agreement, Báthory gave up his claims to Hungary but was recognized by the Emperor as prince of

Transylvania.[23] As previously outlined, Stephan Báthory, the first of the new dynasty, had been strongly under Jesuit influence. When Stephan left Transylvania in 1576 to become King of Poland, he arranged for Christopher, his brother, to succeed him as prince of Transylvania. When Christopher died in 1581, he was followed by his son Sigismund Báthory (1581–1602).[24]

The Danubian principalities dealt the first blow in what might be termed the "little war" of the tributary principalities. The revolt of Michael, Voivode of Wallachia, toward the end of 1594, at first aided the Habsburg cause greatly; the Ottoman state had to face a serious threat on its right flank, which endangered the chief supply routes from the Porte and the lower Danube to Hungary, whether they came by boat up the Danube or overland by way of Adrianople, Sofia, Nish, and Belgrade.

As Grand *Aġā* and then Ban of Craïova, Michael of Wallachia acquired popularity and influence to such an extent that he aroused the jealousy of the Voivode Alessandro Bogdan (1592–1593) and only escaped execution at the instigation of the latter by fleeing to Transylvania. It was thus in 1592 that Michael first made contact with Sigismund Báthory. Sigismund wrote to Edward Barton, the influential English ambassador at the Porte, and to Sinān Pasha, the Grand Vezir, on behalf of Michael. These letters, combined with the influence of his Cantacuzinos relatives, obtained the voivodeship for Michael in 1593.[25]

Such favors from high dignitaries at the Porte, however, were not provided for nothing. Soon creditors and office seekers descended on Michael from every side. Thus, in addition to the normal commitments of the office (i.e., the payment of tribute and the supplying of provisions in time of war to the Sultan), Michael had to pay off his creditors. It is difficult to determine exactly what led Michael to revolt against the Ottomans and equally difficult to determine how long he had worked toward this end. Some sources state that he was already planning a revolt while he was in exile in Transylvania. One Ottoman historian calls attention to excessive Ottoman war demands and the lack of a conciliatory Ottoman policy toward the Danubian principalities as underlying causes for the unrest.[26] Ottoman fiscal oppression was particularly onerous to the boyars. In addition to tribute, from 10,000 to 30,000 ducats per year in Moldavia and twice that amount in Wallachia, there were presents, gratuities, and the forced sale of foodstuffs at fixed prices, both for troops on campaign and for the inhabitants of Istanbul.[27]

In March 1594, some six months after he had become Voivode, Michael received a visit from Komulovič, who was styled the "apostolic visitor of the Latin Churches in the European part of the Ottoman state." There is no doubt that these contacts with individuals outside the Ottoman milieu, first with Sigismund Báthory and then with Komulovič, encouraged Michael in his plans to revolt.

By the end of the same month, the then Voivode of Moldavia, Aaron, called "the Tyrant" (1591–1592 and 1592–1595), also received the apostolic visitor and gave him assurances that he would take part in an anti-Ottoman league. Moreover, Aaron sent with Komulovič personal letters to the Cossacks, to the Chancellor of Poland, Zamoyski, and to the Tsar of Muscovy.[28] Aaron had one major reservation about the league. He demanded special protection against the Tatars if he should break with the Porte. A report of June 1594 shows that the Moldavian voivode took no chances. He had prepared already for the expected passing of the Tatars through his territories en route for Hungary by provisioning the way stations along routes customarily traveled by the Tatars. Also, until the end of 1593, Michael did not fail to maintain amicable relations with the Tatar Khan.[29]

Poland remained aloof from the anti-Ottoman league, considering such a course to be the best means of preserving her own position between the Habsburg realm and Muscovy. Sigismund Vasa, son of John III of Sweden, had succeeded to the Polish throne in 1588. After defeating an attempt by Archduke Maximilian to unseat him, he had turned to the crisis of 1589 with the Ottomans, which developed out of the indiscriminate raiding of the Cossacks on Ottoman and Tatar possessions at this time.[30] The movement of settlers and soldiers of fortune from western into the eastern Ukraine during the late sixteenth century had become rapid and widespread with the extension of serfdom in Poland. Following this influx of peoples into the Ukraine in the sixteenth century, the Polish state, in order to protect her settled areas, attempted to register some of the more turbulent elements, such as the Zaporozhian Cossacks who lived on the edge of the open steppe in more or less self-sustaining communities.[31] These attempts had failed, because the registered Cossacks continued to associate freely with the unregistered ones, thus rendering discipline impossible. The problem of indiscriminate raiding against the Ottoman territories combined with the encroachment of certain Cossack groups on the lands of powerful Polish nobles, led to an attack upon and the defeat of the Cossacks by a force composed of Hungarian mercenaries and of Polish nobles with their retainers. This battle fought at Piatka in 1590 and the subsequent repressive measures of a local nature which continued until 1593 have been termed by Hrushevsky the "First Cossack War."[32]

Not until 1594 did the Zaporozhian Cossacks feel themselves secure enough to become embroiled once more in international events. Having been duly prepared for a role in the Habsburg-Ottoman struggle by visits from Father Komulovič and from representatives of the Emperor, Rudolph II, the Cossacks welcomed Erich Lassota, a special envoy of the Emperor, during the summer of 1594. As a result of negotiations taking place at that time, the Cossacks accepted insignia and supplies of money from the Emperor and thereafter harassed the Crimean Tatars and laid waste Moldavia in 1594 and 1595.[33]

These activities helped to bring about the intervention of Poland in

Moldavian affairs in 1595 and led directly to the complete repression of the Zaporozhian Cossacks by the Polish state in 1596. This "Second Cossack War" scattered the Cossacks far and wide, and accounts for the relative weakness of the Zaporozhian Cossacks throughout the remaining years of the Hungarian War. The Cossacks, on this occasion, had negotiated with the Emperor and the Tsar as an independent power, a political development which the Polish state could not have tolerated.[34]

5 The First Year of the Hungarian War and the Advent of the Crimean Tatars

The Crimean Tatars, during the Persian War, had been called upon to participate in a struggle between the Safavids and the Ottomans. In the new struggle, the Tatars were destined to take part in a war the stakes of which were the control of the Danube basin, including the heartlands of Hungary and the tributary principalities of Wallachia, Moldavia, and Transylvania. This time the principal contenders were the Habsburgs and the Ottomans with Poland playing an important secondary role commensurate with her own interests.

The campaign season was already far advanced when Sinān Pasha left Istanbul in 1593 to undertake the first major operation of the war. He reached Belgrade in September, reviewed his troops at Stuhlweissenburg, and then proceeded to reduce Veszprem and Palota before taking up winter quarters. The Grand Vezir had gained a tactical advantage for the following year by setting up his headquarters in Belgrade. The Austrian forces, however, were not averse to taking advantage of the Ottoman distaste for winter campaigns. Christopher Teuffenbach, commander-in-chief of the Styrian forces, joined his troops with those of Count Palffy and siezed several lesser strongpoints, amongst them Szabandna and Divin. Weather permitting, the Imperial forces could often take advantage of the Ottomans' slowness in assembling their troops in the spring. Thus, for example, Archduke Matthias began a siege of Gran in early May 1594, but he was forced to withdraw upon the approach of Sinān Pasha at the beginning of June. The main Imperial army crossed the Danube and camped near Raab. Another army, under the command of Archduke Maximilian, operated on the Croatian border, taking several lesser border forts, but lost most of them again to the Ottomans upon the eventual withdrawal of the Archduke.

Sinān Pasha in 1594 had received reinforcements from Istanbul which were led by the Janissary Aġā. The Grand Vezir, after driving the Imperial forces from before Gran, besieged Raab. It was at this juncture that the Crimean Tatars, led by their Khan, Ġāzī Girāy, joined the Ottomans and rendered assistance in the conquest of Raab and Papa during the campaign of 1594. The Ottomans now turned to the reduction of Komorn but, the season being far advanced, the army abandoned the siege and moved to winter quarters.[35]

In summary, during the year 1594 the superior organization and resources of the Sultan gave to the Ottomans a strategic advantage which was emphasized by the fall of Raab, one of the most important of the Christian border strongholds, situated only a little more than 100 kilometers from Vienna. The Imperial forces had suffered because of a change in leadership. Archduke Matthias had replaced the decisive Archduke Ernst, and Matthias, lacking energy and shunning hard discipline, ignored the council of Georg Zrinyi and listened only to drunken David Ungnad.[36]

The Khan, upon receiving the instructions of the Sultan to join Sinān Pasha in Hungary, had brought his negotiations with the Tsar to a fruitful conclusion.[37] In preparation for the Ottoman campaign, he mustered a force estimated at 30,000 to 40,000 horsemen. According to the Khan's own description as quoted by Peçewī, the mustering of the Tatar contingents followed a traditional pattern. Every ten or twelve men brought their own cooking pot (kazġān) and such a unit was termed a *ḳōş*. Moreover, it was known how many *ḳōş* came from each village unit.[38]

The most difficult problem that now faced the Khan, after he had made peace with Moscow, was to move his forces to the plains of Hungary. During the entire spring and early summer of 1594, the diplomatic correspondence of the Danubian principalities which were friendly to the Emperor, shows a marked preoccupation with whether the Khan was coming and, if so, by what route and in what strength. Furthermore, on behalf of the Imperial cause, three separate attempts to block the coming of the Tatars can be discerned—by the Principalities, by the Zaporozhian Cossacks, and by Transylvania. The role played by Poland was equivocal. She did not wish to be dominated by the Porte, but the possibility of having the Habsburgs as a neighbor on her Transylvanian border was equally distasteful. An examination of the map will show that the Tatars had available to them two main routes into Hungary, the one across Moldavia and Wallachia and then along the southern shores of the Danube, the other through southern Poland and across Transylvania. Both routes had been used by Tatar forces en route to Hungary in the past. Under normal circumstances the easiest route would have been the one along the Danube. Moldavia, a relatively weak state, could not, on its own, offer much resistance to a large Tatar contingent. Wallachia, with its greater resources and a strong voivode like Michael could present difficulties.

The diplomatic exchanges between Wallachia, Moldavia, and Transylvania and the representatives of the Pope and the Emperor did not pass unnoticed by the Porte. Already Sinān Pasha, after the first year of campaigning, had found it necessary to rebuke the Voivode Michael for the inadequate provisions he had sent to the front. In 1594, the Sultan and the Grand Vezir sent strong letters to the princes of the three principalities in the hope of keeping them in the Ottoman fold.[39] It is no wonder that the Khan, in view of the unsettled situation on the Danube, very early decided upon the northern route through Poland and Transylvania. It is also probable that such a move was made for strategic reasons. If it could be shown to the Prince of Transylvania how easy it was to concentrate Tatar forces on his soil, then he might think twice about changing allegiance. It is evident that Transylvania would have a key position in the event of a rebellion on the Danube since supplies and men sent from the Habsburg lands to Wallachia and Moldavia would have to pass through Transylvania.

Already in December of 1593, Marco Zane, the Venetian Bailo at the Porte, had informed the Doge that the Tatars might pass through Poland en route to Hungary. He also listed the provisions, such as arquebuses, money, spades, tents, pikes, maces, and bows, that the Ottomans were sending to the Crimea. By the spring of 1594, it became apparent that two separate contingents would be going to Hungary. The Bailo Marco Venier reported on May 20 that at least one contingent had been held up by a serious Cossack raid on Tatar territory at the end of March and that, although the Voivode of Moldavia had prepared ample food and halting stations for the Tatars, they had not yet passed into Moldavia.[40]

Indeed both the Khan and the Sultan had made plans well in advance. On March 5, 1594, the Hospodar Aaron of Moldavia wrote to Grand Chancellor Zamoyski that the Khan had sent an envoy to him in order to discuss the provisioning of the routes for the passage of the Tatars through Moldavia. At this time also, the Khan asked the Voivode to provide him with some guides for his forces on their passage through southern Poland into Transylvania. In his correspondence to Zamoyski, Aaron claimed that he would not provide the guides.[41] By April 12 the papal nuncio Speziano, who was residing at the court in Prague, was able to report that a çāvuş (envoy, ambassador) from the Sultan had arrived in Warsaw to request permission for the Tatars to pass through Poland. In a letter of Zamoyski to Christof Radziwill, the Voivode of Vilna, dated March 30, 1594, the Chancellor discussed the arrival of this same çāvuş. Evidently the çāvuş actually denied that the Tatars planned to go to Hungary by the way of Poland, a view that the Chancellor held himself at the time. It was difficult for him to conceive that the Sultan would want to risk war with Poland at a time when he was at war with the Emperor.[42] On May 27 the nuncio Speziano reported from Regensburg that 7,000 or 8,000 Tatars had joined Sinān Pasha, having come through Wallachia because they were blocked from entering Poland by the Duke of Ostrog.[43] For some time the diplomatic missions of the Emperor had sought to block the mountain passes, particularly in Transylvania, in order to bar the passage of the main Tatar force. It seems, however, that before final plans for blocking the Tatars either on the steppe or in the mountain passes had been completed, the Tatars had been able to join the Ottomans in Hungary by way of Poland and Transylvania.

Why did the Poles, who were playing the game of interested neutrals in this way, permit the Tatars to pass unmolested? The obvious answer is that they did not permit it but were unable to take appropriate action in time.[44] The diary of Erich Lassota, special envoy of the Emperor to the Cossacks, and related materials help to resolve this problem. Before Lassota had arrived on the Dnieper in the summer of 1594, a certain Stanislaus Chlopicki had visited the court at Prague and, giving himself out as the head of the Cossacks, had made specious promises about what he and his men might accomplish if they were supported by the Emperor. Chlopicki returned to the Zaporozhians with money, silver drums, an eagle crest, and banners during the winter of 1593–1594. Thus, when an envoy of the Emperor sought an alliance with Poland against the Ottomans in February 1594, the Polish Diet complained about the secret negotiations of the Habsburgs with the Zaporozhian Cossacks, who were subjects of Poland. The envoy of the Emperor excused the government at Prague by stating that Chlopicki had represented the Cossacks as being an independent state. Chlopicki, not being fully content with the support he had obtained from Prague, also went to Moscow in August, where concessions were made to him on the condition that he accept Muscovite troops in his force and that he recognize the suzerainty of Moscow.[45]

While the Habsburg envoys raced against time, the main Tatar force led by Ġāzī Girāy had begun its long journey to the Hungarian front. Lassota's report of a clash between Cossacks and Tatars about June 18, 1594, near Ochakov refers no doubt to an event that occurred during the first stages of this long trek. Lassota learned from a friendly Tatar called Bellek that the Khan himself and his two sons, with 80,000 (!) men, had departed from the Crimea, but that only about 20,000 were troops. Bellek also reported that a force of only 15,000 remained to guard the Crimea.[46] After the Tatar forces were ferried across the mouth of the Dnieper to Ochakov, they quickly passed through Moldavia, probably reaching the Polish frontier in late June. The Khan waited three days near Snyatyn, north of Czernowitz, for a reply from Zamoyski with whom he had presumably been in correspondence about free passage. Some guides for the march appear to have been dissident Poles, "traitors" from Transylvania, and a number of boyar and Greek supporters of Peter the Moldavian (Peter VI, 1592). When the awaited answer from Zamoyski arrived, there was no indication whatsoever that Zamoyski might provide guides for the Tatars to cross Polish territory. The Chancellor, on the contrary, challenged the presence of the Khan and his forces and threatened him with Polish troops, reputed to be 50,000 strong, which were held in readiness some four leagues from the Khan.[47] In actuality, it appears that the Chancellor wanted to stop the Tatars but many Cossacks upon whom he planned to rely proved untrustworthy, doubtless for lack of pay. The Cossacks hastened to join the project of Chlopicki, which developed into a diversionary action against the Ottomans in Moldavia. This adventure of Chlopicki helped bring about the revolt of the Voivode Aaron in 1594.[48] Apparently, during the summer of 1594 the Cossacks were doubly bought off, for the Papal envoy, Komulovič, concluded a treaty with them on August 30, 1594, in which the Cossacks undertook to attack the Tatars.

Although the question of guides for the Tatars is frequently alluded to in Western sources, it is clear that the Tatars had at least a certain number of their own guides, who knew the route to Hungary through the Carpathain passes very well.[49] Several passes could be used by the Tatars to cross the Carpathians but the most likely pass was probably the one still known as the "Tatars' Pass" or Per Yablonitse at a height of 841 meters. This pass connects the source of the Prut and the Tissa (Tchorna Tisa), a branch of the Tisza (Theiss) River. By following the Tisza, the Tatars could very quickly reach the plains of Hungary.[50]

Further news about the Tatars deals with their activities around Huszth, a city on the Tisza in upper Transylvania. Their arrival in northern Transylvania, shortly after Sigismund Báthory had decided to cast his lot with the Emperor, appears significant. A Jesuit correspondent from Transylvania, probably Carillo, accused certain Transylvanian senators of conniving with the Tatars to undo the plans of Sigismund. A report in Ortelius confirms the suspicion that the Tatars were sent to Transylvania for strategic considerations. It is certain that highly placed individuals had earlier informed the Sultan of Sigismund's betrayal; moreover, when it was learned that the Tatars would pass through Transylvania, these same informers were said to have sent forged letters to the Prince—which were signed by Zamoyski—asking the Prince to come to the Polish border for consultations with him. Thus, they hoped to bring about the undoing or the capture of Prince Sigismund near Huszth with the help of the Tatars.[51] In actuality, however, it would appear that these are examples of a garbled account. Kaspar Kornis, Governor of Huszth, was ordered to block the passes. He was later asked by the Prince why he had let the Tatars through. Kornis then showed the Prince letters signed by the Prince himself countermanding the original order.[52]

The Tatars had a number of minor clashes with enemy forces of unknown strength in Poland, but they did not stop to raid or plunder until they reached Transylvania. In Transylvania Kaspar Kornis attacked the vanguard of the Tatars near his city, but he was so badly defeated that he almost did not reach the protection of the city walls. He then sent gifts to the Khan and the latter, not wishing to molest the territory of a Prince who paid tribute to the Sultan, continued on his way. The Tatars, even after reaching the borders of the Ottoman provinces in Hungary, were not sure they had reached their goal, for, as the Ottoman chroniclers admit, they saw hardly anyone wearing turbans![53] In summary, the Tatars had commenced their journey shortly before June 18. Next they were reported at Huszth on June 28 and by August 5 they had joined the army of Sinān Pasha before Raab. Thus their total travel time by the northern route was slightly more than one and a half months. This account affords to Ottoman historians some rare details of the delicacy with which even the Tatar Khan handled relations with Poland and Transylvania in this era.

On 19 Zī'l Ka'de 1002/6 August 1594, Sinān Pasha ordered a full-dress parade in honor of the arrival of the Khan. After meeting one another on horseback and exchanging formalities, they moved off to the ornate pavilion tent of the Grand Vezir where they sat down and feasted together on food that had been prepared. Some Ottoman dignitaries saw in this gesture of the Grand Vezir a kind of mortification for the Khan. They found it unfitting that the Grand Vezir should seat the Khan on his right, or sit down with him at all, particularly as the Khan himself was the higher in rank. They felt it to be highly inappropriate, regardless of the high position of the Vezir, to treat as an equal a ruler whose ancestors had possessed rights of *Sikke* and *Ḫuṭbe* for four hundred years (*sic*). But the Khan paid little attention to these matters. After the banquet he washed his hands in a golden basin with water brought in a golden ewer. Then he received a number of valuable gifts, including a traditional grant of 5,000 gold pieces and a charger. He seated himself on his new mount and was escorted back to his own pavilion.[54]

The presence of the Khan was a matter of no small importance for the success or failure of the Ottoman campaign. The Tatars, in numbers alone, much increased the striking force of the Ottomans. They served as forward scouts, as skirmishers, and even as assault units, particularly across rivers for they needed no bridges; they merely held to their horses' tails and were pulled across the water. Of no mean significance was the psychological impact of their presence on the discipline of the Ottoman troops. As the Sultan rarely took part in the campaigns, the presence of the Tatar Khan without doubt added to the discipline of the troops and the chances of success in any given campaign. The Tatars were considered invincible by ordinary people.[55] Moreover, the Khan, ever conscious of his own exposed position on the borders of the Ottoman state, was true to his name, Ġāzī (warrior fighting the infidel) and able to see in this war the traditional struggle (*Ġāzā*) of Islam against all unbelievers. There were, of course, other fundamental reasons in the nature of political and economic expediency which brought the Tatars to Hungary. Politically speaking, the Sultan could remove or refuse in other ways to assist a disobedient Khan if he failed to join a campaign. Of primary importance to the Tatars were the chances for acquiring booty and captives. The Khan himself received extra grants of money while on campaign, grants which he could use to better maintain his position in the continual intrigues of the Porte and among his own mīrzās.

The Khan received his initial war grant upon his arrival, but difficulties now arose because Sinān Pasha refused to authorize a "scorched earth" policy even under pressure from the Khan and other dignitaries. The Ottoman army had made camp on the plain before Raab on 13 Ẕi'l Ka'de 1002/31 July 1594. The Tatars first saw action in the storming of an enemy *Tābūr* (fortified point) situated across the Danube and next to the main fortress of Raab. The Ottomans placed pontoon bridges across the Danube upon which volunteers, members of the *Serden Geçdī* (~*enfants perdu*) regiment, could pass to the other side. The Tatars, led by the Khan, merely swam their horses across. The fortress itself lay on the bank of the Raab river and was protected by a moat on the land side. In the reduction of the fortress, the Tatars performed the service of dragging up sandbags with their horses because the soil was too wet for entrenching. Later an attempt to dam up the waters of the Raab River which swirled through the moat proved unsuccessful and the citadel was eventually reduced on 17 Muḥarrem 1003/2 October 1594 by the action of sappers (*laġimjīlar*) who systematically mined a portion of the walls.[56] In the light of these details, it is difficult to substantiate the claim of the Tatar chronicler 'Abd al Ġaffār that the Tatars played a decisive role in the conquest of Raab. When it became clear that Raab would soon capitulate under steady bombardment and mining operations, Ġāzī Girāy was sent to the neighboring fortress of Tata, but finding it unoccupied, he was able to report its conquest on the same day as Raab itself fell.[57] After a brief siege of Komorn, the Tatars went their way toward the Crimea and the Ottoman forces took up winter quarters on the frontier. Only a token force of Tatars, camping in their *yāpūnja* or reed-and-mud huts, spent the winter on the plains near Stuhlweissenburg.[58]

Fortune had definitely smiled on the Ottomans in Hungary in 1594. Sinān Pasha had kept a stern discipline over all units in his command even though the Khan and several other dignitaries felt that those troops not actually involved in the sieges should have been permitted to raid enemy territory indiscriminately. But the Grand Vezir felt that the *Re'āyā* (peasantry) had already suffered enough at the hands of bandits and marauders. He reasoned that for the Ottomans to perpetrate similar excesses would only play into the hands of the enemy; no profit would accrue to the Ottomans if they conquered territory from which their own troops had driven the peasantry.[59] This was sound Ottoman policy but it didn't give the Crimean Tatars an opportunity to capture slaves or collect booty. There is evidence from an Italian report that, over and above the question of whether or not the Tatars should be free to raid, the Khan came into conflict with the Grand Vezir in connection with another matter: Ġāzī Girāy wanted to have two of his brothers appointed the voivodes of Wallachia and Moldavia as recompense for the Tatar contributions to the Hungarian War—a desire that Sinān Pasha did not welcome.[60] This is the first indication of a scheme for Tatar territorial aggrandizement which the Khan henceforth nurtured almost to the end of his life. The fact that the Khan expressed such an idea so early in the war may have led directly to his dismissal in 1596 after the death of his personal friend, Sultan Murād III.

6 The Revolt of the Principalities and Polish Intervention

The tributary principalities of Wallachia, Moldavia, and Transylvania, by the end of 1594, had prepared for a revolt against the Ottomans and had begun concluding formal agreements with the Emperor.[61] Voivode Michael made the first open break with the Sultan by exterminating his Ottoman creditors in Bucharest in October of 1594. His troops then drove all Ottomans, except those stationed in fortresses, out of Wallachia and sent them reeling south across the Danube. Aaron, Voivode of Moldavia, had encouraged the Cossacks in his pay to attack Bender and seize the new Ottoman fortress of Ismā'īl. Meanwhile, Sultan Murād III had died on January 16, 1595, and was succeeded by Sultan Meḥemmed III (1595–1603). At the time of the accession, Ferhād Pasha had also replaced Ḳōjā Sinān Pasha as Grand Vezir.[62]

The serious threat to the Ottoman flank posed by the revolt of Michael had to be met immediately. Not until July, however, did Ferhād Pasha move his forces up to Rusçuk (Ruse) where he began the construction of a bridge across the Danube to the Wallachian town of Yergöğü (Giurgiu). Shortly thereafter Ferhād Pasha was dismissed and Ḳōjā Sinān Pasha again assumed the rank of Grand Vezir. Sinān Pasha marched into Wallachia intending to settle the revolt, but Michael withdrew his troops to the border of Transylvania and only sallied forth at the beginning of October in the wake of the withdrawing Ottoman forces. The autumn withdrawal, harassed by attacks from Michael's troops—whose numbers had swelled appreciably through additions from Transylvania—now became a rout.[63] All now converged on the Yergöğü-Rusçuk bridge—cattle, men, supplies, and equipment—resulting in a great traffic jam at the bridgehead toward which the artillery of the Transylvanian-Wallachian forces was now directed. The artillery barrage only heightened the confusion and thousands of men lost their lives by drowning in the Danube.

In spite of the seriousness of the revolt in the Principalities, the Sultan had been reluctant to accept a proposal made earlier by Ġāzī Girāy Khan that his brothers be appointed to the positions of voivode in Wallachia and Moldavia to assure their pacification. Nevertheless, as the rebellion in Wallachia and Moldavia spread rapidly during the winter of 1594–1595, the Ottomans were increasingly forced to make use of the Tatars in all manner of assignments in the provinces.[64]

Meanwhile the Tatars, led by the Khan, had departed from the Hungarian front in the late autumn of 1594. When the Khan, however, learned that all exit routes in Transylvania were blocked, he was forced to remain on the Hungarian plain until the ice was frozen solid on the Danube, a more suitable time to move such a large force along the southern route. Hence, the Tatars were scattered from Szolnok to Temesvar, some scouting out the routes, others raiding, and still others camping in their wretched huts (yāpūnja). The Khan himself stayed with the Pasha of Temesvar. Only in late February of 1595 did the Tatars again start their march for the Crimea.[65] When they reached the lower Danube, three or four factors determined that they conduct themselves in a more military manner. In the first place, they were by now laden with booty and hence less maneuverable. Furthermore, the Ottomans had strong garrisons in the area, notably at Silistria, and the principalities of Wallachia and Moldavia were under arms and in revolt. Marco Venier, the Venetian Bailo, reported to the Doge on February 20, 1595, that about 24,000 Tatars had entered Wallachia earlier in the month, and had been permitted to journey unmolested for two days before they suffered a terrible massacre at the hands of the Vlach and Transylvanian troops of the Voivode Michael. This surprise attack caused the Tatars to recross the Danube whence they had come.[66] Another report provided details of this clash and revealed that the Tatars had entered Wallachia in two separate forces from Nicopolis. When the Tatars returned to the Bulgarian side of the Danube at Rusçuk they encountered Muṣṭafā Pasha who was on his way to Moldavia to install the Voivode Bogdan.[67] (The Sultan had chosen Bogdan to replace Aaron, who had joined the revolt.) In consideration of a generous gift from the new voivode, Ġāzī Girāy detached some 4,000 Tatars under the leadership of one of his sons to aid the cause of the voivode.[68] Behind the scenes both voivodes, new and old, were intriguing to remain in favor with the Sultan. This is perhaps why Aaron permitted the Khan free passage through to the Dnieper. Sigismund Báthory, however, continued to exert pressure on Michael of Wallachia and on Aaron of Moldavia to maintain the struggle against the Sultan. Aaron was able to defeat the forces of Bogdan and Muṣṭafā Pasha and to remain in power until May when he was driven out by Stefan VIII, Razvan, who survived as voivode only from May 1595 to August 1595.[69]

The Khan appears to have spent the months of March through September, 1595, in the Crimea. By then it had become evident to the Ottomans that, if something was not done to stop the spread of Transylvanian influence in Moldavia, they would find it difficult even to receive help from the Tatars overland. The Grand Vezir Sinān Pasha had put pressure on Wallachia. In Hungary, the Austrian imperial forces, during the summer of 1595, attacked the fortress of Gran (Esztergom) and eventually forced its capitulation.[70] The forces of Sigismund Báthory also besieged the fortress of Temesvar but to no avail. In short, most of the Ottoman forces were pinned down and only the Khan, if he chose to take part, was in a position to maneuver. Ġāzī Girāy, however, now played for larger stakes. He had already sought control over the Wallachian and Moldavian principalities. The Sultan or the Grand Vezir may have made some vague promises in this direction, for the Khan at last moved into action. While the Grand Vezir was withdrawing from Wallachia, he received word from the Khan that he had quieted the *Re'āyā* in Moldavia. Now the Khan sought a specific declaration of his rights in Moldavia, but this ambition was thwarted by a directive from the Sultan.[71]

By August 1595, the Poles, having heard that the Ottomans and Tatars were on the march again, had mobilized their forces. They did not view with pleasure the extension of Habsburg influence into Transylvania and from there into Wallachia and Moldavia, nor did the Poles want to see the Danubian principalities turned into Ottoman provinces.[72] Only gradually does any Ottoman plan come to light. The grand design appears to be that Sinān Pasha was supposed to suppress quickly the Wallachian revolt and the Khan was to do likewise with Moldavia. Thereafter one or both of these forces would have marched into Transylvania.[73] Michael and Sigismund had, of course, foiled the Ottomans by withdrawing to the mountains until their adversaries had begun to withdraw to winter quarters. In Moldavia, meanwhile, the Polish forces led by the Chancellor, Jan Zamoyski, checked the Tatar bid to take over Moldavia. Later, after his debacle at Giurgiu bridge, Sinān Pasha attempted to put the blame on the Khan, saying that he had received no support from him.[74] There was probably some truth in this claim. The Khan had not seen fit to move west of the Dnieper until October 1595. In early October, the Khan probably felt that Sinān Pasha had dealt effectively with the rebels in Wallachia, thus leaving him a free hand to turn his attention to Moldavia.[75] The Khan and his brother, Feth Girāy, the Ḳalġay, arrived at Tehine and were regally received by their relative Aḥmed Bey, the Sanjāḳ Bey of Tehine (Bender) and Kilia.[76] The Khan now joined his forces with those of the Bey and marched into Moldavia. He apparently intended to install the Bey as voivode of Moldavia and then proceed into Transylvania.[77] In a dispatch of Zamoyski to King Sigismund III, the succeeding events are clearly spelled out. The Khan advanced to the lines of the Polish forces which were placed near the juncture of the Cecora (Ţuţora) and the Prut rivers. Neither army wanted a full-scale conflict. Thus, after a brief sham battle with only a few casualties, negotiators from both sides met and concluded an agreement. Zamoyski had stipulated that Jeremia Movila, a member of an old Moldavian family, be appointed Hospodar of Moldavia, that no damage be suffered by Moldavia or Poland, and that the Tatars evacuate Moldavia within three days. Aḥmed Aġā, the chief negotiator for the Khan, much to the surprise of Zamoyski, accepted these stipulations upon the undertaking of the Chancellor to eliminate the Zaporozhian Cossack raids on Tatar territory. The agreement of Cecora was concluded on October 22, 1595.[78]

Now that the Poles and Tatars had driven Stefan Razvan, the Transylvanian protégé, from Moldavia, Zamoyski attempted to smooth over the wrath of Prince Sigismund, whose sister was the wife of Zamoyski. He excused the action that he had taken in regard to Moldavia on the grounds thet he was merely restraining the Tatar forces. In actuality, he and the Khan had agreed to a kind of joint tributary protectorate over Moldavia, an agreement which had received the blessing of the Sultan.[79] The Chancellor, leaving a Polish detachment behind, withdrew to Polish territory in November. The Tatars took up winter quarters around Tehine, Akkerman, and Kilia. At this juncture it became known that King Sigismund Vasa was displeased with the action that his chancellor had taken at Cecora. After all, had not the Chancellor's brother-in-law, Sigismund Báthory, driven the Ottomans beyond the Danube! Would not an alliance between Hungary, Transylvania, Wallachia, Moldavia and Poland now be appropriate? These were some of the thoughts which the Polish king must have considered as he discussed the problems with Cardinal Andras Báthory. Meanwhile, King Sigismund received a strongly-worded letter from his cousin, the Prince of Transylvania, reproaching him for interfering with Christian successes over the Ottomans.[80] Thus it is clear that in Poland, as in Transylvania, there was a clash between the humanists, such as Zamoyski, and the Catholic party, who desired to destroy the cooperative arrangements in effect between Poland and the Ottoman state. But clearly the best interests of Poland required the neutralization of Wallachia, Moldavia, and Transylvania. Poland wanted no Habsburg satellites on its southern or western borders.[81]

After the honeymoon year, a new realism was beginning to appear along the Danube. Moldavia was now once more in Ottoman hands. The standards from the Sultan recognizing Jeremia Movila as voivode of Moldavia arrived from the Porte in December. Sigismund Báthory had not, as yet, given up the idea of sponsoring Stefan Razvan again in a new campaign into Moldavia with the help of Michael. But Poland was now, if not friendly, at least more cooperative with the Ottomans; the ambitions of the voivodes of Transylvania and Wallachia were becoming apparent. These ambitions could become the prelude to Habsburg encroachments in the Principalities, or they might upset the position of the buffer states to such an extent that the Ottomans might turn the Danubian Principalities into *Beylerbeyliks*, that is, provinces.[82]

7 The Year 1596: The Victory of Haç Ovasï (Mezö Kerésztés) and the Dismissal of Ġāzī Girāy Khan

The Crimean Tatars, in their turn, although they had commenced their activities late in the season, had generally served to stabilize a very fluid situation in Moldavia by the Peace of Cecora with Poland. But the Khan was not pleased; his ambitions had been thwarted. Already toward the end of 1595, it had become clear that the Khan was ready to play the role of a neutral power in the war in consideration of appropriate gifts and grants of money from the Christians. In spite of various excuses for the Khan's change in attitude late in the year 1595, it was the death of Sultan Murād III, his friend and benefactor, that heralded the change in the fortunes of Ġāzī Girāy. The Khan, at a time when his popularity and importance were beginning to be significant, had aroused the jealousies of certain personalities close to the Sultan. Sinān Pasha had harmed the position of the Khan considerably at the Porte by placing blame upon him for his own mismanagement of the Wallachian campaign. These developments at the end of 1595 led to the dismissal of the Khan in 1596.[83]

Generally speaking, the year 1595 had proved demoralizing for the Ottomans. The great border fortress of Gran had fallen and the Christian principalities of Transylvania and Wallachia had successfully kept the Ottomans at bay, thus leaving a great wedge of territory on the Ottoman flank in enemy hands. The two most pressing problems, army morale and the revolt of the Principalities of Transylvania and Wallachia had to be reckoned with. For the sake of morale it was decided that the Sultan must unfurl the sacred banner of the Prophet and head the campaign in person. As for the problem of the principalities, the frontal attack of 1595 had failed; the difficulties of terrain, the mountains and the forests, had played into the hands of the skilful leadership of Viovode Michael. To check such successes, the Ottomans decided to strike at a most vulnerable spot indeed, the main supply route between the Habsburg lands and Transylvania. The main objective for this campaign became the fortress of Erlau (Eğrī), which was situated close to the narrow corridor of land through which ran the communications between Austria and Transylvania.

Meanwhile, certain changes had taken place in the Ottoman government. Ḳōjā Sinān Pasha had been dismissed on 16 Rabi' I 1004/19 November 1595, after his shameful tactical blunders which led up to Giurgiu. When his successor to the Grand Vezirate, Lālā Meḥemmed Pasha, died only one month later, Sinān Pasha returned to the office for the fifth and last time; he died on 5 Sha'ban 1004/4 April 1596. Ibrāhīm Pasha now became Grand Vezir. By 15 Ẕī'l Hijje 1004/16 August 1596, the main army camped before Belgrade. At this point some dignitaries expressed their preference for a campaign against the Emperor's forces who were camped north of Pest, but the majority held out for the move into upper Hungary. Erlau (Eğrī) fell to the Ottomans on 19 Ṣefer 1005/12 October 1596 before the Imperial forces could come to its relief. The inside story of the capitulation is worth telling: while the new Imperial Commander-in-chief, Archduke Maximilian, dawdled north of Pest until his forces were joined by those of Prince Sigismund, a relief force, meanwhile, of Walloons and Bohemians were sent to Eger (Hung.) [Erlau (Ger.); Eğrī (Turk.)]. These very foreigners, during the siege, locked up the Austrian and Hungarian officers and capitulated, only to be cut down by the Janissaries in retaliation for Janissary murders at the Ottoman capitulation of Hatwan.[84]

Now, however, as the Ottomans turned toward the swampy Plain of Mezö Kerésztés (Haç Ovasï), they ran into the Imperial Army which had fortified itself behind *tābūrs* (rings of wagons). The mobility of the Ottoman forces was greatly reduced because the Habsburg forces controlled the passes through the swamps. The Ottomans, pushed to the last extremity, made one final desperate assault in which the third Vezir, Çiġālāzāde Sinān Pasha, played a prominent role. The Austrian Imperial forces were now routed and driven into the swamps. The Ottomans had won the most decisive victory of the war. Çiġālāzāde, as a reward for his timely services, was now appointed Grand Vezir, a post he held for only a little more than a month, Rabīʿ I-Rabīʿ II/October–December, 1596.[85]

Sigismund Báthory, during the winter of 1595–1596, had betaken himself to Prague where he received some money, troops, and supplies from the Emperor and the Papal Nuncio. The Transylvanian prince had also encouraged another invasion of Moldavia under the leadership of his protégé, Stephen Razvan, in December 1595, after Zamoyski had returned to Poland. The Poles, however, who had closely watched the growing rapprochement between Transylvania and the Habsburgs, had left troops with Jeremia Movila which defeated and executed Razvan.[86] The Poles once again sent a force into Moldavia during the campaign season of 1596.[87]

Meanwhile, Michael himself had been hard pressed by a sudden invasion of Ottomans and Tatars in February or March. The Ottomans intended to put Radu, the son of the former Voivode Mihnea II (1585–1591), into the voivodeship of Wallachia. Michael, catching the drift of events, and perhaps fearing that the extensive preparations for the Erlau campaign were intended for him, petitioned the Porte to accept him back into the Ottoman fold. At the Porte some of the great dignitaries, among them the late Grand Vezir, Sinān Pasha, had supported the project of replacing Michael, with a reliable vassal. After the death of Sinān Pasha, Ibrāhīm Pasha, now raised to Grand Vezir, and the preceptor of the Sultan, H̱ojā Saʿdeddin, were able to have Michael's submission accepted by the Sultan on the condition that he send to the Porte one of his sons as a hostage. This was an important expedient while the Sultan was on the plains of Northern Hungary.[88]

Paralleling all of these events, the Crimean Tatars were also on the move. The first definite word concerning the whereabouts of the Khan, Ġāzī Girāy, came from Jeremia Movila. On August 12, 1596, Jeremia reported to King Sigismund III Vasa that the Khan was known to have celebrated the *Ḳurbān*

Bayramï or festival of the sacrifice on 10 Ẕī'l Hijje 1004/5 August 1596 at Perekop in the Crimea. In this dispatch the Voivode speculated that the Khan would soon thereafter begin his march to Tehine (Bender).[89] In actual fact, shortly after this date a large movement of Crimean Tatars took place. Voivode Jeremia reported to the Grand Chancellor Zamoyski on August 28, 1596, that he expected the Tatars of Tehine (Bender) at the end of the week. The Voivode Michael relayed a similar message from Jeremia to Prince Sigismund Báthory and asked for troops. The Khan himself had written Jeremia Movila that he was coming with a very large army.[90] Indeed, the Khan and his brother, the Ḳalġay Fetḥ Girāy, who was destined to play an important role in the battle of Mezö Kerésztés, led a large body of horsemen toward Moldavia. It would appear, however, from the evidence of a few meager reports, that while the troops under Fetḥ Girāy were hastening to assist the Sultan in Hungary, the Khan himself remained in Wallachia ravaging the countryside. On December 20, 1596, Ġāzī Girāy wrote Jeremia Movila regarding an exchange of prisoners. One must assume that the diversionary tactics of the Khan had helped to keep the Wallachian troops occupied in 1596.[91]

The most significant event of the year 1596 for the Crimean Tatars was the deposition of Ġāzī Girāy. How far this political move was a development arising out of the insubordination and the grandiose schemes of the Khan and how far out of intrigues at the Porte is difficult to determine. Both factors no doubt had some bearing on the actual decision to depose the Khan, but the performances of Fetḥ Girāy and Çiġālazāde Sinān Pasha at Mezö Kerésztés did much to turn the balance against Ġāzī Girāy.

The Khan had been urged by the Porte to take part in the campaign of 1596 with Sultan Meḥemmed III. In view of the turbulence in Wallachia and Moldavia, however, the Khan had decided to remain in the lower Danube region close to his own domain. Perhaps he feared another attack by the Cossacks? In any case, he sent his brother, the Ḳalġay, with fewer forces than the Sultan had expected. The sanjāḳ bey of Szolnok had already reconnoitered the region around Eger (Eğrī) in the spring of 1596. Thereafter, the Ottoman dignitaries had decided to seize Eğrī for two main reasons: (*a*) its control would put them in a position to threaten the narrow corridor through which the Habsburgs were sending men and supplies to Transylvania and the other principalities; (*b*) the Ottomans also considered exploiting the mines in the mountains directly above Eğrī.

The Ottomans, this time led by the Sultan himself, besieged Eğrī from September 21 to October 12, 1596, when the fortress capitulated. Meanwhile, however, the siege gave to the Imperial forces time to move up to Eğrī and to occupy the marshlands in the area, thus posing a formidable threat to the Ottoman troops.[92]

At Mezö Kerésztés the Sultan, upon initial contact with the enemy, had ordered Feth Girāy to seek out the Imperial forces and report on their strength. When the Sultan received this report, he realized that the Infidels had assembled a very large army indeed. In truth, the battle of Mezö Kerésztés (Ḥāç Ovasï), as mentioned above, was destined to be the only significant field battle of the war and was to be ranked by the Ottomans alongside such famous victories as Mohács and Chaldiran.[93] At a critical stage in the conflict, the Tatars were able to attack the Imperial forces at the rear of the tābūr and with this diversionary action to draw off a sufficient number of enemy troops to enable the advancing Ottomans to push back the ranks of the enemy. Feth Girāy had served the Ottoman cause well and in recognition of this he was appointed the new Khan of the Crimean Tatars by Çiġālazāde Sinān Pasha, who had just been elevated to the Grand Vezirate, chiefly because of his services during the battle.[94]

Feth Girāy, a good soldier and rather less ambitious than Ġāzī Girāy, made a good impression on many of his contemporaries. The Ḳalġay at first refused the post of Khan, saying that it rightfully belonged to his elder brother. With the insistence of the Grand Vezir and other dignitaries, however, he reluctantly accepted.[95] It was a fateful step, leading to a rebellion in the Crimea.

The general lines of the ensuing conflict between the two brothers is fairly clear. Ġāzī Girāy, after his incursion into Wallachia, returned to the Crimea where he learned of his deposition in early November. The former Khan had every advantage for he occupied the home territory. Feth Girāy did not even have a very large force at his command in Hungary, 20,000 Tatars at most. Another factor favored Ġāzī Girāy: the Sultan, hard pressed as he was in the war, could not afford to detach a strong troop to aid Feth Girāy in unseating the former Khan. But Feth Girāy Khan also had his friends in the Crimea. He had appointed the former Nūr ed-Dīn, Baẖt Girāy, the son of 'Ādil Girāy, to the rank of Ḳalġay and Selāmēt Girāy, his brother and future Khan, to be Nūr ed-Dīn.[96] As each of these relatives came into new positions of prominence, their traditional supporters and kin fell into line and helped to produce a strong pro-Feth Girāy faction. Meanwhile, Çiġālazāde was dismissed from office in December of 1596. Shortly thereafter, Grand Vezir Ibrāhīm Pasha wanted to reinstate Ġāzī Girāy as Khan if he met certain conditions. Ġāzī Girāy, meanwhile, had decided to go to the capital to plead his cause. He boarded a vessel for Istanbul but before embarking he met Çerkes H̱āndan Aġā, Muteferriḳa Bāşī (i.e., head of a special guard regiment of the Sultan) who had been sent to settle the squabble over the Khanship. He had been directed to give the *muḳarrernāme* (letter of confirmation) of the Sultan to the brother who appeared to have the largest following. H̱āndan Aġā, an old friend of Ġāzī Girāy, gave the muḳarrernāme to him. But Feth Girāy had influential friends at the Porte who were able to have an Imperial patent (H̱aṭṭ-i Şerīf) issued declaring that he was the rightful Khan.

In the end, because the passions of the two factions had been raised to such a high pitch, it became necessary for the interested parties to settle the dilemma by having recourse to the legal institutions of the Empire. Now each contender for the Khanship submitted his credentials to the highest judge in the Crimea, the Ḳādī of Kaffa, ʿAbd al Raḥman Efendi, for his decision. The Ḳādī pronounced in favor of Fetḥ Girāy on the grounds that the H̱aṭṭ-i Şerīf pertaining to Fetḥ Girāy was more valid than the muḳarrernāme of Ġāzī Girāy because the H̱aṭṭ bore the signature of the Sultan. His decision, however, became subject to the opinion and confirmation of the Muftī of Kaffa, highest authority on Muslim law in the Crimea, who, apart from being a supporter of Ġāzī Girāy, was able to throw out the decision of the Ḳādī on the basis of a technicality. The Muftī, Mevlanā Azakī, brought to the attention of the Ḳādī and the assembled dignitaries that although what the Ḳādī had stated was correct, only the patent of Ġāzī Girāy carried the *Ṭūġrā* or seal of the Sultan and, as the Ṭūġrā was the great seal upon which the administration of the empire depended, anyone who failed to obey Ġāzī Girāy was committing sedition against the Sultan. This settled the issue; Ġāzī Girāy became Khan for the second time some three or four months after his dismissal (c. February, 1597).[97] Now Fetḥ Girāy, who had been summoned to the Porte, came to do homage to his brother, but Ġāzī Girāy had him executed and all of his sons put to death.[98] The entire affair only served to heighten the feelings of insecurity that the Khan felt toward the Porte and indeed toward many of his own people.[99] The position of Ḳalġay now fell to the brother of the Khan, Selāmet Girāy, and that of Nūr ed-Dīn to a son of Saʿādet Girāy, Devlet Girāy.

It appears, also, that about the time of these political changes in the Crimea, the Khan published a decree calling on each household to set aside annually twelve sheep and a certain sum of money to enable him to establish a unit of five hundred arquebusiers. Perhaps this is further proof of the insecurity of the Khan; it most certainly reflects the growing awareness of the Khan concerning the importance of hand guns and other firearms in the warfare of the late sixteenth century.[100]

As a postscript to the warfare, the intrigues and the counterintrigues of the year 1596, it is worth recalling that Ġāzī Girāy Khan had to win and to retain the respect of his overlord, the Sultan; he had also to keep in the good graces of the faction closest to the Sultan. This faction included first and foremost, Ṣafiye H̱ānum, favorite wife of the late Sultan Murād III and the mother (Vālide Sultan) of Sultan Meḥemmed III. After her, H̱ōja Saʿdeddin, the preceptor of the Sultan, and Ġazanfer Aġā, the Kapï Ağasï of the court had the Sultan's ear. While Sultan Meḥemmed was on campaign, the influence of H̱ōja Saʿdeddin and Ġazanfer Aġā naturally increased. This was ominous for Ġāzī Girāy, for he had been a friend of the late Sultan Murād III and hence could be expected to retain much of his influence at court through the good offices of the Vālide Sultan. Ġāzī Girāy Khan, of course, by refusing to go on campaign in person and by intriguing for his own benefit in the Principalities, must have alienated any support he may have had among the closest advisers of the Sultan. Viewed in this light, the appointment of Çiġāla-zāde Sinān Pasha, a protégé of the H̱ōja and the Ağā, to the post of Grand Vezir and the subsequent removal of Ġāzī Girāy from the post of Khan did not seem very surprising, any more than did his reinstatement under Ibrāhīm Pasha, supported as the latter was by the Vālide Sultan.[101]

NOTES

1. See Kramers, "Skanderbeg," *E.I.*[1], pp. 466–467.
2. See the writer's article, "Ottoman Imperial Policy and the Economy of the Black Sea Region," *J.A.O.S.* 86/2 (April–June 1966), pp. 86–113.
3. Among many available sources and studies for the period, see Pfeffermann, *Die Zusammenarbeit der Renaissancepäpste mit den Türken*, pp. 122–242. Von Hefele, *Histoire des Conciles*, VIII/I, H. Le Clercq, tr., pp. 239–620; Moncallero, "La Politica di Leone X e di Francesco I nella progettata crociate contro i turchi e nella lotta per la successione imperiale," *Rinascimento*, VIII/1, pp. 61–109, and finally, the important overview of Fueter, *Geschichte des Europaischen Staatssystems von 1492–1559*.
4. See, for example, the proposal of the Fifth Lateran Council for a Crusade and the letter of Sultan Selim to Pope Leo X in Sanuto, *I Diarii XXV*, pp. 95–106, 266–267; and the summary chapter by Pastor, *History of the Popes*, VII, pp. 213–254.
5. For a reconstruction of the Hungarian social background, I am particularly indebted to the following studies: Franz Salamon, *Ungarn im Zeitalter der Türkenherrschaft*; E. (Jenö) Csuday *Die Geschichte der Üngarn*, M. Darvai, tr., and Ladislas Makkai, *Histoire de Transylvanie*. For details of the *Tripartitum*, see C. M. Knatchbull-Hugessen, *The Political Evolution of the Hungarian Nation*. It is also important to note that the outcasts of society, the gypsies and others, became Muslim.
6. Csuday, II, pp. 63–68; Makkai, pp. 162–166.
7. For complete details of the sanjāḳs belonging to the four *eyalets* in Hungary, see Salamon, p. 235, and Csuday, II, pp. 42–44. George Martinuzzi, prior to his death, warned the Emperor Ferdinand that the restrictions on the Christian peasantry should be eased because many were going over to Islam. See Arpád Károlyi, "Fráter György Levelezése . . ." in *Terténelmi Tár*, p. 51 (Note: courtesy of Mr. Andrew Riedlmayer.)
8. Makkai, pp. 63–64.
9. Csuday, II, pp. 67–72. Some of the old Transylvanian noble families were pushed into the background by the nobility coming into the province from Western Hungary. See Makkai, pp. 156–160. The term Haiduk [Hung., hajdu(k); Ger., Haiduken, Heyduken; Turk., haydud, haydud] is believed to have derived from the Hungarian word for roving cattle-drovers (hajtók) who turned to brigandry or joined Habsburg, Transylvanian or Turkish fighting units whenever political or social conditions of the 16th and 17th centuries disrupted the cattle trade. Their ranks were also joined by other dispossessed or disgruntled elements of society. Cf. Eric Hobsbawm, *Bandits*. [This note on Haiduks, courtesy of Andrew Riedlmayer.]
10. Makkai, pp. 182 ff.
11. Makkai, p. 190.
12. See note 7; also J. W. Zinkeisen, *Geschichte des osmanischen Reiches in Europa* II, pp. 807–865, 866–913.
13. Rothenberg, *The Austrian Military Border in Croatia, 1522–1747*, p. 44.
14. Hantsch, *Die Geschichte Österreiches*, I, pp. 336, 344 ff.

15. Thus, for example, the peace concluded in 1568 contains such a clause as the following (mentioned by Hammer, *Histoire de l'Empire Ottoman*, VI, p. 316): ". . . les deux souverains convenaient de faire de mutuels efforts pour enlever aux voivodes tous motifs de troubler la paix; ils s'engageaient a exercer une active surveillance sur les heiduques, les azabs, les martoloses, les levends et les haramiyes ou brigands . . . ."
16. The Uscocs are believed to have been in origin Serbian refugees who settled in the border areas of Croatia and Slavonia. See Rothenberg, *Austrian . . . Border*, p. 28. The Muslim borderers, in spite of pressure put on them by the Ottoman state from time to time, still continued to raid the lands of the infidel, bringing back captives and booty.
17. For details, see *Ibid.*, pp. 40–47. It seems that the Lutheran magnates blocked appropriations out of the fear that such funds might be used to equip an army to enforce the policies of the Counter Reformation.
18. *Ibid.*, pp. 49–54; by the same author, "Venice and the Uskoks of Zeng: 1537–1618," *J. of Mod. Hist.*, XXXIII/2 (June, 1961), pp. 148–156.
19. Although Hasan Pasha had been sent reinforcements from Rumeli by the Grand Vezir, Siyāvuş Pasha, he never received them. The movement of these troops had been stopped by Kōjā Sinān Pasha upon his appointment to the Grand Vezirate, because he held a grudge against the Pasha of Bosnia. Peçewī, *Tārīḫ-i*, II, pp. 128–129. Two relatives of the Sultan also perished in the mêlée.
20. The Pope had hopes of forming an anti-Ottoman league (Von Pastor, *History of the Popes* XXIII, p. 273). A study of the diplomacy of this period has been made by Matoušek, *Turečka Valka v Evropske Politice v Letech 1592–1594* (not seen).
21. *Pamyatniki Diplomaticheskikh Snosheniy Drevnoy Rossii s Derzhavami Inostrannymi 1488–1699*, I, col, 1394.
22. See Fisher, *The Russian Fur Trade 1550–1700*, pp. 137–138.
23. Pierling, *Papes et Tsars 1547–1597*, pp. 451–452; R. Gooss, ed., *Österreichische Staatsverträge Fürstentum Siebenbürgen*, pp. 226–231; Hammer, *Histoire*, VII, pp. 273–275.
24. A. de Bertha, *Magyars et Roumains devant l'Histoire*, p. 197; also, Seton-Watson, *A History of the Roumanians*, p. 110. Even before Sigismund Báthory signed a treaty with the Emperor, certain members of the Transylvanian Diet who opposed Sigismund, including some of his own kinsmen, were put to death (Pierling, pp. 451–452). Of the three estates which were represented in the Diet, namely the Magyars, the Szekely, and the Saxons, the Szekely were particularly hostile to the rule of the Báthory line (De Bertha, p. 198).
25. *Ibid.*, pp. 192–200; Seton-Watson, pp. 62–63.
26. Peçewī, II, p. 158.
27. N. Iorga, *A History of Roumania*, J. McCabe, tr., pp. 106–108, 147 ff; also Beldiceanu, "La crise monetaire ottomane au XVIe siècle et son influence sur les principautés roumaines," *Südost-Forschungen* XVI (1957), pp. 70–86.
28. Pierling, pp. 447–454.
29. Hurmuzaki, ed., *Documente privatóre la Istoria Romanilor*, IV/2, pp. 174–175, 179.
30. A summary of the Polish-Ottoman agreement of 1592 can be found in Abrahamovicz, *Katalog Dokumentow Tureckich . . . 1455–1672*, I, pp. 225–226.
31. For an important study of the formation and development of the Cossack communities, see Stökl, *Die Entstehung des Kosakentums.*
32. Hrushevsky, *History*, pp. 178–181, 182–183.
33. See Schottin, ed., *Tagebuch des Erich Lassota von Steblau, passim.*
34. For the religious and social implications of this repression, see Hrushevsky, *History*, pp. 188–192, 211–214.
35. Hammer, *Histoire*, VII, pp. 267–272.
36. Csuday, II, p. 73.
37. On April 14, 1594, the agreement was signed. For details, see Chap. VI.

38. In one passage Peçewī (II, pp. 156–157) attempts to estimate the number of troops on campaign in Hungary in 1594. He gives the number 30,000 for the total of the *Kapī Kūlarī* alone, and estimates another 30,000 coming from Rumeli. To this he added an unknown number from the garrisons in the border fortresses. Also, as no campaign has been made in Hungary since the days of Sulaymān, as many as another 30,000 camp followers of various descriptions joined the campaign out of their thirst for booty (the usual slave merchants, prostitutes, provisioners, armorers, etc.). Finally, Peçewī included in his count at least 20,000 Tatars and as many more irregulars, bringing the total to something between 120,000 and 150,000 (a modest total of six or eight divisions according to present day standards).

39. Peçewī, II, p. 152; see also Gökbilgin, "Erdel," *I.A.*, IV, p. 300; Hammer, *Histoire*, VII, pp. 273–274.

40. Hurmuzaki, IV/2, pp. 174–5 and 179.

41. Hospodar Aaron to Zamoyski (March 5, 1594), *ibid.*, Suppl. II/I, p. 329. At this time the Hospodar wrote that he had no intention of providing guides for the Tatars.

42. *Ibid.*, XI, p. 432. Accompanying the çāvuş was a certain Pole who had become a convert to Islam. The latter declared that the çāvuş was not to be trusted because the Tatars did plan to go through Poland (*ibid.*, Suppl. II/I, pp. 337–338). The Ottomans may have been sincere. The Khan may have decided to go through Poland at the last minute, to avoid an ambush (*ibid.*, XI, p. 394).

43. This may have been a small detachment sent as a diversionary force. As the editor, Hurmuzaki, has noted, the main Tatar contingent came through Moldavia and then through Maramures in June and July (*ibid.*, XI, p. 446). Some confirmation of this report may be found in Francus. According to his account, the Tatars attempted to force their entrance into Poland by stampeding a large amount of livestock into the waiting Polish forces. The plan failed, however, when the noise of the Polish guns reversed the stampede and forced the Tatars to flee toward the south (Francus, *Quinquennalis*, pp. 504–505).

44. Zamoyski, in a rather apologetic letter to Cardinal Aldobrandini, explained how the Tatars slipped through his fingers. He had taken steps to block the pass near Sambor, the most commodious of the three possible routes and also the route which the Tatars had followed for the Szigetvar campaign of 1566. But the Tatars took the route leading to Huszth. By the time Zamoyski had marched his troops to the other pass, the Tatars were already in Transylvania (Zamoyski, *De Transitu Tartarorum per Pocutiam, Anni M.D. XCIII Epistola.*

45. Schottin, ed., *Tagebuch*, pp. 7–8.

46. *Ibid.*, p. 211. Ochakov was a likely spot for an attack. It was to this point the Ottoman vessels ferried the Tatars across the estuary of the Dnieper from the Crimean side of the river. It is doubtful if this "attack" was anything more than a minor harassment (*Ibid.*, p. 217).

47. See the long report of Morinni Paully to the Kaiser (c. beginning of July), Hurmuzaki, III, pp. 200–206, and also the memoir of Abraham Tocken, *ibid.*, XI, p. 391. At this time the Khan must have quickly moved his forces into Transylvania (Zamoyski to Aldobrandini, *De Transitu Tartarorum*).

48. It must have become clear to Lassota (pp. 8, 215–219) that the Tatar advance could not be stopped; therefore, he negotiated with the Cossacks about either a diversionary attack on the Ottomans through Moldavia and Wallachia to the Danube or an attack on Perekop (Orkapu) in the Crimea or both. One of the chief disappointments of Lassota during the mission was his discovery that Chlopicki was not the head of the Zaporozhian Cossacks of the Sich but of those in Kiev. Nevertheless, Chlopicki, with the gold of the Emperor, was able to win over the Sich Cossacks to the Habsburg cause.

49. Pierling, p. 460. Peçewī, (II, p. 149) described Jānis Aġā, a talented guide and the one who led the Tatars to Hungary. Peçewī implies that Jānis Aġā had more divine inspiration than actual knowledge of the routes.

50. See Bartholomew, *The Times Atlas of the World*, IV, Pl. 82 (J–2.5) and Chardonnet, *Atlas*

International Larousse, Pl. 8 (L-d/e). See letter of Kornis to Zamoyski in which Kornis mentions the pass "circa augustias Snatinensis" (March 21, 1594), Veress, *Documente Privitoare*, IV, p. 71. In the account of Peçewī it is clearly stated that the Tatars, by way of the shores of the Ṭūrlä (Ṭūrlā), i.e., Dniester river, passed out of Poland and into Hungary. Cf. Chardonnet, *loc. cit.*, and Peçewī II, p. 148. For an idea of international boundaries at the time, see *Cambridge Modern History Atlas*, Maps Nos. 3, 20, and especially 21. The account of Kâtib Çelebī (*Fezleke*, I, pp. 34–35), while mentioning the Ṭūrlā (Dnieper), also mentions the name of the pass leading to Huszth which was called "Balkan." Both Kâtib Çelebī and Zamoyski (*De Transitu Tatarorum*) mention that the pass was blocked but that the Tatars dismounted, crept around the barriers of rocks and felled trees, and slaughtered a force guarding the pass.

51. Veress, ed., *Annuae Litterae Societatio Jesu* in *Fontes rerum Transylvanicarum*, V (1921), pp. 41–42.

52. Ortelius, . . . *Beschreibung* . . . pp. 227–228; Zeitung no. 1095 cited by Kertbény, ed., *Bibliografie der ungarischen nationalen und internationalen Literatur*, I, p. 259; Marco Venier to the Doge (November 25, 1594), Hurmuzaki, III, p. 463.

53. Those Tatars who could not forgo opportunities to raid or burn in Poland were put under arrest for a few days and then again released. In short, in Poland the Tatars avoided trouble whenever possible (Peçewī, II, p. 149–150; Munejjimbāşī, II p. 703). See also Decsi, *Magyar Historiaja* (*De Rebus hungaricus*), *1592–1598*, pp. 109–110. Kâtib Çelebī reports that the Khan had a serious skirmish with Báthory near Debreczen but that, fearing the enemy cannon, he withdrew (*Fezleke*, pp. 34–35).

54. Peçewī, pp. 150–151; Munejjimbāşī, III, p. 570.

55. Romaci (?), ed., *La Terza Parte del Tesero Politico*, p. 463.

56. Peçewī, II, pp. 145–147, 153; Munejjimbāşī, III, p. 571.

57. 'Abd al Ġaffār, p. 115. According to the account of Munejjimbāşī (III, p. 571), however, it was the Khan who, together with other commanders, turned the tide by conceiving the plan of crossing the Danube, seizing the tābūr, then attacking the fortress by bridging the moat.

58. Peçewī, II, p. 156.

59. *Ibid.*, pp. 157–158.

60. Marco Venier, Bailo, to the Doge (Para, November 12, 1594), Hurmuzaki, III, p. 463.

61. Peçewī, II, pp. 158–159; Zinkeisen, IV, pp. 598–599; Jorga, *Geschichte des Osmanischen Reiches*, III, p. 303. The Treaty of Prague negotiated by Stephan Bocskay gained Emperor Rudolph's recognition of Transylvanian autonomy in exchange for the recognition of Rudolph as overlord. This Treaty led to an open rupture between Poland and Transylvania and put Poland in the Ottoman camp for the duration of the war (Makkai, pp. 192–193, 195). For details of the Treaty, including an arranged marriage between Prince Sigismund and the daughter of the late Archduke Karl, see Csuday, II, p. 76. The document was signed January 28, 1595.

62. Munejjimbāşī, III, pp. 579–582; Peçewī, II, pp. 123–125, 158–160; Iorga-McCabe, p. 149. Iorga (*G.O.R.*, III, p. 303) gives the date of Michael's treachery as October 15. Carl Göllner, in his important study, *Michael der Tapfere im Lichte des Abendlandes*, dates the uprising November 13, 1594 (p. 31).

63. On May 25, 1595, Michael had signed an agreement recognizing Sigismund Báthory as his King in exchange for supplies of men and other concessions. For details, see Seton-Watson, p. 63. According to Makkai (p. 194), Stephan Bocskay led the Transylvanian troops who so ably assisted Michael at this rout of the Turkish forces.

64. Munejjimbāşī, III, p. 583; Zinkeisen, IV, p. 599. Cf. the remarks of Novosel'skiy, *Bor'ba*, pp. 41, 42. For eyewitness accounts of the Ottoman defeat at Giurgiu, see Göllner, Texts xxii–xxix.

65. Decsi, pp. 147–148.

66. Venier to the Doge (Feb. 20, 1595), Hurmuzaki, IV/2, pp. 188–189; also Voivode Aaron to Zamoyski (Feb. 15, 1595), *ibid.*, Suppl. II/I, p. 341.

67. It was reported that Ġāzī Girāy, in this battle, received a wound from an arquebus and was treated by a barber in Silistria. Marco Venier, Bailo, to the Doge, (March 6, 1595), *ibid.*, III, p.

469 and IV, p. 189.
68. Dispatch of Simeon Genga from Alba Julia to his brother John, ambassador of Sigismund Báthory in Rome, in Veress, "Campania Creştinilor in Contra Lui Sinan Paşa Din 1595," *Academia Romãna Memoriile Sectiunii Istorice*, III/IV, pp. 33–35. See also the Ottoman report of the meeting of Ġazī Girāy and Muṣṭafā Pasha, Peçewī, II, pp. 158, 159. In a letter of Marini Paully to Prague (April 28, 1595), it was reported that this son of the Khan was killed (Veress, *Documente*, IV, p. 207).
69. *Ibid.* Voivode Aaron had been the protégé of Kōjā Sinān Pasha. Bogdan was the new appointee of Ferhād Pasha who had replaced Sinān Pasha as Grand Vezir (Peçewī, II, pp. 158–159); Munejjimbāşī, III, p. 573; Iorga-McCabe, p. 268; and Seton-Watson, p. 63. Stephan Razvan, captain of Aaron's Hungarian guard, had been instrumental in bringing about the arrest of Aaron and his banishment to Hungary. When Stephen Razvan then declared himself voivode, he had the full support of Michael and Sigismund Báthory (Iorga, *G.O.R.*, III, p. 307) and in turn did homage to Sigismund (Makkai, p. 194).
70. Peçewī, II, pp. 178 ff. General Mannstein, the victor of Gran, died after his success. As Archduke Matthias was a weak commander, the indiscipline or *soldatesca* of the Habsburg soldiery brought misery and destruction to the Hungarian countryside (Csuday, II, pp. 77–78).
71. The Khan was reported to have begun to cross the delta of the Dnieper with his troops around the first of July (Jeremia Movila to Sigismund III of Poland, July 1, 1595, Hurmuzaki, Suppl. II/I, p. 343). The Khan however, only took up action in October (*ibid.*, Suppl. II/I, pp. 352–353). Thus if these reports are to be believed, the Khan lingered along the border area for at least two months. For an account of the Khan's schemes, see Peçewī, II, p. 147; Kâtib Çelebi I, pp. 61–62; and Hofdiener to Sigismund Báthory (October 1595), Hurmuzaki, III, pp. 252–253.
72. Francis, p. 90; Iorga, *G.O.R.* III, p. 313. This is an important point revealing to what extent Wallachia and Moldavia were indebted to Poland for their semi-independent position.
73. Hofdiener to Sigismund Báthory, Hurmuzaki, *loc. cit.*
74. Sagredo, *Histoire de l'Empire Ottoman*, V, pp. 45–46; Iorga, *G.O.R.*, III, p. 316.
75. The fortress of Giurgiu did not fall into Michael's hands until October 31, 1595 (Munejjimbāşī, III, pp. 585–586). Cf. Venier to the Doge (September 15, 1595), Hurmuzaki IV/2, p. 205, concerning the reluctance of the Tatars to participate that year.
76. Heidenstein (*Vitae J. Zamoyscii*, pp. 117–121) reports that Aḥmed Beg was the son of the Khan's sister.
77. Statement of a Serbian prisoner, Dimitrasko (October 17, 1595), Hurmuzaki, Suppl. II/I, pp. 352–353. This is confirmed in a letter of "Siaban Bascha," chief vezir of the Khan, to Jeremia (September 16, 1595), Veress, *Documente*, IV, pp. 273–274. The letter reveals that Jeremia had twice sought the standards of investiture from the Khan and Sinān Pasha but without success. The vezir "Siaban," however, encouraged Jeremia to continue seeking the post, assuring him of his support.
78. Zamoyski to Sigismund III (October 24, 1595), Hurmuzaki, Suppl. II/I, pp. 357–358. According to another document, the Khan had also given up his right to demand tribute or damages from Poland (*ibid.*, VIII, p. 196). Decsi (pp. 203–204) denies this. See also, in this regard, the letter of the Khan to King Sigismund III, N. Reusner, *Epistolae Turcicae*, XIV, p. 161. For information about a Cossack raid on Kaffa in September, which may have delayed the coming of the Tatars, see Letter of E. Barton (September 20, 1595), Cotton M.S., Nero B XI, Brit. Mus., f. 215a. See also Iorga, *G.O.R.*, III, pp. 317–318.
79. Filip Pigafetta to Belizar Vinta, grand chancellor to the Duke of Tuscany (October 18, 1595), Veress, *Academia Romana*, III/IV, pp. 34–52. Pigafetta was secretary to Capt. Piccolomini, commander of a group of Tuscan crusaders serving under Michael.
80. Pigafetta to Vinta (November 14, 1595); Veress, *Academia Romana*, II/IV, pp. 61–64.
81. *Ibid.*, also, document of December 2, 1595, Hurmuzaki, IV/2, p. 209.
82. Venier to the Doge (December 2, 1595), *ibid.*, II, pp. 496–497; the same (December 14),

ibid., IV/2, p. 210; and Pigafetta to Vinta (November 26, 1595), Veress, *Academia Romana*, III/IV, pp. 66–67.

83. Csuday, II, pp. 77–78. By January of 1596 it became a very serious question of face-saving with the old Pasha. He manipulated the factions and he particularly aroused the suspicions of the Porte by insinuating that there was danger of collusion between the Khan, the Poles, and the Voivode of Moldavia against the Ottoman State (Venier to the Doge, January 12, 1596, Hurmuzaki, IV/2, pp. 211–212).

84. Csuday, II, pp. 79–80.

85. Peçewī, II, pp. 188–206; Munejjimbāşī, III, pp. 586–592. During this engagement the very tent of the Sultan was under attack for a time. Had it not been for the steadying influence of H̱ōja Sa'deddin, the preceptor of the Sultan, the latter might have fled, or have been captured. See also Hammer, VII, pp. 325–326, 329.

86. Campana, *Istoria del Mondo*, 41b–42a; Seton-Watson, p. 64; Iorga-McCabe, p. 151, and Iorga, *G.O.R.*, III, p. 318.

87. The Poles may have been prompted to take action by information that the Cossacks planned another invasion of Moldavia. See Potacki to Zamoyski (April 19, 1596), Hurmuzaki, Suppl. II/I, p. 385. The main reason for their reoccupation of a portion of Moldavia, however, was to prevent the same action by the Tatars.

88. Venier to the Doge (February 10, 1596), Hurmuzaki, III, p. 504; also dispatch of an unknown (March 2, 1596), *ibid.*, Suppl. II/I, pp. 378–379; Ortelius, p. 304; Hammer, *Histoire*, VII, pp. 319–320; Iorga-McCabe, p. 268.

89. Jeremia to Sigismund III (August 12, 1596), Hurmuzaki, Suppl. II/I, p. 394.

90. Jeremia to Zamoyski (August 28, 1596), *ibid.*, pp. 395–396; Michael to Prince of Transylvania (September 5, 1596), *ibid.*, III, pp. 275–276; Zamoyski to Radziwill (September 6, 1596), *ibid.*, Suppl. II/I, p. 398.

91. Fugger Report (October 30, 1596), *ibid.*, III, p. 271, and Jeremia to King Sigismund III (November 25, 1596), *ibid.*, Suppl. II/I, p. 405. According to Iorga (*G.O.R.*, III, p. 321), this Tatar incursion into Wallachia was only the first of several attempts to put the brother of Jeremia, Simeon Movila, into the voivodeship of Wallachia. Of course Poland would have acquiesced in this for the Movila brothers owed their prominence to Polish support (Ġāzī Girāy to Jeremia, December 20, 1596, Hurmuzaki, Suppl. II/I, p. 408.

92. See Parry, "Egri," *E.I.*², II, pp. 689–691.

93. Peçewī, II, p. 197; Hammer, *Histoire*, VII, p. 329.

94. For a plan of this battle, see Dilich, *Ungarische Chronica*, pp. 297–299; Peçewī, II, p. 205; Munejjimbāşī, III, pp. 591–593. Çiġāla-zāde, who served as Grand Vezir a little over a month (October to December, 1596) before his dismissal, was appointed through the influence of the Kapï Agāsï, Ġazanfer, and of H̱ōja Sa'deddin, but he caused so much trouble through his decision to intervene in Tatar affairs and also to punish or condemn to death those *Sipahiyân* who were absent from the recent battle, that he was quickly dismissed and replaced by Damad Ibrāhīm Pasha at the behest of the Sultan's mother. See Gökbilgin "Ciğala-zade" *I.A.* III, pp. 161–165, and Parry, "Čighalazade Yusuf Sinan Pasha," *E.I.*², II, pp. 33–34.

95. Meḥemmed Rižā, *al Set'es-Seyyār fī aẖbār Mulūk at-Tātār*, pp. 108–109. At least one Turkish historian has suggested that an old emnity existed between Jigāla-zāde Sinān Pasha and Gāzī Girāy from the days when both of them assisted 'Osmān Pasha in the taking of Tabriz in 1585.

96. Meḥemmed Rižā, pp. 108–109.

97. Hasanbeyzāde, *Tārīẖ-i Al-i 'Osmān*, Istanbul, Nūr-u Osmaniyye Ktp. Ms. No. 3105–06.

98. Decsi (pp. 284–285) provides some interesting details about this event. He states that although Feth Girāy had been summoned to the Porte with promises that he would be reinstalled as Khan, Feth actually heard that he was to be killed by order of the Sultan. He thus made plans to flee to Muscovy and it was then that he and his Hungarian wife ("e nobili Ungarorum ad Munkacsium Moricziorum gente procreata") and all his children were killed.

99. Meḥemmed Riżā, pp. 108–109; Peçewī, II. 205–206; Munejjimbāşī, III, pp. 591–594; Soranzo, *L'Ottomano*, pp. 91–92.
100. Kazimirski, "Précis . . . ," *J.A.*, Ser. II/XII, pp. 431–43.
101. Rossi, "La Sultana 'Nur Bānū' (Cecilia Venier-Baffo), moglie di Selim II (1566–1574) e Madre de Murād III (1574–1595)," *Oriente Moderno* (1953), pp. 433–441. See also Gökbilgin, "Cigala-zade," *I.A.*, III, p. 164.

CHAPTER EIGHT
The Final Stages of the Long War and the Bocskay Revolt (1597–1606)

The clear-cut victory at Mezö Kerésztés (1596) once again gave to the Ottomans a mandate, reminiscent of their victory at Mohács (1526), to establish the terms for a new equilibrium in eastern Europe. Yet, the war and the quest for a new equilibrium continued to trouble eastern Europe a further ten years. Henceforth, the Christian forces avoided field battles with the Muslims. The two chief contenders now conducted siege and countersiege year after year until peace was finally concluded in 1606. But even in the siege warfare, the Ottomans slowly gained advantage over the Habsburgs as one by one such important fortress towns as Esztergom (Gran), Székesfehérvar (Stuhlweissenburg), and Kanisza fell into Ottoman hands. Only in the early spring and late autumn of each year when the Ottoman armies had returned to winter quarters were the Habsburg forces, toughened by contingents of Spaniards and Walloons, able to check the progress of Ottoman arms.[1] But the toll in men and equipment of siege warfare on both the Ottomans and Habsburgs exerted steady pressure upon their leaders to end the conflict.

Although the Ottomans had a slight advantage over the Habsburgs in siege warfare, it was the social and political unrest in Hungary that gained for the Ottomans a decisive advantage over the Habsburgs in the last years of the war. The lack of Habsburg sensitivity to Hungarian national feelings and of the Catholic Church to the issue of freedom of conscience following the Reformation assured to the Ottomans the overlordship of Hungary for another hundred years.

1 Siege Warfare and Ottoman Problems to 1606 and the Revolt of Stephan Bocskay

The prince of Transylvania, Sigismund Báthory, whose troops had lost heavily with the Habsburgs at Kerésztés, wrote a long letter to Emperor Rudolph II that winter setting forth a campaign plan for the Christian armies in 1597. In his opinion, the Imperial forces of upper Hungary and the armies in Transylvania and Wallachia should hold back until the Turks and Tatars had committed themselves. If the Ottomans chose to continue the war in Hungary, then the forces of Wallachia and Transylvania would best serve the common cause by an attack on the vital Danube line. If, however, the main attack came through the Danubian principalities, then the Christians must make a united stand against the Ottoman advance. Finally, if the Ottomans advanced on Hungary and the Tatars remained at home, then the Wallachians and the Transylvanian forces would have to maintain a separate watch on their borders.[2]

These views, set forth by Sigismund Báthory, call attention to the weak and strong points of both adversaries. Neither side could provide or arm enough men to knock out the other. The Ottomans had to defend the line of the Danube at all costs as the most feasible way of transporting supplies and ordinance to the Hungarian front. Contrariwise, the Christian powers considered it essential to disrupt this route whenever and wherever it was possible. It is also clear that the Tatar horsemen were a force to be reckoned with.

The year 1597 was uneventful in the war in Hungary. The Grand Vezir, Ibrāhīm Pasha, having just replaced Çigālāzāde, felt that his personal presence at the Porte was necessary and thus appointed Sāṭūrjī Meḥemmed Pasha to be commander-in-chief of the Ottoman forces in Hungary. Sāṭūrjī Meḥemmed Pasha, however, accomplished very little. He recovered Totis, a minor fortress that had fallen to the Habsburgs, and then moved in the direction of Gran (Esztergom). An unexpected revolt of the Janissaries brought the operation of the Serdār to an end and forced him to enter into negotiations with Habsburg representatives on an island in the Danube opposite Waitzen (Vač). The talks proved fruitless and not long afterward the Ottomans returned to their winter quarters. Sāṭūrjī Meḥemmed, when upbraided fòr his inactivity, placed the blame for the uneventful campaign upon the failure of the Tatar Khan to appear in the field.[3]

The Sultan now deposed Ibrāhīm Pasha from the office of Grand Vezir and appointed the eunuch, Ḥasan Pasha, in his stead (23 Rabī'I 1006/3 November 1597). The new Grand Vezir, although aware that the Sultan Vālide was in large measure responsible for the fall of his predecessor as well as for the rise of his own star, came into conflict with Ġażanfer Aġā, the Kāpï Aġāsï, another eunuch and an important member of the entourage of the

Vālide Sultan. Henceforth, the preceptor of the Sultan, H̱ōja Sa'd ed-Dīn, Ġażanfer Aġā himself, and Ṭurnāḳjīzāde, Aġā of the Janissaries, intrigued for Ḥasan Pasha's removal. He was indeed deposed on April 8, 1598, and replaced by the second Vezir, Jerrāḥ Meḥemmed Pasha. The dismissal of Ḥasan Pasha was easily arranged after the arrival of news that the Habsburg Imperial forces had retaken the great fortress of Raab on March 29, 1598. This fortress, which had been bought so dearly, fell to the generals Palffy and Schwarzenberg in a surprise attack which lasted only two days.[4]

In spite of this loss, the Ottoman forces in this same year did not assemble until July at Becskerek, a town 18 kilometers northwest of Temesvar. Sāṭūrjī Meḥemmed waited there forty-five days, until he was joined by the Crimean Khan at the end of August. While the Imperial forces moved against Buda, the Ottomans, at the beginning of October, began a siege of the star-shaped fortress of Varaždin (Vārād, Grosswardein, Oradea), the key fortress guarding the western approaches to Transylvania.[5] When it became evident to the Serdār that the Christian threat to Buda was serious, he raised the siege of Varaždin and made an effort to relieve Buda. The autumn rains, however, had begun in earnest. Every river and every ravine had turned into a torrent, forcing upon the Ottoman army an excessive amount of bridge building and ferrying activities. The journey from Varaždin (Vārād) to Szolnok, which ordinarily would have taken three days, now took the army twelve. Short of rations, exhausted by the siege and the fatigue of the journey, the troops revolted at Szolnok, compelling the Serdār to return to Belgrade and to take up winter quarters there. Fortunately for the Ottomans, the inclement weather also took its toll of the Habsburg forces; they, too, found it necessary to withdraw to their own frontiers. The Khan and his forces had to spend the winter in Szombor and Szegedin. Toward the close of the year (December 8, 1598), the Grand Vezir Jerrāḥ Meḥemmed Pasha and the Serdār Sāṭūrjī Meḥemmed Pasha were removed from office. Dāmād Ibrāhīm Pasha, the brother-in-law of the Sultan, now became Grand Vezir once again and also Serdār.[6]

During the spring of 1599, while the Grand Vezir was marching to Belgrade to assume command of his forces, word came to the Sultan and his Vezir that Sāṭūrjī Meḥemmed Pasha, a close friend of the Tatar Khan, had, prior to his dismissal, conferred upon Ġāzī Girāy the governorship and revenues of Silistria. Such an appointment was subject, however, to the confirmation of the Sultan, whose reaction was immediate. He sent Ṭurnāḳjī Ḥasan, the Aġā of the Janissaries, to the headquarters of Sāṭūrjī Meḥemmed at Hisarjīḳ near Belgrade with an Ottoman imperial decree (Haṭṭ-i Şerif) calling for the death of the former Serdār. Sātūrjī Meḥemmed Pasha was executed on the spot.

Because of the death of his friend, the Khan refused to enter into cordial relations with the new Grand Vezir, whom he distrusted, throughout the remainder of the campaign season. After another uneventful campaign season in 1599, notable only for further unsuccessful negotiations with the Habsburgs, the Grand Vezir assigned his troops to winter quarters. The Khan took the opportunity to return to the Crimea with most of his men.

The year 1600 brought an important success to the Ottomans. Ibrāhīm Pasha besieged the swamp-encircled fortress of Kanisza and thus won a great prize, for this fortress guarded the southern approach to Habsburg and Croatian territories.[7] The Christians in 1601 suffered heavy losses in their unsuccessful attempt to retake Kanisza. They succeeded, however, in capturing Ustūn-i Belgrād (Stuhlweissenburg) on October 10, 1601. Ibrāhīm Pasha had entered into negotiations that year with the Archduke Matthias in an attempt to find a common basis for peace; such progress as had been achieved in this direction came to an end with the death of the Grand Vezir on July 10, 1601. Yemişçī (the Fruiterer) Ḥasan Pasha, the new Grand Vezir, reached the plain of Semlin before Buda on September 6; but it was too late in the year to attempt to relieve Stuhlweissenburg. The Ottomans, however, regained Stuhlweissenburg on August 29, 1602, and by so doing gave clear indication of their strength vis-à-vis that of the Habsburgs. Meanwhile, Yemişçī Ḥasan Pasha had received word that Moïses Székely, a former commander of Sigismund Báthory who had gone over to the Ottomans, had obtained notable successes against the Habsburg Imperial forces of Giorgio Basta. The Grand Vezir thus decided to render aid to this Transylvanian supporter of the Ottoman cause, but as the Ottoman army crossed the Tisza, news that Pest had fallen to the Emperor brought the Ottomans back to the defense of Buda in four days. Too late to save Pest, the army retired to winter quarters on November 2, 1602. At this time, Ġāzī Girāy, who had been absent from Hungary since 1599, again joined the Ottoman forces only to leave again in the spring without even fighting a campaign.[8]

The war in Hungary for the next two years centered on Buda and Pest. Eventually the Ottomans were able to unseat the Habsburg Imperial forces from Pest in 1604; Buda, though under heavy attack, never capitulated.

Meanwhile, as one result of the increased momentum of the Counter Reformation as it gained strength from its successes in Inner Austria, the Emperor unwittingly aided the Ottoman cause by putting into effect repressive measures against Protestants in the Imperial army and in Northern Hungary and Transylvania.[9] The inhabitants of Transylvania, embittered by the constant ravages of war, the exactions of a fickle prince, and the outright occupation—now by Imperial troops and now by Wallachian troops—sought an end to their troubles by supporting Stephan Bocskay, the power behind the throne in the era of Sigismund Báthory. Bocskay, in turn, sought support for his movement from the Ottomans. The venture proved to be one of the decisive strokes of the war. Stephan Bocskay, who with Ottoman support drove the Imperial forces out of Transylvania, was crowned Prince of Transylvania on October 24, 1605, shortly after the reconquest of Gran

(Esztergom). In this last major campaign of the war, the Ottomans recovered, in addition to Gran, several lesser fortresses including Visegrad, Veszprem, and Palota. It was indeed fortunate for the Ottomans that the Habsburg effort in Hungary was on the verge of collapse. In Asia Minor, the Jelālī revolt still continued to simmer and flare up intermitently and Shah ʿAbbās, who had launched a new offensive against the Ottomans in 1603, had succeeded in driving the Ottomans out of most of Transcaucasia and Azerbaijan, the territories that they had recently bought so dearly. Of particular importance for the prospect of peace was the death of Meḥemmed III in 1603. Now Sultan Aḥmed I (1603–1617), a mere boy, had assumed the reins of power.[10]

One might well conclude a study of this era with this traditional overview of the main events in the siege warfare from 1597–1606. Fortunately, however, a number of Turkish and east European scholars, while revealing details of their own national histories, have brought to light important details concerning Ottoman and Tatar affairs of the period. These details help clear up the relationship of Ottoman power in eastern Europe to such important European social developments as the growing national consciousness of the peoples of southeastern Europe and their awareness of the issue of freedom of conscience.

2 Ġāzī Girāy and Hungary (1597–1600)

The Crimean Tatars, led by their newly reinstated Khan, Ġāzī Girāy, played their "own game" in the last years of the Hungarian War. It was clear, however, after the events of 1596 which had led to the Khan's dismissal, that Ġāzī Girāy no longer enjoyed the favor at court that had been typical of the era of Sultan Murād III. During the campaign season of 1597, Poland and the three principalities of Transylvania, Wallachia, and Moldavia fully expected the Khan to rejoin the Ottoman forces in Hungary; consequently, they had their frontiers well guarded and their spies well placed to determine the direction the Khan might take. In actuality, however, the Khan had no intention of assisting the Sultan in that year.[11] He sent envoys to Jeremia Movila and the King of Poland in May, to Sigismund Báthory in September and to Michael of Wallachia, with the intention of re-establishing personal relations with these leaders and of gaining whatever advantage he could from them.[12] To Poland the Khan offered an alliance, even hinting at switching his allegiance to the Polish King.[13] The Khan sent an embassy to Michael of Wallachia expressly to determine his sincerity and to suggest that Michael send appropriate gifts to him or else suffer a raid much more devastating than the one of 1596. The Poles could not be put at ease. From August until November rumors continued to reach the Chancellor, Zamoyski, from Jeremia of Moldavia concerning troop movements of the Tatars.[14] In Transylvania, the envoys of both the Sultan and the Khan encouraged the Prince to resume his old loyalty to the Porte. The Khan also sought a subsidy. One report also suggested that the Sultan and the Khan wanted the Prince to act as an intermediary to bring about peace between the Emperor and the Sultan. The Prince of Transylvania, wishing to keep open the negotiations, now sent one of his confidential secretaries, Ioannes Bernardfius, and another of his colleagues, Georgius Racz, to the Crimea in the company of the returning Tatar envoys. The party had traveled through Wallachia and Moldavia to the Crimea in the early months of 1598, and after being well received by the Khan they started again for Transylvania in May. Accompanying Bernardfius on the return journey to Alba Julia, which they reached in June, were the Tatar legates, Sefer Aġā and Alexander Paleologus. The Tatar envoys stated in the name of their Khan that the letters of Sigismund Báthory had been received and that the Khan was so pleased with the friendship of the Prince that he personally would not go to the assistance of the Ottoman forces until a little before October. In his letters and through his envoys, the Khan showed himself to be entirely disillusioned with the Porte. Ġāzī Girāy complained that for the sake of the Ottomans he had spent years in Persia languishing in chains, the marks of which still remained on his body, and that, at the conquest of Raab, he had given an example to the rest of the troops. Yet the Ottomans had rewarded him by dismissing him.

The Tatar envoys, apart from their talks with Sigismund Báthory, met with two Imperial ambassadors, Stephanus Szuchay (Zuhai) and Nicolaus Isthvanfi (the latter envoy actually recorded these events in his history of the era).[15] Clearly the Khan was already seeking a rapprochement with the Emperor. In his negotiations he appears to be playing the age-old double role, as go-between for the Sultan and as promoter of his own interests. The Imperial ambassadors found the Khan's proposals so significant that they proposed to send one of the Tatar envoys on to the Emperor; however, the envoys proceeded to Wallachia accompanied by the Imperial ambassadors and, after talks with Voivode Michael, they returned to the Crimea with Ioannes Posoniensis (Posony) and Georgius Racz, who delivered a gift to the Khan.[16] The plenipotentiaries to the Khan received clear instructions to consult with the Khan and to urge him to send a reliable envoy to the Emperor to work out the details, if he chose to become an ally of the Christians. Thus the Khan sent Alexander Paleologus, a trusted Greek in his entourage, to Prague.[17]

Meanwhile, Tsar Feodor of Muscovy had died on January 16, 1598, an event that prompted the Khan to send an embassy to Boris Godunov, the new Tsar. The embassy of the Khan, which was headed by a certain 'Alī Mīrzā, was received by the Tsar on July 8, 1598, at Serpukhov on the Oka, south of Moscow, amidst a great assemblage of Muscovite troops. The grand muster of the army had been prompted by a series of false reports, which began as early as April and which had convinced Boris Godunov and his councilors that a Tatar attack was imminent. The Tatar representatives, in spite of this bellicose reception, managed to have the treaty renewed. They were then accompanied to the Crimea by an embassy of the Tsar to receive the sworn oath of the Khan.[18] It appears that the informants of the Tsar had mistaken the preparations of the Khan prior to his departure for Hungary as preparations for a raid against Muscovy.

Not until the Khan had satisfactorily completed negotiations with the Emperor and with the Tsar did he begin preparations for his march to Hungary. Already, by the end of June, the Voivode of Moldavia, Jeremia, was trying to determine the route the Khan would take. Would he cross the fords of the Dniester at Tehine (Bender) or would he cross the bay at Akkerman (Belgorod)? Zamoyski was fearful that the Khan would again pass through Poland en route to Hungary at a time when no funds were available to pay troops to maintain surveillance in the south.[19] In July, Jeremia reported to Zamoyski that the Khan had crossed the Dnieper below Berezna (Berezovka?), i.e., by boat across the bay at Ochakov. The Khan had written the Voivode in a predictable manner. He said that he was no longer pleased with the gifts that Jeremia had sent, and moreover he was planning an attack on Wallachia. But these were simply threats designed to squeeze more tribute from both Wallachia and Moldavia. The Khan was moving quickly. He crossed the Danube at Obloczyce (*sic*) while the Ḳalġay crossed with his contingent at nearby Ismail (Izmail). Quite clearly the Khan planned to go to Hungary along the safe, southern shores of the Danube. Voivode Michael, taking cognizance of this movement of the Tatars, sought money and troops from his nominal overlord, the Prince of Transylvania.[20] The Khan had passed along the Danube with his forces between the 12th and the 16th of July. In dispatches to Jeremia and presumably to Michael also, the Khan made it clear that he intended to raid their lands on his return if their "gifts" were unsatisfactory.

That the Tatars did not hesitate to live off the land en route to Belgrade is quite clear. A Pasha in Vidin was particularly disturbed at the passing of the Tatars. He complained that Serdār Sāṭūrjī Meḥemmed had taken most of his troops for the impeding campaign and therefore he was unable to prevent the Tatar depredations.[21] As the Khan approached the Ottoman army at Becskerek he was subjected to a great amount of diplomatic pressure from an envoy of Sigismund Báthory, who had also been carefully instructed by the representatives of the Emperor. Typical of the kind of pressure the Khan received was a letter that reminded him that the Asian provinces of the Sultan were in revolt and thus it was up to the Khan to negotiate a peace. Furthermore, the letter, pointing to the "great stability" of the Christian lands, spoke of the impending grand invasion of the Ottoman lands, an invasion in which the Khan, if he joined the Christian league, would be able to keep all of the lands which he himself conquered.[22] The Khan of course had already gone back on his agreement to withhold assistance to the Ottomans until October. The secret envoy of Sigismund Báthory, Bernardfius, had gained the confidence of both parties during the course of the negotiations with the Tatars. Therefore, in mid-August, he was again sent to the Khan. Before he departed he received detailed instructions, most likely from one of the Imperial commissioners such as Isthvanfi. In brief the Christian terms were to be as follows:

(*a*) Dalmatia, Croatia, Sclavonia, Transylvania, and Wallachia were to come under Christian control.

(*b*) If the ambassador found the Khan well disposed toward the Christians, then more could be asked for, such as Agria (Erlau), Szolnok, even Gyula (Alba Julia) and Temesvar.

(*c*) The ambassador should avoid any arrangements for tribute from the above-mentioned lands.

(*d*) It should be made known to the Khan that he would be rewarded for any favors.

(*e*) The Khan might also communicate anything he chose to his legate Alexander Paleologus in Prague who might then communicate with the Emperor.

(*f*) The envoy, in a private interview with the Khan, was to show him a letter requesting him to repudiate his alliance with the Ottomans and take arms against them or else remain neutral; the longer he remained neutral, the more money the Khan would receive.

(*g*) Finally, if all other means failed, then the envoy was requested to urge the Khan to use the 10,000 ducats already granted to him to bribe various Vezirs, encouraging them to disrupt the war effort by any means at their disposal.[23]

Prince Sigismund was now well aware of the pending danger to his own land. The Ottoman forces had bridged the Danube at Pancsova (Pančevo) and had marched from Temesvar to Becskerek. In the eyes of Prince Sigismund all Transylvania was threatened.

Before the Khan joined the Ottoman forces near Becskerek at the end of August he had already stipulated that he would not attack the Christians until his envoy, Alexander Paleologus, whom he had sent to Prague, had returned. Sigismund Báthory, during the course of his discussions with Paleologus, had found out some valuable information. It had become apparent that the Ottomans had asked the Khan to arrange a temporary peace with the Habsburgs so that the Sultan could deal with the Jelālī rebellion in Anatolia which, by now, had got quite out of hand. The Khan, moreover, was reluctant to commit himself openly to an alliance with the Christians, although he had this inclination, because of religious considerations and because he doubted if he could bring his Tatar followers over to the Christian camp. These were the principal facts which Sigismund Báthory disclosed to the Emperor in a long dispatch of August 15, 1598. The Prince also reported his dire need for funds with which to pay off his own rebellious troops and those of Voivode Michael.[24]

The Ottoman campaign was now at hand. If Western reports had tended to emphasize the animosity of the Khan for the Ottomans, one must also be aware of the conciliatory attitude of the Sultan. In a letter to the Khan, Sultan Meḥemmed III had expressed his pleasure that the Tatars had crossed the Danube and were hastening to join the main army in Hungary. The Sultan emphasized the importance of a campaign into Transylvania as the best means of keeping Wallachia and Moldavia within the Ottoman fold. The Sultan also demonstrated his concern for the security of the Crimea in the absence of the Khan and assured him that the Ottoman forces at Kaffa were always ready to assist in the protection of the Khanate. Finally, the Sultan urged the Khan to remain on the frontiers during the following winter to ensure that the Christians would be properly held in check. Sāṭūrjī Meḥemmed Pasha was also pleased that the Khan was coming. He facilitated the movement of the Tatar troops by ordering the Ḳādīs or judges in the Ottoman towns along the Danube to ready provisions for them.[25] The bridge over the Danube on the road from Belgrade to Pancsova was completed on 27 Z̲iʿl Ḥijje 1006/31 July 1598, the day the Serdār received positive information that the Khan was at Ruschuk. When the two forces met on 26 Muḥarrem 1007/29 August 1598, the Khan received a regal welcome. Then, after the two commanders decided their course of action, they marched together between the Körös and Mörös (Mures) rivers ("inter Chrysium et Marysum omnes") in the direction of Vārād (Grosswardein; Varaždin; mod., Oradea).[26] The fortress of Vārād on the Sebes was besieged and one hundred and forty of its defenders put to the sword. This was the fortress Sigismund Báthory had intended to hold "to inspire resistance elsewhere."[27] According to Hammer, the siege of Vārād (Grosswardein) began on 29 Ṣefer 1007/1 October 1598; according to Isthvanfi, 4 October ("ad quartum Nonas Octobris"). It was destined to last some forty days or into early November.[28] Provisions were scarce in the Ottoman camp; therefore, the Tatars were sent to scour the countryside for foodstuffs. Georgio Basta, with his small force, moved from Kassa (Cassovia) to Tokaj upon the approach of the Ottomans, partly, as he said, to protect that region from Tatar depredations. Particularly hard hit were the villages around Becskerek and Debreczen.[29]

The year 1598 did not go well for the Ottomans. The Imperial forces had recovered their initiative at a time when the Ottomans were beginning to suffer from want of provisions that ordinarily would have come from the Danubian Principalities. As was indicated in the previous section, no sooner had the Khan and Sāṭūrjī Meḥemmed Pasha commenced the siege of Vārād in earnest than news came that the Christians had seized Totis, Papa, and Weszprim and had laid siege to Buda. Moreover, Voivode Michael had crossed the Danube and defeated Ḥāfiż Aḥmed Pasha at Nikbōlī (Nicopolis).

Against such a background and considering the almost continuous rainfall that had accompanied the expedition, it is not surprising that the Ottoman and Tatar dignitaries decided on October 28, 1598, to send a Tatar relief force to Buda and to raise the siege in eight days if further efforts proved unsatisfactory—a decision that was reported to Basta by one of his lieutenants.[30] Apart from the weather, the siege at Vārād had not gone well for the Ottomans owing to their shortage of artillery pieces. The Serdār had attempted to remedy this by sending a contingent to Egrī (Erlau) to obtain more ordinance, powder, and shot. The inclement weather, however, militated against what ordinarily would have been a simple problem for the teamsters. There was also a shortage of oxen to draw the cannon.[31] After the siege was raised, even greater hardships faced the army. An advance guard had been sent ahead to repair and to build bridges for the march to Szolnok, but where one river had flowed before, there were now several raging torrents and this condition repeated itself across the entire flood plain of the Tizsa. The final blow to the morale of the troops came at Szolnok, the terminus on the Tisza for supplies coming from the Porte or from the lower Danube. When the supply boats did not appear, a rumor swept through the army that their provisions had been sent to Buda. Thereafter, the entire army—hungry, diseased and cold—was on the verge of rebellion. The Serdār had no choice. He now assigned his troops to winter quarters and departed for Belgrade. The Khan went to Szombor (Sombor) and most of his troops were divided between that town and Szegedin.[32]

Toward the end of October and again at the beginning of November, the Khan received communications direct from the Archduke Maximilian and from Emperor Rudolph, respectively. The Archduke urged the Khan to return to the Crimea now that winter was approaching in order that he might gain the eternal friendship of the Christians. Emperor Rudolph only confirmed in vague terms his desire for peace along the lines suggested by the envoy of the Khan. It is significant, however, that the Sultan, fully aware of the Khan's desire to return to the Crimea, exerted his own pressure on the Khan to remain on the frontier. On November 18, the Habsburg Emperor issued "visas" which permitted the Tatar envoy, Paleologus, and his own own legate, Georgio Racz, to leave the Habsburg realm. Negotiations continued during the winter. Basta reported to Archduke Matthias from Vārād his good treatment of the Tatar ambassadors, who proceeded to Kassa (Cassovia) to meet with representatives of the Archduke.[33]

Two important developments in 1598—the defeat of Ḥāfiẓ Aḥmed Pasha at Nicopolis by Michael of Wallachia and the negotiations between the Khan and the Emperor—set the scene for the following year. Even as the Serdār had sent a contingent of Tatars to aid in the relief of Buda, so also he must have acquiesced in the sending of a strong contingent of Tatars to the Danube during the autumn of 1598. In any case, one specific report in European sources supports the conjecture that, by the autumn or early winter of 1598, the Khan already had one of his own Tatar dignitaries commanding a body of men at Silistria.[34] This conjecture receives further support from an undated letter in Italian which Ġāzī Girāy sent to Voivode Michael. In this letter the Khan clearly stated that he had been permitted to winter in the Sanjāḳ of Silistria and that he was placing Aḥmed Aġā in command.[35] He further chastised Michael for breaking his truce by conducting raids across the Danube. The Khan then proceeded to threaten the Voivode with an invasion if he violated his agreement again.[36] These documents show that the Khan had already by the end of 1598 staked a claim to Silistria. But official confirmation in Ottoman sources that Ġāzī Girāy had been assigned the revenues of the Sanjāḳ of Silistria by Sāṭūrjī Meḥemmed Pasha did not reach the ears of the Grand Vezir, Ibrāhīm Pasha, until some time in June, 1599.[37]

When Sāṭūrjī Meḥemmed Pasha was replaced as Serdār by Ibrāhīm Pasha himself, the Khan sent his envoy, 'Abdul 'Azīz Aġā, to seek confirmation from the new Grand Vezir for his possession of Silistria. Although not refusing the confirmation for fear that the Khan might withdraw his support in Hungary, the Grand Vezir immediately informed the Porte but advised caution until Sāṭūrjī could be separated from the protection of the Khan. The reaction of the Sultan and the dignitaries advising him was immediate. The Khan could not be permitted to retain such an important Sanjāḳ, nor could Sāṭūrjī Meḥemmed be excused for this gross violation of Ottoman policy. The Janissary Aġā, Ṭurnāḳjī Ḥasan, received orders to execute the former Serdār. He was killed at Hisarjiḳ near Belgrade on 12 Z̲ī'l Ḥijje 1007/6 July 1599.[38] The tragic outcome of this incident was not surprising in the light of the previously cool reception that had been given at the Porte to the ambitious schemes of Ġāzī Girāy Khan. The Khan must have suspected such a negative reaction for he refused to attend the banquet of Sāṭūrjī Meḥemmed Pasha at which Sātūrjī was executed. Furthermore, the Khan even warned his friend to be wary of the Janissary Aġā, but his words were not heeded.

Upon hearing of the execution of his master, Ibrāhīm Aġā, Ketẖudā (aide-de-camp) to Sāṭūrjī, fled to the camp of Ġāzī Girāy at Szombor. The shock of the news, in spite of the suspicions he had held earlier, forced the Khan to think of his own safety. His first reaction was to return to the Crimea, but when the Khan took up the matter with his own Tatar dignitaries, they opposed his plan on the grounds that to leave at the beginning of a campaign season was merely inviting trouble for the Khanate.[39] The Grand Vezir Ibrāhīm Pasha, having received word from the Khan that he wished to depart, helped placate him by sending him gifts and by showing great deference to him whenever they met. Thus although the Khan remained in Hungary that year and although he gave important assistance to the Ottoman camp by bringing the Ottomans and Christians to the conference table, he never really became reconciled to Ibrāhīm Pasha. Whenever they met, they carried out their conversation on horseback and, as if to emphasize the rift, the Khan always had a large group of armed retainers close at hand. Moreover, as the Grand Vezir proceeded in the direction of Buda on the left bank of the Danube, the Khan remained on the right bank and marched toward Pest.[40]

In passing it is interesting to note that the Christians had not failed to observe the coolness between the Vezir and the Khan. In a report of the time to the Doge of Venice, however, the Sāṭūrjī affair was not mentioned. The reason given for the "diffidentia" between the Khan and the Vezir was that the Vezir distrusted the negotiations that the Kḥan was carrying on with the Emperor and with Transylvania.[41] There appears little doubt, however, that the death of Sāṭūrjī caused Ġāzī Girāy to distrust the Grand Vezir and the Ottoman system which he represented. On 11 Sefer 1008/2 September 1599, the Grand Vezir, while moving with his army in the direction of Buda, received letters from Ġāzī Girāy which stated that the Khan had been contacted by the Emperor for the purpose of opening direct negotiations between the two sides.[42] The contacts between the ambassadors of the Khan and Archduke Maximilian in Vienna had continued into 1599. The Khan had done all he could to squeeze funds for himself out of the Archduke. In one letter the Khan suggested that the Emperor might build a fortress for him to ensure that the Tatars remain "friends of his friends and enemies of his enemies." The Khan sent gifts to the Archduke, and then asked the Archduke to send him a beautiful clock.[43] In a letter of February 5, the Khan informed the Archduke that he was sending to him Bāljī Meḥemmed Agā and an agent who was known as Antonio (Spinola). Once again the Khan, wishing to pressure the Archduke, made it clear that he would spend the entire winter in Hungary and that ". . . wie Euch bewüsst ist, das die Tarttarn nich wallen in einem ort ruehig bleiben, sondern alles verwössten . . ." (as your Excellency knows, the Tatars will not remain quiet in one spot but will lay waste to everything).[44] Alexander Paleologus, whom Isthvanfi describes as having charge of all the revenues of the Khan, by land or by sea,[45] was at the time still negotiating at Prague.

Archduke Matthias now took charge of the probes for peace. He immediately sounded a note of caution by asking the Khan to produce his authority for acting on behalf of the Sultan. The Archduke also informed the Khan that he was sending him two clocks and that his own stables were filled with horses sent by the Khan.[46] By July, the details of a possible peace were already becoming known. In reply to some queries made by the Khan, presumably through the Grand Vezir, the Sultan sent a letter to Ġāzī Girāy. It was clear that, as a preliminary basis for negotiations, the Christians had suggested that Gran (Esztergom), then held by the Emperor, be exchanged for Erlau (Egrī), the cork so to speak in the Transylvanian bottle. The Sultan rejected such a proposal out of hand by reminding the Khan that the ancestors of the Sultan had never restored any territory that had been taken by the sword.[47]

The first negotiations took place on an island in the Danube between Buda and Gran from 24 to 26 Rabiʿ I 1008/14 to 16 October 1599. The chief representatives of the Ottomans included Murād Pasha, Ket͟hudā of Ibrāhīm Pasha; Aḥmed Aġā, the Vezir of the Khan; and the Ḳādī of Buda, Mevlānā Hābīl Efendī, whom Isthvanfi described as an old man of great authority. It appears also that Alexander Paleologus was present. For the Emperor, the Archbishop of Gran, Jan Kutassi; the generals Nadazdi and Palfi; and the special representative of the Emperor, Dr. Pezzen, took part. But the talks were broken off by the Grand Vezir when the Christians insisted on an exchange of fortresses.[48] Once more, as the Ottoman army approached Gran (Esztergom), the two sides tried to come to terms, but the attempt was in vain.[49]

The Grand Vezir at the head of the Ottoman army had crossed the Danube from Buda to Pest and had proceeded up the shore to a point opposite the fortress of Gran. The Habsburg imperial army, which had also been on the Pest side of the Danube, built a bridge across the river at Gran and withdrew in the direction of that fortress. At this time the Khan and his men harassed the enemy withdrawal incessantly but, according to the account of Ṣōlaḳzāde, with little appreciation shown on the part of the Grand Vezir.[50] The Khan, at the end of the season, took his leave of the Ottoman camp with few regrets. He complained of the shortage of rations among his men and argued that it would serve no useful purpose to keep them any longer in Hungary. He departed in late October.[51]

Events in the Principalities had moved quickly in 1599. The Khan, however, played only a subordinate role. The third Vezir, Güzeljī Meḥemmed Pasha, led a successful foray into Wallachia with the aid of Tatar troops. Voivode Michael, however, having his eye on the weak position of Cardinal Andras Báthory, who had replaced his brother Sigismund in Transylvania, made peace overtures to the Sultan and the Khan. At the same time, he received the permission of the Emperor to drive the Cardinal out of Transylvania. Cardinal Báthory was a menace to the Christian cause because of his family and personal ties with the Movila dynasty of Moldavia and the royal family in Poland, i.e., his pro-Ottoman sympathies.[52] After Michael had taken control of Transylvania he petitioned the Emperor urgently for funds with which to bribe the Khan. It was clear that the Christian powers still hoped to wean the Khan away from the Sultan.[53]

Giorgio Basta, the military commander for the Emperor in Transylvania, assisted Michael in his conquest of Transylvania, only to take arms against him in the succeeding years. Basta, a keen tactician, wrote to the Emperor as early as February of 1599 that the best weapon against the Turks and Tatars was the arquebus because they feared it so much. Later in the same year, Basta became more specific in another letter: to be effective against the Tatars, his troops required the arquebuses "di longhezza di cinque palmi" because the Tatars in particular could cause so much damage among cavalry which were equipped with the short arquebuses. The Tatar bow, in other words, still had a longer range than the ordinary arquebus![54]

As the Khan withdrew from Hungary, he again created anxiety in Poland and Moldavia regarding the route that he would take to the Crimea, but the Khan returned the way he had come, south of the Danube and through Ismail into lower Moldavia, about mid-December.[55] The Khan continued to seek a peace treaty with Poland. Jeremia reported to Zamoyski in September that Jantemir (Jāntīmūr) Aġā, an envoy of the Khan, was proceeding through his territory with the interpreter Kossekowski on a mission to the Polish king. The mission of Jāntīmūr Aġā was successful. The treaty between Poland and the Crimea that had been drawn up at Ţuţora (Cecora) was reconfirmed at this time.[56] The years 1597 to 1599 confirmed the importance of the Tatar Khan to the Ottomans in the Hungarian war. Thereafter, his significance—at least in Hungary—gradually declined. This development was brought about partly by his absence from the front and partly because the internal and external position of the Ottoman state gradually improved. The revolt in Anatolia was soon to be partially suppressed at a time when the former cooperation among the rebelling tributary principalities of Wallachia and Transylvania was on the verge of breaking down. The Khan, also, had other interests closer to home than Hungary.

In answer to letters urging him to join Ibrāhīm Pasha in Hungary, the Khan excused himself to the Grand Vezir and H̲ōja Sa'd ed-Dīn by sending them lyric poetry (*ġazels*) of a sarcastic and moralistic quality which he had personally composed. The following extracts from ġazels composed by Ġāzī Girāy during this period of bitterness reflect accurately his attitude. In the first poem the Khan addresses the Sultan; in the second, he expresses the timeless complaint of the warrior against all of those peoples who do not care about his sacrifices (in this instance, at Szombor during the winter of 1598–1599):

> We [i.e., I] are one of your slaves fighting for the faith,
> We sacrifice our life [lit., soul and head]
> My Sultan, what should I say?
> Later you will hear the news [of my sacrifice],
> Do not flee from the sword and the arrow,
> Busy thyself on the pathway of righteousness. . . .
>
> . . . . .
>
> Is it any wonder that we are tasting bitterness?
> Just look at our plight.
> By Heaven, even the bitter waters of Szombor
> Have come out our nostrils.

The infidels have plundered the lands of Islam
[While] you [people], with no fear of God,
Take your bribes and take your ease.
We shall pour out [our] blood and weep blood
On the field of battle,
[While] you enjoy the [blood-red] cup of delight
In the valley of [pleasant] dissipation. . . .[58]

The Khan did send a contingent of Tatars to Hungary in 1600 which gave valuable service to the Grand Vezir in his siege of Kanisza.[59] At the end of the year the Khan was still receiving letters from representatives of the Habsburg Emperor asking him to persist in his approaches to the Porte for the purpose of bringing about a peace in Hungary.[60]

3 The End of the Vlach Rebellion

Mezö Kerésztés had greatly weakened the Transylvanian army of Sigismund Báthory and thus, leaving aside the Austrian forces, the balance of power in the Principalities had now shifted in favor of Michael Viteazul of Wallachia. Between 1596 and his death in 1601, Michael succeeded in uniting for a time the Vlach-speaking peoples of Wallachia, Moldavia, and Transylvania under his leadership but his policy of exalting the Vlachs and Orthodoxy was far ahead of its time. The talent that Michael demonstrated as a commander and local ruler proved insufficient for him to deal with the larger powers and forces of his day, whether Habsburg, Polish, and Ottoman imperialism or the social movements of Hungary and his own land. As a result of the Ottoman victory at Mezö Kerésztés it is not surprising that both Sigismund Báthory and Michael of Wallachia carried on negotiations with the Ottomans in 1597. In July, Michael actually agreed to a reconciliation with the Porte which, formally at least, lasted until he swore allegiance to the Emperor on June 9, 1598. Prince Sigismund meanwhile had given up his sovereign rights in Transylvania to the Emperor in May 1598 in exchange for a feudal dependency in Habsburg Silesia, but Sigismund was soon convinced by his relatives that he should return to Transylvania which he did in August. Neither prince really discontinued diplomatic exchanges with the Ottomans; Michael even paid a token tribute to the Sultan during this period.[61]

In the Principalities during the year 1599, events took a different turn. On March 27, 1599, Sigismund Báthory, while seeking from the Emperor a new dominion for himself, turned over his princely position to his cousin, Andras Báthory, a Cardinal of the Church and the Polish Bishop of Ermeland. The new prince wasted no time in establishing diplomatic ties with Moldavia, Poland, and the Porte. The Ottomans, however, were very wary of his attempts to alter agreements which had long governed the relationships between Transylvania and the Ottoman State. Nevertheless, the trappings of office for Cardinal Andras Báthory and the usual *Ahitname* were sent by the Sultan on November 7, but clearly the Ottomans were moving too slowly. Michael had recognized Cardinal Báthory as his overlord on June 26, but when it became clear that the Cardinal could not rule his land, Michael, who had already received the secret support of the Emperor, defeated the Cardinal decisively on October 28, 1599, near Hermannstadt (Szeben). The Cardinal was subsequently killed. Now Michael quickly occupied Alba Julia and, to ward off trouble from the south, sought and received the tacit support of the Ottomans, a cynical move which proved a fatal mistake.[62] The Habsburgs obviously were not pleased and the Transylvanian notables were even less so when Michael commenced taking cruel repressive measures against the nobility and peasantry of Transylvania. Undaunted, Michael continued his conquests. With a thrust into Moldavia in May, he succeeded in driving Jeremia Movila to the Polish border and having allegiance sworn to him and his son in the principal Moldavian cities by June of 1600.

Obviously neither the Habsburgs nor the Ottomans could acquiesce in the loss of such strategic territories to Michael of Wallachia. Giorgio Basta, encouraged and supplied by the Emperor and enlisting troops from the German and Hungarian population, defeated Michael on September 18, 1600, at Miriszló. At the same time, Grand Chancellor Zamoyski of Poland had marched into Moldavia, re-established Jeremia as Voivode, and attempted to place Simeon, the brother of Jeremia, in the Voivodeship of Wallachia.[63] After his defeat in Transylvania, Michael had withdrawn to Wallachia only to be again defeated, this time by the Poles on the Telejean River. The Ottomans, still wishing to install Radu Mihnea, also sent a force into Wallachia and Michael, now almost devoid of troops, dispersed his forces and avoided a showdown. During the winter months he betook himself to Prague to plead for support from the Emperor. Meanwhile the Transylvanian Diet, which met in Kolozsvar on January 21, 1601, re-elected—much to the chagrin of the Habsburgs—Sigismund Báthory as prince. Better a weak native ruler than a foreign oppressor! The Habsburgs thus saw that they had to patch up the differences between Basta and Michael in order to defeat Prince Sigismund who was abandoning the Habsburg cause for the sake of Hungarian independence. This done, Michael and Basta won a victory over Prince Sigismund at Nagy-Goroszló on August 3, 1601. Now Sigismund Báthory fled to Moldavia. Michael, hearing of a threat to his family through the machinations of Sigismund Báthory and not really keeping on good terms with Basta, wrote a letter to Sigismund assuring him that he would assist him to regain his principality. In a letter to the Ottoman camp Michael offered to work for the Muslims and to reveal all of the enemy secrets. Both letters fell into the hands of Basta, who had Michael executed on August 19, 1601.[64]

The death of Michael, who had carried high the banner of Greek

Orthodoxy and proto-Vlach nationalism did not improve the confused situation in the Principalities. Sigismund Báthory again advanced against Basta, but this proved to be his last campaign. He had vacillated between Ottoman and Imperial support to such an extent that he had lost most of his followers and could no longer obtain subsidies from anyone. Meanwhile Poland in the year 1600 had found itself in an equivocal position with the Khan and the Sultan. Voivode Michael, who had seized Transylvania late in 1599, had received the official recognition of the Sultan.[65] Michael, knowing well that Poland did not view with satisfaction his Transylvanian adventure nor his design on Moldavia, sought to instigate the Ottomans and the Tatars against Poland. The King, however, by sending embassies to the Porte and to the Crimea, dispelled any doubts that the Khan and the Sultan may have had about Polish intentions. The King, in his letter to Ġāzī Girāy, also gave notice that Zamoyski was now being sent to Moldavia to combat the invasion of Michael and he expressed the wish that the Tatar Khan would also render assistance.[66]

Voivode Michael had in fact invaded Moldavia in May. During the month of April, the Poles, the Tatars, and the Moldavians had been planning an attack into Transylvania against Michael in support of Sigismund Báthory, who had taken refuge in Moldavia.[67] Before these plans came to fruition, however, and before the Khan could send any troops, Michael had attacked Moldavia,[68] seized the principal towns, and forced the Voivode Jeremia and also Sigismund Báthory to take refuge in the Polish border fortress of Khotin. Now Michael exacted homage for himself and his sons from the Moldavian population and sent the appropriate annual tribute from Moldavia to the Khan in the hope of gaining the latter's support.[69] But Michael had over-extended himself and had made himself unpopular in Transylvania. The Ottomans also withdrew their support and ordered the Khan to invade Wallachia. Poland, after the defeat of some of her forces which had been sent to support Jeremia, mobilized a large force and drove Michael's forces out of Moldavia. Meanwhile, in Transylvania, as we have already learned, the Wallachian forces of Michael were soundly defeated at Miriszló by Basta, who, after the excesses Michael had taken against the nobility in Transylvania, had been ordered by the Emperor to clip his wings.[70]

These events prepared the way for the final demise of Michael in 1601. Sigismund Báthory made an attempt to enter Transylvania from Varaždin. Apart from local support, his field commander, Moïses Szekely, had received reinforcements from a mixed Ottoman and Tatar force estimated at twelve thousand, which had been sent by Lālā Meḥemmed Pasha, Beylerbey of Buda. This thrust into Transylvania was stopped by Basta in early August near Goroszlo and shortly thereafter Basta ordered the execution of Michael for an alleged conspiracy with the enemy.[71] For the time being, Basta was left in control of Transylvania. The year 1601 also marked the final withdrawal of Sigismund Báthory from the Transylvanian scene.

The Poles had brought their protégé, Jeremia Movila, back into Moldavia in the autumn of 1600. Now once again Moldavia became the center of an attempt to put the brother of Jeremia, Simeon Movila, into the Voivodeship of Wallachia. The Ottomans still preferred Radu Mihnea, but finally made up their minds to support Simeon at a time when Radu Serban, a lieutenant of Michael, had begun to make a successful bid for the control of Wallachia.[72]

4 The Khan Leaves the War

During the summer of 1601, Ġāzī Girāy Khan faced a serious threat to his rule in the Crimea. His Nūr ed-Dīn, Devlet Girāy, plotted with the mīrzās of the most prominent Crimean tribe, the Şirin oğullarï (sons of the Şirin), to murder the Khan and to make himself Khan. To some extent, this plot can be considered a sequel to the previous movements opposing Ottoman domination in the Crimea, which were led by Meḥemmed Girāy Khan in 1583–1584 and by his son, Sa'ādet Girāy, in 1584–1585. Devlet Girāy, the son of Sa'ādet Girāy and the grandson of Meḥemmed Girāy Khan, was following a well-established precedent in his family. The Khan learned of the plot shortly before the important feast day of the Ḳurbān Bayrāmī of 10 Ẕī'l Ḥijje 1009/12 June 1601, and invited the Nūr ed-Dīn, Devlet Girāy, and some of the principal dignitaries of the Şirin tribe to a banquet. Ġāzī Girāy secretly assembled his arquebusiers, as a counterforce to the armed retainers of the visiting dignitaries, and then, during the banquet, had Devlet Girāy and two of the Şirin Beys, one of whom was his own son-in-law, executed. Two other Şirin Beys escaped to Kaffa. The Khan now sought out the younger brothers of Devlet Girāy, Meḥemmed Girāy and Şahīn Girāy, to eliminate them also. They were warned of the Khan's intentions, however, and managed to escape.[73] Meḥemmed Girāy took refuge in Circassia and his brother, Şahīn Girāy, joined the Jelālī uprising in Anatolia. The flight of these two ẖānzādes was shortly followed by that of the Ḳalġay and brother of the Khan, Selāmet Girāy, who escaped to Aḳkermān and then also took refuge with the Jelālīs in Asia Minor. The Khan, meanwhile, had become ill and therefore had sent in his place, to the Hungarian front, with a contingent of Tatars, his nephew, Batir Girāy.[74]

Ġāzī Girāy Khan had been forced to put his own realm in order in the year 1601, but by the following spring, the Sultan once more ordered the Khan to the Hungarian frontier. Ġāzī Girāy, however, had learned that Selāmet Girāy had fallen into the hands of the Sultan; he was, therefore, very reluctant to leave the Crimea for fear that he might be replaced by his brother.[75] When the Khan voiced these fears in his correspondence with the Porte, he received firm assurances from the Sultan that, although Selāmet Girāy would not be executed, as the Khan had requested, he would be exiled to a place where he would be unable to intrigue against Ġāzī Girāy. The Sultan warned, however, that the Khan would be expected to carry out his obligations to the realm and to serve on the Hungarian front.[76]

After clearing up the problem of family rivalries, Ġāzī Girāy, in a burst of activity, prepared himself for the campaign season in 1602. He renewed the existing peace agreement between himself and Boris Godunov, Tsar of Muscovy.[77] A series of Zaporozhian Cossack raids along the Dnieper and the coast of the Black Sea during the spring of 1602 had forced the Khan to make retaliatory raids into the Polish borderlands. Incidents like these had become a bone of contention leading to a series of diplomatic exchanges between the King of Poland and the Khan which will be discussed in Section 5.[78] By August, however, it became clear from a series of dispatches sent to the King of Poland by John Potocki, Starost (holder of a crown estate) of Kameniac, and M. Sobieski, the Voivode of Lublin, both of whom were stationed with troops on the southern frontier of Poland, that the Khan had received the tacit support of Poland in a new attempt to establish Simeon Movila in the voivodeship of Wallachia. The Khan apparently had received orders from the Sultan to march into Transylvania and Ġāzī Girāy, ever alert to an opportunity to advance his own interests, attempted to place Simeon in the voivodeship of Wallachia en route to Hungary. This appeared to be an easy task because it was generally known that Radu Serban, who was at the time Voivode of Wallachia, had a very shabby army of about ten thousand men.[79] By the middle of September 1602 the Khan was advancing rapidly on the forces of Radu Serban, who had been forced to withdraw into the mountains of Northern Wallachia. Unknown to the Khan, however, Georgio Basta, although he was occupied in Transylvania with an Ottoman-supported invasion from Temesvar led by Moïses Szekely, had been able to reinforce Serban with some regiments of seasoned Walloon infantry. After some tough fighting on September 23 and 24 near the town of Telzayn, the Khan withdrew with heavy losses, inflicted by the entrenched Walloons and four well-placed cannon (*Falconi*). As the Khan withdrew, he placed the body of his brother-in-law, who had fallen in the battle, on a horse in front of him, according to Tatar custom, and covered him with beautiful rugs. The Khan was so grieved by this mishap that he was moved to tears.[80] Ġāzī Girāy now sent out scouts to find a pass to Hungary through Transylvania but all were blocked by Basta's men; thus, the Tatars withdrew to Silistria and proceeded on their way to Hungary along the south shore of the Danube. As the Khan withdrew, he received a dispatch from the Porte ordering him to send Simeon Movila to Istanbul for the Sultan had now, once again, appointed Radu Mihnea to the position of Hospodar of Wallachia.[81]

The Khan reached Belgrade at the end of Rabīʿ II 1011/mid-October 1602 just as the Grand Vezir, Yemīşçī Ḥasan Pasha, was entering Belgrade from the north. The Grand Vezir received the Khan with full honors and made arrangements for him to stay in the residence of the Defterdār Etmekjīzāde. After several days of feasting, Ġāzī Girāy took up winter quarters in the town of Péc (Fünfkirchen) as a guest of the then young historian Ibrāhīm Peçewī. It was during this winter that the Khan lived what Von Hammer has described as an epicurean life—writing poetry, instructing Ibrāhīm Peçewī in the Persian language and script, hunting wild game, feasting, and walking in the gardens of the Peçewī lands. There were also frequent receptions and entertainments for visiting dignitaries. As the spring of 1603 drew near, the Khan went on raids into neighboring enemy territory. Upon the arrival of Lālā Meḥemmed Pasha in Hungary, who had been appointed Serdār for the campaign season of 1603, he, too, paid a visit to Péc and spent several days with the Khan and Peçewī.[82]

In spite of this conviviality, Ġāzī Girāy was fearful for his position as Khan. After viewing the large retinue of Delī Ḥasan, the former Jelālī leader under whom his brother Selāmet Girāy had served, and who had been pardoned by the Sultan, the Khan became even more uneasy and resolved to return to the Crimea. Apparently the Khan considered that it was not only risky but beneath his dignity to serve on the front with these former rebels; moreover, he did not wish to take orders from anyone less exalted than the Grand Vezir, who had in this year been sent against the Jelālī rebels in Asia Minor. Lālā Meḥemmed Pasha, upon learning of the Khan's intention to depart, sent Peçewī and Etmekjīzāde to the Khan in the hope that they might persuade him to remain, but their efforts were futile. The Khan once more complained about the presence of the rebels and also mentioned how poor the rations were for the Tatars.[83] There is no doubt that Selāmet Girāy, when he fell into Ottoman hands after the capitulation of Delī Ḥasan, had revealed to the Sultan all of the information he possibly could about the secret negotiations of Ġāzī Girāy with the Emperor and other Christian rulers. Thereafter, the Sultan appears to have granted an amnesty to Selāmet Girāy at the end of Z̲ī'l Ḥijje 1011/beginning of June, 1603, just at the time when Ġāzī Girāy was leaving the Hungarian front. This amnesty may well have increased the doubt of the Khan about his retaining control of the Khanate. In a letter to the Sultan, the Serdār Lālā Meḥemmed Pasha complained bitterly about the withdrawal of the Khan, and even Peçewī added a wry comment in his chronicle about the uselessness of the Khan on this campaign: His Tatars had laid waste six sanjāḳs and had gone on only one raid; moreover, he had come at the end of one campaign season and had left at the beginning of another.[84]

While the Khan marched in the direction of Wallachia along the southern route leading through Nicopolis, Moïses Szekely, to whom the Khan had given some Taṭar forces, now led an attack into Transylvania from Temesvar. ring the siege of Alba Julia, these same Tatars set fire to the city with ng arrows and firebrands.[85] This thrust into Transylvania kept Basta occupied while the Khan, meantime, entered Wallachia and devastated the countryside. Radu Serban sought aid from Vienna, but as the Ottomans had launched an offensive in upper Hungary and as Basta was fighting Szekely, he received little help. This was just the position in which Ġāzī Girāy hoped to place Radu Serban. The Voivode became very emenable to negotiations with the Khan and was only too happy to agree to pay him an annual tribute. The Tatar envoy, during his negotiations with Serban, made it quite apparent that a new rupture had taken place in the relations between the Khan and the Sultan. The Khan seemed prepared to accept the fact that Serban owed his ultimate allegiance to the Austrian Emperor.[86]

In the year 1603, the Khan had been able to collect gifts and subsidies, not just from Moldavia, Wallachia, and the Porte, but also from Poland.[87] During 1603 and 1604, Aḥmed Aġā, envoy of the Khan, was sent to Clausenburg (Kolozsvar, Cluj) in Transylvania to negotiate a separate peace between the Khan and the Emperor. The Khan sought a subsidy of 40,000 ducats a year as a form of ransom to keep the cities of the Emperor free from Tatar raids.[88]

The Khan did not return again to the Hungarian front after 1603 but in 1604 he continued negotiations with Serban and with the representatives of the Emperor. The Khan came to an agreement with Serban in 1604 and, during the same year, Serban received the standards and other trappings of his office from the Sultan. Thus, it would appear that the Khan, while gaining his own ends, also maintained sufficient influence at the Porte to prolong official recognition of Serban as the Voivode of Wallachia.[89]

Ġāzī Girāy sent his son and Ḳalġay, Tōḳtamīş Girāy, to the Hungarian front in 1604. The Khan himself had been ordered to Ochakov by the Sultan to build a strong fortress there. The Imperial representatives negotiating with Aḥmed Aġā in Clausenburg (Cluj) were particularly interested in having the Ḳalġay Tōḳtamīş recalled from the Hungarian front. While these negotiations were reaching an advanced stage—the Emperor had offered the Khan 20,000 ducats a year—Stephan Bocskay was beginning to drive the forces of the Emperor out of Transylvania.[90] As the offensive of Bocskay and the Ottomans gained momentum, the balance of forces in Hungary and in Transylvania and Wallachia shifted sharply in favor or the Sultan.[91]

Apart from isolated raids by the Tatars, and the assistance Tōḳtamīş Girāy continued to render to Bocskay and the Ottoman army during the years 1605 and 1606, the contributions of the Crimean Tatars to the Ottoman war in Hungary were virtually at an end. The Ottoman and Crimean Tatar lands were now faced with a serious shortage of food. Ġāzī Girāy Khan had sent a sizable contingent to the front each year of the war, and during the thirteen years of the war, he himself had spent seven on campaign either in Hungary or in the tributary principalities. Occasionally also during the Hungarian War, rumors had circulated through the capital that the Sultan would be replaced by the Tatar Khan or that the Khan had placed his personal supporters in high places at the Porte—rumors which attest to the great influence of the Khan at the time.[92]

5 An Important Polish Embassy to the Crimea (1601–1603)

While the Hungarian War was in progress, an important embassy was being undertaken to the Crimea. Before the tide shifted in 1604 so clearly in favor of the Ottomans and their Crimean Tatar allies, the Kingdom of Poland made a serious attempt to capitalize on her neutral position in the war. Because of her exposed positions, facing a number of bellicose German states to the west—particularly the Habsburgs, and a turbulent Muscovy to the east, the sixteenth-century Polish-Lithuanian Commonwealth had preferred to keep on good terms with the Ottomans. But the cost of cooperation with the Sultan came high. By the beginning of the sixteenth century, the Ottomans had secured for themselves control over Wallachia and Moldavia, the latter of which had formerly been a virtual satellite of Poland in the fifteenth century. Moreover, by becoming masters of the Black Sea and overlords of the Crimean Tatars, the Turks were able to block further exploitation by Poland of her traditional routes of access to the Black Sea along the Dnieper, the Dniester, and the Prut rivers.

But just as the Princes of Transylvania maintained the memory of an independent Hungary, an idea that had helped to win Transylvanian adherence to the "Holy League" against the Turks in this war, so also the Polish crown continued to hope for a time when Poland-Lithuania once again would stretch from the Baltic to the Black Sea. Such ideas, when not supported by superior resources and planning, could only lead to futile, devastating wars such as the one we now study. Unlike the Hungarians, however, Poland, under the able leadership of Jan Zamoyski, the Grand Chancellor, emphasized their loyalty to the Ottomans but did not hesitate to push Polish interests with firm diplomacy and an occasional show of force.

As we have seen, the almost constant and irresponsible raiding by the Zaporozhian Cossacks had brought Poland to the brink of war with the Ottoman Sultan and the Tatar Khan in the years 1589 and 1590. When the Tatars were summoned to participate in the Hungarian War in 1594, they embarrassed the Polish government, and particularly Jan Zamoyski, by taking a shortcut to Transylvania through Pokutia in southern Poland. The pride of Poland had reached new heights under the leadership of the Transylvanian King, Stephan Báthory (1575–1586), but had recently suffered humiliation at the hands of the Habsburgs, who had attempted forcibly to put their own candidate on the Polish throne during the interregnum of 1587. Thus the sensitivity of Poland to Ottoman demands in 1590 and to the Tatar incursion of 1594 is quite understandable. A comprehension of these previous events serves as the indispensable background for understanding the Ţuţora incident of 1595 and the three embassies of Laurin Piaseczinski to the Crimean Khanate in the years 1601, 1602, and 1603.

The Ţuţora incident, which is described in Chapter VII, developed directly out of the rebellion of the three Principalities—Wallachia, Moldavia, and Transylvania. To recapitulate briefly, Sigismund Báthory of Transylvania had promised his support to Austria in 1594 and he, in turn, had gained the overlordship of the Voivodes, Michael of Wallachia and Stephan Razvan of Moldavia. Zamoyski, who was close to the Báthory family (Griseldis, sister of Sigismund, was Zamoyski's wife), saw in this system of alliances the outflanking of Poland by the Habsburgs. Moreover, even if it were a gamble, Poland might mildly reassert its claims to Moldavia by a show of force—a small invasion of Moldavia's northern provinces while the Ottomans were heavily committed in Hungary. The Poles clashed with Ottoman and Tatar forces in October 1595 on the Ţuţora River, a tributary of the Prut near Jassy. But the clash was not serious and after three days of skirmishes the contestants broke contact and negotiated an armistice which the Poles considered a "victory" and the Ottomans looked upon as "friendly cooperation." As a result of the negotiation Jeremia Movila, a protégé of Poland, was appointed hospodar and was permitted a palace guard of Polish soldiers. The Tatar Khan, who had conducted the negotiation on behalf of the Sultan, had hoped to have appointed hospodar his own protégé, Aḥmed Aġā, the sanjāḳ bey of Tehine. But the latter official ended up arbitrating the differences between Zamoyski and Ġāzī Girāy. Apart from the aforementioned arrangements for Movila, the Khan agreed to depart from Moldavia within three days of the signing, to exchange prisoners, and to avoid violating Polish territory. Poland also made vague reference to its ancient rights on the Black Sea. Poland was to use its good offices with the Cossacks and Jeremia Movila, and to avoid Tatar raids; and promised to give the Khan seven villages and yearly gifts including a few thousand pounds of honey. After an exchange of gifts, the two armies separated amicably.[93]

It was the understanding of all parties that the armistice of Ţuţora would serve as the basis of future negotiations. The Khan also expected to receive periodic gifts not only from Moldavia but also from Poland. But as we know, Sultan Murād III, a confidant of the Khan, died in 1595 and hence Ġāzī Girāy of necessity became preoccupied with maintaining himself in the Khanship and fighting in Hungary during the next few years. Sigismund Vasa, the Polish King (1587–1632), improved his Catholic credentials and brought relative peace to the borders by suppressing the Cossacks whenever possible and establishing the Uniate Church to wean them away from Orthodoxy. These events had temporarily diminished diplomatic contact between Poland and the Khanate. In 1597, for example, Ġāzī Girāy, in a letter to Zamoyski, promised to serve the Polish King against his enemies if gifts were forthcoming. The Khan, however, demanded the destruction of the Cossacks and received the evasive answer: "Who can say to the wolf that he cannot dwell in the forest?"[94]

In 1599 while the Khan was on campaign in Hungary, the Ḳalġay, Selāmet Girāy, brother of the Khan, agreed not to damage the King's land "up to the Black Sea" but in turn asked the Polish King not to give sanctuary to spies and enemies of the Crimea. When Ġāzī Girāy returned from the front in 1600, he agreed to the freedom of movement of all Tatar and Polish merchants who paid the proper dues, but he insisted that the King, in exchange for his support, must send yearly gifts as of old, half in cash and half in merchandise, to Akkerman. Because of the vagueness of these exchanges over the years since Ţuţora, the Polish King decided in 1601 to send his secretary and Vice-Chancellor of Breslau, Laurin Piaseczinski, on a personal embassy to the Crimea.[95]

Pulaski, in notations for his edition of the diaries of Piaseczinski, summarized the letters prepared for Ġāzī Girāy in which are detailed significant goals of Polish diplomacy:

(*a*) The Khan should keep the peace.

(*b*) The Khan and the other Tatar Princes should refrain from restricting Polish access to the Black Sea.

(*c*) There should be no violation of the King's lands or borders.

(*d*) At the King's request, the Khan should make war on Muscovy.

(*e*) Neither the King nor the Khan should protect traitors, but the Khan should not expect the King to control actions of "outlaw" Cossacks.

(*f*) The King asked that the Khan be friends of the Voivodes of Wallachia and Moldavia, pointing out that Ottoman control of the Principalities had made the Sultan strong.

(*g*) Out of long-standing friendship with Poland, the Khan should serve the King; but if there were no service in a given year then no gifts would be sent. Gifts which formerly were delivered on the last day of November in Akkerman would now be delivered in Kamenetz for which the Khan should give a proper receipt.[96]

The ambassador further received instructions that the Khan should be informed of the recently signed twenty-year treaty with Moscow (March 11, 1601) and that he should remain evasive about the value of the gifts except "in accordance with old custom." When the time for delivery of the gifts was set, the ambassador was urged to be prompt in order to maintain the "autoritas" of the crown. Other letters were sent by the King and by Zamoyski to leading dignitaries of the Crimea. The total cost of the embassy was estimated at 40,000 red-gold zloti of which about 17,500 zloti represented itemized gifts and the remainder, travel costs. Plans called for the storage of the gifts in Kamenetz, but they were destined to follow the embassy later because the crown could not raise sufficient gold coin at short notice.

Piaseczinski reached Jassy on June 27 where he was royally entertained by Jeremia Movila and given much news about the Ottoman scene. These details were sent to the King in a long letter from Jassy. This was the year prior to the death of Kara Yaziji (d. 1602), leader of the Jelālī rebellion which had laid waste a number of provinces in Asia Minor.[97] Apart from the Jelālī rebellion, there appeared to be no news about the Ottoman victory of Kanisza but the envoy heard much of importance about the Crimea. It seems the Sultan had sent to the Khan gifts worth 100,000 zloti and enough money to pay the entire Tatar court for one year, and all this to induce the Khan to take his Tatars to Hungary. But just as the Khan planned to comply, he learned of a plot on his life by Devlet Girāy, his Nūr ed-Dīn, and certain Şirin Beys. As a result, the Khan had eliminated his cousin in traditional manner, by executing him at a banquet held at the end of the fast of Ramazan.[98]

Perhaps the most striking evidence of the reliability of Piaseczinski's sources of information is the report that the Khan was planning also to eliminate his brother, Selāmet Giray. There was also news that Muscovy was renewing its treaty with the Crimea in the same year. The Muscovite gifts were at the border but the Khan had been asked to provide an escort to protect them against the Zaporozhian Cossacks. And from whom did such reliable information derive? From 'Alī Mīrzā and Szachmancir (Şeyh Mansur), two Tatars who had been sent to escort the ambassador. Their tongues had been loosened by strong drink and a couple of measures of gold.[99]

To exploit fully the richness of the diary of Piaseczinski would require a detailed exposition of many more lines than are available to us here. It is important to note, however, the most important details of the journey of 1601. The ambassador left Jassy on July 8 and arrived in Akkerman on July 13. Prior to his departure by galley for the Crimean port of Gözlev (modern Evpatoriya), he noted that a number of Poles were being sold into slavery and complained to the Sanjāḳ Bey. The bey was sympathetic but noted that the Tatar merchants possessed letters of the Khan permitting this trafficking. The envoy, before leaving town, was grossly overcharged for the care of his horses at the public livery stable, witnessed the beating of his servants, and finally had to pay twice for a one-way trip to the Crimea. Upon his arrival in the Crimea (July 19), he received his official food supply (*Stacya*, *Statsiya*, *Ulufe*) and transportation (carriages drawn by oxen *sic.*) The *Statsiya* consisted of 1 ox, 10 sheep, 400 loaves of bread, 10 boxes of smoked fish, 1 jug of olives, 1/2 barrel of wine ("turning to vinegar"). The ambassador was soon received by a high official of the Khan, Jan Ahmed Çelebi, who stated that the Khan was ill but that he would see the ambassador at the earliest possible moment after his recovery. On August 2, a further allotment of Statsiya was sent, this time including caviar, but already various Tatar officials were complaining openly because they had not yet received gifts from the ambassador.[100]

Finally on August 23, after much hesitation on the part of the court, Piaseczinski was led into the presence of the Khan by Ahmed Ağa, the Khan's vezir, by Abdul Aziz Çelebi, treasurer, and by Jan Ahmed Çelebi, son-in-law of the Khan. The ambassador bowed and kneeled before the Khan who sat upon a dais in a carpet-covered chamber (kiosk) located in the garden of Bagçesaray. The Khan was clad in a long robe of brown silk brocade. Around his waist he wore a red silk sash into which was tucked a dagger (*hançer*), ornately decorated with white gold. Upon his head, he wore a sable head-dress held together with scarlet material and at his side lay a saber.

The Khan, looking very pale and thin, rose to receive the kneeling ambassador, and as the latter presented his letters the Khan asked about the health of the King. When satisfied with the assurances of the ambassador, the Khan asked him to state his business, saying the letters would be read later. When the envoy complained about Tatar raids and the Polish slaves in Akkerman, the Khan reminded the ambassador that only twice had he received gifts. The Tatars had merely retaliated after the Cossack attacks. Piaseczinski repeated that the King could not take responsibility for such a mixed group of bandits.

The Khan, excusing himself for his illness (which was most evident to the envoy), stated that if the Cossacks were punished and proper gifts were sent, then the Khan would show true friendship to the King and would not permit Tatar raids. Piaseczinski, upon a sign from the Khan, retired from the audience after presenting the Khan with a beautiful musket (*resznica*) in Spanish gold and ebony with pearl decorations, a powder flask, and a golden key. As was customary, the Khan had the ambassador and his entourage draped in robes of honor (*H̱il'a*). The Khan ordered the translation of the letters and assigned an ambassador to return to Poland with Piaseczinski. On September 4, the ambassador paid a similar visit to the Ḳalġay, Selāmet Giray, who resided in Kïzïl Kaya but who was dwelling in a tent outside of his palace because of the bad air (i.e., the plague).

Prior to his departure, Piaseczinski twice proved his skill as a diplomat. On September 10, Selāmet Girāy, shortly after his interview with the ambassador, fled the country and rode to Istanbul, fearful that his brother planned his destruction. Immediately suspicion centered on the ambassador but his calm exterior and ample witnesses to his audience with the Ḳalġay saved him from seizure. As a result of the flight of Selāmet Girāy, the Khan mobilized his troops and also summoned to his camp near Gözlev (Kozlov) the Ottoman bey of Kaffa who upon arrival assured the Khan that he would seek the extradition of Selāmet Girāy from the Sultan. On this occasion, the Khan appointed his own son, Tōḳtamiş, a boy of twelve, as Ḳalġay or heir apparent, and made his second son Nūr ed-Dīn.

The proximity of the Khan to the Polish camp gave Piaseczinski the opportunity to bid a personal farewell to the Khan. Thus on September 20 the envoy was led into the Khan's tent where he was attended by Jan Anton Spinola of Kaffa who often served as the Khan's negotiator in western lands. During the brief encounter the Khan twice fainted. The Khan, however, had already got to the heart of the King's letters as was demonstrated when he said, "The Black Sea is not mine, hence I cannot give it away." The Khan further stated his intention of sending Jan Ahmed to Poland with his own response. Later that same evening, Jan Anton disclosed that the Khan had consulted his seers (*Ḥāfiż*) who predicted that the Khan would live only two years but would die in power.

Finally, while waiting for good winds to facilitate his return to Akkerman, the ambassador was approached on October 3 by a delegation of Kaffa merchants who demanded of him full payment for debts of Martin Bronowski, former Polish Ambassador to the Crimea (1578). The merchants threatened to have the envoy killed unless he gave them satisfaction. To these threats Piaseczinski retorted that a petition must be sent to the King asking that he recover this private debt from the Bronowski family. The following day the ambassador took ship for Akkerman and, after further hardships, he arrived in Poland where he visited his own estates near Wolyn prior to his arrival in Vilna on November 29.[101]

During the winter months, from November 1601 to January 1602, it became the turn of the Polish government to provide *ulufe* (upkeep) and to entertain some thirty-odd Tatar messengers and dignitaries. Clearly the Khan gained the support of his family and close friends by sending them on such lucrative missions. Beg Timūr, the Khan's messenger, and Alexander Paleologus, the Ḳalġay's messenger, both of whom claimed to be Circassians and Catholic, seemed quite friendly to Poland. The messengers had been sent ahead to announce the coming of Jan Aḥmed Çelebi, the Khan's ambassador, who, by contrast, was quite hostile to Poland. After the reception for the Khan's ambassador, which was held on December 27, the King decided to send Piaseczinski back to the Crimea with Jan Ahmed.

The Khan, in his letter to the King, had failed to deal with the problem of Polish rights of access to the Black Sea which appeared to be the most important issue for Poland. The Khan concerned himself rather with rights of free passage for beggars, women, "white hats" ('Ulemā'), widows, and merchants and showed himself to be particularly concerned with Cossack raids. On an informal basis, Piaseczinski had learned from the Tatar messengers that the Ottomans and Tatars had considered war with Poland a possibility after peace was restored in Hungary. First the Tatars would help the Sultan end the war; then the pro-Polish Voivodes of the Principalities would be replaced and an actual invasion of Poland would follow. These plans, the messengers hastened to point out, depended upon the present cordial relations of the Khan and the Sultan; Ġāzī Girāy had sent a request to the Sultan asking him to execute his brother, Selāmet, but instead the Sultan had him removed either to Bythinia or Rhodes.[102]

Piaseczinski left Vilna for Jassy and Belgorod (Akkerman) on March 3, 1602, but the portion of the Khan's gifts to be paid in gold had not yet been collected. Poland had been fighting a war against Sweden for the control of Latvia and the war had taxed the resources of the crown to the utmost. The Polish crown now planned to exact a capitation tax from the Jews to complete the Khan's gift shipment to Kamenetz. To dispel accusations during this embassy that the Polish King was stingy, the ambassador made a point of showing a portion of the gifts, which were stored in Lublin, to the Tartar envoys.

En route to Akkerman, the Polish ambassador again picked up word of Ġāzī Girāy which he faithfully relayed to the King and to Zamoyski. The Khan still was reported to be ill but this time it was claimed that one of his wives had bewitched him. She and her accomplices were promptly executed. Among the Poles, the Khan was recognized as being learned and brave, but also quite merciless. A number of accounts support this appraisal.

About the time the embassy approached Akkerman for the second time, the town and locality had been attacked by the Cossacks. Thirty Cossack boats had slipped past the fortress in early May with Ottoman galleys in pursuit. The Sanjāḳ Bey of Akkerman accordingly restricted the Polish ambassador to his inn. He also was quick to see a connection between the Polish desire for a Black Sea outlet and the current Cossack raid on the lower Dniester. Furthermore, Piaseczinski came under criticism because the Polish princes, Kniaz Wasyl and Kniaz Jazlowiecki, were building castles close to Tehine (Bender) on Ottoman territory.

All of these accusations could be traced to the machinations of Jan Ahmed Çelebi who had journeyed with Piaseczinski from Jassy to Akkerman. It is interesting, even significant, to follow his reasoning. Jan Ahmed even criticized the Khan for dealing too gently with Poland. To remain strong, to his way of thinking, the Crimea must maintain friendship, not with Poland, but with Circassians, Georgians, Kabardinians, Nogays, and the Ottoman Sultan.

When the embassy arrived at Gözlev on May 26, Jan Ahmed went straight to the Khan while the Polish ambassador was forced to wait until the Khan had completed his reception of the Muscovite ambassador, Gregory Volkovsky, who had brought twenty wagonloads of gifts to the Khan. It is interesting that even the Muscovites feared the Cossacks to the extent that they required the Tatars to send an armed escort to their southernmost outpost at the confluence of the Hoszin and Buzuk (*sic*) rivers. Only on June 24 was Piaseczinski called to an audience with the Khan. The words of Jan Ahmed had indeed done their damage. The Khan made it very clear that it was not in his power to give Poland access to the Black Sea, nor could he accede to any special position for Poland regarding Wallachia and Moldavia. His position hardened to the point that he expected Polish gifts or his Tatars would raid

Polish soil and take what they wanted. The ambassador was then summarily dismissed and Ġāzī Girāy made immediate preparations to join the Sultan's forces in Hungary. Still wary of his brother Selāmet Girāy, he left his son Tōḳtamiş in charge of the Khanate together with a large army and a contingent of his personal Circassian guards. The Khan also entrusted responsibility to his sister's son, Şahrak Bey, the new mīrzā of the influential Şirin tribe. Thus ended the second mission of Piaseczinski.[103] On his return, in the letters sent from Jassy, the Polish ambassador indicated clearly his pessimism about ever coming to an agreement with the Tatar Khan. He sent urgent dispatches to the Castellon of Halics, Jerzy Strus, alerting him to a possible Tatar attack either through Halics to the Transylvanian mountains or by way of the "Black Way" (Czarny Szlak) through Podolia. He similarly alerted Jan Potocky, military commander of all Podolia. Piaseczinski had received no "living" while in the Crimea, an unheard of discourtesy, and no one was allowed to speak with him. When the ambassador reported to the King in Cracow on August 17, 1602, he stated that the Khan had warned the voivodes of the three principalities to discharge the Poles in their service and to provide him and the Sultan with all possible intelligence about Poland. The Wallachian voivode had sent rich gifts to the Khan, but had so far not sent his tribute to the Polish King.[104]

In the letters of Piaseczinski to Zamoyski, it is clear that many Polish noblemen of Podolia wanted to attack the Tatars but Zamoyski, true to his previous policies, preferred an active policy against Muscovy. In these letters some other interesting details about the Crimea come to light. Ahmed Aġā, the Khan's Vezir and first cousin, was appointed custodian of the Khan's treasure which he housed in the impregnable fortress of Inkerman. Moreover, a slave rebellion was threatening the Crimea from the mountains to the south where a number of slaves had taken refuge.[105]

Toward the close of the year 1602, it had become clear to the King of Poland that time was not on his side. The Turks were making gains on every front in spite of the Jelālī rebellion in Asia Minor and the threatening position of Persia toward Ottoman possessions in the Caucasus. When the Tatar embassy reached Poland in September, the various delegates were well treated. The King instructed Piaseczinski to ready the gifts at Kamenetz so they could be delivered to the Tatars against a receipt. To cover the shortages, Poland put pressure on Wallachia and received 50,000 zloti (2 thalers = 3 zloti). In the dispatches of Piaseczinski to Zamoyski, we learn just how impoverished the Crown of Poland was. The ambassador was forced to cover his expenses in Kamenetz out of his own pocket! As the Khan planned to winter in Buda (i.e., Hungary), 'Alī Mīrzā was sent to Kamenetz but he refused to take delivery of the gifts except in Akkerman. 'Alī Mīrzā finally consented to receive the gifts from Piaseczinski in Jassy at the end of January, 1603. The ambassador had discharged his task, had received the receipts of 'Alī Mīrzā, and had returned home to Crakow where he received a royal citation. Moscow, the Sultan, and now Poland had given in to the high-pressure tactics of the Khan. Whether or not the Khan would honor his pledges still remained in doubt; meanwhile the steppe continued to be as turbulent as ever.[106]

6 The Counter-Rebellion of Bocskay Against Habsburg-Catholic Imperialism and the Peace of Szitva-Török (1606)

In the era under discussion, there is considerable overlapping of action between Ottoman affairs in Istanbul, the warfare on the Hungarian front, and the internal politics of Transylvania, Wallachia, Moldavia, and the Crimean Khanate. While a number of these complex interrelationships have been touched upon in the preceding pages, a full understanding of the events in Ottoman Eastern Europe at the turn of the seventeenth century would not be complete without a close look at some of the Counter Reformation activities of Austria and their impact on events in Hungary. It is this activity in particular which created in Hungary a climate of acceptability for another century of Ottoman rule.

In Chapter VII we discussed the impact of the Protestant Reformation on Hungary and observed that a significant majority of Saxons and Hungarians from all strata of society broke away from the Roman Catholic faith and became members of a variety of Protestant sects.[107] It was also shown that there was a relationship between the sect to which a given stratum adhered and the extent to which that stratum felt itself alienated, for economic or social reasons, from the rest of Hungarian society. In short, one need not be reminded that changing one's religious allegiance has often served as a means either of political protest or of economic gain. For better or for worse, only three significant Catholic dioceses survived the Protestant Revolution: Esztergom (Gran), Nyitra (Neutraer), and Györ (Raab).[108] There were historical precedents for this. On the borders of Hungary, nationalistic Slav princes, prior to the Ottoman conquest, had often supported the heterodoxy of the Manichean Bogomils as a check on the imperialist designs of Roman Catholic Hungary or of latter day Greek Orthodox Byzantium.[109] It is perhaps too much to conclude that Protestantism flourished in Hungary during the era of the Zápolyai simply because the Zápolyai, not unlike the Bosnian princes of an earlier era, saw in the Protestant movement a chance for their own political survival or economic aggrandizement.[110] At this stage we know too little about how much the Zápolyai or the other magnates encouraged the spread of Protestantism as a check on Habsburg-Catholic imperialism in relation to the popularity of Protestantism as a means of protest against political and ecclesiastical abuse, in general, of which there was much in Hungary.

Even as the era of the Zápolyai was opportune for the spread of Protestantism in Hungary, primarily because the Ottoman Turks and not the Habsburgs were the overlords, the coming to power of the Catholic Báthorys in Transylvania after 1571 appeared to the Habsburgs and to the Papacy as an appropriate time to begin winning back the "lost souls" to Catholicism. While the Papacy might have made inroads in its own right against the multitude of sects in Hungary had it practiced tolerance in Catholic lands, it made the mistake of trying to reimpose Catholicism by means of Habsburg armies in the Hungarian War, 1593–1606. Such a policy went against the national feelings and religious convictions of the Hungarians and thus assured Ottoman control until 1699 and anti-Habsburg sentiment in Hungary throughout the eighteenth century.[111]

The Counter Reformation had gained some notable successes in the Austrian home territories of the Habsburgs. The peasants had to face the hard choice of remaining Catholic or emigrating. But the nerves of the Habsburg ruling house had been frayed considerably by communal wars with the Protestant German princes which had led up to the Peace of Augsburg (1555). Meanwhile the Papacy could do little but watch the dismantling of bishopric after bishopric as one sect or another of Protestantism won converts under the protection of the Ottoman Sultan. It is not surprising thus that Emperor Rudolph, controlled by the Catholic party and the papal nuncios, Ferreri and Serra, did everything in his power to destroy Protestantism and its institutions in Hungary. In fact, he went so far as to alienate Hungarians loyal to the Habsburgs by decreeing that no Hungarian might serve as an officer in the Austrian army units.

In the 1570s Catholicism made its first major counterplay in Transylvania by obtaining the election of Stephan Báthory as prince. One must observe in passing that Báthory, owing to his known military prowess and his anti-Habsburg stance, was the Sultan's choice also. While Stephan Báthory had done little more than provide for the toleration of Catholics (1572) and the establishment of a Jesuit Academy in Kolozsvar (1579) during the time that his influence was strong in Transylvania, his nephew, Prince Sigismund, after the death of Stephan Báthory (1586), experienced a reaction to these Catholic inroads. The Transylvanian Diet ordered the closing of the Jesuit Academy in 1588 and banished all Catholic clergy. Only Alphonse Carillo (Cariglios), Spanish Jesuit and confessor of Sigismund, remained at court.[112]

But Carillo was no ordinary man. Through long training and experience, he had accurately evaluated the weak position of the Catholic Church in Hungary. He knew that after the extinction of the Zápolyai line, a polarization had gradually taken place among the notables of the country. A number of the Hungarian patriots such as Georg Bocskay (father of Stephan), in spite of their Protestant convictions, considered that Hungarian national life could only be preserved through close cooperation with the Habsburgs. For his loyalty to the Habsburgs, Bocskay was imprisoned in Koloszvar, but ironically was released in time to lead the Transylvanian forces against Emperor Maximilian in 1568, thus assuring to John Sigismund Zápolyai his princedom until the end of his life.

It is thus clear that until the great Hungarian War between the Ottomans and the Habsburgs (1593–1606), there were Protestants and Catholics occupying the entire political spectrum from pro-Habsburg to pro-Ottoman. It is also clear that Hungarians and Saxons in the vast majority were Protestant. Hence the proverb so many writers quote about the era, "*Ein Katholik auf tausend Ketzer komme*" (One Catholic may encounter a thousand heretics). Our task here is to show that Habsburg imperial policies and attitudes toward Hungary, together with Papal interference, awakened a strong national and religious consciousness that polarized Catholic and Protestant in Hungary, and that this served Ottoman interests for at least a century. The Islamic-Ottoman system did not basically disturb national or religious sensibilities, although it is well known that the Ottomans tacitly gave support to the Protestant clergy.[113]

Before turning to the seemingly endless military operations that led up to the Bocskay revolt, it would seem worthy of our attention to determine how the Habsburgs lost so much popularity in Hungary during the sixteenth century and yet almost succeeded in imposing the Counter Reformation. Stated simply, when Ferdinand I was chosen King of Hungary in 1526, it was assumed that he would make Hungary his place of residence, but when he became Emperor after the resignation of Charles V in 1556, it was clear that the Habsburgs would rule from Vienna and Prague. Maximilian II and Rudolph II were brought up in Spain and during their youth Habsburg grandeur and absolutism made further strides. Hence during the sixteenth century concepts of absolutism based on "Divine Right," rule from Prague, and Catholicism became clearly the pillars of the "Habsburg system."[114] If the Crown had, on occasion, enjoyed the counsel of wordly and farseeing advisers who had been sensitive to the plight of Hungary in the past, such counsel had abandoned the Crown in its late sixteenth-century "Wars of Religion" and the struggle with Ottoman Turkey. Important financial and military assistance had been arranged by Pope Clement VIII but even this did not suffice.[115] This state of affairs gave to the Catholic bishops of Hungary residing in Prague an inordinate voice in the imperial councils even though their bishoprics often existed only on paper. The bishops, many of whom were as materialistic as their Renaissance predecessors, naturally coveted the power and wealth that had belonged to their bishoprics prior to the Reformation.

Although one might choose in this secular era to stress the venality of a Pope Clement VIII (1592–1605), the zealousness for the Counter Reformation of such Jesuits as Carillo, or the greediness of the Hungarian bishops, it would be a mistake to overemphasize the villainy of the Catholic Church. In fact,

Pope Clement VIII was one of the most pious and upright popes of all time. His motives in fostering a "Holy League" against the Turks derived from a genuine fear for the survival of Christendom.[116]

But the Church lost its credulity, as did the Habsburgs, because of the excesses perpetrated in its name against a basically Protestant or Orthodox population in Hungary, and particularly in Transylvania, during this war.

Through this brief review of events covered in Chapter VII, we are able to piece together the case for war as seen, even planned, by the Pope and the Emperor. The basic concept of a "Holy League," which had enjoyed partial success against the Ottoman advance in the past, was once again encouraged by the Pope in 1592 in view of Ottoman belligerency in Croatia in that year when Wihitsch (Bihac) fell. The idea of a "Holy League," together with the promise of financial help, was very appealing to Rudolph II, who was a fanatic Catholic and autocrat and who was surrounded primarily by men of like mind, including the Hungarian prelates. The idea picked up momentum as Ottoman Turkey declared war on the Habsburgs and the Pope sent Alexander Komulovič on his mission to win over Transylvania, Moldavia, the Cossacks, and Muscovy.[117] This activity triggered an important shifting of forces at the court of Sigismund Báthory in Transylvania. Báthory had quietly lined up all of the notables favorable to Habsburg-Catholic interests, placed them in strategic positions about the land, and then signed an agreement to cooperate with the Emperor and the "Holy League" against the Turks. He was thus prepared to move against what some have termed the "humanists" and others, "the neutralists," whose opinions actually represented the majority of the Transylvanian nobility up to 1594. This entire plan of union with the Habsburgs had been worked out by the Jesuit Carillo.[118] The community of interest of Papacy, Jesuits, Emperor, and Hungarian bishops would have been insufficient, however, to strike a blow at the Turks if the Voivodes of Transylvania, Wallachia, and Moldavia had not been in a position to exploit the latent hostility of many of their subjects to Ottoman rule. If the so-called "humanists" or upholders of the *status quo* considered the time inopportune to revolt against the Ottoman Empire, their opposition was quickly neutralized by the pro-Habsburg faction. A key role in the coup of 1594 was played by Stephan Bocskay, son of Georg Bocskay and uncle of Sigismund Báthory.

Stephan Bocskay was born in a Kolozsvar prison where his father and mother were interned. He spent most of his youth in Prague and Vienna where he received a thorough education among the other royal pages who were sons of noblemen. When he returned to Transylvania, he began his public career favored by his nephew the Prince. In 1592 Sigismund Báthory, doubtless at the behest of Carillo, appointed his uncle Counselor of State, Commander-in-Chief of Nagyvarad (Grosswardein), the principal fortress, and Count of Bihar—three offices which he held until 1598. Bocskay was known as a believing Christian, a good Protestant, and a Hungarian patriot. The plans of Carillo, which would help free Hungary from the Turks, held great appeal for Bocskay in the years 1592 to 1598. He had witnessed the suffering of Hungary under the Turks, particularly in the border areas where the peasantry was subjected to continuous warfare and raiding.

Though his pro-Habsburg sympathies were genuine, his support for the Habsburg cause began to cool appreciably as the war progressed.[119] The plans of Carillo, the Hungarian bishops, and Sigismund Báthory, apart from placing all military forces and imperial posts in the hands of "good Catholics" or pro-Habsburg families, also called for the destruction of the economic power of the "uncooperative" Protestant magnates. The Hungarian Saxon communities, while basically Lutheran, tended because of their ethnic origins to be favorable to the Habsburgs. Except for the Saxons, the Protestant movement depended fundamentally upon the financial support of the leading magnates. Thus, their wealth, goods, and influence came under sharp attack by one of the typical instruments of the Counter-Reformation, the so-called "fiscal processes." Most notable of the Hungarian magnates to fall victim to these illegal confiscations was the grand marshal to the Habsburg Court, Stephan Illéshazy, a leading Lutheran. Out of fear for his life, he fled to Poland and his lands and possessions were confiscated. Sigismund Rákoczy, whose family was second only in wealth and prestige to the Báthorys, was forced to pay 50,000 guilders, Valentin Homonnay, 20,000, and Georg Homonnay, 150,000—all to the imperial fisc.[120] As the pro-Habsburg coup progressed in 1594, a number of Protestant magnates who opposed a league with Austria were executed and thereby the Transylvanian Diet was intimidated sufficiently to ratify the Habsburg treaty (1594). Hand in hand with the political and economic changes, Jesuit monasteries were given permission by the captive diet to open in Klausenburg (Kolozsvar) and Karlsburg (Alba Julia) and in 1598 Sigismund restored the Catholic bishopric of the latter place.[121]

The year 1595 had seen the establishment of Transylvanian hegemony over Wallachia and Moldavia and the disastrous defeat of an Ottoman army at Giurgiu by a combined Transylvanian and Wallachian force, but Transylvanian ascendency lasted only until the Ottomans had adjusted to the new situation. Stephan Razvan, Sigismund's puppet in Moldavia, was killed by Polish and Tatar action at Ţuţora in 1595 and the Transylvanian troops fighting with the Habsburgs at Mezö Kerésztés were badly mauled in 1596. Meanwhile the Szekelys had revolted and were ruthlessly crushed by Bocskay. It soon became clear that Sigismund Báthory was as impotent in his bedchamber as on the battlefield. Carillo, seeing his master plan wavering, negotiated with the Emperor to give to Sigismund the duchies of Oppeln and Ratibor in Silesia. He also arranged an annulment of Sigismund's marriage with the Emperor's niece and turned Transylvania over to Imperial Commissioners. But popular opinion was against both Rudolph and his comissioners who in 1598 maladroitly removed the last pillar of respectability in the former regime, Stephan Bocskay, from his leadership of the army.[122]

Between the years 1598 and 1602, Transylvania changed its leadership five times. Sigismund Báthory resumed the voivodeship from August 1598 until he turned it over to his cousin Andras, the Polish Cardinal, in March 1599. But Cardinal Andras Báthory, under the influence of Zamoyski, negotiated an accord with the Ottomans. Michael of Wallachia now saw himself encircled by Poland, Transylvania, and the Ottomans and hence struck at the weakest foe, Andras Báthory, whom he killed (October, 1599) at the battle of Sellemberk near Szeben (Sibiu) with the aid of the Szekelys, many of whom hated the Báthorys for their repressive policies of 1570–1571 and 1596. Thereafter Michael quartered himself in Alba Julia and, acting as an ally of the Habsburgs, he and his troops established control throughout Transylvania.[123] Michael then took steps to consolidate his control of both Transylvania and Wallachia. He sought an accommodation with the Turks, appointed bishop Napragyi as his chancellor, and Caspar Kornis, Moïses (Moses) Szekely, and Stephen Csaky as his counselors. He also assured to the three estates their ancient privileges. But Prague had other ideas about the future of Transylvania and sent two royal commissioners, David Ungnad and Michael Szekely, to negotiate. In actuality Michael enjoyed local support only from the Vlach and Szekely peasants. Feeling isolated and fearing intervention from Polish forces in Moldavia, he unseated Movila temporarily in May 1600 with a lightning attack—but his army was slowly falling to pieces. He was defeated by Basta and a faction of noblemen led by Moïse Szekely at Miriszlo on the Maros River and retreated to Wallachia. But now the anti-Habsburg forces were increasing and rather than see Transylvania fall into the hands of the Habsburgs, Zamoyski urged his brother-in-law, Sigismund Báthory, to return for the third time. With the aid of Turkish troops, Sigismund launched a successful campaign from Temesvar in February 1601. However, at the instigation of Prague, a temporary alliance was hammered out between Basta and Michael who then defeated Báthory at Goroszlo on August 3, 1601. Shortly thereafter, Basta had Michael executed on acquiring evidence of his diplomatic exchanges with the Turks. Once again at the beginning of 1602, Sigismund, with the aid of Turk and Tatar troops, drove Basta out of Transylvania. But when Sigismund departed Transylvania for the last time, some Szeklers, led by Moïses Szekely, and the remaining noblemen took arms against the Habsburg troops. They were crushed at the battle of Tovis on July, 2, 1602. Many of the survivors, hunted by Austrian troops took refuge with the Turks, principally in Temesvar; Basta, meanwhile, set up a harsh military rule using as his base the Saxon towns.

Sigismund Báthory and his confessor, the Jesuit Carillo had made serious attempts to re-Catholicize Transylvania but only after Giorgio Basta and his Spanish, Italian, and Walloon troops took control of the principality in the summer of 1602 could harsh repressive measures be carried out (in the name of pacification) against all heretics. On September 1, Basta, in announcing to Emperor Rudolph II, his victory over local opposition at Tovis, sketched his plan of action for the months ahead. First he planned to re-Catholicize the Saxon towns starting with Hermannstadt (Szeben, Sibiu); the others would follow. Next he would suppress by force all followers of Arian (Unitarian), Sabbatarian, or Jewish beliefs. Public offices must all be turned over to Catholics. Suppression of Calvinism (owing to its wide diffusion) would not be undertaken directly until a more appropriate time. Meanwhile Basta's troops, quartered on the Saxons, had their way with the hapless townsmen. Demetrius Napragyi, who had served as the newly appointed Catholic bishop for a time but who had been driven out after Sigismund Báthory lost his power, also advised the court not to disturb the Calvinists but to count first of all on the Szekelys, many of whom were still Catholic. As for the leading Unitarians, their wealth should be confiscated forthwith and their edifices in Kolozsvar (Klausenburg) destroyed. Not surprisingly, Napragyi was again appointed by Pope Clement VIII as bishop of Transylvania on January 15, 1603.[125] Along with Basta, the royal commissioners once again returned to Transylvania to represent the bureaucratic aspects of Habsburg rule, but they quickly undermined their credulity by ignoring the Saxon plea for religious freedom.

The chronology is rather confused for the period from the final defeat by Basta of Sigismund Báthory and of the Transylvanian nobles at Tovis on July 2, 1602, until Bocskay received the *Ahitname* of the Sultan on November 20, 1604. But a careful study of the sequence of events in this two-year period gives one much insight into the growth of the Bocskay revolutionary movement and of the important role that the Ottomans played in it.

While the full weight of the Habsburg military, religious, and bureaucratic system was descending on the exhausted principality, a few Hungarian nobles led by Moïses Szekely, a former commander for King Stephan Báthory and long involved in Transylvanian affairs, sought and gained help from the Turks.[126] Moïses Szekely, a Szekler (Szekely) nobleman (*lófö*) of Unitarian proclivities, had only recently served on the staff of Michael of Wallachia who had championed Szekler grievances. It is thus no surprise to find him taking refuge with the Turks after the Battle of Tovis (July, 1602), together with other Hungarians who sought refuge in Turkish-protected cities such as Temesvar. Moïses Szekely, a good military leader, had doubtless first been received by Yemişçī Ḥasan Paşa, the Grand Vezir, sometime during the summer of 1602 and related to him some easy ways (*bāżī asān tarīḳ*) to reconquer Transylvania. He, of course, showed his willingness to lead the attack. Yemişçī Ḥasan found the plans of Moïses very attractive and encouraged him to carry them out. The Grand Vezir had already, however, planned to retake Stuhlweissenburg (Ustun-i Belgrad) during the summer of 1602. After taking the fortress on August 29, 1602, Yemişçī Ḥasan led his army across the Buda bridge to the plain below Pest and prepared to lend support to Moïses. At this point his local staff tried to dissuade him from going to Transylvania so late in the season. Kādīzāde 'Alī Pasha, the Beylerbey of Buda, Ḳōjā Habil Efendi, the Kādī of Buda, and Sufi Sinān Pasha, the Commander of the Buda garrison, went together to talk to the Grand Vezir. Kādīzāde 'Alī had to be brought in a stretched because he had been wounded by a bullet from an arquebus at Stuhlweissenburg. In particular, Kādīzāde 'Alī became insistent, saying that one of his most trusted spies reported that the enemy camp near Esztergom (Gran) possessed forty large cannon and a fighting force of more than 80,000 men. But as Peçewī observed, Yemişçī Ḥasan was an Albanian and, ridiculing the enemy, stubbornly held to his original intention. Thus, as the main Ottoman army moved in the direction of Transylvania, the Habsburg troops besieged Pest and captured it (October, 1602) before the headstrong Grand Vezir could return to its relief.[127]

Meanwhile the Tatar Khan appeared on the scene in mid-October and was assigned winter quarters in Péc (Fünfkirchen). Here one notices a certain amount of anachronism in the account of Peçewī upon which the article of Gökbilgin is dependent. Peçewī unfolds the story of Moïses Szekely as if the Khan and Yemişçī Ḥasan had spoken with Moïses in Péc prior to the 1602 campaign—that is, in the winter of 1601–1602—while it is evident that the "Epicurean Winter" of Ġāzī Girāy's residence in Péc took place between October 1602 and the spring of 1603. Before that time the Khan was in the Crimea. If Moïses had the tête-à-tête with Ġāzī Girāy that Peçewī describes, it was during the winter of 1602–1603.[128] Evidence from other sources would suggest that the Khan and Moïses indeed did meet because the Khan supplied Moïses with Tatar horsemen in the spring of 1603, but he himself departed for Wallachia and the Crimea without campaigning. Thus in the spring of 1603, a relatively small troop of Hungarians, Turks, and Tatars lead by Moïses Szekely departed from Temesvar to do battle with Basta. At first Moïses saw success at Lippa and Jenö and his victories were crowned at Alba Julia by his election as prince of Transylvania. After he took Kolozsvar the local population burned the Jesuit quarters to the ground. This and other excesses, however, made his movement unpopular with the Saxons and peasant Szekely. Basta, who was unable alone to repulse Moïses Szekely, had called upon his puppet, Radu Serban, the Voivode of Wallachia, for assistance. Thus caught between Basta and Serban at Brassó, Szekely and the "flower of the Transylvanian nobles" perished on July 17, 1603. The true picture was, though incredibly grim, somewhat otherwise. It was doubtful if any Unitarian Szekler, such as Moïses representing the *lófö* exploiting class, could acquire a broad base of support in Hungary at this time. Ottoman support also appeared to be inadequate.[129]

After Brassó, the wrath of Basta's troops could not be controlled. Wholesale murder, rape, and pillaging engulfed the principality. The land appeared to be incapable of resisting the *soldatesca.* Even Rudolph's secret order to Basta of August 20, 1603, had racist overtones. Only Catholic spiritual possessions and ore-mining operations were to be spared, apart from the "faithful Saxons." Clearly the "foreign" nations, and particularly the Vlachs, were to be given no quarter. All men of property were required to pay in gold or silver one quarter of their estimated wealth, and as many could not raise this much money, their goods were confiscated. Wherever enforceable by troops, evangelical preaching was forbidden. Basta now had a free hand to Germanize and to Catholicize the entire principality; Basta and his officers in fact confiscated much of the land as their personal domains and slaughtered Hungarians at every turn.

A decree, particularly irksome to the Protestants, was issued on November 11, 1603: the St. Elizabeth Church of Kaschau (Kassa), Protestant for over fifty years, was turned over to the Erlau (Eger) Catholic community which had fled to Kaschau after their town had fallen to the Turks. When the city magistrates of Kaschau resisted this illegal act, the Kaschau military commander, Jakob Barbiano Belgiojoso, occupied the church with his mercenaries, expelled the ministers, and punished the city with the confiscation of its granary and twenty-eight surrounding villages. Little did the Ottomans realize what misery was brought upon a whole region when a given town was conquered and its principal churches converted into Mosques! Now Catholic and Protestant fought to control the remaining Christian edifices.

Following shortly upon such acts of military rule, the Imperial Reichstag of the German Nation opened on February 3, 1604. The occasion was a bitter one because the majority of its members were Protestant. The Habsburgs and the Papacy had carried the principal burden of fighting the Ottomans; moreover, most of the anti-Protestant or anti-Hungarian decrees had originated with Emperor Rudolph and his entourage. Now ironically it was Archduke Matthias who was caught in the middle. He had to make a plea for subsidies to a Reichstag made hostile by the senseless acts of Rudolph and his military commanders. The Reichstag lost no time in drafting twenty-one articles to ensure the security of person and property and the free practice of religion in Hungary. No subsidies would be forthcoming from the North German princes until the articles were endorsed by the Emperor. While Rudolph grudgingly endorsed the twenty-one articles on May 1, he appended the infamous Article 22 which revealed his bigotry to the whole empire. In short, the cities of Hungary were set apart from the 21 articles and placed directly under control of the Emperor to whom was entrusted the "correctness" of their religious beliefs, "the Roman-Catholic beliefs and confession."

The declaration of Article 22 broke up the Reichstag and because of its wide distribution did much to create almost total opposition to Habsburg rule in Hungary.[130] Meanwhile close upon the military occupation of every region, property, gardens, and vineyards were set aside and quickly occupied by

Jesuits and other Catholic clerics. But even Basta, in the summer of 1604 when he was recalled from Transylvania to assume over-all command of the war against the Turks, passed through Kaschau and sensed that a revolt was brewing. Not only had the cities of northern Hungary lost their religious freedom by a stroke of the pen; the very nature of their rights to possess land and property had been called into question by the Imperial decrees. During the meeting of the Reichstag, a statement had been recorded that summarized the frightening mentality of the whole Counter Reformation: "*Es ist besser, dass die handvoll evangelischen Volkes untergehe, als dass die katholische Kirche Schaden erleide*" (It is better that the handful of Protestants should perish than that the Catholic Church should suffer harm).

But if the Habsburgs felt that the time to root out Protestantism had arrived, the Protestant communities of Hungary had likewise come to the realization that, difficult as life was under Turkish rule, the Turks paid little attention to one's religious preferences and, apart from tribute, they left the economic and social order intact. In Transylvania in the year 1604, famine was driving people to cannibalism and pestilence was raging in the land. The realization that Habsburg rule meant complete subjugation and humiliation had come already in 1602 and 1603 to a dedicated band of émigrés which had escaped the slaughter at Tovis and Brassó. Gabriel (Gabor) Bethlen, who would later become Prince of Transylvania (1613–1629), acted as the chief spokesman of the émigrés.

Gabriel Bethlen stemmed from the Iktári branch of an ancient Hungarian family.[131] As a young man he served at the court of Sigismund Báthory where he knew the chief dignitaries of the land including Moïses Szekely and Stephan Bocskay. He had taken refuge in Turkey, presumably after Tovis (1602), where he had been appointed a *müteferrika* (~royal body guard) by Yemişçī Hasan Pasha (with a wage of 120 aḳçe) and assigned winter quarters in Semendere on the Danube. In 1603 Lālā Meḥemmed Pasha was appointed commander-in-chief of the Hungarian front. It was his intention, probably with the advice of Yemişçī Ḥasan, to assist the Moïses Szekely movement with an attack on the key fortress of Vārād (Grosswardein). But while Gabriel Bethlen had joined the forces of Szekely, the main Ottoman support had not materialized in time to save Szekely's troops from destruction at Brassó (Kronstadt) on July 17, 1603. Moreover, once the siege of Vārād had begun in September, the Serdār was forced to raise it and go to the rescue of Buda, then under siege. Bethlen once again took refuge in Temesvar. He had developed a marked facility with the Ottoman language and numerous friendships with Ottoman dignitaries; consequently, Lālā Meḥemmed Pasha urged him to accept the *Ahitname* of the Sultan and to make his bid for the voivodeship. But the experience of Moïses had shown that a prince would require a broad following. Bethlen, a devout Calvinist, now turned the attention of the émigrés to Stephan Bocskay, as a man with sufficient prominence and acceptability to both Protestant and Catholic factions to bring unity to Transylvania in its struggle with the Habsburgs.

Stephan Bocskay, who had been removed from his post as commander of Transylvanian forces in 1598, languished on his estates. He too had fallen under suspicion in 1600 and had seen his own estates confiscated. Only after a personal plea to the Emperor had his estates near Debreczin and Vārād (Grosswardein or Oradea) been returned. But Bocskay, who had once been a leading supporter of the Habsburgs, had also lost his zeal upon seeing the cruelty of Basta and his men and the arbitrariness and capriciousness of Habsburg power.

Whether the Transylvanian émigrés contacted Bocskay or, as Peçewī contends, a dervish prisoner-of-war, serving as Bocskay's gardener, had convinced Bocskay that with Ottoman help he could drive the Austrian army out of Hungary, an exchange of views took place among Bektaş Pasha, Beylerbey of Temesvar, Bocskay, and Bethlen with the idea of appointing Bocskay as voivode with Ottoman support.[132] The attractiveness of Bocskay was manifold: the Catholics looked upon him as a protector of their civil rights and the others knew that he would defend the Hungarian nation. As Bocskay later stated, "This would be a league with the Turks, not to abandon political and religious freedom, but to preserve it." Bocskay was quickly assured, through correspondence with Bethlen, that he would receive the *Ahitname* for the voivodeship. The émigrés now waited only for an appropriate moment to start the rebellion. When Basta moved his troops to the relief of Gran (Esztergom) in 1604, Gabriel Bethlen and the Pasha of Temesvar considered the time right for an attack, first on Lippa and then into central Transylvania. But the plot was sprung. Some Haiduks and the Lippa commander made a surprise attack on the Hungarians and Turks. While the émigrés and Turks were able to escape, the Haiduks intercepted a letter from Bocskay to Bethlen that revealed the master plan. Fortunately Bocskay learned of the betrayal before Belgiojoso, commander at Kaschau, could encircle him on his estates. As Bocskay was in close contact with another group of Haiduk chiefs—Blasius Nemet, Johann Szilasy, and Blasius Lippay—he called upon them to defend the Transylvanian statutes and the Protestant faith. Many, perhaps most, of the Haiduks were Calvinists, who had turned to banditry either during the rebellion of 1570–1571 or during the ravages of the present war. As Bocskay, to gain their support, had promised them land after the war, they quickly flocked to his standard.[133]

Bocskay now rapidly began to take control of upper Hungary while Bethlen lined up his supporters in Transylvania. His first great victory took place on October 15, 1604, when his troops fell upon Colonel Pezzen who was attempting to make a rendezvous of his troops with Belgiojoso near Adorjan. Now Belgiojoso retreated to Kaschau (Kassa) by way of Tokaj, thus leaving Transylvania unprotected by Habsburg troops except in the fortified towns

Erratum

Add on p. iv:

This book is published with the help of a grant from the late Miss Isobel Thornley's Bequest to the University of London.

of Vārād, Szamosujvar, and Fogoras. But Belgiojoso was locked out of his own command headquarters at Kaschau. The burghers in fact secretly let in the Haiduks without the knowledge of the *Mustermeister* (~Quartermaster), Erich Lassota, erstwhile envoy of the Emperor to the Cossacks, who had been left in nominal command.[134] With this humiliation of the Habsburg commander for upper Hungary, the occupation began to give way to the Haiduks of Bocskay in every region not occupied by the Turks.

On November 20, 1604, the Çavuş of the Grand Vezir arrived in Kaschau, where Bocskay had halted, and presented him with the *Ahitname* confirming him as Prince of Transylvania and King of Hungary.[135] The Turkish support appeared unqualified. Basta, meanwhile, who had engaged the Turks for a time before Esztergom, departed from that city on November 5 with 14,000 troops to attempt to halt the rebellion. Two sharp clashes with Bocskay's Haiduks at Besenyö and Edeleny ended in Basta's favor, but when Basta reached Kaschau on December 3, he too was forced to withdraw. The cities of Löcse, Szeben, Bartfa, and Kaschau, even at this late date, tried to negotiate with Basta for their religious freedom and for the renewal of the city privileges and licenses. Basta, while indicating that he personally was favorable to such overtures, was seeking reinforcements and Rudolph was doing all in his power to discredit the movement. But Rudolph was totally out of touch with Hungary. He continued to issue orders to nonexistent Catholic magnates and counties that they should stand against Bocskay.

At this point, according to an important observation by Professor Gökbilgin which is not apparent in the Hungarian sources, the defeat of Bocskay and the Haiduks by Basta (November 1604) might well have put an end to the Bocskay revolt had not the Ottomans quickly given direct support to Bocskay with Ottoman and Tatar troops. In the words of Peçewī, "The accursed Austrians . . . sent the wretched commander Georgi Basta, together with the Austrian troops, against him [Bocskay], defeated his troops and caused them to take flight. Later [i.e., 1605] the [Ottoman] commander-in-chief [Lālā Meḥemmed Paşa] having again sent a number of Tatars, Ottoman troops ['asker] and the provincial troops of Temesvar to [his] aid, Bocskay, by the Grace of God, took courage and routed the aforementioned Georgi Basta, together with the Austrian troops and caused them to take flight . . . ."[136]

During this period of stress, we catch a glimpse of an interesting sidelight. The Bocskay revolt awakened in Slavonia the fear that Hungarians and Turks might henceforth cooperate more closely, "*als die stammverwandten Ungarn mit der Türkei Hand in Hand gehen*" (since the ethnic-related Hungary cooperates closely with Turkey).[137] Rudolph, in the name of German unity, appealed to the North German princes for assistance but he could awaken no response. Leaders like Christian VI of Saxony blamed the Jesuits for the troubles and complained that they even went against the Confession of Augsburg. Only one small loan was forthcoming, from the Spanish ambassador. This meager response forced Basta to turn more seriously to negotiation on December 19, 1604. The northern counties of Hungary supported seven points:

1. Freedom of religion;
2. The integrity of other civil liberties and the withdrawal of illegal citations;
3. Military supremacy of Hungarians in Kaschau (Kassa);
4. Diminution of imperial authority in the exchequer;
5. Withdrawal of Article XXII and negation of any such future illegalities;
6. An honorable position for Bocskay;
7. Letters of amnesty for all participants in the rebellion.[138]

In mid-January the negotiations were broken off because Bocskay held out for recognition as Prince of Transylvania. Archduke Matthias and the entourage of the Court could not bring themselves to support religious freedom. Meanwhile, the Bocskay movement gained momentum and all of Basta's troops were forced out of upper Hungary by April 8. The Walloons, as they withdrew, burned and pillaged everything in their path.

In Transylvania the Bocskay movement under the leadership of Gabriel Bethlen also made rapid progress against the Saxon-speaking regions. The imperial commissioners, Imhoff and Hoffmann, moved from Kolozsvar (Klausenburg) to Nagyszeben (Hermannstadt) where they remained at the mercy of the Saxons. Meanwhile, on February 17 at Marös-Szereda the Hungarian counts and Szekely had chosen Bocskay as Prince. This election was important because it eventually brought to Bocskay the support of the magnates. Bocskay now felt that his support was strong enough to assemble the estates of Hungary and Transylvania which took place at Szerencs on April 17, 1605. On April 20, Bocskay was chosen Prince of Hungary and given the title of "Highness" which he, however, refused. To commemorate the occasion and to provide a cohesive rational for the nation, a *Flugschrift* was drawn up in which it was clearly stated that Emperor Rudolph had enlisted the sympathies of Christendom to fight the Turks but had used the help and assistance aroused to subjugate Hungary. These wrongs and many more, including attacks on Habsburg commanders and officials, were listed in the document. Thus, the document concluded, the Hungarians were forced to turn to the Turks for assistance in this hour of need. At Szerencs Bocskay also organized the whole country to further the rebellion. Georg Széchy was named commander of the praetorian soldiers, and Valentin Homonnay to head the fighting army. The Catholic, Michael Katháy, was chosen chancellor.

The Imperial camp hastened to meet this show of unity in Hungary with a meeting of the Archdukes Maximilian, Ferdinand, and Matthias in May. On May 28, full powers were given to Matthias to sue for peace. On July 4 in Kassa, Bocskay gathered his negotiators. Stephan Illésházy served as the representative of Matthias while Bocskay selected Georg Thurzó, Nikolos

Deraffy, Paulus Nyáry, and Emerich Doczy. Fifteen points were then drawn up:

1. Freedom for the Lutheran, Swiss (Calvinist), and Catholic confessions (the omission of the Greek Orthodox appeared intentional);
2. Peace with the Porte;
3. A "Palatine" to be chosen to represent Hungarian interests to the Emperor;
4. The Crown to be authenticated in Hungary;
5. The fiscal officers formerly answerable to the presidium of Catholic bishops to be removed;
6. The number of bishops to be reduced because they have no followers and income (they had been generally unpatriotic and subject to bribery);
7. The ecclesiatical courts to be disestablished and no non-Catholic need answer their summons;
8. His majesty to remove the Jesuits from the country;
9. His majesty also to appoint only men of Hungarian origin to bureaucratic posts (formerly the bureaucrats, the bishops, and the fiscal officers had cooperated to fleece the public);
10. Border guards to be Hungarian and also the King's counsel;
11. In the absence of the King, the Palatine to preside over the [Hungarian] Reichstag.
12. Plaintiffs against crimes of state to be heard and dealt with in the Reichstag.
13. Complete amnesty to be given to all participants in the rebellion;
14. Confirmation of the donations of Bocskay [to his Haiduk supporters];
15. All remaining matters to be settled by the Reichstag.[139]

After setting forth these basic conditions for further negotiations, Bocskay entered Transylvania on July 26, 1605. The Saxon community received him cordially and on August 5 he signed an offensive and defensive agreement with Radul Serban of Wallachia. In Kolozsvar Bocskay was particularly well received because he had previously ordered the return of the principal church and school to the Unitarians. On September 14, Bocskay was installed as prince at Medgyes with full pomp and splendor.

The Sultan, not wishing to be outdone by the local ceremonies, commanded the Grand Vezir, Lālā Meḥemmed Pasha, to bestow on Bocskay the rights and protection which John Zápolyai had enjoyed. On November 11, 1605, on the plain beneath the cannon of Pest, Stephan Bocskay was met by the Grand Vezir. Here Bocskay, in the presence of the Hungarian nobles, was girded with a sword and presented with a sceptor and a banner. A magnificent crown, which had been sent by the Sultan especially for the occasion, was then solemnly placed on his head. But to the Hungarians, the crown meant something different than it did to the Turks. For Hungarians it symbolized an "accommodation"; for the Turks, a sign of their overlordship.[140]

Meanwhile the Turks, taking their cue from Bocskay, launched their offensive in the summer of 1605. First Visegrád and then the strategic Esztergom fell. Ersekujvar (Neuhäusel) capitulated to the Bocskay forces, by design, as Illésházy had promised its return to Austria. Rudolph meanwhile attempted to make a separate peace with the Ottomans and then use Turkish forces to force a settlement on the Protestants. Finally, however, the patience and good will of Bocskay and Illésházy produced the Peace of Vienna on June 23, 1606. Its principal clauses included the following:

1. His Majesty the Emperor will not interfere in the religious matters in the Imperial counties.
2. All churches shall return to the status that they enjoyed prior to the war.
3. A Palatine shall be chosen at the next Reichstag; Matthias is to have full powers in Hungary and his measures are to be carried out by Hungarian counselors.
4. The Commanders of the fortresses are to be Hungarian without regard to religion.
5. Stephan Bocskay is recognized as Prince of Transylvania and Count of the Szeklers; should he die without an heir the principality would revert to the (Habsburg) crown. Bocskay is also to control Tokaj and the Northern Hungarian countries of Ugocsa, Bercq, and Szatmár.

It is interesting to contrast the articles of the Peace of Vienna with those of the Peace of Szitva-Török. The Hungarians had clearly learned to fear the intentions of the Habsburgs and the Papacy and they sought every means in their power to keep these "foreign" elements out of Hungary and Transylvania. The treaty signed by the Habsburgs and the Ottomans also characteristically represented the principal interests and concerns of these protagonists. In summary, the principle clauses include the following:

1. Both monarchs shall henceforth deal with one another as father and son.
2. Both in writing and in personal relations, the two monarchs shall deal with each other courteously and each should address the other as "Emperor."
3. So long as this treaty is in force, the Tatars and other nations are bound by it.
4. Between the lands of the two emperors and also on the high seas, peace shall obtain and particularly in Hungary and neighbouring provinces.
5. All forms of disturbance shall cease; robbers apprehended shall be dealt with by local commanders and stolen goods returned.
6. Castles and fortresses shall neither openly nor secretly be subverted and no prisoner may be spirited away.

7. Prisoners of war shall be mutually returned and exchanged.
8. Lesser affairs on the borders shall be dealt with by the Commander at Raab and the Pasha of Buda; matters of greater importance shall be referred to both emperors.
9. Old fortresses and castles may be restored to their former condition but new ones may not be erected.
10. Both emperors will exchange ambassadors and the Sultan shall send more suitable gifts than heretofore; the Archduke Matthias and the Grand Vezir Murād Pasha shall also exchange ambassadors.
11. The ambassador of His Majesty shall, as promised, bring to Constantinople a final gift of 200,000 guilders, once and for all.
12. The peace shall last from January 1 of 1607 for twenty years and after three years embassies shall be exchanged; said treaty shall be valid for the heirs of both rulers and shall require no renewals.
13. The fortress of Waizen (Vać) shall remain in Habsburg hands and may be repaired and extended.
14. The ambassador of the Emperor to the Porte may freely express his desires to the Sultan.
15. The villages [named in the treaty] shall no longer be subject to Turkish fiscal exactions.
16. Likewise, the villages around Gran which are subject to Turkish control shall not be disturbed by the Habsburgs.
17. With regard to the villages pertaining to Kanisza, the Pasha of Buda and Franz Bathyani are empowered to sort out the separate parts; noblemen living with their possessions in a village deemed taxable by the Turks, shall remain tax free; all taxes are to be collected by the local judge and only upon default may one resort to force.[141]

It is noteworthy that most textbooks and histories, when referring to this treaty, cite it as a great landmark in the history of Ottoman relations with the Habsburgs. In actual fact, with or without the new courtesies and a diminution of the "gifts," the peace appears to be a convenient accommodation for both parties.

Gabriel Bethlen, one of the most distinguished of the young noblemen of Transylvania and a friend of the Turks, had played an important role in the Bocskay revolt. After the untimely death of Bocskay on December 29, 1606, three candidates were put forth: George Homonnay, the successor designated by Bocskay and favored by the Porte; Gabriel Báthory, supported by his relative, Bethlen; and Sigismund Rákoczi, scion of another leading family and a compromise candidate. Rákoczi was elected prince for the brief term of two years (1606–1608) and then was followed by Gabriel Bocskay (1608–1613). But the latter prince became jealous of the superior talents of Bethlen and hence Bethlen was forced to take refuge once again in the Ottoman Empire. He eventually received Ottoman support for the voivodeship and served

Ottoman and Hungarian Protestant interests during his long years as voivode (1613–1629).

1. See Sir Charles Oman, *A History of the Art of War in the Sixteenth Century*, especially pp. 748–769, for interesting observations on Ottoman warfare in this era.
2. Veress, *Documente Privitoare la Istoria Archealului Moldavei şi Tarii Romaneşti, Acte şi Scrisori*, V, pp. 57–58.
3. Peçewī, *Tārīḫ*, II, pp. 206–209; Von Hammer, *Histoire de l'Empire ottomane*, VII, pp. 339–346.
4. For details, see *ibid.*, pp. 340–345 and Jenö Csuday, *Die Geschichte der Ungarn*, II, pp. 81–83. The term "second vezir" refers to the vezirs of highest rank, who were ranked in a series and considered a reservoir of top administrators and commanders. As their picturesque names, "Knifemaker (Sātūrjī)," "Ṭurnāḳjī (Manicurist)," and "Jerrāḥ (Surgeon)" indicate, most of these high officials originated from the palace school and the palace service.
5. For a contemporary drawing of this fortress, see Veress, *Documente*, V, p. 195.
6. Peçewī, II, pp. 209–223; Von Hammer, *Histoire*, VII, pp. 343–349.
7. Peçewi, II, pp. 223–235; Von Hammer, *Histoire*, VII, pp. 350–361.
8. Peçewi, II, pp. 235–252; Von Hammer, *Histoire*, VIII, pp. 5–20.
9. Rothenberg, *The Austrian Military Border*, p. 61.
10. Peçewī, II, pp. 252–328 *passim.* Hammer, *Histoire*, VIII, pp. 21–114 *passim.* For a discussion of the wider implications of the Jelālī movement in Asia Minor, see Akdağ, "Celâlî Isyanlarïnïn Başlamasï (Der Beginn der Celaliden Aufstaende)", *Ankara Üniversitesi Dil ve Tarih-Coğrafya Fakültesi Dergisi*, IV, pp. 23–50.
11. Hammer, *Histoire*, VII, p. 341. For additional information on the era of Sultan Murād III, see Kütükoğlu, "Murad III," *I.A.*, VIII, pp. 615–625.
12. Jeremia to Zamoyski (May 18, 1597), Hurmuzaki, ed., *Documente privatóre la Istoria Romanilor*, Suppl. II/I, pp. 417–418; Lassota to Rudolph II (July 31, August 27, September 30, 1597), Veress, *Documente*, V, pp. 80–81, 89, 97–98; Jeremia to Sigismund III (August 29, 1597), Hurmuzaki, Suppl. II/I, pp. 424–425.
13. Jeremia to Zamoyski (May 18, 1597) and Zamoyski to all Polish nobles (June, 1598), *ibid.*, pp. 417–418, 465–466.
14. Jeremia to Zamoyski (August 29, 1597), *ibid.*, pp. 424–425. Zamoyski to Radziwill (August 13, 1597) and Jeremia to Zamoyski (September 21, October 4, November 26, 1597), *ibid.*, pp. 421, 428, 431, 437.
15. Ortelius, . . . *Beschreibung* . . . , p. 383; Lassota, Mustermeister, to Emperor Rudolph (September 26, 1597), Veress, *Documente*, V, pp. 97–98; Decsi, *Magyar Historiaja . . . , 1592–1598* in *Monumenta Hungariae Historica, Scriptores*, XVII, pp. 323–325. ". . . ad legatos Casi Queraii Tartarorum Precopensium sive Tauricanorum principis nuncii, Sefersahes et Alexander Paleologus, natkone et religione Graecus, . . ." (Isthvanfi, *Historiarum de Rebus Ungaricus Libri XXXIV*, pp. 725–726).
16. Isthvanfi, *loc. cit.* and Decsi, *loc. cit.*; the letters of Isthvanfi reveal that the legates had found the Khan to be so well disposed toward the Christians and so distrustful of the Sultan that they decided to send 10,000 ducats with Posoniensis (John Posony) and Racz to the Khan. One of the Tatar envoys became drunk during a banquet in Wallachia and spoke quite openly of the Khan's good disposition toward the Christians. Isthvanfi to Pezzen (June 10, 1598), Szuchay and Isthvanfi to Emperor Rudolph (June 12, 1598), and Szuchay and Isthvanfi to Baron Rumff (June 12, 1598), Hurmuzaki, III, pp. 289, 292–293.
17. Instructions of Szuchay and Isthvanfi to Posony and Racz (June 10, 1598), *ibid.*, pp. 291–292, and Sigismund Báthory to the Emperor (August 15, 1598), *ibid.*, pp. 300–302. Solov'ev, *Istoriya Rossii*, VII, p. 323.

18. Derzhavin, ed., *Vremennik Ivana Timofeeva*, pp. 224–225, 480. One eyewitness clearly depicts the farcical preparations of the time and concludes, "Mais pour finir ceste guerre, il ne se trouva autre ennemy qu'un Ambassadeur avec environ cent hommes vestus de peaux de mouton selon leur cousture, mais tres-bien montez, qui venoient pour traicter quelque accord de la part du Tartare . . . ," (Margèrét, *Estat de l'Empire de Russie et Grande Duchie de Moscovie*, p. 8). See also Karamsin, *Histoire de l'Empire de Russie*, XI, pp. 10–19, and Solov'ev, VIII, pp. 353–354.
19. Zamoyski to the Polish nobles (June, 1598) and Jeremia to Zamoyski (June 26, 1598), Hurmuzaki, Suppl. II/I, pp. 463–466. It is known that the Khan, disappointed with the reception his proposals for close cooperation with Poland had received, had in turn treated the Polish ambassador, Piaseczynski, rather badly. Jan Herborth to Diet of Wisnicz (October, 1598), *ibid.*, pp. 503–513.
20. Jeremia to Zamoyski (July 11, 1598) and Jeremia to Voivode of Braclow (July 14, 1598), *ibid.*, pp. 467–469. Michael to the Prince of Transylvania (July 6 and July 11, 1598), *ibid.*, III, pp. 294–295.
21. This was actually Ḥāfiz Aḥmed Pasha, Beylerbey of Bosnia, who was ordered to defend the Danube line during the campaign season of 1598. He suffered a significant defeat at Nikbōlī (Nikopol) at the hands of Voivode Michael (Munejjimbāşī, *Ṣaḥā'if al aẖbār*, III, p. 598). Capello to the Doge (August 8, 1598), Hurmuzaki, Supp. IV/II, p. 228.
22. Anonymous to the Khan (in excellent Latin), August 11, 1598, *ibid.*, III, pp. 297–298.
23. Instructions to Bernardfius (August 13, 1598), *ibid.*, pp. 298–299.
24. Prince of Transylvania to Emperor Rudolph (August 15, 1598), *ibid.*, pp. 299–300.
25. Ferīdūn Bey, *Münşe'āt es-Selāṭīn*, II, pp. 118–119, as cited by Rypka in Menzel, ed., *Festschrift Georg Jacob*; Inalcïk, "Ġāzī Girāy," *I.A.*, IV, p. 735; Na'īmā, *Tārīh*, I, pp. 200–213.
26. Isthvanfi, pp. 729–730; Munejjimbāşī, III, p. 587.
27. Prince of Transylvania to Emperor Rudolph (August 15, 1598), Hurmuzaki, III, pp. 300–302; Hammer, *Histoire*, VII, p. 345.
28. Isthvanfi, pp. 729–730; Hammer, *Histoire*, VII, pp. 546–547; Munejjimbāşī, III, p. 597.
29. Isthvanfi, p. 731; Dilich, *Ungarische Chronica*, p. 315; Basta György, "Levezese es Iratai," Veress, ed., *Monumenta Hungariae Historica, Diplomataria*, Vol. XXXIV, pp. 43–45; Ḳâtib Çelebī, *Fezleke*, I, pp. 110–112.
30. *Ibid.*; Hammer, *Histoire*, VII, pp. 546–547; Peçewī, II, p. 217; Munejjimbāşī, III, pp. 597–598; Basta, pp. 105–106.
31. Kâtib Çelebī, *loc. cit.*; Veress, *Basta*, pp. 56–57. It is interesting to note that draft animals were as scarce in the Christian camp as they were in the Muslim camp. Basta complains of not being able to bring all of his artillery from Kallo to Tokaj for the same reason (p. 135). Doubtless the draft animals made good eating!
32. Peçewī, II, pp. 215–223; Kâtib Çelebī, I, p. 113; Munejjimbāşī, III, p. 598.
33. Ferīdūn, II, pp. 138–139. Archduke Maximilian to Ġāzī Girāy (October 17, 1598), Emperor Rudolph to Ġāzī Girāy (November 1, 1598), and Issuance of Passes (November 18, 1598), Hurmuzaki, III, pp. 303–305, 314. Basta to Matyás (December 18, 1598), Veress, *Basta*, p. 154.
34. In one instance the commander is spoken of as "Aḥmed Pasha . . . general of the Tatar Khan." See Relation of Ambassador of Wallachia (October 8, 1598), Hurmuzaki II/I, p. 486.
35. This is the Aḥmed Aġā whom Peçewī describes as the Ḳapū Aġāsï of the Khan, an individual occupying a position among the Crimean Tatars comparable to that of the Grand Vezir of the Ottomans (II, pp. 251–252).
36. Ġāzī Girāy Khan to Voivode Michael (*c.* 1598–1599), Hurmuzaki III, p. 422. Quite possibly he refers to the treaty that confirmed Michael as Voivode of Wallachia, July 21, 1597 (Hammer, *Histoire*, VIII, p. 2).
37. One must suspect here a kind of double game on the part of the Porte. A report from Istanbul dated March 16, 1599, informed the Doge that ". . . Micali havesse ricevuta una gran rotta dal Bei di Silistria fratello del Tartaro . . . ." If one were to make a conjecture on the basis of this

report, one might say that the Porte was glad enough to receive the protection of the Tatars at Silistria when Michael presented a serious threat, but when the Tatars began to gain successes against the rebellious voivode, the Khan was chastised and Sāṭūrjī Meḥemmed executed (Capello to the Doge March 16, 1599, Hurmuzaki, IV/II, p. 229). Yanbolu, attached to the Sanjāḳ of Silistria, was the town in which Ġāzī Girāy had resided between 1585 and 1588. As M. Tayyib Gökbilgin mentions in his *XV-XVI Asïrlarda Edirne ve Paşa Livasï*, p. 17, dismissed or retired Tatar Khans sometimes received a pension (arpalïk) from the Edirne Livasï, of which Silistria was a part.

38. Na'īmā, I, pp. 213–218; Peçewī, II, pp. 224–226.

39. Munejjimbāşī, III, p. 599; Kâtib Çelebī, I, pp. 117–118. The Mīrzās, moreover, would not wish to leave a campaign that held promise of bringing them rich booty (Na'īmā, I, p. 217).

40. Munejjimbāşī, III, p. 600; Kâtib Çelebī, I, pp. 123–125.

41. Capello to the Doge (September 4, 1599), Hurmuzaki, IV/II, p. 238.

42. Na'īmā, I, pp. 221–222.

43. Ġāzī Girāy to Archduke Maximilian (January, 1599), Hurmuzaki, III, p. 323.

44. Khan to the Archduke (February 5, 1599), *ibid.*, pp. 324–325.

45. "In Tartarorum principi charus et consiliorum particeps, eius vectigalibus et portoriis tam terra guam mari praeerat" (Isthvanfi, pp. 742–744).

46. Two letters from Archduke Matthias to Ġāzī Girāy Khan (February 8, 1599), Hurmuzaki, III, pp. 325–327.

47. Sultan Meḥemmed to the Khan (July, 1599), *ibid.*, pp. 332–333.

48. Na'īmā, I, pp. 223–225; Peçewī, II, pp. 296–297; Isthvanfi, pp. 742–744.

49. Na'īmā, *loc. cit.* During and after the peace negotiations, the Tatars raided the Hungarian and Austrian countryside almost continually, a factor that greatly disturbed the progress of the talks. These depredations appear to have taken place against the wishes of the Khan and the Grand Vezir. Strife broke out even between Ottoman and Tatar troops over the meager rations. The Tatars described themselves as "Cossacks" to dupe the peasantry. Ortelius, pp. 447–457 and *passim.*

50. Ṣōlāḳzāde, *Tārīh*, pp. 651 ff.

51. Peçewī, II, pp. 226–228; Kâtib Çelebī, I, pp. 123–125.

52. Munejjimbāşī, III, pp. 600, 605–606; Jeremia to Zamoyski (November 10, 1599) and Radibrad to one of the Archdukes (November 29, 1599), Hurmuzaki, Suppl. II/I, p. 558, XII, pp. 518–9.

53. Voivode Michael to Emperor Rudolph (November 29, 1599), *ibid.*, III, pp. 363–364.

54. Basta to the Emperor (February, 1599) and Basta to Miksa (Michael) (April 13, 1599), Basta, pp. 169, 191. I am particularly grateful to Mr. Vernon Parry, Reader at the School of Oriental and African Studies, London University, for calling my attention to this text.

55. Zamoyski to King Sigismund (November 10, 1599), King Sigismund to Zamoyski (November 23, 1599), Jeremia to Zamoyski (December 18, 1599), Hurmuzaki, Suppl. II/I, pp. 559, 563, 569.

56. Jeremia to Zamoyski (September 16, 1599) and King Sigismund to Ġāzī Girāy Khan (July 24, 1600), *ibid.*, pp. 546, 627.

57. Hammer, *Histoire*, VII, pp. 358–359.

58. Bir mujāhid ḳūlunuz terk eyderiz jān-u seri
Pādişāhim ne diyem sonra duyārsin ẖaberī

Ḳāçmañiz tīġ ve tīrden çālīşin dīn yōluna. . . .

. . . . .

Telẖ-i kām ōlsaḳ 'ajeb mī ẖālīmizni bir gōrun
Būrnumuzdan geldi bi'llah ajī ṣuyi Ṣōnburun
Ehl-i Islām īllerin kuffār gāret eyledi

Ey Ḫuda nātersler siz rüşvet ālin ōtūrun
'Arṣayi rezm īçere biz kānlar tōkūb ḳān āğlariz
Vādi-ye 'eşratte siz jām-i ṣafā-i z̲evḳni sūrun. . . .

Copies of these poems and further comment can be found in O. Burian, "Bozuk Idareden Şikayetçi iki Şair," *Ankara Universitesi Dil ve Tarih-Coğrafya Fakültesi Dergisi*, VIII/4 (1950), pp. 675–681. (I am grateful to Dr. V. Ménage, Professor of Turkish, School of Oriental and African Studies, London University, for checking my translations and making helpful suggestions.)

59. Na'īmā, I, p. 235. The Tatars, at a critical point during the siege, were able to cut off the supplies being brought to the tābūr by the enemy relief force, thus rendering their position untenable (Munejjimbāşī, III, p. 604; Sagredo, *Histoire de l'Empire Ottoman*, V, pp. 167–168).

60. Letter to the Khan from Transylvania (December 6, 1600), Hurmuzaki, IV/I, p. 199.

61. Iorga, *Geschichte des Osmanischen Reiches*, III, pp. 319–327. Sigismund Báthory, at the time of his first alliance (1595) with the Emperor, also contracted to marry a niece of the Emperor. It shortly became common gossip, however, that the Prince was impotent and his embarrassment helped convince him that he should retire to Silesia. See Makkai, *Histoire de Transylvanie*, p. 195.

62. Jorga, *G.O.R.* III, pp. 327–332.

63. *Ibid.*, p. 332.

64. De Bertha, *Magyars et Roumains devant l'Histoire*, pp. 211–214. Leaving Transylvania for the last time on July 26, 1602, Báthory urged the Transylvanian estates and the administrators of the principality to cooperate with Basta.

65. Jeremia to Zamoyski (March 29, 1600), Hurmuzaki, Suppl. II/I, p. 589. The son of Michael was also confirmed as voivode of Wallachia.

66. King Sigismund to Adrian Rembowski, ambassador to the Porte (July 6, 1600), Zamoyski to Radziwill (July 20, 1600), and King Sigismund to the Khan (July 24, 1600), *ibid.*, pp. 616–617, 625, 627.

67. Anonymous reports from Transylvania (April 24 and May 29, 1600), Veress, *Documente*, VII, pp. 90–91, 112–113.

68. Voivode Michael to Dr. Pezzen, representative of the Emperor (April 28, 1600) and Michael to King Sigismund (May 21, 1600), Hurmuzaki, IV/I, p. 43, and Suppl., II/I, p. 602.

69. This traditionally included money, sheep, honey, and horses. Anonymous reports from Moldavia (May 29, June 25, and July 12, 1600), Veress, *Documente*, VI, pp. 113–114, 132–133, p. 144.

70. Anonymous report from Moldavia (August 5, 1600), Veress, *Documente*, VI, p. 154; Bailo Capello to the Doge (August 12, 1600), Hurmuzaki, IV/II, pp. 26–27; Ortelius, pp. 480–482.

71. Basta to Archduke Matthias (July 9, 1601), Basta, p. 562; Meḥemmed Pasha to Andrei Negroni, Imperial Dragoman (August 1, 1601), Hurmuzaki, IV/I, p. 264; Anonymous from Transylvania (June 30, 1601), Constantini to Chancellor of Mantua (July 23, 1601), and Anonymous from Transylvania (August 13, 1601), Veress, *Documente*, VI, pp. 389, 403, 423.

72. During this confused period, it appears that the Ottoman hospodar, Radu Mihnea, was in possession of Silistria and Giurgiu while supporters of Simeon and Radu Serban held other areas. Jorga, *G.O.R.*, III, p. 332; anonymous reports of events in Transylvania (December 23, 1600, and March 18, 1601), Veress, *Documente*, pp. 285, 339. Nani to the Doge (October 7, 1601), Hurmuzaki, IV/II, p. 256.

73. The details of this incident are found in a letter of the Polish ambassador, Laurin Piaseczinski, to King Sigismund III (July 3, 1601), Hurmuzaki, Suppl. II/II, pp. 45–47. In the same letter, the ambassador also describes how the Khan recruited his arquebusiers; they were drawn from the villages (of the Khan) facing those in the lands of the Polish king.

74. Peçewī, II, pp. 250–252; Meḥemmed Rizā, *Es-Seb'es-Seygān fī aḫbār Mulūk at-Tātār*, pp. 108–110; Munejjimbāşī, III, pp. 591–594; Soranzo, *L'Ottomano*, pp. 91–92; Kazimirski, "Précis . . . ," *J.A.*, Ser. II/XII, pp. 431–432; Jeremia to King Sigismund III (July 26 and September

30, 1601), Hurmuzaki, II/II, pp. 54, 65–66. See the geneological chart in the Appendix.
75. When the Jelālī leader, Delī Ḥasan, was pardoned, Selāmet Girāy, a member of his rebel force, also made his peace with the Sultan and sought his own appointment to the Khanship of the Crimea. See Peçewī, II, pp. 250–251.
76. Letter of the Sultan to Ġāzī Girāy Khan (c. June, 1602), Ferīdūn, *Munşe'at*, II, pp. 166 ff. In a report of March 12, 1602, Jeremia told the King of Poland that the Ḳalġay (Selāmet) had already been banished by the Sultan. See Hurmuzaki, Suppl. II/II, p. 115. Augustino Nani, in a report to the Doge (November 3, 1602), actually states that the Ḳalġay was banished to the island of Rhodes. See *ibid.*, IV/II, p. 269.
77. Karamsin, XI, p. 32.
78. Letters of Laurin Piaseczinski, Polish ambassador, to the King of Poland (May 17 and June 16, 1602), Hurmuzaki, Suppl. II/II, pp. 153, 167; also, dispatch of Gontaut-Biron, French Ambassador, to Villeroy (May 2, 1602), "Ambassade en Turquie . . . ," (*Archive Historique de la Gascogne,*) Fasc. 19, p. 43.
79. See Potocki to the King of Poland (August 18, 1602), Hurmuzaki, Suppl. II/II, pp. 196–197; Sobieski to an unknown (August 22, 1602), *ibid.*, p. 204; Sobieski, in another dispatch to the King (September 18, 1602), suggests that Jeremia actually called in the Tatars to assist him in establishing his brother in order to be free of Polish influence; *ibid.*, p. 217.
80. Zucconi to the Duke of Mantua (September 2, 1602), Veress, *Documente*, VII, pp. 75–76; Cavriolo to Piero Duodo, Venetian Ambassador at Prague (September 2 and October 1, 1602), Hurmuzaki, VIII, pp. 250, 252–253; Basta to Venetian Ambassador (September 18, 1602), *ibid.*, p. 251. See also John Smith, *Travels* (London, 1630), pp. 19–28. This appears to be the battle after which Smith was captured and sold into slavery.
81. Jeremia to the King of Poland (October 21, 1602) and Sobieski to the King of Poland (November 4, 1602) Hurmuzaki, Suppl. II/II, pp. 235, 241–242.
82. Jeremia to the King of Poland (January 9, 1603), *ibid.*, p. 245; Peçewī, II, pp. 251–252; Kâtib Çelebī, I, pp. 183–184; Na'īmā, I, pp. 305–306; Dilich, pp. 351–352; Hammer, *Histoire*, VIII, pp. 20–21.
83. Peçewī, II, pp. 267–270; Munejjimbāşī, II, p. 703, and III, p. 711; Jeremia to the King of Poland (November 28, 1603), Hurmuzaki, Suppl. II/II, pp. 319–320; Hammer, *Histoire*, VIII, p. 35. See also concerning the Khan's departure, Danişmend, *Izahlī Osmanlī Tarihi Kronolojisi*, III, p. 220.
84. Peçewī, II, pp. 269, 292; Jeremia to the King of Poland (July 28, 1603), Hurmuzaki, Suppl. II/II, pp. 293–294; Na'īmā, I, p. 325.
85. Venetian Ambassador in Prague to the Doge (May 5 and 19, 1603), Hurmuzaki, VIII, pp. 266, 1603–1604; Veress, "Annuae Litterae Societatis Jesu," *Fontes Rerum Transylvanicarum*, V, pp. 83–84.
86. Radu Serban to Vienna and letter of Wallachian Boyars to Vienna (October 24, 1603), Hurmuzaki, IV/I, pp. 346–347; Report of Vimercato to General Basta (December 25, 1603), *ibid.*, p. 353; Contarini, Bailo, to the Doge (December 29, 1603), *ibid.*, VIII, p. 273.
87. 'Alī Mīrza to the King of Poland (January 24, 1603) and Jeremia to the King of Poland (November 28, 1603), *ibid.*, Suppl. II/II, pp. 249, 319–320; Contarini, Bailo, to the Doge (December 6, 1603), *ibid.*, IV/II, p. 275. See also the following section in this chapter "An Important Polish Embassy."
88. Hammer, *Histoire*, VIII, pp. 78–79.
89. Basta to the Archduke Matthias (January 5, 1604), Hurmuzaki, IV/I, p. 361; Imperial Commissioner Paul Krausenegg to Radu Şerban (August 2, 1604), Veress, *Documente*, pp. 218–219; Venetian Ambassador in Prague to the Doge (September 20, 1604), Hurmuzaki VIII, p. 284; Octavian Bon to the Doge (December 13, 1604), *ibid.*, IV/II, p. 279.
90. Instructions of Rudolph II to his commissioner, Krausenegg (January 6 and 20, 1604), *ibid.*, IV/I, p. 362; Munejjimbāşī, III, pp. 619–620; Hurmuzaki, Suppl., II/II, p. 336; Venetian

ambassador in Prague to the Doge (July 19, 1604), *ibid.*, VIII, p. 276; Krausenegg to Radu Şerban (August 2, 1604), Veress, *Documente*, VII, pp. 218, 219.

91. Peçewī, II, p. 300; Veress, *Fontes*, V, p. 120; Sagredo, V, pp. 253–257; Von Pastor, History of the Popes, XXIII, pp. 304–308.

92. Isthvanfi, p. 830; anonymous report (January 8, 1605), Hurmuzaki, IV/II, p. 280; Peçewī, II, p. 309; Barozzi and Berchet, *Le Relazioni degli Stati Europei*, Ser. V/I, pp. 203–204; Sagredo, V, pp. 132–133; Hammer, *Histoire*, VIII, pp. 94–95. In fact, whenever a given Sultan showed himself to be inept, rumors circulated in the capital that he would be replaced by a Tatar Khan.

93. See above Chapter VII, part 6, and the following Polish sources: J. Sasa, "Wyprawa Zamojskiego na Moldawie," *Prsegląd powszechny* (1897), pp. 74–89, and Casimir Pulaski, "Trzy poselstwa Lawryna Piaseczinskiego do Kazi Gireja hana Tatarow (1601–1603)," *Przewodnik naukowy i literaeki* (Lvov, 1911), pp. 136–140 and the text of Ţuţora, pp. 139–140. I am pleased to acknowledge the great assistance Mrs. Roman Holod rendered in helping me translate this valuable study.

94. Pulaski, pp. 141–142.

95. *Ibid.*, pp. 242–245.

96. *Ibid.*, pp. 245–246.

97. See Akdağ, "Kara-yazïcï," *I.A.*, VI, pp. 339–343.

98. Here we learn that the trusted arquebusiers, who killed Devlet and his Shirīn accomplices, had been trained by retired Janissaries! See Pulaski, pp. 252–256.

99. *Ibid.*

100. *Ibid.*, pp. 358–360.

101. *Ibid.*, pp. 360–366, 467–478.

102. *Ibid.*, pp. 475–480, 553–566.

103. *Ibid.*, pp. 650–660, 756–763.

104. *Ibid.*, pp. 763–768.

105. *Ibid.*, pp. 846–848.

106. *Ibid.*, pp. 852–864.

107. Stephen Fischer-Galati, in his *Ottoman Imperialism and German Protestantism 1521–1555* (Cambridge, Mass., 1959), has concentrated on the role the Ottomans played in the official recognition of Protestantism at the Treaty of Augsburg of 1555. Here he concludes that the secular interests of the Habsburg monarchs, notably their plans to annex Hungary, led them to neglect Germany and hence "the consolidation, expansion, and legitimizing of Lutheranism in Germany by 1555 should be attributed to Ottoman imperialism more than any other single factor" (p. 117). One of the conclusions of this study is that the Protestant movement took such a hold on Hungary that the Counter Reformation tactics of the Habsburgs, which were linked closely to Habsburg imperialism, alienated the Hungarians to such an extent that they opted for Ottoman rule.

108. Lencz, D. Géza, *Der Aufstand Bocskays und der Wiener Friede.*

109. See Steven Runciman, *Le Manichéisme Mediéval*, pp. 62, 65–66, 92–95, 101, "La religion bogomile était portée par les forces du nationalisme, qui en faisaient une opposition nationale tant à l'orthodoxie, inséparable de l'influence byzantino-serbe, qu'au catholicisme de la Hongrie et de la Dalmatie" (*ibid.*, p. 104).

110. Certainly a number of magnates in the entourage of the Zápolyai enriched themselves at the expense of Roman Catholic land holdings throughout Hungary.

111. See Seton-Watson, *A History of the Roumanians*, in particular: Chapter VII, "Transylvania under Habsburg Rule (1699–1792)," pp. 169–191. The best study in English dealing with the preliminary stages of Protestantism in Hungary is the article by Betts, "The Reformation in Difficulties: Poland, Hungary and Bohemia," *New Cambridge Modern History*, II, pp. 186–209.

112. Makkai pp. 186–187, Betts, pp. 208–209.

113. Lencz, pp. 35–36. See, in particular, the accounts and documents showing overt Ottoman support to Protestant churches and preachers in Bucsay, *Geschichte des Protestantismus in Ungarn*, pp.

37–64. (This footnote courtesy of Andrew Riedlmayer.)
114. Depner, *Das Fürstentum Siebenbürgen im Kampf gegen Habsburg*, pp. 21–23.
115. Lencz, pp. 29–31.
116. Von Pastor, XXIII, pp. 18–42, 265 ff.
117. See above Chap. 7 and Pastor, XXIII, pp. 273 ff.
118. Lencz, pp. 35–36, citing the letters of Carillo written between 1591 and 1599 preserved in the *Monumenta Hungariae Historica* XXXII.
119. *Ibid.*, pp. 35–37.
120. *Ibid.*, pp. 30–33.
121. *Ibid.*, pp. 36–39. For greater detail about the role of Bocskay, see Makkai, *Histoire de Transylvanie*, pp. 191–195. After aiding in the intimidation of the Diet, Bocskay was sent to Prague to negotiate the so-called Treaty of Prague which recognized Báthory as an autonomous prince in a Habsburg Hungary and also provided for his marriage to the Habsburg princess, Marie-Christine. Bocskay understood well the strength of the pro-Turkish faction and hence was responsible for the execution of the twelve wealthiest pro-Turkish members of the Diet, who were led by Alexander Skendi and Balthasar Báthory. See Benda, *Bocskai István (1557–1606)*, p. 51 and *passim* (the latter source, courtesy of Andrew Riedlmayer).
122. Makkai, pp. 195–197.
123. *Ibid.*, pp. 196–201, and the accompanying maps showing troop movements in Transylvania. See also Göllner, *Michael der Tapferer*, Texts XLIV–LI, pp. 175–193.
124. Lencz, p. 39; Makkai, p. 203. See also Göllner for eyewitness and *Zeitung* reports, Texts LII–XCIII, pp. 193–225.
125. Lencz, pp. 40–41.
126. The Turkish historian, M. Tayyib Gökbilgin, in his article, "XVII Asïr Başlarïnda Erdel Hadiseleri ve Bethlen Gabor'un Beyliğe Intihabï," *Tarih Dergisi* I/I (Sept., 1949), pp. 1–28, drawing upon Ottoman sources, has added some important new insights to the history of this era.
127. Peçewī, II, pp. 244–246.
128. See Peçewī, II, p. 244 where he gives an interesting description of the Khan's *Divān*.
129. Lencz, pp. 44–45; Makkai, pp. 204–205, Csuday, *Die Geschichte der Ungarn*, II, pp. 84–85. Makkai suggests that the ethnic imbalance against Hungarians in the Transylvanian regions dates from this era. See also Csetneki, "Die Székler-Frage," *Ungarische Revue*, I, pp. 411–428. (This note on Szeklers, courtesy of Andrew Riedlmayer.)
130. See Csuday, II, p. 85, and particularly Lencz, pp. 70–71 for complete text of Article 22.
131. Baine, "Bethlen," *Encyclopedia Britannica*, Eleventh Edition, III, p. 829. Peçewī declares Bethlen to be *Báthory neslinden* "of the Báthory line" (II, pp. 349–350).
132. Peçewī (II, pp. 298–299) reproduces an interesting argument that took place between the dervish and Bocskay concerning the merits of cooperation with the Ottomans.
133. Csuday, II, pp. 87–89; Lencz, pp. 80–86; Makkai, pp. 205–206.
134. See Chap. VI, above.
135. Lencz, 86–89, citing Áron Sziládi es Alex. Szilági, *Török-magyarkori történeti emlékek* (Historical monuments of the Turkish-Hungarian Era), III (Budapest, 1868), p. 46.
136. See Peçewī, II, p. 300 and Gökbilgin, *Tarih Dergisi*, I, p. 10.
137. Lencz, pp. 96–99, citing "Antwort Honts an Matthias von 24 Nov., 1604," *Wiener Hof-, Haus-und Staats archiv, Hungarn.*
138. Lencz, pp. 101–103.
139. Lencz, pp. 105–130.
140. Peçewī, II, p. 300.
141. Csuday, II, pp. 91–95; See also, Iorga, *Geschichte des osmanischen Reiches*, III, p. 338. The older sources tend to omit the European relationships. In this regard see also J. W. Zinkeisen, *Geschichte des osmanischen Reiches in Europa*, III, pp. 613–615.

THE OTTOMAN EMPIRE IN EUROPE

CHAPTER NINE
Decision-making in the Ottoman Empire on the Eve of the Seventeenth Century 1578–1606

Although we have examined an era of serious stress in the life of the Ottoman Empire, very little attention has been paid to dynastic history in any traditional sense. Rather, interest has centered on the interplay between foreign powers and the Ottoman state. On another level the study has also analyzed the interrelationship between external events and internal structures. There is, however, a very important reason why one cannot ignore altogether the study of a dynastic household. Within the sultan's household and entourage, one finds a high concentration of the elements that determine how decisions are made: the marriage alliances, the ethnic and regional loyalties, the petty greeds and jealousies, and the self-evident incapacity of some men in high places. One also becomes aware of the ways in which traditional values often reassert themselves in the decision-making process, in the face of, or possibly because of, adverse conditions.

In this chapter, we place under closer scrutiny than heretofore a number of major decisions of the era under study, showing where possible the influences brought to bear on such decisions.

A high percentage of the men holding the most influential positions in the land shared certain characteristics in common. They came to their high positions by promotion, slowly or rapidly, through the ranks of the palace. Most of them served as Ağā of the Janissary Corps about midway in their careers before becoming Grand Vezir. About 50 per cent of their number were closely tied to the fortunes of the dynasty through their marriage to one or more daughters or granddaughters of sultans. Finally, during thirty-five of the forty-one years surveyed, the office of Grand Vezir was held by men of Bosnian-Croatian or Albanian origin, that is, men originating from the western Balkans where conversions to Islam were exceptionally high. (See Tables II–IV.)

1 War With Safavid Persia (1578)

Ṣoḳōllū Meḥemmed Pasha (Bosnian) was appointed Grand Vezir in 1565. By the year 1577 when the decision to make war on Persia was taken, he had gradually lost his influence over Sultan Murād III to the Sultan's Vālide, Nūr Banū Sultana, a Venetian; his favorite, Sāfiye Sultana, an Albanian; Üveys Pasha, the Defterdār, a Türk; H̱ōja Sa'deddin Efendi, and others.[1] When Ṣoḳōllū Meḥemmed came out strongly against the war because of his experience with the difficulties, costliness, and ultimate futility of previous Persian campaigns, this new court faction opposed him (doubtless partly on principle) and they were joined by the two old "war horses" and rivals, Lālā Muṣṭafā Pasha (Bosnian) and Ḳōjā Sinān Pasha (Albanian). It was very easy, of course, to stir up the rank and file of the ruling classes for a war against Safavid Persia because the Sheykh Safa sect of Shi'ism was still very popular among the tribes and peasants of eastern Asia Minor, so popular in fact that to many observers it presented a serious threat to Ottoman rule in that area.[2]

Against such formidable opposition, and also seeing his old friends in key positions either dying, being executed, or otherwise eliminated, Ṣoḳōllū accepted the inevitability of the war.

Only after plans for the campaign had been completed can one speculate on the importance ethnic politics must have played behind the scenes. After an altercation between Lālā Muṣṭafā Pasha and Ḳōjā Sinān Pasha over sectors of the Persian front—each had been allotted a command—Ḳōjā Sinān charged favoritism, as well there may have been, and hence the command went to Lālā Muṣṭafā, a member of the old Bosnian elite, who had occupied the center of the Ottoman political stage since the days of Sulaymān. It is important to note also that both Ṣoḳōllū and Lālā Muṣṭafā were married to daughters or granddaughters of sultans.

2 The Assassination of Ṣoḳōllū (1579) and Its Aftermath

With the assassination of Ṣoḳōllū Meḥemmed in 1579 by a Bosnian dervish, what might be termed the "system of Sultan Sulaymān" came to an end. Neither Sultan Murād III nor Sultan Meḥemmed III showed much talent for independent judgment in matters of state. It follows then that both Sultans were greatly influenced by their respective entourages. Initially such men as

Şemsi Aḥmed Pasha, the Sultan's gentleman-in-waiting, and Kara Üveys, both of whom had served the Şehzāde in Manisa, were influential.[3] Later the advise of the preceptor, H̱ōja Sa'deddin, a protégé of Sultan Sulaymān's Şeyẖ ul-Islām, Ebüssu'ud Efendi, gained a position of great prominence. And probably no less important on occasion was the influence of Ġażānfer, the Kapï Ağasï, and of the Vālide Sultan, the Sultan's sisters and nieces, and his harem favorites (*Haseki Sulṭānlar*).

These background matters continued to be important. Ṣoḳōllū was replaced by Aḥmed Pasha, a relative by marriage of the Sultan and an Albanian. Sinān Pasha, another Albanian, quickly influenced Aḥmed Pasha to dismiss Lālā Muṣṭafā and to have himself appointed to the post of Serdār on the Persian front.[4]

Now Lālā Muṣṭafā returned to Istanbul and Sinān Pasha took command of the troops in Erzurum. Thus, with the death of Aḥmed Pasha in April, 1580, Lālā Muṣṭafā was in a good position to succeed him. There is some question whether he ever did; it is probably fortunate that he died before his old rival returned to the Bosphorus. Yemişçī Ḥasan Ağa, an Albanian, at the time serving as *Kapujular Kethüdasï*, delivered the Imperial Seal to Sinān Pasha and thus gained the lifelong support of the old soldier. Sinān Pasha, after two years in office, grew weary of the eastern front and hence conducted peace negotiations during the gaudy circumcision ceremonies of Meḥemmed III in the summer of 1582. But while the Grand Vezir relaxed in Istanbul, Persian forces retook Shirvan and seized a supply train. When the Sultan expressed his displeasure, the brash Albanian suggested that the Sultan should personally go on campaign.[5] The women of the harem reacted sharply against this suggestion, rightly fearing that their own influence over the Sultan would diminish should he take to the field. This audacity and the sterility of the negotiations led to the immediate dismissal of Sinān Pasha and his replacement by Siyāvüş, the second Vezir, who was of Croatian or Hungarian origin.

As an interesting sidelight of this period, England had sent William Harbonne to Istanbul in 1578 and very soon H̱ōja Sa'deddin became a strong supporter of English projects. In particular, together with the English ambassador, he sought an early end to the Persian War so that the Ottoman Empire and England might form a united front against Spain.[6]

During the Vezirate of Siyāvüş Pasha, the two seasoned commanders Ferhād Pasha and Özdemīroğlu 'O̱smān Pasha temporarily broke Persian resistance, especially in Transcaucasia. 'O̱smān Pasha rewarded his troops with promotions and salary increases which Siyāvüş considered excessive. After a triumphal entry into Istanbul, the troops protested to the Sultan who removed Siyāvüş Pasha from office and appointed 'O̱smān Pasha in his stead. Upon his death in Persia in 1585, his place was filled, after considerable wrangling behind the scenes, by Mesiḥ Pasha, a compromise candidate ninety years old. ʻOs̱mān Pasha had advocated that he be replaced by Çiġālazāde while a faction led by Saʻdeddin had sought the appointment of Ferhād Pasha.[7]

3 Financial Problems and the Growth of Corruption and Insubordination

Although Mesiḥ Pasha occupied his position for only four months, he made an impression on the pages of history because he resigned after the Sultan revoked his recommendation for the dismisal of the Reʻis ul-Kuttāb. He was a vezir of the old school who suffered neither bribery nor insubordination. Siyāvüş Pasha, called to the Grand Vezirate a second time, had to face the terrible financial problems that had accumulated as a result of lavish spending by the household, the great burden of the war, and the pressure on Ottoman production brought about by the increase in population and the introduction of cheap silver from the New World. The silver content of the Aḳçe had been debased in 1585. Siyāvüş attempted to pay his troops in that currency in 1589 and faced a serious revolt of the salaried cavalry of the Porte (*Bölük Halkï*) who had only just returned from the Persian front. Pushing their way right up to the doors of the Imperial Dīvān, the troops called for the heads of Maḥmūd Efendi, the Bāş Defterdār, and Doğancï Meḥmet Pasha, an intimate of the Sultan who, it was alleged, had turned over the task of improving the silver content of the currency to a Jewish subordinate for the sake of a bribe.[8]

After the executions, Siyāvüş was replaced by Ḳōjā Sinān, who took effective steps to improve the quality of the coinage. Apart from concluding the peace with Persia, which took place on March 21, 1590, Sinān Pasha also lent his support to the completion of the Black Sea–Bay of Izmit Canal Project which was to pass by way of the Sakarya River. While the Grand Vezir was on a tour of inspection of his pet project, a cabal formed against him which included Ferhād Pasha, the *Kapūdan-i Deryā*, Ḥasan Pasha, and the *Kapï Ağasï*, Mehmet Ağa. They went before the Sultan and convinced him that the canal project was bringing unnecessary hardship on the peasantry and that funds being channeled to that project should be used to make ready the fleet for a sortie into the Mediterranean. The Sultan, ever ready to listen to the advice of those closest at hand, removed Ḳōjā Sinān and replaced him with Ferhād Pasha.

The Grand Vezir, Ferhād Pasha, and his immediate successor, Siyāvüş Pasha, who was returned to power for the third time, were both dismissed because of Janissary disturbances sparked by the awareness that pay was being distributed inequitably. As Ḳōjā Sinān had dealt satisfactorily with the previous financial problems, he received the support of the *Kapï Kūllārï* for a return to the Grand Vezirate.

Meanwhile the inner circle of the household involved itself more and more in a complex system of bribery, extortion, and petty politics which turned responsible decision-making into a mockery. The women of the harem, already generously endowed with estates and "livings", greedily took control of war subsidies that had been extracted from the peasantry especially to pay the rebelling military units.

4 The Decision for War in Hungary against the Habsburgs (1592–1593)

Although it is clear that there were many abuses in the system during the reign of Murād III—particularly the irresponsible instigation of a war against Persia and attempts by certain dignitaries to make a quick profit from the inevitable social dislocations of that war and from the apparently Mediterranean-wide inflation—the abuses never became so outrageous as in the reign of Meḥemmed III. The decision to make war in Hungary, however, gives one a clear idea of the shape of events to come. It was indeed unfortunate for the Ottoman Empire that twice in one generation a bloodthirsty campaigner like Ḳōjā Sinān was so close to the seat of power when decisions for war or peace were made. His insistence had helped throw the Empire into war against Persia. As Ṣoḳōllū had predicted, the arrogance of the military had increased during the Persian war. War with Poland had only narrowly been averted during Ḳōjā Sinān's second occupancy of the Grand Vezirate (1589–1591).

The background for the war in Hungary, as in the case of Persia, had deep roots which were discussed in Chapter VII. To review briefly, the immediate causes were basically four:

1. The Habsburg Emperor was in arrears in his annual tribute payment of 30,000 ducats that had been specified in the treaty of 1568.
2. Ḥasan Pasha, the Beylerbey of Bosnia, who had formerly been a personal retainer of the Sultan, had exceeded the normal border-raiding practices and during a siege of the Austrian fortress of Sīsḳe (Sissek) had suffered a humiliating defeat and death; moreover, two sons of the former Grand Vezir Semiz Aḥmed Pasha, who were also cousins of the Sultan, died in the battle.
3. The country was still on a "war footing," (i.e., a large number of men were still mobilized) which accounts, in part, for the number of minor rebellions taking place in the capital.
4. Finally, Ḳōjā Sinān, being a vain, jealous-hearted, and vindictive person, wanted, in view of the recent popularity of Ferhād Pasha, to add one more spectacular victory to his title of "Victor of Yemen and Tunis."[9]

In view of the foregoing, Sinān Pasha advised the Sultan (late 1592) to declare war against the Habsburgs. The Sultan, who had not completely withdrawn from reality, called together a *Meclis-i Meşveret*, or council of his chief dignitaries and, contrary to custom (*mu'tad değil iken*), permitted them to debate the issue before him. According to an eyewitness account told to Peçewī by Dervīş Pasha, Ferhād Pasha, Bostānzāde, and H̱ōja Sa'deddin opposed a war on grounds that the army and the state finances were exhausted and that, in any case, the ambassador of the Emperor, had arrived in Buda bearing the arrears of his annual tribute. But Ḳōjā Sinān once more made a passionate plea for war, stating that he would bring the Habsburg "king" to the Sultan's threshold! H̱ōja Efendi was greatly annoyed by such exaggeration and answered sharply, "I am fearful indeed for the consequences of the presumption of these words!"[10] Ḳōjā Sinān had his way and departed for the front in the late summer of 1593.

5 The Execution of Ferhad Pasha

Meḥemmed III was placed on the throne in January 1595, under the watchful eye of his mother, Sāfiye. Ḳōjā Sinān Pasha was still on the Hungarian front and not making spectacular progress; hence, he was replaced by Ferhād Pasha, the Ḳā'immakām, who was in Istanbul and thus was in a good position to gain favor with the new Sultan. It is clear, however, that Ferhād Pasha, who was an Albanian, gained the position through the support of Sāfiye, the Queen Mother who was Albanian also. She had doubtless found Ḳōjā Sinān completely unamenable to her will.

Ferhād Pasha had to deal immediately with the deterioration of the Ottoman position on the Danube. Michael the Brave, of Wallachia, had caused considerable damage to both Giurgiu and Ruschuk. While forming an army for a campaign into Wallachia, Ferhād Pasha had to quash a revolt in the capital, led in part by some of his former troops, the so-called "Sons of the Janissaries" (*Ḳūl-Oğullarï*), actually draftees to whom he had promised full "Cavalry of the Porte" status and pay if they would remain on garrison duty in Genje for three years. Although the veterans' claims were legitimate, they were joined by a great street rabble with no claims at all. When they asked for the Grand Vezir's head, they were dispersed by the Janissaries. Ferhād Pasha was able to claim, perhaps correctly, that the uprising was arranged by Sinān Pasha who was dwelling near the city. He obtained a decree which called for the blinding of Ḳōjā Sinān, but after considering the religious proscriptions against such a deed, he simply ordered Sinān Pasha back to his estate in Malkara.

After moving his army to Edirne, Ferhād Pasha decided to change the status of Wallachia and Moldavia from "protected" principalities to that of

Ottoman provinces. Meanwhile the friends of Ḳōjā Sinān—Dāmād Ibrāhīm Pasha, the Ḳā'immakām; Bostānzāde, Şeyh ul-Islām; Baki, the poet and Kādi'asker; and the Vezirs, Jerrāh Meḥemmed and Çiġālazāde—convinced the Sultan that Ferhād was unsuited for his position. Hence Ḳōjā Sinān was recalled to become Grand Vezir for his fourth tour of duty. He wasted no time in taking advantage of the Sultan's cupidity to have Ferhād Pasha executed in spite of the protests of Sāfiye, the Vālide Sultan, and the mercy Ferhād Pasha had shown him some months previously. It would appear that when two Albanians became rivals, the outcome was not pleasant, either for the loser or for the affairs of state.[11]

Once an individual attained the post of Grand Vezir, with all its privileges and responsibilities, the men in the entourage of the Sultan who had put aside their grievances with one another in order to change the leadership would begin to make new political alliances, either with the Grand Vezir or with new elements seeking power. This process is typical of all political organizations. Sinān Pasha, hardly without notice, had enhanced the power of the Grand Vezir at the expense of the Sultan during his multiple tenure of that office. He was the first Grand Vezir to take the Janissary Corps on campaign. Until the Hungarian War, the Janissaries had left the city en masse only to accompany the sultan. Furthermore, by meeting the Crimean Khan on horseback and dining with him in the autumn of 1594, Sinān Pasha had indicated, in the eyes of his contemporaries, that the Grand Vezir was on the same footing as the Crimean Khan in spite of the latter's Jenghiz Khan ancestry.[12]

Sinān Pasha was a master of power politics. When he came to the Grand Vezirate for the fifth and last time (December 1595–April 1596), he had long since grasped the relationship between attaining success against an external enemy and maintaining stable and reliable support in the household. When he realized that Ibrāhīm Pasha had become the chosen favorite of the Vālide Sultan, he knew that if he once again led a campaign to a distant point in Hungary, he would soon be dismissed. Yet the troops were so ill-disciplined and the campaigns so strenuous that they would listen only to someone with absolute authority over them such as only the Grand Vezir and the Sultan possessed. Fearing that his authority would be challenged and his supplies mischanneled in the rear, he now urged, as he had in 1582 under similar circumstances, that the Sultan lead the campaign of 1596 in person. With the encouragement of H̱ōja Sa'deddin and in spite of the objections of his mother, the Sultan agreed to go on campaign.

6 The Vicissitudes of the Sons and Brothers-in-Law, Damād Ibrāhīm Pasha and Yemişçi Ḥasan Pasha

When Ḳōjā Sinān died in April 1596, Dāmād Ibrāhīm, a Bosnian, became Grand Vezir and vigorously made preparations for the important campaign of that year. Dāmād Ibrāhīm had obtained his post with the support of Sāfiye, the Sultan's mother, and his wife, Ayşe, sister to the Sultan, but later he would run into difficulties with the Sultan Vālide while trying to manage the Empire with the superior administrative skills that he possessed. One cannot begin to describe the venality of the Sultan Vālide in a few pages of text; rather, her pernicious influence on affairs of state should be the subject of a special monograph. Perhaps only the report of Lello, the English ambassador to the Porte who arrived after the death of the influential Edward Barton, conveys, in the course of a few pages, the blight that harem-meddling brought to the Empire during the reign of Meḥemmed III.[13]

Dāmād Ibrāhīm's career was typical of the careers of many men of Christian origin serving in the top echelons of Ottoman government. He was conscripted into Ottoman service (*devşirme*) from a Bosnian background. He moved slowly through the ranks of the palace, only becoming Janissary Ağā in April 1580. He was promoted out of the palace service in 1581 as Rumeli Beylerbeyi and was married to Sultan Murād III's daughter in 1582, after which he was appointed to the highest echelon of government, the so-called "Vezirs of the Dome" (*Kübbe Vezirleri*). In 1583 he replaced the eunuch Mürteşi (Briber) Hasān as Governor of Egypt and brought order and justice where his predecessor had brought havoc. He returned to Istanbul in 1585, having quelled a revolt of the Druze of Lebanon in that year. In view of these services and the "great bribe" (pişkeş-i 'ażīm) or gifts that Ibrāhīm brought to the Sultan from Egypt and Lebanon, he was appointed to the rank of Second Vezir. By this time, Ibrāhīm Pasha began to consider his influence to be more valuable to the Sultan than that of Doğancï Meḥmet and thus he became implicated in the Janissary Rebellion of 1589 during which Meḥmet Pasha lost his life. When the Sultan learned of Ibrāhīm's implication in the rebellion, he was dismissed from office, never again to return to prominence until the reign of Sultan Meḥemmed III; then, his family position changed from son-in-law of Murād III to brother-in-law of Meḥemmed III.

In 1596, Ibrāhīm Pasha, as Grand Vezir, had done a great deal of the "staff" work that made the victory at Mezö Kerésztés (Ḥaç Ovasï) possible. In the best Ottoman tradition, he was a master of detail. During the actual battle, three heroes emerged: H̱ōjā Sa'deddin who had forced the Sultan to stand firm when the enemy threatened his very life; Feth̩ Girāy, emissary of his brother, Ġāzī Girāy Khan, who, with his Tatars, had fought bravely; and Çiġālāzāde Sinān Pasha, whose sudden appearance at a critical moment with his fresh reserve forces broke the resistance of the enemy.

Sultan Meḥemmed III, far removed for a time from the influence of his mother and excited by the great victory, appointed Çiġālāzāde Sinān Pasha the Grand Vezir in place of his brother-in-law Dāmād Ibrāhīm. Çiġālāzāde in turn made two sweeping changes. First, he appointed Fetḥ Girāy to the Khanship of the Crimea, which very soon led to the revolt of Ġāzī Girāy and the death of Fetḥ Girāy and his family as described in Chapter VII. Next he held an inspection of all the troops and ordered a roll call. All troops not present were struck from the payroll, but the consequences were far reaching because these men, the so-called *Firārīs* or "Deserters," were caught unawares by this unexpected muster; they thus, perforce, joined the Jelālī movement in Asia Minor. As many of them were skilled commanders, they fought the central government adroitly for decades.[14]

Forty days after this surprise appointment, the Sultan received a letter from his mother demanding that he reinstate Dāmād Ibrāhīm immediately. H̱ōja Sa'deddin, for his role in this affair, received a special *ferman* ordering him to desist henceforth from meddling in political and military affairs or from interfering with the appointments of various members of the 'Ulemā.'

Space does not permit us to detail here the vicissitudes of Dāmād Ibrāhīm's succeeding years as Grand Vezir, a position which at one interval was held by the despicable eunuch Hasān Pasha, nicknamed *Mürteşi*, that is, the briber. His appointment represents the prime example of a post that was purchased with a bribe to the Sultan Vālide. When he openly admitted that any post could be "purchased," he lost his life. Dāmād Ibrāhīm had superior talents as an army administrator and as a counselor who was able to pacify the war-weary peasantry of Hungary. His untimely death in 1601 at a time when he was conducting delicate negotiations with Austria and with Michael of Wallachia undoubtedly extended the length of the war.[15]

H̱ōja Sa'deddin, another of the old guard, died in October 1599 after having been appointed Şeyẖ ul-Islām. His many years of influence-peddling for his sons and friends, and of destruction or banishment for his enemies, were at an end. It is clear that his unfortunate example as a member of the 'Ulemā' class contributed no small amount to the decline in standards of the learned community in subsequent years.[16]

Yemişçī (The Fruiterer) Ḥasān Pasha first came into prominence when he was appointed Janissary Aġā by Ḳōjā Sinān Pasha in 1594.[17] In 1596 he was sent to Shirvan where he remained until about 1600 and on one occasion helped to destroy a fortification constructed by the Russians on the shores of the Caspian. On September 4, 1600, Yemişçī Ḥasan attracted attention when he made a 50 per cent improvement in the value of the aḳçe in relation to the florin (Venetian ducat). He replaced H̱ādim Ḥāfiż Ahmed as Ḳā'immakām in February 1601, and following the death of Ibrāhīm Pasha became Grand Vezir on July 22, 1601. He fell heir to the wealth and equipment of Ibrāhīm Pasha which awaited his march to Belgrade; moreover, he was immediately engaged to Ayşe Sultan, the former wife of Ibrāhīm and a sister of the Sultan. As the experienced commander Lālā Meḥemmed had been left in charge of the Hungarian front, Yemişçī sought permission to remain in Istanbul, to effect his marriage and to prepare for the campaign season of 1602. But the Sultan, at the time listening to the advice of Sun'ullah Efendi, the Şeyh ul-Islām, ordered Yemişçī to the front immediately. This order, in the opinion of Hasānbeyzāde, the Chronicler, was a serious tactical mistake which notwithstanding its effect upon the fall of Stuhlweissenburg (Ustūn-i Belgrad), most certainly helped the enemy to seize Esztergom (Gran). Had full powers been given Lālā Meḥemmed Pasha, proper precautions might have been taken. Yemişçī had to leave the capital without proper provisions and without having the opportunity to replace some of his enemies such as Sun'ullah Efendi. He reached Belgrade after a series of forced marches on September 6, 1601, actually too late to conduct an effective campaign. When his main body of troops refused to march to the relief of Kanisza, at the time commanded by Tiryâki (the Addict) Ḥasān Pasha, Yemişçī attempted to march his personal retainers to the besieged fortress, but they too revolted and he was forced to retire to winter quarters. In the year 1602, Yemişçī recaptured Stuhlweissenburg and having met with a group of refugees from Transylvania, notably Gabriel Bethlen and Moïses Szekely, he promised to march on Gross Wardein (Vārād) at the end of the 1602 campaign season. This plan was never fulfilled because the Pasha, after crossing the Tisza River at Szolnok, was forced to return to the relief of Pest.[18]

Having heard that a plot was developing against him in Istanbul, Yemişçī resupplied the fortified places in Hungary and then hastened to the capital. While Yemişçī Ḥasān had been occupied on the Hungarian front, the Jelālī Rebellion had reached frightening proportions in Asia Minor. The ordinary troops in the capital and provinces, who had to bear the brunt of the fighting, began to blame the poor leadership furnished them by the Imperial Household. The combination of serious external crises and a critical inflation with the corruption of the Sultan and his immediate entourage continued to produce explosive incidents in the capital, all of which tended to be blamed on whichever hapless general happened to be serving as Ḳā 'immakām. All such incidents were more dangerous than in the past because so many men of the crack Household regiments had perished in Persia and now in Hungary that perhaps as many as half of the troops were Ḳūl Oğullarï, that is, raw recruits who had not received the training and discipline of bygone days. These facts lay behind a series of revolts in the capital, aimed at the Vālide Sultan and her "creatures."

In April 1600, the troops had called for the head of Esther Kira, the trusted Jewess who had long served the Vālide Sultan. She was reputed to have had control of the customs receipts for the port of Constantinople. The execution of Esther Kira was only the first measure against the Vālide Sultan.

The rebellion that had caused Yemişçī Hasan to hasten back to the capital took place on January 6, 1603. This time the troops demanded an *Ayak Dīvānī*, or public audience with the Sultan, during which they obtained the execution of Ġażānfer Ağa and 'O̱smān Ağa, who had long carried out the bidding of the Vālide Sultan. It is said that the Sultan wept during the execution.

A little more than a month later, on the night of February 18, Yemişçī Ḥasan, accompanied by the historian Hasanbeyzāde, reached Büyük Çekmeji—about twenty miles from the capital. He was met there by some trusted informants who told him that his life was in danger. Hearing this, he nevertheless continued his journey and passed through the city gates at dawn. Güzelje Mahmūd Pasha, the Ḳā'immakām, with the connivance of the Şeyẖ ul-Islām, had obtained a *fetva* for the Grand Vezir's execution, citing the loss of Pest and other blunders as justification. He had also hired some disgruntled *Sipāhiyān* (~provincial cavalrymen) to kill him. Yemişçī Ḥasan, acting quickly, nullified the fetva and had his adversaries, Güzelje Mahmūd and Sun'ullah, dismissed. To eliminate the danger to his person posed by the disgruntled soldiery, he ordered the execution of the ringleaders of the Sipāhiyān and when it appeared that both the Sipāhiyān and the Janissaries would revolt against him, he took the unforgivable step of turning the Janissaries against the Sipāhiyān who were grossly outnumbered. This move heralded his own end. He was known to be a rude fellow and had proven that he was no mean adversary, but this personal victory over the machinations of the Porte caused him to become exceedingly vainglorious—he even spoke openly against the Vālide Sultan. His execution quickly followed on October 16, 1603. Never one to give up easily, Yemişçī barricaded himself in the villa of his wife, Ayşe Sultan, and fought off the palace guard until he was overpowered. To the very end, Ayşe had sought his pardon from her brother, the Sultan, but to no avail.[19]

7 Sultan Ahmed I and His Generals

Many of the ills of the previous reign continued and new ones were to be added. Fortunately for the future of the dynasty, when Sultan Aḥmed came to the throne in December 1603, he immediately banished his grandmother, Sāfiye, and her following, to the old Palace in the district of the Beyazid mosque. Initially the Sultan was hampered more by his youth and inexperience than by any malevolent courtiers. His commonly accepted age at accession was thirteen years. For a time he followed the advice of his mother, the Sultana, H̱āndan, and after her death in 1605, he at first listened to the fickle counsel of Dervīş Meḥmet who had become Bostānji-Başï in 1604 and, in that position, had worked through the Vālide Sultan to influence state decisions.

Shortly after the beginning of his reign in 1603, Sultan Aḥmed removed Yavuz ʻAli (Malkoç), whom he had inherited from the last days of the previous reign and appointed Lālā Meḥemmed as Grand Vezir. Lālā Meḥemmed led his troops with distinction, lent his support to the Bocskay Rebellion, and conducted the delicate negotiations that resulted in the Treaty of Szitva-Török of 1606. He died in June 1606, just prior to his departure for the Persian front. Dervīş Meḥmet, who had meanwhile been appointed Kapūdān-i Derya (High Admiral), was responsible for having Lālā Meḥemmed Pasha removed from the Hungarian Front. The young Sultan ordered Dervīş Mehmet, to proceed to Hungary as Commander-in-Chief and Grand Vezir. His understanding of the Vezirate was so limited that, with the prompting of Sunʻullah Efendi who had once again become Şeyẖ ul-Islām, Sultan Aḥmed had Dervīş Pasha dismissed and killed in December 1606.

Although it is clear that the Ottomans had profited in Hungary from the good generalship of such commanders as Dāmād Ibrāhīm and Lālā Meḥemmed, they had enjoyed few successes against the Jelālī Revolt in Asia Minor. To make matters worse, in 1603 Shah ʻAbbās had opened his campaign in the East to regain his territories in Transcaucasia—Azerbaijan and Kurdistan. Çiġālāzāde had been sent against the forces of the Shah after the latter had taken Erivan and Kars, but shortly after his defeat at Salmās on Sept. 9, 1605, a terrible blow for this proud commander, he took his own life in Diyarbakïr. Shah ʻAbbās, maintaining his momentum, then retook Genje and Shirvan.

Meanwhile a commander of superior stature had been groomed by the Ottoman system to bring order out of chaos in the Empire. He bore the unlikely name of Kuyūjū (The Well-digger) Murād, a nickname given to him supposedly because he fell into a well during ʻO̱smān Pasha's campaign in Persia in 1585, an incident which led to his capture. Other writers claim that he gained the title by filling wells with the bodies of the Jelālī rebels. Kuyūjū Murād had become Beylerbey of Cyprus in 1590 after his release from captivity. After a number of similar posts he attained the rank of Fourth Vezir in 1605 and was appointed Serdār of the Persian front following the death of Lālā Meḥemmed. Upon the execution of Dervīş, he was appointed Grand Vezir (December, 1606) through the support of Sunʻullah Efendi. It would go beyond the scope of this study to detail the incredible successes of this commander against the Jelālī movement, but it is worthy of note that such great leaders, when they had successfully gained the confidence of their Sultan, not infrequently brought the system back to some measure of efficiency. Kuyūjū Murād led a campaign every year of his Vezirate. He was so loved by the young Sultan that he affectionately addressed him as "father."

It is said of Kuyūjū that he was efficient, respectful of tradition, and devout, owing allegiance to the Nakşbendi order of Dervishes. He was over eighty years old when he died on the Persian front in August, 1611. By that time he had quieted the rebellion at home, silenced his critics in Istanbul, and had brought Shah ʻAbbās to the peace table.[20]

NOTES

1. See Gökbilgin, "Mehmed Paşa Sokullu," *I.A.*, VII, pp. 602–604, for a full discussion of this process of alienation.
2. The background has been discussed in Chap. 3.
3. Manisa served formerly as the provincial seat of the heir apparent.
4. Turan, "Sinān Paşa, Kōcā," *I.A.*, X, p. 672.
5. *Ibid.* See also Kütükoğlu, "Mustafa Paşa," and "Murad III," *I.A.*, VIII, pp. 735–736, 618–619; and Hammer, *Histoire de l'Empire Ottoman*, VII, p. 107.
6. Turan, "Sa'd-ed-Din," *I.A.*, X, p. 28.
7. Hammer, *Histoire*, pp. 214–215.
8. For a discussion of this complex issue, see Inalcïk, "Türkiye'nin Iktisadi Vaziyeti," *Belleten*, XV/60 (Oct., 1951), pp. 629–690; Kortepeter, "Ottoman Imperial Policy and the Economy of the Black Sea Region in the Sixteenth Century," *J.A.O.S.*, Vol. 86/2 (April-June 1966), pp. 86–113; Parry, "The Ottoman Empire 1566–1617," *New Cambridge Modern History*, III, p. 370; Danişmend, *Izahlī Osmanlï Tarihi Kronolojisi*, III, pp. 111–113; Roth, *The House of Nasi: The Duke of Naxos*, p. 204.
9. Roth, *Duke of Naxos*, Chap. VIII. Also see Alderson, *The Structure of the Ottoman Dynasty*, Pl. XXX; and Turan, "Sinān Paşa, Kōcā," *loc. cit.*
10. Peçewī, *Tārīh*, II, pp. 132–133.
11. Ḳōjā Sinān gave considerable attention to the so-called *Jins* (ethnic) question. Peçewī points out that Lālā Meḥemmed Ağa, a Bosnian, and a relative alike of Peçewī and Ṣoḳōllū, was removed from his post as Janissary Aġā in 1594 and was replaced by his Albanian protégé, Yemişçī Ḥasan Ağā. This should not have surprised Peçewī. Ṣoḳōllū Meḥemmed Pasha never did much for Ḳōjā Sinān! See Peçewī, II, p. 145; Danişmend, III, pp. 144–147, 155–156; Gökbilgin, "Mehmed III," *I.A.*., VII, p. 537.
12. Peçewī, II, pp. 145, 150–151. The Khan, it is to be remembered, was received like a king. The Grand Vezir ordered a full parade and banquet in his honor right in the middle of a battle zone!
13. See Burian, *The Report of Lello* (Ankara Üniversitesi D.T.–C. Fak. Yayïnlarï, No. 83); also Skilliter, "Three Letters from the Ottoman 'Sultana' Safiye to Queen Elizabeth I," in Stern, ed., *Documents from Islamic Chanceries* (Oxford Oriental Studies, No. 3), pp. 118–157.
14. For details, see Hammer, *Histoire*, VII, pp. 330 ff.; and Gökbilgin, "Mehmed III," in which is disclosed the location of the actual list of "Deserters" in the Baş Vekâlet Arşivi, Ali Emirî Defterleri, Mehmed III, nr. 107.
15. See the excellent article, "Ibrahim Paşa, Dāmād," by Parmaksïzoğlu, *I.A.*, V, pp. 915–919.
16. See Turan, "Sa'd-ed-Dīn," *I.A.*, X, pp. 27–32.
17. See note no. 11 above.
18. Discussed in Chapter VIII.
19. See Peçewī, II, pp. 255–257; and Köprülü, "Hasan Paşa, Yemişçi," *I.A.*, V, pp. 330–334.
20. Peçewī, II, pp. 329–337; and Orhonlu, "Murad Paşa, Kuyucu," *I.A.*, VIII, pp. 651–654.

CHAPTER TEN
The Last Years of Ġāzī Girāy Khan

In the last quarter of the sixteenth century and for almost a decade in the seventeenth century, Ġāzī Girāy, Khan of the Crimean Tatars, had taken an intimate part in the affairs of the Ottoman Empire. Almost without exception, he was the one dignitary of consequence in the realm to maintain a position of prominence from the beginning to the end of the period. The reasons for his longevity are readily apparent. He was well endowed both mentally and physically; thus, he managed to keep not only abreast but well ahead of the intrigues of his enemies. Yet as a man of letters, he wrote poetry of such a quality that his work still appears in present-day anthologies. Most important of all, he possessed a power base that was beyond the reach and comprehension of the Ottoman Household. His independence increased as the Ottoman state became enmeshed in conflicts in Hungary, Persia, and Asia Minor.

Information on the activities of Ġāzī Girāy in the last years of his life is relatively scarce. Such materials as are available, however, indicate that the Khan remained vigilant to his death in the defense of what he considered the best interests of the Khanate in its relations with Persia, Muscovy, Poland, and the Porte.

Ġāzī Girāy Khan had spent four years on campaign in the Caucasus during the twelve years of the Persian War (1578–1590). When he was captured by the Persians in 1581, he spent some two or three years in prison before the Safavids decided that it might be profitable to cultivate the friendship of the Crimean Tatars. Thereafter, Ġāzī Girāy was treated in a manner worthy of a h̲ānzāde until his escape in 1585. Isthvanfi, who was in a position during his negotiations with the representatives of the Khan to find out intimate details of the Khan's life, even stated that the Khan was married during his captivity to one of the sisters of Shah 'Abbās.[1] Ġāzī Girāy, because of his proximity to the Caucasus, certainly had more reasons than most of his contemporaries to maintain amicable relations with Shah 'Abbās. Even after the Shah had opened hostilities with the Ottomans in 1603, the Khan remained on good terms with him. After capturing a friend of the Khan, Çerkes H̲andān Aġā—doubtless the very same Muteferriḳa Bāşī who had brought the *Muḳarrernāme* to Ġāzī Girāy in 1597—Shah 'Abbās sent him on an embassy to the Khan. The Shah, it appears, was uneasy lest the Crimean Tatars might come to the assistance of the Ottomans in the Caucasus as they had in the past. But Ġāzī Girāy assured the Shah, through an embassy to Persia that arrived in Isfahan during the year 1607, of his desire for peace and friendship. At that time, the Khan sought the release of two sons of H̲āndān Aġā. These exchanges of embassies continued until the Khan's death in 1608. When the news of these embassies reached the Porte, the Khan was naturally viewed with greater distrust than ever before.[2]

Diplomatic relations between the Tsar and the Khan in the last years of the life of Ġāzī Girāy made very little progress. Boris Godunov, Tsar of Muscovy (1598–1605), consistently sought to maintain peace between his realm and the Crimean Khanate by the regular payment of subsidies. Toward the end of his short reign, however, amicable relations between the Khan and the Tsar were disturbed by incessant Don Cossack raids on the territories of the former. Moreover, the diplomatic activity taking place between Poland and the Crimea gave the Tsar cause for concern. Shortly before his death in 1605, Boris Godunov was able to deter the Khan from assisting the Polish-supported movement in favor of "False Dmitri" (1605–1606);[3] nevertheless, at a time when the Pretender, Dmitri I, was gaining support on the western borderlands of Muscovy, other signs of the disintegration of central authority became evident on the Terek. The voivode at this outpost reported that the Kabardinians no longer wished to serve the Tsar and that they were making common cause with the Little Nogays and the Kumucks to drive out the Muscovite garrisons. In 1604 the voivode was actually forced to withdraw from the fort on the Sunzhu and, although a Muscovite force had defeated the Şamh̲al of Tarku in the same year, a garrison stationed in Tarku was besieged and ultimately massacred by a combined Ottoman and Kumuck force in 1605.[4] The Pretender, who entered Moscow in triumph in June 1605, at first pursued a conciliatory policy toward the Khan,[5] but shortly before his murder in 1606, False Dmitri had made preparations for a campaign against the Crimea.[6] During the reign of Vasiliy Shuiskiy (1606–1610), it became no longer safe for couriers, not to mention embassies, to pass between Muscovy and the Crimea; consequently, ties between the two states were broken off until 1613.[7]

Relations between the Khan and the King of Poland deteriorated seriously in the summer of 1606. During the winter months of 1606–1607, the French ambassador at the Porte reported that Ġāzī Girāy had personally led a raid into the Polish borderlands.[8] These incursions led to the signing of an agreement between the Sultan and the King of Poland in 1607 in which the Sultan undertook to restrain the Crimean Tatars in exchange for the payment of the traditional subsidies to the Khan. The Khan, in return, would be expected to assist the King, if need be, against his enemies.[9]

From the foregoing scraps of information and a few sparse statements in the Ottoman and Tatar sources, it is possible to piece together the general outlines of the last few years of the life of Ġāzī Girāy Khan. The series of negotiations with Poland between 1601 and 1605 resulted in an arrangement, if not an agreement, for the Crimean Tatars to assist Poland in an attack on Muscovy. Such an understanding, of course, could not have become operative had not the Hungarian War taken a decided turn in favor of the Ottomans. As the Russian sources boldly described the situation, King Sigismund paid the Tatars to assist him in an attack on Muscovy.[10] The death of Zamoyski (1605), an old adversary of the Khan, may also have temporarily eased relations between Poland and the Crimea. Ġāzī Girāy, however, once he learned of the rise of False Dmitri and of the support the latter was receiving from Poland, could not forego the temptation to reap a double harvest of "gifts"; consequently, he sent an envoy to Boris Godunov. He informed the Tsar that it was growing increasingly difficult to keep his Tatars at home as a result of the favorable incentives he was receiving from King Sigismund to make common cause with him. Boris Godunov, already facing a serious threat to his position at home, hastened to appease the Khan with appropriate "gifts." The Khan was quite content to remain aloof from any Polish involvement at the time because if Muscovy were humbled by Poland, then the Crimea could no longer expect assistance from Muscovy if Poland attacked the Crimea.

By the middle of 1605, Boris Godunov was dead and False Dmitri, a friend of Poland, was in control in Muscovy. It does not seem surprising, then, that by 1606 plans for Muscovite attack on the Crimea—to be launched from Elets were already far advanced. Moreover, Polish troops had been mobilized in preparation for an attack on the Crimea in response to an incursion into the Polish borderlands that had been led by Ġāzī Girāy. The Polish-Lithuanian Commonwealth still hoped to gain full access to the Black Sea. One must suspect that a measure of collusion was planned between Muscovy and Poland for an attack on the Crimea in 1606. At this point, however, the Pretender was killed by a faction led by Vasiliy Shuiskiy and better relations again developed between Muscovy and the Crimean Khanate. As the war in Hungary also dragged to an end in this same year, negotiations between the Porte and Poland leading to the treaty of 1607 relieved the pressure on the Khanate from the northwest.

The Sultan now turned to the Khan with new demands for assistance against the Jelālī uprising, against the Shah of Persia, and against the son of Jeremia Movila who, with Polish support, was attempting to unseat the son of Simeon Movila, the Sultan's selection for the voivodeship of Moldavia. The Khan sent a token force to assist only in quelling the Jelālī rebellion. He did not, however, wish to interfere in the Moldavian affair and, in the light of previous assurances to Shah 'Abbās, he excused himself from sending a force to Persia.[11] The Khan knew that the young and impetuous Sultan Aḥmed I (1603–1617) would want to remove him from the Khanship as a result of his disobedience; therefore, he took steps to entrench himself for the inevitable conflict in a manner reminiscent of the defensive measures he had taken during his struggle with the Feth Girāy faction in 1596 and 1597. At that time he had begun building the fortress of Ġāzī Kermān on the Kuban River in Circassia.[12] In 1607 and 1608, Ġāzī Girāy completed the construction of Ġāzī Kermān and, at the same time taking advantage of the internal dissension in Muscovy, exacted allegiance to the Khanate from the Şamḫal and the Kabardinian Circassians.[13] While the Khan was returning from a visit to his "eastern domain," he fell ill with the plague (Ṭa'ūn) in the spring of 1608 and died in the fortress of Temruk near the Straits of Kerch.[14] Tōḳtamiş Girāy, the son of the Khan, who had led the Tatar forces in Hungary during the closing years of the war, was now chosen for the position of Khan by a *Kuraltay* of assembled dignitaries from the Şīrīn, Bārin, Sijavut (Sijavīt), and Manṣur tribes of the Crimea and the Sultan was then petitioned to recognize him. The Sultan, however, chose to make Selāmet Girāy the new Khan. The long and exceptional rule of Ġāzī Girāy was at an end.[15]

In 1597 the Tatar ambassador, Antonio Spinola, a descendant of the famous Genoese house of that name, had related to William Bruce, a fugitive Scot serving Poland, that the Sultan (Meḥemmed III) had sought to do away with Ġāzī Girāy but, as he was much respected by his own people, all his efforts had come to nothing. The Khan, he added, was a ruler of great wisdom and prudence such as Tatary had not seen for a long time.[16]

Although the Crimean Tatars first came into close contact with the Ottoman state in 1475, the nature of the authority that the Sultan exercised over the Crimean Khans thereafter was always rather ill-defined. At first the relationship between the Khanate and the Ottoman Empire was more in the nature of an offensive-defensive treaty. The good faith of the Tatar Khan was assured by a practice requiring him to send a close relative to the Porte as a hostage. Early in the sixteenth century, however, the Tatar Khans, particularly Meḥemmed Girāy I (1514–1523), acted in a manner considered by the Ottomans to be contrary to the best interests of the Ottoman state. The Sultans thus felt it necessary to control more closely than previously the appointment and dismissal of the Khans. At the same time, the Sultans provided funds to enable the Khans of their choosing, for example Ṣāḥib Girāy (1532–1551), to establish a reliable personal guard (*Sekbān*) in order that their personal position vis-à-vis the tribal dignitaries of the Crimea might be more stable. The Crimean Tatar Khans were also granted regular subsidies which came, in part, out of the customs dues levied by the Ottomans at Kaffa. While participating in an Ottoman campaign, the Khans could expect to receive additional subsidies and on occasion even grants of land, as had Mengli Girāy after the Moldavian campaign of 1484.[17]

During the late sixteenth century, the exact nature of the vassalage of the Crimean Khanate had not yet been finally determined. Much of the friction between the Porte and the Khanate must be considered in relation to this problem. The Khanate, as a Muslim state within the Empire and also as a buffer state to the north of the Black Sea, had to be handled with extreme tact. Thus, if the Porte wished to bring about a change in the Khanate, it preferred, except in cases of extreme urgency, to work with the ever-present conflicting factions inside the Khanate.

The Porte generally had its way with such Khans as Islām Girāy (1584–1588) who had spent much more time as a hostage in the Ottoman milieu at Istanbul than he had as a h̲ānzāde accustomed to the more spartan way of life among the Tatars. It was another matter with such Khans as Devlet Girāy (1551–1577), the "taker of the capital" (Moscow), Meḥemmed Girāy II (1577–1584), and Ġāzī Girāy II (1588–1608). During the reigns of these Tatar Khans, the best interests of the Khanate, as construed by the Khan himself, were often placed ahead of considerations relating to the Ottoman Empire as a whole. Thus, Devlet Girāy saw in the Astrakhan campaign of 1569 a threat to his own position—and opposed it. Meḥemmed Girāy II, after stripping the provinces of Shirvan and Genje of whatever booty was to be found there, felt no longer obliged to serve in Transcaucasia, particularly as he had good reason to view with some alarm the intentions toward the Khanate of so active a Polish king as Stephan Báthory. On this occasion, the Porte found it necessary to deal directly with his insubordination. This would have been difficult in wartime, however, had not the powerful Şīrīn Beys given their support to the new Ottoman candidate, Islām Girāy. Meḥemmed Girāy Khan had also wished to perpetuate the Khanship in his own family, a desire which the Ottoman Sultans certainly did not encourage.

During the khanship of Ġāzī Girāy the tension between the Sultan and the Khan again became acute, largely beçause Ġāzī Girāy was an intelligent and capable Khan. The power groups that influenced the Crimean political scene had not altered appreciably since the days of Devlet Girāy, the illustrious father of Ġāzī Girāy. Within the Khanate one could differentiate among four groups at any one time: the Khan and his household, the other Girāy H̲ānzādes and their followers, the Mīrzās of the principal Crimean Tatar tribes, and finally the dignitaries of the Nogay and Circassian tribes who had family alliances with the other three groups. There were of course traditional alignments within and among these various groups as well as more transient and changing alliances. The Ottoman Sultans and their vezirs maintained contacts with the various factions that developed out of these four main groups.

In view of his great services to the Ottoman state at the time of the Persian conflict (1578–1590), Ġāzī Girāy, when he was chosen khan, enjoyed excellent relations with the Porte. After assisting the Ottomans in the Polish affair of 1589–1590, he proceeded to settle the immediate problems facing the Khanate on the steppe by means of the treaty with Muscovy. Thereafter he complied with the Sultan's wishes by joining the Hungarian campaign in 1594. Very early in this conflict, however, Ġāzī Girāy came to feel that in the light of the contribution that the Khanate was making to the prosecution of the war, and in view of the poor showing of the Ottomans, the Tatars ought to be compensated with better rations, greater subsidies, and possibly with territories—even as his ancestors had been. It was natural that the Khan should seek to extend his way in the direction of Wallachia and Moldavia. He already controlled portions of Bessarabia; moreover, within Moldavia there was a sizable community of Tatar agriculturists and merchants.[18] When Ġāzī Girāy refused to go in person on campaign in 1596, the Sultan, as in the previous case of Meḥemmed Girāy II, was encouraged by his entourage to bring about the Khan's dismissal. Here again there is evidence that the Şīrīn tribe, as in the time of Meḥemmed Girāy, sided with the Ottomans against the ruling Khan.[19] But at this juncture, Ġāzī Girāy was too well respected—by the rank-and-file of the Tatar army, as a warrior of the faith, and by the learned community of the 'Ulemā' as a man of culture and learning—to be easily removed from office, particularly while the Ottomans were directing their energies elsewhere. Upon receiving his reappointment in 1597, the Khan eliminated systematically the various threats to his independent position. First, he eliminated the family and the supporters of Fetḥ Girāy (1597). When the Şīrīn Mīrzās—even including his own son-in-law—attempted to replace him with a h̲ānzāde from the Meḥemmed Girāy line, Ġāzī Girāy took the occasion to bring vengeance on the Şīrīnoğullarī (1601). When his brother Selāmet Girāy, fearing some intrigue from the Khan, took refuge with the Ottomans in 1602, Ġāzī Girāy refused to go on campaign again without the customary subsidies and firm assurances that he would not be dismissed from the Khanship.

The question now arises: how was the Khan able to take such an independent position toward the traditional elements of power within the Khanate and toward the Ottoman Sultan? The answer must be sought in the internal and external policies of Ġāzī Girāy. At home, he had strengthened his personal power by maintaining a retinue of Circassians loyal to him personally. Moreover, he had built up a contingent of arquebusiers, trained by retired Janissaries, who were drawn chiefly from Tatar villages bordering on Poland. Finally there is some evidence that he was able to maintain better surveillance over his own territories than previous khans had done by devoting considerable care to his relations with the Tatars and other peoples on the Crimean Peninsula and by building some new fortifications in the region stretching from the Dnieper to the Kuban.

The relations of Ġāzī Girāy with foreign powers also helped to enhance the independent position of the Khanate. It was through his contacts with the Tsar of Muscovy, the Kings of Poland and Sweden, and with the Holy Roman Emperor that Ġāzī Girāy, in a manner somewhat reminiscent of his Golden Horde ancestors, obtained subsidies and perquisites that aided him in furthering his own ambitions in the Khanate and provided him with funds that he could use to bribe the great dignitaries at the Porte. These revenues, of course, were supplements to his normal grants from the Sultan and the tribute that he was able to extract from Wallachia, Moldavia, and also from the Nogays and the Circassians. During the last years of his life, owing to the "Time of Troubles" in Muscovy and to the pressure placed on the Ottoman state by Shah 'Abbās I, the Khan was even able to extend his rule into the northern Caucasus to such an extent that the Şamḫal of Tarku paid tribute to him. It is doubtful if Ġāzī Girāy could have maintained himself as Khan as long as he did had there not been a "Time of Troubles" in Muscovy, a "long war" on the Danube, and also serious internal troubles in Poland. But in some measure at least, he had been successful because he had been able to project a favorable impression of himself upon his subjects, upon his supporters at the Porte, and upon the representatives of various foreign powers.

Although Ġāzī Girāy solved temporarily the problem of political survival for himself, he was unable to grasp the importance of the steppe as something more than a place for slave raids, a buffer zone, and an environment for the raising of livestock. The lessons that he and his successors might have learned from the permanent agricultural colonies established by Jan Zamoyski in Poland, by the Don Cossacks to the east of the Khanate, or from similar settlements of the Tatars in Moldavia seem to have gone unheeded by the Khan.[20]

Once again, even as the Ottoman elite had discovered, to remain in power during an era of social and economic change required all of one's energies. Regimes such as the Ottoman Sultanate and the Crimean Khanate had to allot such a high proportion of their resources to maintaining the "system of Sulaymān" under changed social and technological conditions that little time or resources remained to improve upon or change that system.

NOTES

1. Isthvanfi, *De Rebus Ungaricus*, pp. 637–638.

2. Iskāndar Beġ, *Tāriḫ-e 'Ālām*, II, pp. 686, 753; Bellan, *Chah 'Abbas I*, (*Les Grandes Figures de l'Orient*) Vol. III, pp. 163, 169; Gontaut-Biron au Roy (de France) (June 20, 1607), *Arch. Hist. de*

la Gascogne, 19, p. 150. A. de Govvea, *Relation des guerres et victoires obtenues par le roy de Perse Cha Abbas*, p. 326.

3. Platonov, ed., "Pamyat. Diplomat. Snosh. Moskov. Gosudarstva s Pol'sko-Litovskim, 1598–1608," *Sbornik I.R.I.O.*, 137 (1912), pp. 179, 249–250.

4. Belokurov, *Snosheniya Rosii s Kavkazom*, pp. cxi, cxii.

5. Karamsin, *Histoire de l'Empire de Russie*, XI, p. 335.

6. I. I. Smirnov, *Vosstanie Bolotnikova, 1606–1607*, p. 147. The attack was to be launched from Elets in the spring (Obolenskiy, ed., *Novyy Letopisets*, p. 73).

7. Novosel'skiy, *Bor'ba Moskovskogo Gosudarstva . . .*, pp. 51–52.

8. Gontaut-Biron, Baron de Salignac au Roy (de France), "Ambassade en Turquie, 1605 à 1610," *Comité d'Histoire et d'Archeologie de la Province Ecclésiastique d'Auch*, Fasc. 19, pp. 65, 120.

9. Hammer, *Histoire de l'Empire Ottoman*, VIII, pp. 146–147.

10. Platonov, *loc.cit.*

11. Inalcïk, "Ġāzī Girāy Khan II," *I.A.*, IV, pp. 735–736; Ferīdūn, *Münşe'āt*, II, pp. 119–120; "Report on Moldavia (January 8, 1608)," in Hurmuzaki, ed., *Documente privatóre la Istoria Romanilor*, IV/II, p. 292.

12. Kâtib Çelebī, *Fezleke*, I, p. 96; Belokurov, *Snosheniya*, p. cxiv, citing *Nogayskie Dela* (1608), doc. no. 1.

13. Belokurov, pp. cxi–cxii.

14. Meḥemmed Riżā, *Es-Seb' es-Seyyār*, p. 111. There is some disagreement in the sources about the date of Ġāzī Girāy's death. Meḥemmed Riżā reported that the Khan died in Şa'bān 1016/ November-December 1607; Kâtib Çelebī (I, p. 300), 16 Z̲i'l Ka'de 1016/ March 3, 1608; Munejjimbāşī, (*Ṣaḥā'if al Aḫbār*, III, p. 629) concurs with Kâtib Çelebī. The French ambassador, in a dispatch of April 9, 1608 (Gontaut-Biron, *Arch. Hist. de la Gascogne*, Fasc. 19, pp. 208–209) reported to his king that the Khan had died and that Selāmet Girāy had been designated the new Khan.

15. Meḥemmed Riżā, p. 126.

16. William Bruce, *De Tartaris diarium*, pp. 3–5.

17. Inalcïk, "Yeni Vesikalara göre Kïrïm Hanlïğïnïn Osmanlï Tabiliğine Girmesi ve Ahitname Meselesi," *Belleten*, VIII/30, pp. 185–229; and by the same author, "Girāy," *I.A.*, IV, pp. 786–788.

18. Romaci (?), ed., *La Terza Parte del Tesoro Politico*, p. 197.

19. Kâtib Çelebī, *Fezleke*, I, p. 96.

20. Bestyzhev-Ryumin, ed., "Pamyatniki Diplom. Snosh. Moskov. Gosud. s Angliey 1881–1604," *Sbornik I.R.I.O.*, Vol. 38 (1883), p. 376; Tarnowski, *Dzialalność Gospodarcza Jana Zamoyskiego, Kanclerza i Hetmana w. Kor. (1572–1605)*, pp. 415–427.

CHAPTER ELEVEN
Conclusions: The Apparent and the Elusive

In this study, a number of conclusions have been set forth at the end of each chapter. It is clear that historical items which appear important to this writer may, indeed, seem a commonplace to some readers. My intention here is a most subjective one. I propose to call attention to those events and trends that may help the student of Ottoman and East European history to understand the era in question and to grasp the extent to which the Ottoman leadership, given its own *Weltanschauung*, was guiding or determining the course of events in Eastern Europe.

1. By considering within the confines of one study the entire band of countries that come into the Ottoman perspective, from the plains of Hungary to the mountains of Azerbaijan, I have attempted to show the unity and interdependence of each unit of the Ottoman state. In so doing, I have dealt with regions that, even though thoroughly familiar to the Ottoman bureaucracy and warriors, are very little known or explored by Islamic historians outside of Turkey or the Soviet Union.

2. On the basis of recurring themes in this study, it is also clear that the pattern of alignments between the Ottoman Empire and other European and Asian states can be closely correlated with basic Ottoman political and economic interests. The Balkan peninsula and part of Hungary, for example, still continued to be areas of primary production, not only for Ottoman needs, but for the agricultural, pastoral, and mining requirements of Poland-Lithuania and other neighboring lands. Thus, not only political considerations, i.e., antipathy toward the Habsburgs, kept Poland-Lithuania within the Ottoman orbit, but also pressing economic needs. The same can be said of Ottoman relations with France, England and, above all, Venice, who depended sorely on Ottoman exports of foodstuffs. If indeed the Ottoman state

shared important economic interests with certain of its neighbors, it was equally influenced by the strategic importance of laying waste the enemy's economic base while protecting its own. Clearly, tension developed frequently between the Ottoman commanders and their Tatar allies, both in Hungary and Transcaucasia, because the Ottoman commanders knew how difficult it was to keep the Tatars from molesting peasants and townsmen who were essentially loyal to the Ottoman state.

3. The structure of relationships between the Ottoman Empire and its vassal states in this era also provides us with an important pattern. At some point in the accumulated experience of Muslim political relationships with non-Muslim blocks of population, Muslim rulers had learned that it was wiser to rule such populations indirectly rather than directly—as long as vital interests, such as sensitive borders, were not placed in jeopardy. (The Mongols had applied such a system in Russia and in Seljuk Asia Minor; perhaps the pattern originated thus.) The essence of such a system consisted in (*a*) collecting an annual tribute in bullion and "gifts"; (*b*) making the local leadership responsible for the discipline of its own community; (*c*) controlling changes in that leadership; (*d*) controlling the export and import of certain commodities, especially commodities required to nourish the capital or the armies; and (*e*) reserving the right to demand special subsidies and services in time of war. This was essentially the system applied to the buffer states of Transylvania, Wallachia, and Moldavia and it was this system that was challenged unsuccessfully by the Principalities during the "Long War." By contrast, the Crimean Khanate, a Muslim vassal state, received subsidies and economic and military assistance from the Sultan. In turn, the Sultan maintained the right of appointment and dismissal of the Khans. Quite often also the Crimean Tatars were called upon to enforce Ottoman political arrangements in the Principalities.

4. The bone of contention between the Ottoman Empire and Safavid Persia was one of major proportions. From the accession of Sultan Meḥemmed II (1451) until the death of Sultan Sulaymān, the Magnificent (1566), the Ottoman Empire had steadily grown more centralized. Traditionally two or three elements in Islamic society—the tribes, the peasantry and sometimes the artisans—resisted centralization because with centralization they lost much of their mobility. In Asia Minor these elements often expressed their discontent by giving their allegiance to Shi'ite forms of Islam and particularly to the cult of Shaykh Safī of Ardebil whose followers were known as *Kïzïlbāş* or "redheads" because of the red turbans worn by them. Many groups further expressed their discontent by emigrating to Persia or by rebelling against Ottoman authority on a number of occasions during the sixteenth and seventeenth centuries.[1] By the end of the sixteenth century, the position of these lower-class elements in society had deteriorated further, but not simply because of population growth and the galloping inflation. (Generally speaking,

those classes in society who are living close to a subsistence level but who are primary producers suffer less than do city dwellers from inflation.) Rather, they suffered indirectly because the Ottoman central authority, in its quest for material assets with which to pay the vocal and armed elements of society living in the cities, began relentlessly to call back to central control all of the provincial assets available (tīmārs, zi'āmets, etc.) so that revenues from these lands could be squeezed by tax farmers or by other agents of court favorites. The losers in every case were the peasants and townsmen and, to a lesser extent, the tribesmen. These discontented members of society were thus joined by the dispossessed Tīmārli-Sipāhiyān class of warrior which had become obsolescent by the end of the sixteenth century when the nature of warfare required well-disciplined troops and garrison soldiers tutored in the use of firearms. In short, even as the Ottoman Empire provided a protecting umbrella for dispossessed classes, religious innovators and revolutionaries in Christian Hungary, Safavid Persia became a refuge area and a source of inspiration for the political and economic misfits within the Ottoman state. The Persian War did of course have a practical outcome for Persia itself. Prior to the war, the Kïzïlbāş Turcoman tribes were politically dominant in Persia, but after the war, partly no doubt because of their defeat at the hands of the Ottomans, the Turcoman Kïzïlbāş ascendancy was challenged successfully by Persian and other groups seeking power. The relative balance of forces between Turcoman and Tājiḳ (Persian) during the reign of Shah 'Abbās gave to Persia an era of greater stability than it had enjoyed previously. Clearly then, the Persian wars are closely connected to the Ottoman civil war in Asia Minor (the Jelālī "Rebellion") which continually gnawed away at Ottoman resources, both human and material.

5. By the early years of the seventeenth century, Kuyūjū Murād Pasha, in traditional manner, had stamped out opposition to central control in Asia Minor. On a second level of government, Ottoman 'Ulemā began to advocate the sending of prayer leaders trained in Sunnite doctrine to the villages of Asia Minor, a proposal which was not practical for the seventeenth century any more than it has proved practical to train physicians for service in remote parts of Asia Minor in the twentieth century.[2] While the Ottoman state was able to gain some superficial successes in Asia Minor on the political level of empire, one must maintain the suspicion, pending further studies, that those tribes, peasants, and artisans who did not, so to speak, "vote with their feet" and emigrate to Persia remained in Asia Minor as crypto-Kïzïlbāş and subtly helped to undermine the effectiveness of the central government through membership in semiacceptable dervish orders or by giving support to local families which in turn became the *derebeys* of the Ottoman eighteenth century.[3] Thus an old principle of government seems to have had its inevitable way in the Ottoman state, to wit: remove the provinces from contact with and a share of the power at the center (i.e., no longer send princes or men of stature

as governors) and the provinces will soon reciprocate the neglect by driving out or subverting imperial controls.

6. On a purely military level, if the Ottomans could have defeated the Turcoman-Persian Safavids without becoming involved in the self-defeating guerrilla warfare of the Caucasus and of the Armenian and Kurdish highlands, they might well have crippled Persia indefinitely. But Ottoman leaders invariably miscalculated with respect to the geopraphy of eastern Anatolia and the determination of the rugged mountain peoples to be masters of their own fate. Geography also always worked against the Ottomans in their wars with Persia from the rise of the Safavids until well into the nineteenth century. From the Persian side of the mountains, Shirvan, the eastern Georgian Principalities, Armenia, and Kurdistan were always closer to centers of Safavid power and hence more amenable to Safavid control and influence than to those of the Ottomans. The Ottomans could control the Georgian and Circassian emirates bordering the Black Sea, but whenever the Ottomans fought a war to secure strategic, commercial, or ideological gains in the heart of Persia their lines of communication were so dangerously stretched across the mountainous and hostile territories of Georgia, Armenia, and Kurdistan that their exploits were doomed to failure.

If the Ottomans were tempted to humble Persia at a time of Persian internal weakness, however, the young Shah 'Abbās did not forget the role firearms had played in Safavid defeats at the hands of Ottoman Janissaries or of Janissary-instructed Uzbeks in Khorasan. After the humiliating *'ahidname* of 1590, he bided his time until the Ottomans were fully committed in their war against Habsburg Austria. He then sent forth his well-known mission to the West under the leadership of Anthony Sherley (1599), pushed through important political reforms, better equipped his army with firearms and cannon, and launched an offensive which drove the Ottomans out of the recently conquered Georgian, Turcoman, Armenian, and Kurdish areas (1603).[4] To offset the attacks of the Uzbek allies of the Ottomans in Central Asia, some 15,000 Kurds were settled in Khorasan. Armenian and Georgian opposition to Safavid rule was dealt with by outright massacre or mass deportation to the interior; hence the appearance in Isfahan of a large Armenian community in this era and of Kurds in Khorasan. In conclusion, in the course of Persian-Ottoman relations, the equilibrium or balance of forces of a previous era broke down initially because of structural weaknesses within the Persian state, which sorely tempted the Ottoman "war party" to put an end to a multiplicity of grievances against Persia. Twenty-five years later, the Safavids, having put their house in order, partly by imitating Ottoman models and partly by profiting from Turcoman weaknesses evinced in the Persian Wars, took easy advantage of the overextension of the Ottoman state, which was fighting a civil war at home (the Jelālī rebellion) and a war against the Habsburgs.

7. Somewhat more remotely, we see the first Muscovite strivings for an eastern alliance against the Ottomans and Crimean Tatars and for a share of the lucrative silk, carpet, and other handicraft commerce of the Caucasus and Persia. It is interesting also to note that close upon the advent of Muscovite political interests in the Caucasus (1557), English traders made their debut on the Caspian Sea. The Terek Cossacks, using as a base the friendly Circassians with whom Tsar Ivan IV had earlier contracted a marriage and an alliance, attacked the Ottoman-Tatar supply route to Derbent across the Kuban-Terek steppe. Muscovy also sent some light and heavy arms and other western goods to the Shah of Persia. Herein lay the origins of the three-sided rivalry for control of the Caucasus which henceforth determined the course of history in that region until late in the nineteenth century. During the period of this study, however, Muscovy, thanks to the erratic leadership of Tsar Ivan IV, Grozniy (d. 1584), was approaching its Time of Troubles; hence, most Muscovite activity of the era exhibits a strong commitment to non-involvement and conciliation.[5]

8. To the north of the Black Sea the Crimean Khanate, apart from rendering assistance in the expansion and defense of the Empire, attempted to keep its own buffer elements in line, whether Nogay or Circassian, and to maintain surveillance for the interests of the Ottomans and themselves over the vast expanse of steppe from Bessarabia to the Caucasus. How well the Tatars performed these tasks depended partly on the attitude of the Khans toward Ottoman power and partly on how much the Khans were involved with their own internal and external problems. Meḥemmed Girāy Khan (1577–1584) guarded his own prerogatives jealously and, fearful of Cossack attacks at a time when the Ottomans were heavily committed in Persia, refused to aid the Sultan. Ġāzī Girāy Khan, who had served with the Ottomans in Persia and was therefore more aware of Ottoman capabilities than his predecessor, welcomed Ottoman assistance against his enemies and, in turn, provided almost continual Tatar support for the Ottoman armies in the Hungarian War (1593–1606). One must not underestimate the incredible prestige and morale which the presence of the Tatar Khan lent to the Ottoman fighting forces. Perhaps because of their enormous commitments elsewhere, the Ottomans relied too heavily on the Crimean Khans to police the steppe in the sixteenth century. They may have thereby missed opportunities to keep in touch with Russian methods of conquest and developments in technology —albeit often borrowed from western Europe— which helped to turn the tide against the Muslims on the steppe in the seventeenth century.[6] The Mongol-Tatar methods of controlling the steppe through tribal loyalties and well-disciplined mobile horsemen diminished in importance and effectiveness in the sixteenth century as the settled peoples on the periphery of the steppe developed hand guns that could compete with the accurate Tatar bow, built fortifications of stone, and perfected methods of moving across the steppe

and down the rivers in armored wagons and gunboats. These were the developments that lay behind the destruction of the Nogay tribal power at the end of the sixteenth century and that also helped to make it less and less profitable for the Crimean Tatars to enrich their own marginal pastoral and agricultural economy by raids on border settlements for slaves and booty. But a martial society with limited economic resources must feed on its wealthier neighbors while also living a Spartan existence. Thus the Crimean Khanate remained an important power on the steppe until the time of Peter the Great of Russia.[7]

9. The Polish bid for more equitable terms with the Ottoman Empire between 1588 and 1590 was poorly timed. The Ottomans had just reduced their chief rival, Safavid Persia, to a second-rate power—if only for a short time—and were in no mood to tolerate Cossack attacks or changes in the *status quo* with a Poland which was deeply divided internally after three interregna, and which continued to face the threat of a two-front war with the Austrian Emperor and the Tsar. It is true that Poland, under the able chancellorship of Jan Zamoyski, helped to check Habsburg ambitions in the Balkans and to assert a sphere of influence by means of small-scale military operations in Moldavia during the "Long War," but it was frustrated in its attempts to reach a separate understanding with the Crimean Khan for free access to the Black Sea. The activities of the Zaporozhian Cossacks and the relentless pressure of Slavic agricultural settlements on the steppe continued to disturb amicable relations between Poland-Lithuania and the Ottomans. It is to the Cossack and related questions in the seventeenth century that we must look for an understanding of the Ottoman invasions of Podolia and the steppe by the Köprülü vezirs and the ultimate destruction of the Ottoman-Polish Entente at Vienna in 1683 prior to the dismemberment of Poland in the eighteenth century. Whether or not the Ottomans had chosen to strengthen Poland economically by permitting access to the Black Sea is immaterial; it was the dead hand of the Polish political system and of clerical power, both working against more egalitarian social forces such as the Cossacks, that brought destruction to the Commonwealth.

10. As political events unfolded in sixteenth-century Hungary, we are able to observe an historical development that exhibits similarities to, and possibly historical connections with, the Kïzïlbāş-Jelālī movement of Asia Minor. The Protestant movement in Hungary shows certain similarities because the peasants of Hungary and Transylvania were subjected to the worst exactions and humiliations of any peasantry in Europe at the hands of Hungarian magnates and Roman church prelates.[8] As to the historical connections between Protestant and Unitarian beliefs in Hungary and the Kïzïlbāş beliefs in Asia Minor, one should not forget that peoples living in the mountains of both regions have always fought against religious conformity and political centralization and, consequently, both regions experienced

strong attachment to heterodox Manicheism in early Christian times and to Monophysite and Paulician doctrines in Byzantine times.

When the reforming spirit of the Fifth Lateran Council was deflected toward the preparation of another crusade against the Turks in 1517, Sultan Sulaymān reacted by annexing Belgrade and invading Hungary. Meanwhile, Martin Luther had expressed the disappointment of the reform-minded German bishops by tacking up his Ninety-five Theses, also in 1517, on the door of Wittenberg Cathedral. Soon, the Lutheran and Calvinist doctrines spread rapidly all over Europe. In territories such as Hungary after the Battle of Mohács (1526), the lesser nobility and the peasantry began clearly to see the advantages of joining the new revolutionary movement. By 1550, either Islam or one or another sect of the Protestant Revolution had attracted a majority of the Christians in the Turkish province of Buda (*Budīn Beylerbeyliği*) and the Turkish-protected Transylvania (Erdel). In the era of Isabella, the widow of John Zapolyai, and her son John Sigismund Zapolyai (d. 1571), Protestantism became dominant and Unitarianism became the adopted creed of the prince.

Stephan Báthory, elected Prince of Transylvania in 1571, quietly tried to turn back the clock but he had to be careful not to alienate the support of the Sultan. Moreover, he soon left the scene to become King of Poland. When Stephan's brother Christopher died, he was succeeded by his son, Sigismund Báthory, a mere boy, who was urged into a pro-Habsburg alliance against the wishes of the majority of his subjects and courtiers by Carillo, his Jesuit confessor, and by Stephan Bocskay, his maternal uncle and head of the Transylvanian army. In all the later praise of Bocskay, it is often forgotten that he was chiefly instrumental in initiating the blood bath of Transylvanian nobles, the majority of whom favored neutrality or Ottoman protection in 1594. Bocskay later made a dramatic switch of allegiance in 1604, partly to save his own skin. He did lead the Hungarian revolt, consisting principally of Calvinist nobility and the Haiduks, against the Habsburgs, but he would have failed without the strong support of the Turks. To the end of the Haiduk revolutionary movement, however, the magnates and the lesser nobility, in spite of their Protestant or Unitarian proclivities, refused whenever possible to give any civil rights to the Haiduks and the peasantry. A general peasant revolt against the nobility was averted with difficulty in the second Haiduk rebellion of 1607 and 1608, a rebellion produced when the nobility attempted to circumvent the promises made to the Haiduks and to the towns in the Treaties of Vienna and Szitva-Török. The Pasha of Buda threatened to join forces with the Haiduks in 1607, which caused the nobility to reassure the Haiduk leadership that they would receive the lands promised to them by Bocskay. In 1608 when the revolt looked as if it might lead to the destruction of the nobility, the Ottomans withdrew their support of the Haiduks.[9]

The Ottomans clearly understood the importance of sectarian politics and they supported Protestant causes and leadership whenever possible.

Fischer-Galati ended his study, *Ottoman Imperialism and German Protestantism*, with the Peace of Augsburg. By so doing he recognized that the Ottoman presence impeded Papal-Habsburg intentions of crushing the Protestant Revolution, but he failed to show how closely Ottoman rule in Hungary was related to the good will shown by the Turks to the various Protestant sects. Apparently it was as much the warfare and bitterness among rival Protestant sects as the prowess of Habsburg armies that destroyed the Ottoman position in Hungary in the late seventeenth century.

11. One cannot underestimate the importance of the worldwide "Price Revolution" at the turn of the seventeenth century. Western Europe, with its ready access to New World silver, was siphoning off with high prices any Ottoman grain and other foodstuffs to which merchants could obtain access. Added to this basic factor affecting the flow of bullion, foodstuffs, and luxuries, the Ottomans placed severe strains on their resources with two long wars. Professors Braudel and Barkan have amassed enough data to convince this writer that there was a Mediterranean-wide population rise. Countries farther to the east, notably Persia, were willing to pay an even higher premium than the Ottomans for bullion, either gold or silver. Thus the Ottoman Empire suffered a shortage of bullion, of foodstuffs, and of luxury goods—the latter in particular when Persia interrupted the flow of silk and the English and Dutch obtained control of the spice trade. One must not assume, as have many previous writers, that the Ottomans were totally unaware of these economic problems and their consequences.

It is, of course, not possible to conclude that the wars with Persia and the Habsburgs had narrow objectives such as the control of the silk production in Transcaucasia, the silk traffic from the Far East, the silver mines in Transylvania, or grazing and agricultural rights on the steppe. But it is clear that certain Ottoman factions saw their best interests served by promoting these two wars. It is to be remembered that the Sultans could turn new territories into tīmārs with which to pay troops. New conquests also meant new tribute and new "gifts" from rulers falling within the Ottoman sphere. Ottoman rulers on the eve of the seventeenth century, reminiscent of the plight of 'Abbasid rulers in the tenth century, could not afford patiently to cultivate wealth derived from agriculture and commerce because inflation had made the demands of the military too pressing. The Ġāzī approach to political economy—that is, "take the wealth of thy neighbor,"—was a very appealing political philosophy to those Ottoman leaders who solved their problems by expediency rather than according to the political norms of classical Islamic (Hellenistic) political philosophy, the practical advice of previous vezirs (i.e., *Nasihat* literature), or the "Mirrors for Princes."[10]

12. The numerous revolts noted in Chapter IX are closely connected with the main features of contemporaneous Ottoman life: the size of the corps of salaried troops, estimated at 45,000; the alienation these troops felt because

of the inflation with its effect on their salaries, and the corruption in high places; and finally the sympathy for and yet the uncertainty indicated by the Jelālī revolution. To augment the confusion we are aware that the settled population of the towns of Anatolia were generally the first targets of the revolt. Consequently, refugees by the thousand (government officials, merchants, artisans, Timarlï-Sipāhiyān) flocked to Istanbul to make their grievances known. As for the aims of the rebels, it is also clear that many were so alienated from Ottoman society that they contemplated establishing separate states.[11]

13. Behavioralist scientists have recently found it a useful practice to observe a political system while it is undergoing stress in the belief that the strengths and weaknesses of that system are more readily observable during such periods than at "normal" times. As a working hypothesis this approach might well be applied to the present study, with the likelihood of obtaining interesting results. Between the years 1578 and 1608, the Ottoman Empire participated in two major wars and also experienced a serious civil war and a major inflation. It is hoped that the major areas of stress in Ottoman society resulting from these events have been adequately portrayed. If one takes a parting glance at the decision-making process through the eyes of the behavioralist, one is struck by the changes within the Imperial Household in the interval between the death of Sultan Sulaymān (1566) and the year 1608. When the Sultans finally abandoned the decision making to their vezirs, one may observe that three elements—*intisāb* (client-patron relationship), *akrabalïk* (blood relationship) and *jins* (ethnic ties)—became the determining factors by which powerful men and the women of the harem set up and maintained their circles of power. Within these circles, one finds further concomitants of successful power manipulation: a family member or courtier with ready accessibility to the Sultan and credibility in his eyes; an *'ālim* who can manipulate his fellow 'Ulemā and the *fetva*—legalizing mechanism; a man of military prowess who can manipulate the Janissaries; an individual well versed in state finance; and finally an individual privy to affairs beyond the Ottoman realm.

In spite of such formidable collusion on the part of men in high places, one can also observe the stern measures to which other factions resorted in their struggles for control of the Ottoman system. In such counterploys and *coups d'etat*, rapid execution or murder silenced adversaries in a given "circle of power" before the friends of the victim could arrange for his protection. One is struck by the terrible waste of good men in such a system where men of broad training and experience were, in the best of times, in short supply. Moreover, once the leadership was forced to devote so much time to keeping itself in favor, the sensitive machinery of government, which had once permitted administrative "feedback" and had thus provided a corrective for blatant abuses, could no longer function properly.

As power relationships shifted and readjusted at the top of the system, it is inevitable that corresponding shifts and readjustments took place in the lower echelons. Finally, the peasants, the tribesmen, and the *levendât*, the Ottoman dispossessed[12] on the bottom of the social pyramid, struck back at the system revealing at once the inelasticity of their own misery and the inadequacy of the once great *devşirme* system, now based on privilege rather than merit, to bring men to the top who could deal with sensitive issues such as the Jelālī rebellion, truly an Ottoman civil war.

In fact, the Ottoman leadership clearly dealt more judiciously with problems in Hungary arising out of the Protestant Reformation than they did with problems in Anatolia connected with tribalism, restructuring of the landholding system and the spread of Shi'ism. Even while realizing that virulant tribalism and Shi'ism were not simple problems, one is lead to believe that the Ottoman political elite in this era, because they were primarily recruited from the western Balkans (see the Appendix), had a better understanding of local conditions there than of the quite different conditions prevailing in eastern Asia Minor. While such an observation itself constitutes a serious criticism of the Balkan Christian orientation of much of the *devşirme* recruiting for the Palace School, it is clear that the political leadership was constantly subjected to pressures from other competing elite power blocs which would tend to offset the influence of a childhood spent in the western Balkans.

Whether or not one may agree with these observations, it is clear that social unrest and constant warfare were eroding the Ottoman dream of an ordered Islamic society. The Ottoman elite, acting upon expediency, found it easier to employ its armies to make war upon a neighboring state, in the hope of seizing that country's movable wealth and population, than to create a healthy social environment and to use wisely its own vast physical and human resources. The great Ottoman state, on the eve of the seventeenth century, was slowly being destroyed by the cupidity, venality, and insensitivity of its own ruling classes. To some readers, the seventeenth century may appear to be quite remote from our own twentieth century, but the problems of the Ottoman Empire are typically the problems of all empires and as such, their recognition has special relevance to the dilemmas of our own time.

While it is clear that the Ottoman system had serious failings, it is important to remember that the Ottoman State, typical of all complex systems, was able to re-adjust its internal structure on a number of successive occasions, with or without external pressures, and to survive into the twentieth century. Few multi-national states can match the longevity of the six century old Ottoman Empire.

NOTES

1. Kütükoğlu, *Osmanlı-İran Siyasî Münasebetleri I, 1578–1590*, pp. 1–10; Tveritinova, "K voprosu o krest'yanstve i krest'yanskom zemlepol'zovanii," *Uchenye Zapiski Instituta Vostokovedeniya* XVII (Moscow, 1959), pp. 3–50. The disastrous rigidity of Ottoman religious doctrines may be attributed in part to the influence of one man. See Baysun, "Ebüssu'ûd Efendi," *I.A.*, IV, pp. 92–99.

2. Şapolyo, *Mezhepler ve Tarikatlar Tarihi*, p. 338.

3. Although at this point I cannot quote chapter and verse for this conjecture, owing to the poor state of our knowledge of the Ottoman seventeenth century, there is obviously an underlying similarity between the Shah Kuli, the Kalenderoğlu, the Jelâlî, and the Kara Yazïjï Revolts. See, for example, the details of general importance to this question in Faruk Sümer, "Avşarlar'a Dâir," in O. Turan et al, eds., *Fuad Köprülü Armağanï*, pp. 453–478; J. K. Birge, *The Bektashi Order of Dervishes* (London, 1937), pp. 62–70; Tschudi, "Bektashiyya," *E.I.²*, I, pp. 1161–1163, and Gölpïnarlï, "Kïzïlbaş," *I.A.*, VI, pp. 789–795.

4. For an important fresh viewpoint on the era of Shah 'Abbās, see the article by R. M. Savory, "The Sherley Myth" in *Iran*, V (1967), pp. 73–82.

5. Please consult Chapter X for further details. An interesting recent study summarizes the exploits of the Sherley family: Davies, *Elizabethans Errant* (Ithaca, 1967). There is also the apologia of one of the Persians who took part in the embassy to Europe: G. Le Strange, ed., *Don Juan of Persia, a Shi'ah Catholic* (London, 1926).

6. See Esper, "Military Self-Sufficiency and Weapons Technology in Muscovite Russia," *Slavic Review*, 38/2 (June 1969), pp. 185–208, for an important discussion of weapons technology during the period of this study.

7. Please consult Chapter X and the previously cited conclusion of A. A. Novosel'skiy, *Bor'ba Moskovskoğo Gosudarstva s Tatarami v pervoy polovine xvii veka*.

8. These facts are well documented in Hungarian and Ottoman sources but are, quite understandably, touched upon lightly in Austrian and other West European sources.

9. See especially the article by K. Benda, "Der Haiduken Aufstand in Hungarn . . . ," in D. Csatári, *et al.*, eds., *Nouvelles études historiques*, pp. 299–313.

10. See Appendix, Pl. VIII, the wheel of justice of Kïnalïzade Ali, *Aḫlāḳ-ï 'Alāyï*, Book III, p. 49; and Luṭfi Pasha, *Âsafnâme, passim*.

11. See especially Baysun, "Ahmed I," *I.A.*, I, pp. 161–164; Orhonlu, "Murad Paşa, Kuyucu," *I.A.*, VIII, pp. 651–654.

12. Uzunçarşïlï, "Levend," *I.A.*, VIII, pp. 46–48. The levendât (sing., levend) often served as troops in the entourage of local Pashas and Beys. Almost equally often they roved in bands throughout much of Asia Minor, looting and pillaging wherever they met little resistance. They often appear to be members of the dispossessed classes, *Timarlï* and others, and hence are a class homologous to the Hayduks of Hungary.

	Edibles: Beverages, Fruit & Vegetables	Slaves	Draft and Service Animals	Cereals	Meat, Fish, Edible Oils, Fats (Includ. Milk Products)	Fibers, Furs, & Hides	Minerals, Chemicals, & Dyes	Naval Stores & Construction Timber, Firewood	Combustibles (petroleum, wax, tallow, etc.)	Crafts, Manufactures
Balkan Peninsula	wine raisins honey	slaves (*devşirme*)	draft horses cavalry mounts oxen donkeys	chiefly: barley wheat rye rice	cheese dried & salt fish meat: mutton beef goat	hides furs wool (high quality)	Fe Au Ag Cu Pb	firewood charcoal timber building stone	wax tallow	shipyards mining weaving metalwork etc. (Istanbul, the center)
Kipchak Steppe & the Crimea	wine fruit vegetables honey	slaves (from raiding)	cavalry mounts	millet wheat	butter cheese salt fish caviar olive oil	wool flax furs hides	salt		wax (best) tallow	salt mining food processing wineries
The Caucasus	wine figs hazelnuts honey tea(?)	slaves (mostly from trading)	falcons	millet rice wheat	butter cheese fish *raugan*	furs hides wool cotton flax silk	Ag Fe Au Sb Pb saffran kermes alum	boxwood	wax petroleum (Baku region)	metalwork silkworms mining petroleum carpets
Asia Minor	fruit wine *nardenk* nuts vegetables spices	slaves (few, highly selective, *devşirme*)	draft horses cavalry mounts oxen donkeys camels	wheat rice	dried fish butter cheese	wool cotton flax silk hides	Ag Cu Pb Fe saltpetre	boxwood oak walnut plane fir naval stores charcoal	tallow	carpets *basma* linens silks woolens mohair (*tiftik*) mining smelting shipyards

I RESOURCES OF THE BLACK SEA LITTORAL BY REGION // SIXTEENTH CENTURY

II OTTOMAN LEADERSHIP DURING THE REIGN OF SULTAN MURĀD III (b. 1546) 1574–1595

Mother Nūr Banu (Venetian) (Esther Kira, influential Jewess in Harem)
Wife Sāfiye (Albanian)
Favorite Jān Fedā, etc.
Preceptor Sa'deddin

Other Court Influences

Kara Üveys—Defterdār Bākī, poet and kadi'asker.
Gażānfer—Kapî Ağasî (Hungarian)
Bostānzāde Meḥemmed—Şeyẖ ül-Islām (1589–1592, 1593–1598)
Ġāzī Girāy—Khan of the Crimea (1588–1596, 1596–1608)
Edward Barton—English Ambassador (d. 1598)
Şemsi Aḥmed Pasha—Musâhip
Dervīş Ḥasan—Musâhip, protégé of Siyavüş
Doğānjî Meḥmet Pasha, Musâhip

Grand Vezirs

1565–1579 (d. Oct. 12)		Sōḳollū Meḥemmed (Bosnian); wife, Ismahān, sister of Murad III
Oct. 1579–Apr. 1580		Semiz Aḥmed (Albanian); wife, 'Ayşe, granddaughter of Sulaymān
Apr. 1580–Aug. 1580		Lālā Musṭafa (Bosnian); wife, Hüma, granddaughter of Sulaymān; Lālā to Selīm II; victor of Cyprus and Georgia; Elder Brother Deli Hüsrev Pasha; called "Vekil-i Sultanat"
Aug. 1580–Dec. 1582	(1st x)	Kojā Sinān (Albanian) (Victor of Yemen and Tunis); aided by his brother Ayas Pasha
Dec. 1582–July 1584	(1st x)	Kanijeli Siyāvüş (Croat); wife, Fatma, sister of Murād III (d. 1580)
July 1584–Oct. 1585		Özdemiroğlu 'Osmān (Circassian)—commander and victor of Yemen and Shirvan, his father a famous Pasha in Yemen and Sudan
Dec. 1585–Apr. 1586		Ḫādim Mesīḥ
Apr. 1586–Apr. 1589	(2nd x)	Kanijeli Siyāvüş
Apr. 1589–Aug. 1591	(2nd x)	Kojā Sinān
Aug. 1591–Apr. 1592	(1st x)	Ferhād (Albanian)—commander and victor in Persia
Apr. 1592–Jan. 1593	(3rd x)	Kanijeli Siyāvüş
Jan. 1593–Feb. 1595	(3rd x)	Kojā Sinān

Other Commanders

Kîlîç 'Alī Pasha (Calabrian), Kapūdān Pasha

III OTTOMAN LEADERSHIP DURING THE REIGN OF SULTAN MEḤEMMED III (b. 1566) 1595–1603

Mother Sāfiye (Albanian) (Esther Kira)
Wife Hândan
Preceptor Sa'deddin; Bāḳī, the famous poet

Other Court Influences

Sun'ullah—Seyh ül-Islām
'Osman Ağa—Kîzlar Ağasî
Edward Barton, English Ambassador
Gazānfer—Kapî Ağasî
Ġāzī Girāy, Khan of the Crimea
Sulaymān Ağa, Çavūş Başî
Solomon Ashkenazi—Physician

Grand Vezirs

to Feb. 1595	(3rd x)	Kojā Sinān
Feb.–July 1595	(2nd x)	Ferhād
July–Nov. 1595	(4th x)	Kojā Sinān
Nov. 1595		Lālā Meḥemmed (d.) (Türk); wife, wet nurse of Meḥemmed III; Lālā to Meḥemmed III
Dec. 1595–Apr. 1596	(5th x)	Kojā Sinān
Apr.–Oct. 1596	(1st x)	Damād Ibrahīm (Bosnian); wife, 'Ayşe, daughter of Murad III
Oct.–Dec. 1596		Jigālāzāde Sinān (Genoese); wives, great granddaughters of Sulaymān
Dec. 1596–Nov. 1597	(2nd x)	Damād Ibrahīm
Nov. 1597–Apr. 1598		Ḫādim Ḥasān (Albanian), "Mürteşi"
Apr. 1598–Jan. 1599		Jerrāh Meḥemmed; wife, a sister of Murād III; surgeon at circumcision of Meḥemmed III
Jan. 1599–July 1601	(3rd x)	Damād Ibrahīm
July 1601–Oct. 1603		Yemişçi Hasān (Albanian); wife, 'Ayşe, widow of Ibrahīm; protégé of Kojā Sinān
Oct. 1603–July 1604		Yavūz (Malkōç) 'Alī (Bosnian), his uncle, Janissary Ağa, Sāliḥ.

Other Commanders

Sātūrjī Meḥemmed (Albanian), Serdār of Hungarian Front
Turnakçi Ḥasān
Tiryāki Ḥasān, Defender of Kanizsa; wife, sister of Aḥmed I
Halīl (Italian, Paggi), 1st husband of Faṭma, sister of Meḥemmed III, Kapūdān Pasha.

IV OTTOMAN LEADERSHIP DURING THE REIGN OF SULTAN AHMET I (b. 1590?) 1603–1617

Mother H̲āndān
Wives Mahfirūz and Mahpeyker
Preceptor Dervīş Meḥmet, Bostānjî Başî; later, Mustafa Efendi

Other Court Influences

Sun'ullah—Şeyh̲ ül-Islām; Nef 'ī, the famous poet

Grand Vezirs

Oct. 1603–July 1604	Yavūz (Malkōç) 'Alī (Bosnian)
Aug. 1604–June 1606	Lālā Meḥemmed (Bosnian), a preceptor of Meḥemmed III
June–Dec. 1606	Dervīş (Bosnian)—as Bostanjî Başî, befriended by Vālide Sulṭān, H̲āndān
Dec. 1606–Aug. 1611	Kuyuju Murād (Croat)
Aug. 1611–Oct. 1614	Nasuh Paşa (Albanian); wife, sister of Aḥmed I
Oct. 1614–Nov. 1616	Öküz Meḥmed (Türk); wife, daughter of Aḥmed I
Nov. 1616–	Halīl (Armenian), brother to musâhip of Murād III

V DYNASTIC AND ETHNIC INFLUENCE IN THE GRAND VEZIRATE 1574–1617

Sultan	Length of Rule	Grand Vezirs (by Nationality)	Proportion Married to Women of Dynasty
Murad III (Dec. 22, 1574–Jan. 16, 1595)	20 yrs., 1 mo. (Grand Vezir changed eleven times)	Bosnian-Croatian (11 yrs.) Albanian (7 years.) Circassian (1 1/2 yrs.) Unknown (6 mo.)	50 per cent.
Meḥemmed III (Jan. 27, 1595–Dec. 22, 1603)	8 yrs., 11 mo. (Grand Vezir changed twelve times)	Bosnian (4 yrs.) Albanian (3 yrs., 10 mo.) Türk (1 mo.) Sicilian (2 mo.) Unknown (9 mo.)	55 per cent.
Aḥmed I (Dec. 21, 1603–Nov. 22, 1617)	11 yrs., 11 mo. (Grand Vezir changed six times)	Bosnian-Croatian (6 yrs., 10 mo.) Albanian (3 yrs., 2 mo.) Türk (2 yrs., 1 mo.) Armenian (1 yr., 1 mo.)	29 per cent.* *the Sultan was too young to have sisters and daughters of a marriagable age.
Totals	40 yrs., 11 mo.	Total Slav (21 yrs., 10 mo.) Total Albanian (14 yrs.) Other (4 yrs., 7 mo.)	

VI THE HOUSES OF ZAPOLYAI AND BATHORY IN THE LATE SIXTEENTH CENTURY

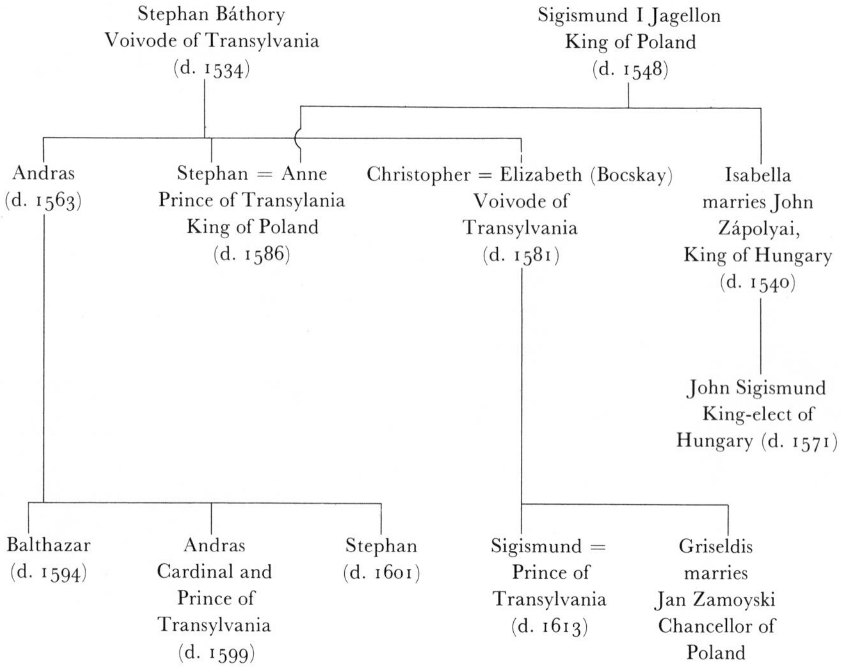

(After Makkai)

VII THE LINE OF DEVLET GIRĀY

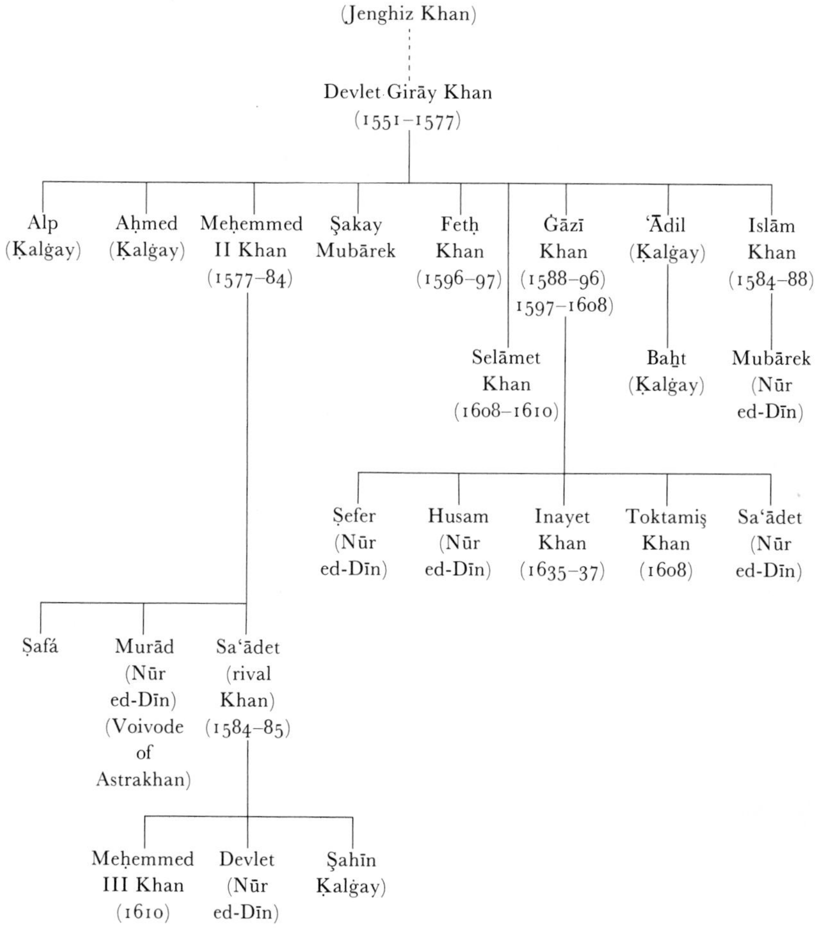

H. Inalcïk, "Giray," Islam Ansiklopedisi, IV, p. 788
[Ṣafā Girāy is an addition, not]
found in *I.A.*

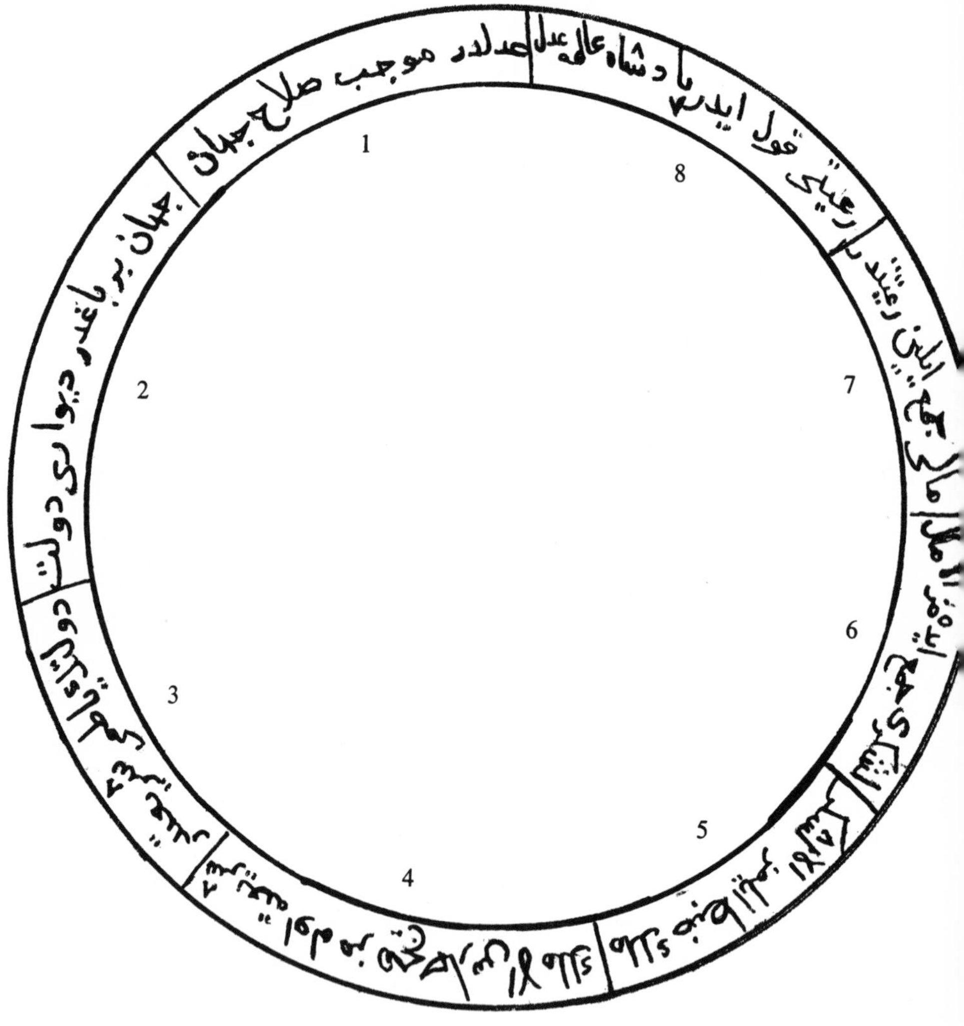

VIII

1. Justice is necessary for the righteousness of the world.
2. The world is a garden, the mainstay of the state.
3. The *Shari'ah* (the Holy Law) is the regulator of the state.
4. No one can be vigilant for the *Shari'ah* save the ruler.
5. The ruler cannot govern without troops.
6. He cannot muster troops without wealth.
7. It is the *Ra'iyah* (subjects) who produce the wealth.
8. Justice calls forth the allegiance of the *Ra'iyah* to the Lord of the World.

IX THE ISLAMIC-OTTOMAN SOCIAL STRUCTURE (SIMPLIFIED)

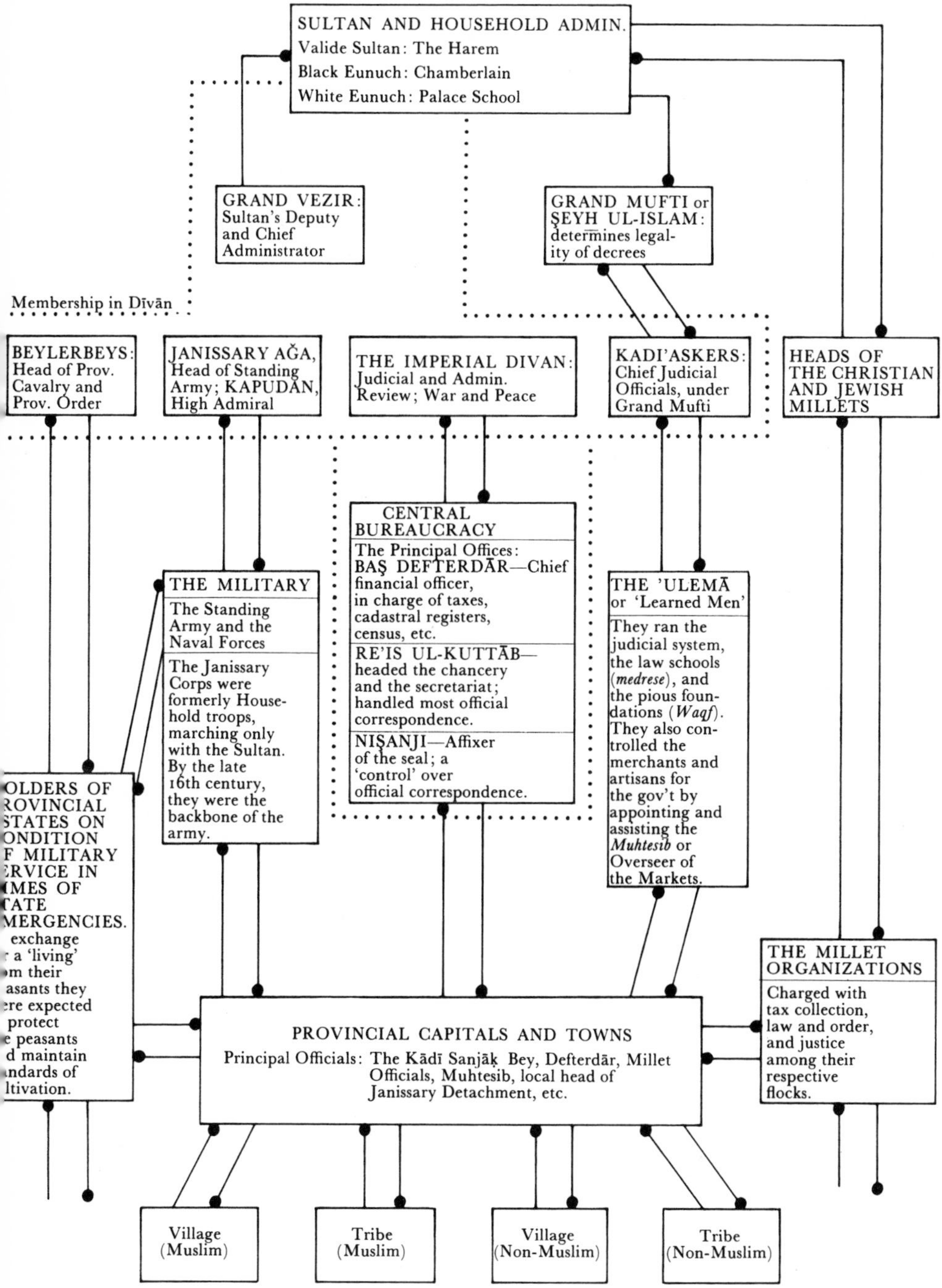
SULTAN AND HOUSEHOLD ADMIN.
Valide Sultan: The Harem
Black Eunuch: Chamberlain
White Eunuch: Palace School
GRAND VEZIR: Sultan's Deputy and Chief Administrator
GRAND MUFTI or ŞEYH UL-ISLAM: determines legality of decrees
Membership in Dīvān
BEYLERBEYS: Head of Prov. Cavalry and Prov. Order
JANISSARY AĞA, Head of Standing Army; KAPUDAN, High Admiral
THE IMPERIAL DIVAN: Judicial and Admin. Review; War and Peace
KADI'ASKERS: Chief Judicial Officials, under Grand Mufti
HEADS OF THE CHRISTIAN AND JEWISH MILLETS
CENTRAL BUREAUCRACY
The Principal Offices: BAŞ DEFTERDĀR—Chief financial officer, in charge of taxes, cadastral registers, census, etc.
RE'IS UL-KUTTĀB—headed the chancery and the secretariat; handled most official correspondence.
NIŞANJI—Affixer of the seal; a 'control' over official correspondence.
THE MILITARY
The Standing Army and the Naval Forces
The Janissary Corps were formerly Household troops, marching only with the Sultan. By the late 16th century, they were the backbone of the army.
THE 'ULEMĀ or 'Learned Men'
They ran the judicial system, the law schools (medrese), and the pious foundations (Waqf). They also controlled the merchants and artisans for the gov't by appointing and assisting the Muhtesib or Overseer of the Markets.
OLDERS OF ROVINCIAL STATES ON ONDITION F MILITARY ERVICE IN IMES OF TATE MERGENCIES. exchange a 'living' m their asants they re expected protect e peasants d maintain ndards of ltivation.
THE MILLET ORGANIZATIONS
Charged with tax collection, law and order, and justice among their respective flocks.
PROVINCIAL CAPITALS AND TOWNS
Principal Officials: The Kādī Sanjāķ Bey, Defterdār, Millet Officials, Muhtesib, local head of Janissary Detachment, etc.
Village (Muslim)
Tribe (Muslim)
Village (Non-Muslim)
Tribe (Non-Muslim)

Bibliography

I PRIMARY SOURCE MATERIALS

Note: Authors are listed alphabetically according to their best-known name.

'Abd al-Ġaffar, N. 'Aṣim, ed., *'Umdet al-Aḫbār*, in *Türk Tarih Enjümeni Mejmu'así* (*T.T.E.M.*), No. 85, Suppl. 2(1343/1924–1925), pp. 1–207.

Abrahamowicz, Zygmunt, *Katalog Rekopisow Orientalnych Za Zbiorow Polskich*, Vol. I, *Katalog Dokumentow Tureckich . . . 1455–1672* (Warsaw, 1959).

Alberi, E. ed., *Le Relazioni degli Ambasciatori Veneti al Senato durante il secolo decimosesto*, Ser. III/ Vols. I-III (Florence, 1839–1863).

'Ali, Muṣṭafa bin Aḥmed, *Nuṣratnāme*, London, British Museum, Ms. Add. 22,011.

Andreyevsky, E., ed., "Novgorodka," *Entsiklopedicheskiy Slovar'* (St. Petersburg, 1897) XXI, p. 235.

Archivum Jana Zamoyskiego (Cracow, 1904 . . . 1949), 4 vols.

Barozzi, N., and Berchet, G., *Le Relazioni degli Stati Europei lette al Senato degli Ambasciatori Veneti nel secolo decimo settimo*, Ser. V, pts. 1–2 (Venice, 1856–1878).

Basta: See Veress.

Behrnauer, W. F. A., tr. of Koçu Bey's *Risâle*, "Kogábeg's Abhandlung über den Verfall des osmanischen Staatsgebäudes seit Sultan Suleiman dem Grossen," *Zeitschrift der deutschen morgenländischen Gesellschaft*, Vol. XV (1861).

Belokurov, S. A., *Snosheniya Rossii s Kavkazom, 1578–1613* (Moscow, 1889).

Berchet, G., *La Repubblica di Venezia e la Persia* (Torino, 1865).

Bestyzhev-Ryumin, K. N., ed., "Pamyatniki Diplomaticheskago Snoshenii Moskovskago Gosudarstva s Angliey 1581–1604," *Sbornik Imperatorskago Russkago Istoricheskago Obshchestva*, Vol. 38 (1883), pp. 1–443.

Bronowski (Bronovius, Broniowski), Marcin (Martin), "Collections out of Martin Broniovius," Samuel Purchas, ed., *Purchas his Pilgrims*, XIII (Glasgow, 1906), pp. 461–491.

——— "Opisanie Kryma (Tartariae Descriptio)," *Zapiski Odesskago Obshchestva Istorii i Drevnostey*, Vol. VI (Odessa, 1867), pp. 333–367.

Bruce (Brussius), William, *De Tartaris diarium* (Frankfurt a/M, 1598).

Burian, O., "Bozuk Idareden Şikayetçi iki Şair," *Ankara Üniversitesi Dil ve Tarih-Coğrafya Fakültesi Dergisi*, VIII/4 (1950), pp. 675–681.

——— ed., *The Report of Lello*, Ankara Üniversitesi Dil ve Tarih-Coğrafya Fakültesi Yayïnlarï No. 83 (Ankara, 1952).

Burrough, Christopher, "Advertisements and Reports of the 6th voyage into parts of Persia and

Media . . . ," Richard Hakluyt, ed., *The Principal Navigations, Voyages, Traffiques and Discoveries of the English Nation*, III (Glasgow, 1903), pp. 214–248.
Calendar of State Papers, Great Britain, edited by A. J. Butler, S. C. Lomas, A. B. Hinds and R. B. Wernham, Vols. VIII–XXIII (London, 1901–1950).
Charrière, E., *Négociations de la France dans le Levant* 4 vols. (Paris, 1848–1860).
C.S.P.: See Calendar of State Papers.
Cotton Manuscript, British Museum, Nero B XI.
Da Lucca, Giovanni, "Relation des Tatars, Perecopites et Nogaies, des Circassians, Mingrelians, et Georgiens," in *Relations de Divers Voyages Curieux*, Part I (Paris, 1663), pp. 14–30.
Decsi, János, *Magyar Historiaja* (*De Rebus ungaricus*) *1592–1598*, in *Monumenta Hungariae Historica, Scriptores*, Vol. XVII (Pest, 1866).
Derzhavin, O. A., ed., *Vremennik Ivana Timofeeva* (Moscow-Leningrad, 1951).
——— and Kolosova, E. V., eds., *Skazanie Avraamiya Palitsyna* (Moscow-Leningrad, 1955).
Dilich, Wilhelm, *Ungarische Chronica* (Cassel, 1609).
Don Juan of Persia: See Le Strange.
Dorev, P., ed., *Dokumenti za Bulgarskata Istoriya*, III/ Vol. I, *Dokumenti iz Turskite Derzhavni Arkhivi* (Sofia, 1940).
Estienne, Henry, *The Frankfort Book Fair*, J. W. Thompson, ed. (Chicago, 1911).
Evliya Çelebi, *Narrative of Travels in Europe, Asia, and Africa in the Seventeenth Century*, tr. by Joseph von Hammer, 2 vols. (London, 1846).
———, *Seyāhatnāme*, vols. II and III (Istanbul, 1341/1896–1897).
Ferīdūn. Aḥmed, *Munşe'āt es-Selāṭīn*, 2 vols. (Istanbul, 1264–1265/1848).
Fletcher, Giles, *Of the Russe Common Wealth*, Hakluyt Society, ed. (London, 1856).
Francus, Jacobus, *Relatio Historica Quinquennalis . . . von Anno 1590 bis 1595* (Frankfurt a/M, 1596).
Gerlach, S., *Dess Aeltern Tagebuch* (Frankfurt a/M, 1674).
Göllner, Carl, *Michael der Tapferer im Lichte des Abendlandes* (Hermannstadt, 1943).
Gontaut-Biron, J. de, Baron de Salignac, "Ambassade en Turquie, 1605 à 1610," *Archive historique de la Gascogne* (publié par la Comité d'Histoire et d'Archeologie de la Province ecclésiatique d'Auch), 2 vols. (Paris, 1888–1889), Fascs. 16, 19–20.
Gooss, R., ed., *Österreichische Staatsverträge Fürstentum Siebenbürgen*, Veröff. der Kom. für neu. Geschicht Österreiches, vol. IX (Vienna, 1911).
Govvea, Antonio de, *Relation des guerres et victoires obtenues par le roy de Perse Cha Abbas* . . . (Rouen, 1646).
Ḥalīm Girāy, *Gülbün-ü Ḫānān* (Istanbul, 1327/1909).
———, *Gülbün-ü Ḫānān*, British Museum, Or. Ms. 11, 164.
Hasanbeyzāde, Ahmed, *Tārīh-i Al-i 'Os̱mān*, Istanbul, Nūr-u 'Osmaniye Mss. 3105/3106.
Heidenstein, Reinhold, *Rerum Polonicarum ab excessu Sigismundi Augusti Libri XII* (Frankfurt a/M, 1672).
———, *Vitae Joannis Zamoyscii* (Posnan, 1861).
Hurmuzaki, E. de, ed., *Documente privitóre la Istoria Romanilor*, 19 vols. (Bucharest, 1876–1922).
Iorga, N., ed., *Les Voyageurs français dans l'Orient européen* (Paris, 1929).
———, ed., *Documente privitōre la Istoria Romanilor*, Suppl. I (Bucharest, 1886).
Iskānder Beg, Munşī, *Tariḫ-e 'Alām Arāye 'Ābāsī*, 2 vols. (Teheran, 1335).
Isthvanfi, Nicolaus, *Nicolai Isthvanfi Pannoni Historiarum de Rebus Ungaricus Libri XXXIV* (Cologne, 1622).
Jenkinson, A., "A compendious and brief declaration of the journey of M. Anthony Jenkinson," R. Hakluyt, ed., *The Principal Navigations, Voyages, Traffiques, and Discoveries of the English Nation*, III (Glasgow, 1903), pp. 15–38.
Karamsin, M., *Histoire de l'Empire de Russie*, 11 vols. (Paris, 1826).
Károlyi, Arpád, "Fráter György Levelezése . . . ," in *Terténelmi Tár* (Budapest, 1881).
Kâtib Çelebī, Muṣṭafa bin 'Abdullah, Ḫajjī Ḫalfa, *Fezleke-i Kâtib Çelebī*, 2 vols. (Istanbul, 1286–1287/1869–1870).

Kazimirski, M., ed., "Précis de l'Histoire des Khans de Crimée . . . ," *Journal Asiatique*, 2nd Ser., XII (1833), pp. 349–428.

Kïnalïzade, 'Alī, *Aḫlāḳ-i Alāyi* (Bulaḳ, 1248/1832–1833).

Knolles, Richard, *General Historie of the Turkes from the first beginning of that Nation* (London, 1603).

Kritovoulos, *History of Mehmed the Conqueror*, C. T. Riggs, ed. and tr. (Princeton, 1954).

Kumykov, T. Kh, and Kusheva, E. N., eds., *Kabardino-Russkie Otnosheniya v xvi–xviii vv.*, 2 vols. (Moscow, 1957).

Kusheva, E. N., *Narodny Severno-Kavkaza i ix Svazi c Rossiey v xvi–xvii vv.* (Moscow, 1963).

Lamberti, P., *Relatione della Cholchide Hoggi detta Mengrellia* . . . (Naples, 1654).

Lashkov, Th., *Pamyatniki diplomaticheskikh Snosheniy Krymskago Khanstva s Moskovskim Gosudarstvom v xvi i xvii vv.* (Simferopol', 1891).

Lassota, von Steblau, Erich: see Schottin.

Le Strange, Guy, ed. and tr., *Don Juan of Persia, a Shi'ah Catholic* (London, 1926).

Leunclavius: see Löwenklau.

Löwenklau, Hans (Leunclavius), *Neue Chronika türkischer Nation* (Frankfurt a/M, 1591).

Luḳmān bin Seyyid Ḥusayn, *Mujmīl at-Tūmār*, British Museum ms. no. Or. 1135.

Luṭfī Pasha, *Âṣafnāme* (Istanbul, 1326/1895–1896).

Lykhachev, D. S., ed., *Puteshestviya Russkikh Poslov xvi–xvii vv.* (Moscow, 1954).

Malcolm, J., *The History of Persia*, 2 vols. (London, 1815).

Margèrét, Jacques, *Estat de l'Empire de Russie et Grande Duchie de Moscovie* (Paris, 1607).

Meḥemmed Rižā, *Es-Seb' es-Seyyār fī Aḫbār Mulūk at-Tātār*, A. Kazembeg, ed. (Kazan, 1832).

Minadoi, G. T., *Historia della Guerra fra Turchi, et Persiani* . . . (Venice, 1588).

Minorsky, V., ed., *Tadhkirat al-Mulūk*, Gibb Memorial Series, N. S. XVI (London, 1943).

Mühimme Defterleri; Baş̧ Vekâlet Arşivleri (the series on "Important Documents," located in the Ottoman Archives of Istanbul).

Munejjimbāşī, Aḥmed bin Luṭfullah, *Ṣaḥā'if al-Aḫbār*, 3 vols. (Istanbul, 1285/ 1868–1869).

Na'īmā, Muṣṭafa, *Tārīḫ-i Na'īmā*, 6 vols. (Istanbul, 1280–1283/ 1863–1867).

Obolenskiy, M. A., ed., *Novyy Letopisets* (Moscow, 1853).

Ocherki po Istorii zapadnoy Rusi i Ukrainy (Kiev, 1916).

Ortelius, Hieronymus, *Chronologia oder Historische Beschreibung . . . so in Ober und Under Ungarn auch Siebenburgen mit dem Turcken von Ao. 1395 biss auff gegenwartige Zeitt* . . . (Nürnberg, 1602).

Öztelli, Cahit, *Karacaoğlan, Hayatī, Sanatī, Şiirleri* (Istanbul, 1952).

Palitsyn: see Derzhavin and Kolosova.

Pamyatniki Diplomaticheskikh Snosheniy Drevnoy Rossii s Derzhavami Inoṣtrannymi 1488–1699, 10 vols. (St. Petersburg, 1851–1871).

Peçewī (Peçevī), Ibrāhīm, *Tārīḫ-i Peçewī*, 2 vols. (Istanbul, 1281–1283/1864–1867).

Platonov, S. Th., ed., "Pamyatniki Diplomaticheskikh Snosheniy Moskovskago Gosudarstva s Pol'sko-Litovskim, 1598–1608," *Sbornik Imperatorskago Russ. Istor. Obshchestva*, vol. 137 (1912), pp. 1–736.

Polo, Marco, *Marco Polo da Venice sia de la meranegliose cose del Mundo* (Venice, 1496).

Pulaski, Casimir, "Trzy poselstwa Lawryna Piaseczinskiego do Kazi Gireja Hana Tatarow (1601–1603)," *Przewodnik naukowy i literacki* (Lvov, 1911), pp. 135–960, *passim.*

Refik, Ahmet, *Anodoluda Türk Aşiretleri* (Istanbul, 1930).

———, *Türk Idaresinde Bulgaristan* (Istanbul, 1933).

"Relatione de Perse," *Le Trésor Politique* (Paris, 1611).

Reusner, N., *Epistolae Turcicae* (Lemberg, 1595?).

Romaci, F. (?), ed., *La Terza Parte del Tesero Politico* (Turino, 1605).

Salamon, Franz, *Ungarn im Zeitalter der Türkenherrschaft* (Leipzig, 1887).

Sanuto, Marino, *I Diarii XXV* (Venice, 1889).

Savary de Brèves, François, "Discours abrége des tartares . . . ," *Recueil Historique* (Paris, 1666), pp. 101–145.

———, *Relation des Voyages* (Paris, 1628).
Schottin, R., ed., *Tagebuch des Erich Lassota von Steblau* (Halle, 1866).
Scriptores Rerum Polonicarum, 22 vols. (Cracow, 1872–1917).
Selānīkī, Muṣṭafa, *Tārīḫ-i Selānīkī* (Istanbul, 1281/ 1864–1865).
Şeref, 'Abd ur-Raḥmān, "Özdemīroğlū 'O̱smān Pāşā," *Tārīḫ-i 'O̱smānī Enjumenî Mejmu'asī* (*T.O.E.M.*) IV/21–24 and V/25 (Istanbul, 1913–1914).
Sīdī 'Ali Re'īs, *Mir'at al-Memālik*: see Vambery.
Smith, John, Captain, *Travels in Europe, Asia, Africa and America* (London, 1630).
Ṣōlāḳzāde, *Tārīḫ* (Istanbul, 1297/1879–1880).
Solov'ëv, S. M., *Istoriya Rossii*, vols, VII and VIII (Moscow, 1960).
Soranzo, Lazaro, *L'Ottomano* (Venice, 1598).
Taranowski, Jedrzej, "Podrozei Poselstwa Polskie do Turcyi," *Biblioteka Polska*, Part 9 (Warsaw, 1860), pp. 42–63.
Tarnowski, A., *Dzialanosc Gospodarcza Jana Zamoyskiego, Kanclerza i Hetmana w. Kor.* (*1572-1605*) (Lvov, 1935).
Tavernier, J. B., *Les Six Voyages . . . en Turquie en Perse et aux Indes*, 2 vols. (Paris, 1676).
Tectander, Georg, *Iter Persicum* (Altenburg-Meissen, 1609).
Timofeev: see Derzhavin.
Tocilescu, G. G., and Odobescu, A. J., eds., *Documente privitóre la Istoria Romanilor*, Suppl. II (Bucharest, 1893, 1895), 2 vols.
T.O.E.M.: see Şeref.
T.T.E.M.: see 'Abd al-Ġaffār.
Trésor politique, Le (Paris, 1611).
Urechi, G., *Chronique de Moldavie depuis le milieu du xiv*[e] *siècle jusqu'a 1594*, E. Picot, ed., Public. de l'École des Langues orientales vivantes, Ser. 1, vol. 9 (Paris, 1878).
Vambery, A., ed. and tr., *The Travels and Adventures of the Turkish Admiral Sidi Ali Reis in India, Afghanistan, Central Asia, and Persia during the years 1553–1556* (London, 1899).
Velyaminov-Zernov, V., *Materiali dlya Istorii Krymskago Khanstva* (St. Petersburg, 1864).
Ventura, C., ed., *Thesoro Politico* (Cologne, 1589).
Veress, A., ed., *Documente Privitoare la Istoria Archealului, Moldavei şi Tarii Romaneşti, Acte şi Scrisori*, vols. I–VIII (1580–1613) (Bucharest, 1932–1935).
———, ed., *Epistolae et Acta Generalis Georgii Basta* (1597–1607), in *Monumenta Hungariae Historica*, Diplomataria, Vol. XXXIV (Budapest, 1909).
———, ed., *Fontes Rerum Transylvanicarum*, 5 vols. (Budapest, 1911–1921).
Vesselovskiy, N. I., ed., "Pamyatniki Diplomaticheskikh i Torgovlennykh Snosheniy Moskovskoy Rusi s Persiey," *Trudy Vostochnago Otdeleniya Imperatorskago Russkago Arkheologicheskago Obshchestva*, vols. XX–XXI (St. Petersburg, 1890–1892).
Vraye Relation de la Route et Deffaicte des Tartares et Turcs (Lyon, 1590).
Zamoyski, Jan, *De Transitu Tartarorum per Pocutiam, Anni M.D. XCIIII* (Danzig, 1595).
———, see also *Archivum* and Heidenstein.

II SECONDARY SOURCE MATERIALS

Akdağ, Mustafa, "Celâlî Isyanlarïnïn Başlamasï (Der Beginn de Celaliden Aufstaende)," *Ankara Üniversitesi Dil ve Tarih-Coğrafya Fakültesi Dergisi* IV (1953), 23–50.
Aktepe, M. Münir, "Naima Tarihi'nin Yazma Nushalarï Hakkïnda," *Tarih Dergisi* I (1949), 35–52.

Alderson, A. D., *The Structure of the Ottoman Dynasty* (Oxford, 1956).
Allen, W. E. D., *A History of the Georgian People* (London, 1932).
———, "Notes on Don Juan of Persia's Account of Georgia," *B.S.O.S.* (now *B.S.O.A.S.*, VI (1930–1932), 179–186.
———, *Problems of Turkish Power in the Sixteenth Century* (London, 1963).
Anhegger, R., *Beiträge zur Geschichte des Bergbaus im osmanischen Reich*, 2 vols. (Istanbul, 1943–1945).
Ayalon, D., "The European-Asiatic Steppes: a Major Reservoir of Power for the Islamic World," *Trudy XXV Mezhdunarodnogo Kongressa Vostokovedov* (Proceedings of the 25th International Congress of Orientalists), II (Moscow, 1963), 47–52.
Babinger, Franz, *Die Geschichtsschreiber der Osmanen und Ihre Werke* (Leipzig, 1927).
Bartholomew, J., ed., *The Times' Atlas of the World*, vols. II (1959) and IV (1956).
Bartoszewicz, J., *Poglad na Stosunki Polski z Turcya i Tatarami* (Warsaw, 1860).
Baysun, M. Cavid, "Hasanbegzade Ahmed Paşa," *Türkiyat Mecmuasï* X (1953), pp. 321–340.
Beldiceanu, N., *Les Actes des premiers Sultans*, École pratique des hautes Études, VIe section, Documents et Recherches, III, 2 vols. (Paris, 1960 & 1964).
———, "La crise monètaire ottomane au xvie siècle et son influence sur les principautés roumaines," *Südost-Forschungen* XVI (1957), pp. 70–86.
Bellan, L. L., *Chah 'Abbas I, Les Grandes Figures de l'Orient*, Vol. III (Paris, 1932).
Benda, Kalman, *Bocskai István, 1557–1606* (Budapest, 1942).
———, "Der Haiduken Aufstand in Hungarn . . . ," in D. Csatári *et al.*, eds., *Nouvelles études historiques*, Vol. I (Budapest, 1965), pp. 299–313.
Bertha, A. de, *Magyars et Roumains devant l'Histoire* (Paris, 1899).
Betts, R. R., "The Reformation in Difficulties: Poland, Hungary and Bohemia," *New Cambridge Modern History* II (London, 1958), pp. 186–209.
Biaudet, H., "Les Origines de la candidature de Sigismund Vasa au trône de Pologne en 1587," *Annales Academiae Scientiarum Fennicae*, Ser. B, II/10 (Helsinki, 1910), pp. 1–82.
Birge, J. K., *The Bektashi Order of Dervishes* (London, 1937).
Blum, J., "The Rise of Serfdom in Eastern Europe," *American Historical Review* LXII/4 (July, 1957), pp. 807–836.
Braudel, F., *La Méditerranée et le Monde méditeranéen à la Époque de Philippe II* (Paris, 1949).
Bucsay, M., *Geschichte des Protestantismus in Ungarn*, H. Krimm, tr., (Stuttgart, 1959).
Cambridge Modern History Atlas (Cambridge, 1924), Maps nos. 3, 20, 21.
Campana, *Istoria del Mondo* (Venice, 1603?).
Caro, J. *Das Interregnum Polens im Jahre 1587* (Gotha, 1861).
Chardonnet, J., *Atlas international Larousse* (Paris, 1950).
Chirovsky, N. L., Fr., *Old Ukraine* (Madison, N.Y., 1963).
Creel, H. G., "The Role of the Horse in Chinese History," *American Historical Review* LXX/3 (April, 1965), pp. 647–672.
Csuday, E. (Jenö), *Die Geschichte der Ungarn*, M. Darvai, tr., 2 vols. (Vienna, 1900).
Danişmend, I. H., *Izahlï Osmanlï Tarihi Kronolojisi* III (Istanbul, 1961).
Davies, D. W., *Elizabethans Errant* (Ithaca, 1967).
Depner, Maja, *Das Fürstentum Siebenbürgen im Kampf gegen Habsburg* (Stuttgart, 1938).
Dowsett, C. J. F., tr., *The History of the Caucasian Albanians of Movsès Dasxuranci* (London, 1961).
E.I.[1] and *E.I.*[2]: see next entry; also, list of encyclopedia articles at the end of this bibliography.
Encyclopedia of Islam, 1st ed., vols. I–IV and Suppl. (Leyden, 1913–1938); 2nd ed., vols. I, II, etc. (Leyden, 1960, 1965, etc.).
Erdmann, Franz von, "Iskender Munschi und sein Werk," *Z.D.M.G.* XV (1861), pp. 457–501.
Ertaylan, I. H., *Gazi Geray Han* (Istanbul, 1958).
Esper, T., "Military Self-Sufficiency and Weapons Technology in Muscovite Russia," *Slavic Review* 38/2 (June, 1969), pp. 185–208.
Fillipov, Y. V., *Geograficheskiy Atlas* (Moscow, 1954).

Fischer-Galati, S. A., *Ottoman Imperialism and German Protestantism, 1521–1555* (Cambridge, Mass., 1959).
Fisher, R. H., *The Russian Fur Trade, 1550–1700*, Univ. of Cal. Publications in History, vol. 31 (Berkeley, 1943).
Fekhner, M. V., "Torgovlya Russkogo Gosudarstva so Stranami Vostoka v xvi veka," *Trudy Gosud. Istorich. Muzeya*, No. XXI (Moscow, 1952).
Fitzler, M. A. H., "Die Entstehung der sogenannten Fuggerzeitungen in der Wiener National-Bibliothek," *Veröffentlichungen des Wiener Hofkammerarchivs* II (Vienna, 1937), pp. 1–81.
Fuetèr, E., *Geschichte des europaischen Staatssystems von 1492–1559* (Munich, 1919).
Gibb, H. A. R., and Bowen, H., *Islamic Society and the West*, vol. I, pts. 1 & 2 (London, 1950, 1957).
Gökbilgin, M. Tayyib, *XV-XVI Asïrlarda Edirne ve Paşa Livasï* (Istanbul, 1952).
———, "XVII Asïr Başlarïnda Erdel Hadiseleri ve Bethlen Gabor'un Beyliğe Intihabï," *Tarih Dergisi* I/i (Sept., 1949), pp. 1–28.
Gottwald, J., "Phanariotische Studien," *Leipziger Vierteljahrsschrift für Südosteuropa* V, pp. 1–57.
Güçer, L., "Le Commerce intérieur des céréales dans l'Empire ottoman pendant la seconde moitié du xvi siècle," *Iktisat Fakültesi Mecmuasï* XI/Suppl. (Istanbul, 1953), pp. 163–188.
Guignard, François E., Count de Saint Priest, *Memoires sur l'Ambassade de France en Turquie et sur le Commerce des Français dans le Levant*, Public. de l'École des Langues Orientales Vivantes, Ser. I/6 (Paris, 1877).
Guignes, Jos. de, *Histoire generale des Huns, des Turcs, des Mongols et des autres Tartares occidentaux*, 5 vols. (Paris, 1756–1758).
Hahn, W., "Die Verpflegung Konstantinopels durch staatliche Zwangswirtschaft," *Vierteljahrschrift für Sozial- und Wirtschafts Geschichte*, Beiheft VIII (Stuttgart, 1926).
Hakluyt: see Burrough, Fletcher and Jenkinson.
Halecki, O., *A History of Poland* (London, 1955).
Hammer, J. von, *Geschichte der Chane der Krim unter osmanischer Herrschaft* (Vienna, 1856).
———, *Geschichte des Osmanischen Reiches*, 10 vols. (Pest, 1827–1835).
———, *Histoire de l'Empire Ottoman*, J. J. Hellert, tr., 18 vols. (Paris, 1835–1843).
Hantsch, H., *Die Geschichte Österreiches*, 2 vols. (Graz, 1951).
Hefele, C. J. von, *Histoire des Conciles*, H. LeClercq, tr., VIII/I (Paris, 1917).
Hellert, J. J., *Atlas de l'Empire Ottoman* (Paris, 1843).
Heyd, W., *Histoire du commerce du Levant au moyen-âge*, 2 vols. (Leipzig, 1923).
Hinz, W., *Irans Aufstieg zum Nationalstaat im fünfzehnten Jahrhundert* (Berlin and Leipzig, 1936).
———, "Schah Esmā'īl II. Ein Beitrag zur Geschichte der Safaviden," *Mitteilungen des Seminars für orientalische Sprachen*, vol. 36, pt. II (Berlin, 1933), pp. 19–100.
Hobsbawn, Eric, *Bandits* (New York, 1969).
Holter, K., "Studien zu Aḥmed Ferīdūn's Münše'āt es-Selāṭīn," *Mitteilungen des oesterreichischen Instituts für Geschichtsforschungen*, vol. XIV/Suppl. (Innsbruck, 1939).
Howorth, H., *History of the Mongols*, vol. II (London, 1880).
Hrushevskiy, M. S., *Istoriya Ukrayni-Rusi* VII (New York, 1956).
Hrushevsky, M. S., *A History of the Ukraine* (New Haven, 1953).
Husameddin, Hüseyin, *Amasya Tarihi*, 4 vols. (Istanbul, 1927–1935).
I.A.: see *Islam Ansiklopedisi* and also the list of encyclopedia articles at the end of this bibliography.
Inalcïk, H. "Osmanlï-Rus Rekabetinin Menşei ve Don-Volga Kanalï Teşebbüsü (1569)," *Belleten* XII/46 (Ankara, 1948), pp. 349–402.
———, "Ottoman Methods of Conquest," *Studia Islamica* II (1954), pp. 103–129.
———, "Türkiye'nin Iktisadi Vaziyeti," *Belleten* XV/60 (Oct., 1951), 629–690.
———, "Yeni Vesikalara göre Kïrïm Hanlïğïnïn Osmanlï Tabiliğine Girmesi ve Ahitname Meselesi," *Belleten* VIII/30 (1944), pp. 349–402.
Inan, Âfet, *Aperçu général sur l'histoire economique de l'Empire Turc-Ottoman*, Türk Tarih Kurumu Seri VIII/6 (Istanbul, 1941).

Iorga, N., *A History of Roumania*, J. McCabe, tr. (New York, 1926). [cited as Iorga-McCabe]

Iorga (Jorga), N., *Geschichte des osmanischen Reiches*, vol. III (Gotha, 1910).

Islam Ansiklopedisi, vols. I-X (Istanbul, 1943–1967).

Jarring, G., "Gustaf II Adolf och tatarna på Krim," *Ny militär Tidskrift* V, pp. 306–314.

Jorga: see Iorga.

Karttunen, K. I., "Die Königswahl in Polen, 1575," *Suomalaisen Tiedeakatemian toi mit uksia*, Ser. B, vol. 12, no. 4.

Kerner, R., *The Urge to the Sea* (Berkeley, Calif., 1942).

Kertbény, K. M., "Ungarn betreffende deutsche Erstlings-Drücke, 1454–1600," *Bibliografie der ungarischen nationalen und internationalen Literatur* I (Budapest, 1880), pp. 17–758.

Kluchevsky, V. O., *A History of Russia*, C. J. Hogarth, tr., II (New York, 1960).

Knatchbull-Hugessen, G. M., *The Political Evolution of the Hungarian Nation*, 2 vols. (London, 1908).

Kortepeter, C. M., "Ġāzī Girāy II, Khan of the Crimea, and Ottoman Policy in Eastern Europe and the Caucasus, 1588–1594," *Slavonic and East European Review* XLIV (1966), pp. 139–166.

———, "German *Zeitung* Literature (as historical sources)," in R. Schoeck, *Editing Sixteenth Century Texts* (Toronto, 1966), pp. 113–129.

———, "The Islamic-Ottoman Social Structure: the Quest for a Model of Ottoman History," in R. B. Winder, ed., *Near Eastern Round Table 1967–68* (Turkish Politics and History) (New York, 1969), pp. 1–40.

———, "Ottoman Imperial Policy and the Economy of the Black Sea Region in the Sixteenth Century," *J.A.O.S.* 86/2 (April–June, 1966), pp. 86–113.

Kraelitz, F. von, "Der osmanischer Historiker Ibrahim Pečewi," *Der Islam* VIII (1918), pp. 252–260.

Kurat, A. N., "The Turkish Expedition to Astrakhan in 1569 and the Don-Volga Canal," *S.E.E.R.*, XL (December, 1961), pp. 7–24.

———, *Türkiye ve Idil Boyu*, Ankara Üniv. D.T.-C. Fak. Yay., 151 (Ankara, 1966).

Kütükoğlu, B., *Osmanlī-Iran Siyasî Münasebetleri I, 1578–1590*, Istanbul Üniv. Edeb. Fak. Yay., 888 (Istanbul, 1962).

Lattimore, O., "Inner Asian Frontiers," *Journal of Economic History* VII (New York, 1947), pp. 24–52.

Lencz, D. Géza, *Der Aufstand Bocskays und der Wiener Friede* (Debreczen, 1917).

Levend, A. S., *Gazavatnameler* (Ankara, 1956).

Lewis, B., *The Emergence of Modern Turkey* (London, 1961).

———, "The Islamic Guilds," *The Economic History Review* VIII/1 (Nov., 1937).

———, *Notes and Documents from the Turkish Archives* (Jerusalem, 1952).

———, "The Ottoman Archives: A Source for European History," *Report on Current Research* (Washington, D.C., 1956).

MacDermott, M., *A History of Bulgaria 1393–1885* (London, 1962).

Makkai, Ladislas, *Histoire de Transylvanie* (Paris, 1946).

Mantran, Robert, *Istanbul dans la seconde Moitié du XVIIe Siècle*, Bibliothèque Archéo. et Histor. de l'Institut Français d'Archéologie d'Istanbul XII (Paris, 1962).

Matoušek, J., *Turecka Valka v Evropska Politice v Letech 1592–1594*, Acad. of Sc. of Czechoslovakia, Ser. I/82 (Prague, 1935).

Matthews, W. K., "The Latinisation of Cyrillic Characters, "*Slavonic Review* (now *S.E.E.R.*)" XXX (1951–52), pp. 531–548.

McNeill, W. H., *Europe's Steppe Frontier 1500–1800* (Chicago, 1964).

Miller, B., *The Palace School of Muhammed the Conqueror*, Harvard Historical Monograph, XVII (Cambridge, Mass., 1941).

Minorsky, V., *Studies in Caucasian History* (London, 1953).

Mirkovich, N., "Ragusa and the Portuguese Spice Trade," *Slavonic and East European Review*

XXI/1 (March, 1943), pp. 174–187.

Moncallero, G. L., "La Politica di Leone X e di Francesco I nella progettata crociata contro i turchi e nella lotta per la successione imperiale," *Rinascimento* VIII/1 (Florence, 1957), pp. 61–109.

Namitok, A., "The 'Voluntary' Adherence of Kabarda (Eastern Circassia) to Russia," *Caucasian Review* 2 (Munich, 1956), pp. 17–33.

Németh, J., "Neuere Untersuchungen über das Wort *Tabor* 'Lager'," *Acta Linguistica* III (Budapest, 1953), pp. 431–446.

Nistor, I., *Handel und Wandel in der Moldau bis zum Ende des 16. Jahrhunderts* (Czernowitz, 1912).

Novak, F., "The Interregna and Stephen Bathory, 1572–86," *Cambridge History of Poland to 1696* (Cambridge, 1950), pp. 369–391.

Novosel'skiy, A. A., *Bor'ba Moskovskogo Gosudarstva s Tatarami v pervoy Polovine xvii veka* (Moscow-Leningrad, 1948).

Oman, Sir Charles, *A History of the Art of War in the Sixteenth Century* (New York, 1937).

Orhonlu, Cengiz, *Osmanlï Imparatorluğunda Aşiretleri Iskân Teşebbüsü* (Istanbul, 1963).

Orzelski, Swietoslaw, "Eight Books on the Interregnum," *Scriptores Rerum Polonicarum* XXII (Warsaw, 1925).

Parry, V. J., "The Ottoman Empire 1566–1617," *New Cambridge Modern History* III (London, 1965).

Pàstine, O., *Genova e l'Impero Ottomano nel Secolo XVII*, Atti della Società Ligura di Storia Patria, vol. LXXIII (Genova, 1962).

Pastor, L. von, *History of the Popes from the Close of the Middle Ages*, vols. VII, XIX-XXII (London, 1930–32).

Pfeffermann, H., *Die Zusammenarbeit der Renaissancepäpste mit den Türken* (Winterthur, 1946).

Pierling, P., *Papes et Tsars, 1547–1597* (Paris, 1890).

Podea, I. I., "A Contribution to the Study of Queen Elizabeth's Eastern Policy, 1590–1593," *Mélanges d'Histoire Générale* (Bucharest, 1958).

Polievktov, M. A., "Iz perepiski severno-kavkazskikh feodalov xvii veka," *XLV Akademiku N. Ya. Marru*, I. I. Meshchaninov, ed. (Moscow, 1935), pp. 745–756.

Primaudaie, F. Elie de la, *Histoire du commerce de la Mer Noire et des Colonies Génoises de la Crimée* (Paris, 1848).

Pritsak, O., "Das erste türkische-ukrainische Bündnis (1648)," *Oriens* VI (1953), pp. 266–298.

Retovsky, B., "Moneti Gazi-Geraya Khana II ben Devlet," *Izvestiya Tavricheskoy Uchonoy Arkhivnoy Kommissii*, No. 8 (Simferopol', 1889), pp. 90–98.

Rieu, C. V., *Catalogue of the Turkish Manuscripts in the British Museum* (London, 1888).

Roberts, M., *Gustavus Adolphus, A History of Sweden, 1611–1632*, 2 vols. (London, 1953).

Roemer, H. R., *Der Niedergang Irans nach dem Tode Ismā'īls des Grausamen, 1577–1581* (Würzburg, 1939).

Rossi, E., "La Sultana 'Nūr Bānū' (Cecilia Venier-Baffo), moglie di Selim II (1566–1574) e Madre di Murād III (1574–1595)," *Oriente Moderno* (1953), pp. 433–441.

Roth, C., *The House of Nasi: Doña Gracia* (Phila., 1948).

———, *The House of Nasi: The Duke of Naxos* (Phila., 1948).

Rothenberg, G. E., *The Austrian Military Border in Croatia, 1522–1747*, Illinois University Studies in the Soc. Scs., vol. 48 (Urbana, 1960).

———, "Venice and the Uskoks of Zeng: 1537–1618," *Journal of Modern History* XXXIII/2 (June, 1961), pp. 148–156.

Runciman, Steven, *Le Manichéisme Mediéval* (Paris, 1949).

Rutkowski, J., *Histoire économique de la Pologne avant les Partages* (Paris, 1927).

Rypka, J., "Briefwechsel der Hohen Pforte mit den Krimchanen im II. Bande von Ferīdūn's Münše'at," in T. Menzel, ed., *Festschrift Georg Jacob* (Leipzig, 1932), pp. 241–269.

Sadikov, P. A., "Pokhod Tatar i Turok na Astrakhan' v 1569 g.," *Istoricheskie Zapiski* 22 (1947),

pp. 132–166.
Ṣafvet Bey, "Ḫazer Denizinde 'Osmānlï Ṣanjāğï," *T.O.E.M.* III/114.
Sagredo, G., *Histoire de l'Empire Ottoman*, M. Laurent, tr., 7 vols. (Paris, 1724).
Sakazov, I., *Bulgarische Wirtschaftsgeschichte* (Berlin, 1929).
Samoylovich, A., "Beiträge zur Bienenzucht in der Krim im 14–17. Jahrhundert," in T. Menzel, ed., *Festschrift Georg Jacob* (Leipzig, 1932), pp. 270–275.
Şapolyo, E. B., *Mezhepler ve Tarikatlar Tarihi* (Istanbul, 1964).
Savory, R. M., "The Principal Offices of the Safavid State during the Reign of Tahmāsp I (930–84/1524–76)," *B.S.O.A.S.* XXIV/1 (1961), pp. 65–85.
———, "The Sherley Myth," *Iran* V (1967), pp. 73–82.
———, "The Significance of the Political Murder of Mīrzā Salmān," *Islamic Studies* III/2 (Karachi, 1964).
Seton-Watson, R. W., *A History of the Roumanians* (Cambridge, 1935).
Shepherd, W. R., *Historical Atlas* (London, 1922).
Sherman, L., *Russkie Istoricheskie Istochniki X-XVIII vv.* (Khar'kov, 1959).
Skilliter, S., "Three Letters from the Ottoman 'Sultana' Ṣofiye to Queen Elizabeth I," S. M. Stern, ed., *Documents from Islamic Chanceries*, Oriental Studies, 3 (Oxford, 1965), pp. 118–157.
Skwarczynski, P., "The *Decretum Electionis* of Henry of Valois," *Slavonic and East European Review* XXXVII (Dec., 1958), pp. 113–130.
Smirnov, I. I., *Vosstanie Bolotnikova, 1606–1607* (Moscow-Leningrad, 1951).
Smirnov, N. A., *Rossiya i Turtsiya v XVI-XVII vv.*, 2 vols. (Moscow, 1946).
Smirnov, V. D., *Krymskoe Khanstvo pod verkhovenstvom otomanskoy Porti do nachala xviii veka* (St. Petersburg, 1887).
Smith, Bradford, *Captain John Smith* (New York, 1953).
Spooner, Frank C., *L'Économie mondiale et les Frappes Monétaires en France, 1493–1680* (Paris, 1956).
Stoianovich, T., "The Conquering Balkan Orthodox Merchant," *Journal of Economic History* XX (1960), pp. 241–243.
Stökl, G., *Die Entstehung des Kosakentums* (Munich, 1953).
Taeschner, F., "Das Bosnische Zunftwesen zur Türkenzeit (1463–1878), *Byzantinische Zeitschrift* 44 (1951).
Tikhomirov, M. N., *Istochnikovedenie Istorii SSSR s Drevneyshikh Vremen do Kontsa xviii veka* (Moscow, 1940).
Togan, A. Z. V., *Bugünku Türkistan ve Yakïn Mazisi* (Cairo, 1929–1930).
———, *Umumi Türk Tarihine Giriş* I (Istanbul, 1946).
Turan, O., *et al.*, eds., *Fuad Köprülü Armağanï* (Istanbul, 1953).
Tveritinova, A. C., "K voprosu o krest'yanstve i krest'yanskom zemlepol'zovanii," *Uchënye Zapiski Instituta Vostokovedeniya* XVII (Moscow, 1959), pp. 3–50.
Vasmer, M., *Russisches Etymologisches Wörterbuch* I (Heidelberg, 1953).
Vaughan, D. M., *Europe and the Turk: A Pattern of Alliances 1350–1700* (Liverpool, 1954).
Vernadsky, G., A History of Russia, vol. III, *The Mongols and Russia* (New Haven, 1953); vol. IV, *Russia at the Dawn of the Modern Age* (New Haven, 1959).
Veress, A., "Campania Creştinilor in Contra Lui Sinan Paşa Din 1595," *Academia Rŏmâna, Memoriile Sectiunii Istorice*, Ser. III/IV (Budapest, 1925), pp. 1–84.
Walsh, J. R., "Giovanni Tomasso Minadoi's History of the Turco-Persian Wars of the Reign of Murad III," *Proceedings of the 25th International Congress of Orientalists* II (Moscow, 1963).
Zettersteen, K. V., *Die Arabischen, Persischen und Türkischen Handschriften der Universitäts-Bibliothek zu Uppsala*, 2 vols. (Uppsala, 1945).
———, *Türkische, Tatarische und Persische Urkunden im schwedischen Reichsarchiv* (Uppsala, 1945).
Zinkeisen, J. W., *Geschichte des osmanischen Reiches in Europa*, 7 vols. and Index vol. (Hamburg and Gotha, 1840–1863).

ENCYCLOPEDIA REFERENCES

The quoting of these excellent articles requires no apology; in many instances, they represent the most advanced work on their respective subject matter. Please note that *E.I.*[1] and *E.I.*[2] refer to first and second editions respectively of the English *Encyclopedia of Islam; I.A.* refers to the Turkish *Islam Ansiklopedisi.*

Akdağ, M., "Kara-yazici," *I.A.* VI, 339–343.
Arat, R., "Kazan," *I.A.* VII, 505–522.
Bala, M., "Çerkesler," *I.A.* III, 380.
Barthold, V., "Dağistan," *I.A.* III, 451–456.
———, "Derbend," *I.A.* III, 537.
Baysun, M. C., "Ahmed I," *I.A.* I, 161–164.
———, "Ebüssu'ûd Efendi," *I.A.* IV, 92–99.
Beldiceanu, N., "Eflāḳ," *E.I.*[2] II, 687–689.
Cahen, C., "Atabak," *E.I.*[2] I, 731–732.
Darkot, B., "Amasya," *I.A.* I, 393–394.
———, "Kastamonu," *I.A.* VI, 399–403.
Decei, A., "Karadeniz," *I.A.* VI, 238–246.
Dunlop, D. M., "Baḥr-i Rūm," *E.I.*[2] I, 934–936.
Gökbilgin, M. T., "Ciğala-zade," *I.A.* III, 161–164.
———, "Mehmed III," *I.A.* VII, 535–547.
———, "Mehmed Paşa, Sokollu," *I.A.* VII, 595–605.
———, "Erdel," *I.A.* IV, 300.
Gölpïnarlï, A., "Kïzïlbaş," *I.A.* VI, 789–795.
Inalcïk, H., "Boghdan," *E.I.*[2] I, 1252–1253.
———, "Buḍjak," *E.I.*[2] I, 1286–1287.
———, "Bulgaria," *E.I.*[2] I, 1302–1304.
———, "Cherkes," *E.I.*[2] II, 21–25.
———, "Gazi Giray Khan II," *I.A.* IV, 734–736.
———, "Girāy," *I.A.* IV, 783–789.
———, "Haci Giray," *I.A.* V, 25–27.
———, "Islam Giray," *I.A.* V, 1105.
———, "Ḳalġay," *I.A.* VI, 131–132.
———, "Kïrïm," *I.A.* VI, 741–756.
Köprülü, O., "Hasan Paşa, Yemişçi," *I.A.* V, 330–334.
Kramers, J. H., "Skanderbeg," *E.I.* IV, 466–467.
Kütükoğlu, B., "Murad III," *I.A.* VIII, 615–625.
———, "Mustafa Paşa, Lala," *I.A.* VIII, 732–736.
Minorsky, V., "Laz," *E.I.*[1] III, 20–22.
———, "Shekki," *E.I.*[1] IV, 346–348.
Orhonlu, C., "Murad Paşa, Kuyucu," *I.A.* VIII, 651–654.
Parmaksïzoğlu, I., "Ibrahim Paşa, Damad," *I.A.* V, 915–919.
Parry, V. J., "Barūd," *E.I.*[2] I, 1061–1066.
———, "Čighālāzade Yusūf Sinān Pasha," *E.I.*[2] II, 33–34.
Savory, R. M., "'Abbās I," *E.I.*[2] I, 7–8.
Spuler, B., "Astrakhan," *E.I.*[2] I, 721–722.
———, "Bāġchesarāy," *E.I.*[2] I, 893–894.
Streck, M. and H. Inanç, "Ermeniye," *I.A.* IV, 317–326.

Taeschner, F., "Anadolu," *E.I.*^{2} I, 461–480.
Tschudi, R., "Bektashiyya," *E.I.*^{2} I, 1161–1163.
Turan, Ş., "Sa'd-ed-Din, Hoca," *I.A.* X, 27–32.
———, "Sinan Paşa, Koca," *I.A.* X, 670–675.
Uzunçarşïlï, I. H., "Levend," *I.A.* VII, 46–48.

Index